ESSAYS ON

SEXUALITY & ETHICS

ESSAYS ON
SEXUALITY & ETHICS

J. Martin Stafford

ISMERON
SOLIHULL
1995

J. Martin Stafford, 298 Blossomfield Road, SOLIHULL B91 1TH

British Library Cataloguing in Publication Data

Stafford, J. Martin
Essays on Sexuality and Ethics
I. Title
176

ISBN 0-9512594-4-x

Printed in Great Britain by
Antony Rowe Ltd. Chippenham

Contents.

Preface

This preface is designed with two ends in view: to serve as both *apologia* and reader's guide. Though written over a period of more than twenty years, most of the pieces here presented deal with two subjects of continuing interest and sufficient importance to justify their appearance in this form. The first three deal with issues in the history of ethics; the following five with sexuality - four of these with the place of homosexuality in the school curriculum. They are reprinted not in the order in which they were originally written or published but in a logical order (progressing from the general to the particular) in which they might best be approached by an intending reader who already has some proficiency in philosophy. Some (Nos. 1 and 5) are both long and demanding; while others (Nos. 6, 7 and 8) were written with a wider readership in mind. The two groups of subjects (the history of ethics and the place of homosexuality in the curriculum) are interrelated inasmuch as that anyone who makes practical recommendations of the kind embodied in my work should be able to support them by appeal to some underlying non-arbitrary ethical principles. I believe that the fruits of my researches in the history of ethics support my work on homosexuality in just such a way. It is a conspicuous weakness (and in my submission a very serious one) of much recent writing in applied philosophy that it is undertaken with little or no historical awareness. Philosophy, like music, is a subject which is largely co-extensive with its own history. Philosophers who write with no acquaintance with the theory or history of the subject may be likened to untrained musicians who yet pick up an instrument and make it sound. The results may be pleasing to some.

The first paper 'Hutcheson, Hume and the Ontology of Morals' was written in the last half of 1982. I started reading David Norton's then recently published book on a train journey from Manchester to Plymouth and realised at once that his account of Hume's moral ontology was starkly at variance with what Hume actually wrote. I subsequently reread Hutcheson's primary ethical treatises and discovered that Norton's interpretation of Hutcheson too was sustainable only when Hutcheson's texts were misrepresented - in some instances so grossly that Hutcheson clearly says the opposite of what Norton claims he meant. The pronouncements of Hutcheson and Hume on this subject, though made nearly three centuries ago, are, I believe, substantially true. I was therefore keen to defend them against Norton's bizarre 'reinterpretation'. That such a book as his was published by a university press and sympathetically reviewed by several people who are well paid to know better constitutes a serious indictment of the state of scholarship at the end of the twentieth century. Early in 1983, as was then my usual practice, I sent the typescript to my former teacher, Professor Peter Nidditch. Unfortunately, by this time he was too ill to take any interest in it and died on 12th February at the tragically early age of fifty-four. The piece is respectfully dedicated to his memory.

Article 2, 'Hume, Spencer and the Standard of Morals', deals with the most fundamental question of ethics and was derived from an M.A. thesis on which I was working in the summer of 1972. When it was recast in its new form in the early 1980s, most of the material was reproduced *verbatim*: it can therefore claim to be the earliest of all my work reprinted here. By contrast, Article 3, 'Egoism and Rigorism' is of very recent composition, dating from 1993-5 and the only piece in this collection not published hitherto. It discusses with reference to the writings of several eighteenth century philosophers a controversy about the nature of virtuous action and shows how Herbert Spencer suggested a resolution to a paradox arising therefrom.

'On Distinguishing between Love and Lust' (1977) was my first philosophical essay to appear in print. It was written in the autumn and winter of 1974-5 and was a conscious reaction to the licentiousness of those times, as yet unchastened by the advent of AIDS and by awareness of the dire consequences moral and social which sexual promiscuity has brought in its wake. Its companion piece 'Love and Lust Revisited' (1988) was written in the winter of 1986-7 in response to Roger Scruton's then recent book *Sexual Desire*. While the first establishes and defends the distinction between love and lust, the second contends that the distinction between homosexual and heterosexual desire is morally insignificant, which insignificance moral educators have a clear duty to proclaim. I pointed out - perhaps naïvely - that if Roger Scruton were consistent, he would surely endorse my views. Its composition marked a personal watershed in that after thirteen years of self-imposed silence I was provoked by reading Scruton's book to return to campaigning for gay rights, albeit from my ivory tower. At the same time I also wrote Article 6, 'In Defence of Gay Lessons', a less rigorously philosophical piece written primarily in response to a tract by Rachel Tingle called *Gay Lessons - How Public Funds are used to promote Homosexuality among Children and Young People*. Articles 5 and 6 and my short book *Homosexuality and Education* were all published in the first four months of 1988 just before the notorious Clause 28 of the Local Government Act was put on the statute books.

Article 7 is a concise but trenchant reply to a hostile review of my book by a radical gay activist commissioned by the *Cambridge Journal of Education*. The note at the foot of its first page stating that the editors were happy to allow me to reply is not strictly true. In advance of publication the editor made clear to me that he intended in his editorial to dissociate himself and fellow editors from the contents of my reply and suggested -

quite wrongly - that I might wish to withdraw the piece rather than see it accompanied by such denunciation. What prompted him to adopt this attitude was presumably not my contention that homosexuality should be positively treated by moral educators but rather my emphatic stance that promiscuity should not be, along with my qualified endorsement of a highly controversial remark made by Mr James Anderton, then Chief Constable of Greater Manchester. (See pages 83 and 90.)

When in the spring of 1987 'Love and Lust Revisited' was accepted as a contribution to the *Journal of Applied Philosophy*, the editors invited Roger Scruton to reply. He refused, saying that he had insufficient time. I suspect that this stated reason was not the real one, such reluctance on his part to engage in controversy being quite out of character; for he is usually keen to defend his corner when he believes he is on firm ground. So far as I am aware, Scruton has never disputed the cogency of the arguments I there adduced against him. In 1989, however, he came up with a new argument to justify homophobia. It was first enunciated in a lecture (later reprinted in a book) and subsequently repeated in a tub-thumping article in the *Sunday Telegraph*. 'The Two Minds of Roger Scruton' highlights the flaws in the new argument and reiterates the inconsistencies between the fastidious deliberations of Scruton the philosopher and the demotic rantings of Scruton the man.

The last two articles are quite unrelated to the rest and to each other. Between 1979 and 1989 I contributed five articles to the *Journal of Philosophy of Education*. All but one were *ad hominem* pieces of ephemeral interest and I decline the opportunity to reprint them here. One, however, 'Public Schools, Private Privilege and Common Sense' was an ardent defence of independent education and incorportates a salutary message not as yet taken to heart in many quarters; for which reason it is here reproduced. Article 10 draws attention to previously unnoticed but significant textual similarities between Mandeville and Hume.

By assembling this selection from my occasional writings and publishing it at my own expense I am deliberately treading in the footsteps of Herbert Spencer, whose name figures prominently in the following pages. In the last century, when the real costs of book production were much higher than they are today, he spent on the publication of his own works large sums, the recovery of which often took many years to achieve. While I do not expect anyone a hundred years hence to be as indebted to me as I am to Spencer, I am inspired to imitate his example. Moreover, as he observed with self-effacing candour: 'Every author is naturally sanguine about his books: he has hopes which nobody else entertains.' (*Various Fragments*, 1897 p.23)

All articles previously published are here reproduced from the pages of the originals. Half a dozen minor corrections and one major one have been made. In all but one case, the original pagination has been preserved. This is supplemented by a continuous pagination in square brackets. Article 9 was first published in a format incongruous with the present one. The typeface has therefore been reduced slightly in size and the text accommodated on four pages instead of five.

Acknowledgements

Copyright of seven of the pieces was assigned to the journals in which they appeared. I am grateful to their respective editors or publishers for permission to reprint them here: 1 and 4 *The Journal of Value Inquiry*, (Martinus Nijhoff); 2 *Philosophy*; 5 *The Journal of Applied Philosophy*; 7 *The Journal of Moral Education*; 8 *Studies in Philosophy and Education* (Kluwer Academic Publishers); 9 *The Journal of Philosophy of Education*.

J. Martin Stafford September, 1995

Illustrations.

The Journal of Value Inquiry 19:133–151 (1985).

Discussions

HUTCHESON, HUME AND THE ONTOLOGY OF MORALS *

J. MARTIN STAFFORD

I

"Hume's ontology of morals is elusive." With this remark Professor David Fate Norton embarks upon one of the longest footnotes in his book *David Hume – Common Sense Moralist, Sceptical Metaphysician*. Norton's conviction that Hume believed that we have moral knowledge, that our moral sentiments serve as signs of moral facts, and that there is some kind of objective 'moral reality' consisting of 'moral entities'[1] certainly engenders more than a mere suspicion that Hume's ontology of morals has eluded him. In this paper I shall criticise the very forced interpretation of this aspect of Hume's theory to be found in Norton's book and shall defend the more traditional account: namely, that neither Hutcheson nor Hume was a cognitivist who believed that moral distinctions are features of an external reality which we somehow apprehend, but rather that they believed moral distinctions simply to be founded upon the uniform sentiments of mankind. This account has the advantage both of being ontologically more economical and of according far more perfectly with Hume's professed empiricism; it enables Hutcheson, Hume and Herbert Spencer to be seen as members of a developing tradition, each offering an explanation of morality more comprehensive and more plausible than that of his predecessor[2]; and it is unburdened by the need to overturn two centuries of consensus about the naturalistic character of Hume's and Hutcheson's moral theories.[3]

While Norton agrees that Norman Kemp Smith was right in seeing Hume's moral philosophy as developing from Hutcheson's, he contends that Kemp Smith went "badly astray for the very simple reason that he...misread Hutcheson, and hence missed much of the point of Hutcheson's moral philosophy."[4] Norton maintains that this alleged misreading of Hutcheson consisted in seeing his moral theory as non-cognitive, and as a prolegomenon to his study of Hume's ethics he devotes a chapter to trying to establish that Hutcheson was a moral realist, and that the moral sense which he postulated and by which Hume was influenced was essen-

* To the memory of Peter Nidditch (1928–1983), Professor of Philosophy, University of Sheffield, a diligent scholar, an inspiring teacher and a generous friend.

tially a cognitive faculty. Since he refers to very few critical works earlier than Kemp Smith's, Norton tends to give the impression that Smith was the first to regard Hutcheson's moral theory as affective rather than cognitive, I think it proper to emphasise that this is by no means true. On the contrary, so far as I can discover, Kemp Smith's account of this aspect of Hutcheson's work is quite concordant with those of a long line of distinguished predecessors. It is not therefore Kemp Smith who is here departing from tradition and received opinion but Norton. While this circumstance does not of itself discredit Norton's enterprise or vindicate Kemp Smith, it should make us extremely circumspect when we assess Norton's innovatory claims; for they necessarily carry with them the implausible corollary that Hutcheson and Hume were widely misunderstood in their own time and did nothing to counteract this; that they have been universally misapprehended ever since; and that Norton is perhaps the first person to understand them aright. The extent and weight of the tradition which Norton needs to subvert may be apparent from the following brief quotations (set out in chronological order) from writers of some standing who all avow that Hutcheson's moral sense was affective and relative to human nature.

> From the term *sense*,...from his rejection of all the arguments that have been used to prove it to be an intellectual power, and from the whole of his language on this subject; it is evident, he considered it as the effect of a *positive constitution* of our minds, or as an *implanted* and *arbitrary* principle by which a *relish* is given us for certain moral objects and forms and aversion to others...[5]
>
> RICHARD PRICE

> Hutcheson himself was evidently apprehensive of the consequences which his language might be supposed to involve; and he has endeavoured to guard against them, though with very little success... Mr. Hume..., with his usual acuteness, pushed this scheme of morals to its ultimate and its legitimate conclusion. The words right and wrong, he asserted, ...can signify nothing in the actions to which they are applied, but only certain *effects* in the mind of the spectator.[6]
>
> DUGALD STEWART

> Hutcheson opposes very resolutely all those moralists who seek to give morality a deeper foundation in the nature of things.[7]
>
> JAMES McCOSH

> The ultimate source of moral distinctions is, of course, placed by Hutcheson ...in the original make of human nature.[8]
>
> THOMAS FOWLER

> The doctrine of the moral sense is a sensationalist, individualistic doctrine, through which Locke's metaphysical assumptions can easily be seen.[9]
>
> L.A. SELBY-BIGGE

Non-cognitive interpretations of Hutcheson are also implied more or less definitely by T.H. Green[10], T.H. Huxley[11], W.R. Scott[12], and John Laird[13].

II

Why is Norton so steadfastly determined to overturn an opinion so well established? His primary reason for placing Hutcheson and Hume firmly on the side of the moral objectivists is that he rightly sees their moral philosophy as part of the reaction against the sceptical and cynical school of Hobbes and Mandeville.[14] Hobbes had claimed that moral distinctions are entirely dependent on the arbitrary will of an all-powerful sovereign, and Mandeville that morality as a social phenomenon had arisen solely from the artifice of politicians, who in the distant past had planted and fostered the notions of shame and honour and whose successors continued still to exploit these in order to render selfish men sufficiently tractable to live together socially. To the wholly justified premise that Hutcheson and Hume were opposed to this tradition Norton conjoins the much more contentious assumption that there is a clear-cut dichotomy between such nihilistic moral scepticism as was widely imputed to Mandeville on the one hand and moral realism on the other. From these two premises he draws the valid but false inference that Hutcheson and Hume must have been moral realists.

This second premise of Norton's is intimated in a footnote to his Introduction[15], where moral scepticism is characterised by its denial that moral distinctions are founded in objective features of the world (in contrast to observers) and by assertions that there can be no good reason for a moral judgment nor any valid moral arguments; that morality has no rational basis; and that the difference between right and wrong is merely a matter of opinion, taste, or convention. Those who oppose this scepticism (Cudworth, Shaftesbury, Hutcheson, Hume and Turnbull are actually named and conjoined) Norton calls "moral realists". This group, according to him, concurred in thinking that moral distinctions are objective and that moral judgments are assertions of moral fact whose truth or falsity can be known. Now these characterisations of scepticism and realism in morals and the implied dichotomy between them are surely too simplistic by far. It should have been apparent to Norton from his own long discussion of different kinds of scepticism in his fifth chapter that there might be species of moral scepticism other than the assertive nihilistic type. By some of the criteria specified by Norton himself[16] the critical and reflective attitude to morality advocated by Hume could constitute a more moderate, questioning kind of scepticism. Moreover, I would say that between nihilistic scepticism and metaphysical realism there must be at least one other major category to accommodate non-nihilistic anthropocentric theories such as those of Hutcheson and Hume. These could, I suppose, be styled "socio-psychological realism", though it could be argued that a reality which is merely anthropocentric or merely psychological is not real enough to warrant the name of realism at all. The deficiency of Norton's dualistic characterisation is suggested also by the fact that all the features which he imputes pejoratively to the moral sceptics could be, and in fact have been, with some important qualifications, attributed to Hume. It is, moreover, at best insensitive to subsume under the same category writers as avowedly antithetical as Cudworth and Hume: for Hutcheson and Hume were at least as staunchly opposed to the rationalism of Cudworth, Clarke and Wollaston as they were to the unmitigated scepticism of Hobbes and Mandeville. (Selby-Bigge actually says that they were engaged in "a war with two fronts"[17].) That both the empirico-sentimentalists and the rationalists were hostile to nihilistic scepticism is in my view a very tenuous reason for asserting, as Norton does[18], that they represent a single philosophical tradition. Accordingly, I think it is the sharp dichotomy which Norton creates between moral scepticism and moral realism which misleads him so badly. There are gradations between moral absolutism in its several forms and total nihilism and Hume and Hutcheson do not belong at either end of the scale. (Norton himself, ironically enough, remarks on Hume's "tendency to steer between philosophical extremes"[19].) For while they were undoubtedly opposed to the cynical doctrine of Mandeville with its claim that morality is the fabrication of politicians, the explanation of morality which Hume propounds is no less a socio-psychological one than is Mandeville's. However, whereas Mandeville saw morality as the product of political artifice, Hume saw it as arising spontaneously from features of an essentially benevolent human nature exposed to the exigencies of social living. Hutcheson's explanation is less dynamic than Hume's since he postulated a divinely implanted and unanalysable moral sense by which we instinctively approve or disapprove of certain characters and actions, but it is true of them both that while their opposition to Mandeville committed them to the view that moral experience is real in that it is integral to human nature without the mediation of political artifice, it did not commit them in any way to postulating moral (as opposed to natural) facts and entities, non-natural qualities, or other metaphysical fictions. As I shall later show, any such ontological fripperies are of Norton's choosing and are entirely alien to the spirit of Hume's work.

Norton believes that Hutcheson had two purposes: (i) to oppose the doctrine that men are motivated only by self-interest; and (ii) to establish the reality of virtue. Of these Norton thinks the second is the more fundamental, the question being "whether or not the moral sense is a faculty capable of apprehending independently existing, intersubjective features...of the world about us, just as the other, ordinary senses presumably do."[20] I think that Norton has mistaken both the priority which Hutcheson accorded to these two questions and the manner in which he conceived the second; for he was primarily concerned to counteract the egoistic psychology of Hobbes and Mandeville and thought that his triumph over this cynical account of human nature was itself sufficient to establish (though clearly not in a sense as strong as Norton would wish) the reality of virtue. Selby-Bigge expressed this point succinctly in the Introduction to his *British Moralists*.

> ...the moral sense theory is a theory of motive rather than of criterion.... It is really a counter-theory to the selfish theory, which is essentially a theory of motives. Virtue is real and natural, says the sentimentalist, because there is in every man a sufficient motive to it.[21]

Norton, however, perseveres in maintaining that for Hutcheson the moral sense *must* be cognitive if he is to combat moral scepticim effectively. He says:

> Fortunately there is surprisingly strong support for this claim [that the moral sense has a cognitive function]. In fact much of what has been said earlier in this chapter serves as evidence to this end. Hutcheson's intentions...included the refutation of egoism and attendant moral scepticism; in opposition to those sceptical views he sought to establish the reality of virtue. But if there is no means by which virtue can be known – no faculty capable of apprehending it – then his enterprise must have ended in failure, even in his own eyes. It would not be enough for Hutcheson to establish in some abstract way that virtue and vice are genuine features of reality. To accomplish only this would be to leave the field open to the moral sceptics. To refute these sceptics effectively he would also need to show that man is equipped to discover and distinguish these features of reality; if the moral sense were not a cognitive sense its discovery would have been of little use to the warm-hearted Hutcheson...[22]

All this would be true only if Hutcheson had conceived the problem in the constricting terms of Norton's sharp dichotomy between moral realism and scepticism. Since there is absolutely no reason to suppose that Hutcheson did so conceive the problem, what Norton here claims as evidence in support of his interpretation is in fact no evidence at all.

III

I come now to consider the very sparse textual evidence (as distinct from the supposed circumstantial evidence) which Norton adduces to support his thesis that Hutcheson was a moral realist. He makes three brief citations[23] which, he claims, support his contention that the moral sense apprehends an external moral reality.

> Esteem...Dislike...are entirely excited by some moral Qualitys, Good or Evil, apprehended to be in the Objects....[24]

> We may observe, that no Action of any other Person was ever approv'd by us, but upon some Apprehension, well or ill grounded, of some really good moral Quality.[25]

> The *Apprehension* of morally good Qualities, is the necessary Cause of *Approbation*, by our moral Sense...[26]

These quotations appear to support Norton's thesis only when thus divested of their context. When this is restored, the first two of them relate virtue to benevolent motives and benficial actions, while the third is in a passage where Hutcheson specifies the formal objects of emotions.[27] Norton also presents us with a longer edited quotation from the later editions of the *Inquiry into the Original of our Ideas of Beauty and Virtue.*[28]

> The Quality approved by our moral Sense is conceived to reside in the Person approved, and to be a Perfection and Dignity in him...The admired Quality is conceived as the Perfection of the Agent, and such a one as is distinct from the *Pleasure* either in the Agent or the Approver tho' 'tis a sure Source of Pleasure to the Agent. The Perception of the Approver, tho' attended with Pleasure, plainly represents something quite distinct from this Pleasure; even as the Perception of *external Forms* is attended with Pleasure, and yet represents something distinct from this Pleasure.[29]

Now it is not disputed by Hutcheson, Hume, or myself that the objects on which our moral sense pronounces (i.e. the feelings and/or deeds of rational agents[30]) are quite distinct from and independent of our moral sentiments. But that they are thus independent does not imply that they have, also independently, a specifically moral nature – an inherent moral excellence or depravity distinct from (in the case of motives) their own phenomenological character or (in the case of actions) their natural tendencies or actual consequences. In my submission, we have no reason either to suppose that there are any such *sui generis*[31] moral qualities or to believe that Hutcheson, at least in his early works, postulated any; for when he speaks of "morally good qualities" or even "really good moral qualities" he probably means simply those qualities (most notably benevolence) which excite our moral approval. In his *Inquiry* Hutcheson says of the moral sense only that it "makes benevolent actions appear beautiful"[32] and, more specifically, that it is "only a Determination of our Minds to receive the simple Ideas of Approbation or Condemnation, from Actions observ'd."[33] He does not, therefore, appear inclined to endow actions or characters with a moral nature having some kind of supra-sensory ontological independence. We must, however, infer from much of what Norton writes that he (Norton) *does* believe that there are *sui generis* moral qualities (for if there were not, the moral sense *as a cognitive faculty* would be superfluous and redundant) and that he is trying to foist his own ontological commitment onto Hutcheson.

In *A System of Moral Philosophy* there is a sentence which might support Norton's case, though Norton does not in fact mention it. Here Hutcheson says:

> There is....a natural and immediate determination to approve certain affections, and actions consequent upon them; or a natural sense of *immediate excellence in them not referred to any other quality perceivable by our other senses or by reasoning.*[34]

Now this passage does, I admit, suggest that Hutcheson might well have begun to espouse a non-naturalistic moral ontology by the time he wrote this later work. However, since *A System of Moral Philosophy* was completed in manuscript by the late 1730's[35] and yet subsequent editions both of the *Inquiry* (1738) and of the *Essay on the Passions with Illustrations upon the Moral Sense* (1742) include passages which tend to discount non-natural ethical qualities, we must conclude either that Hutcheson did *not* mean the above sentence to suggest that actions or characters have non-natural attributes or that he deemed the ontology of morals to be of so little importance that he was content to overlook these manifest inconsistencies.[36] There is in any case an overwhelming reason why this later work should not be admitted as evidence in the controversy concerning the nature of Hutcheson's moral theory and its possible influence on Hume: since *A System of Moral Philosophy* was not published until 1755 (nine years after Hutcheson's death), it could not have had any influence on Hume's ethical writings, all of which predate it.

IV

Section V of Norton's chapter on 'Hutcheson's Moral Realism' attempts to force, much further than does Hutcheson himself, the analogy between our external senses and our moral sense by claiming that just as the former make us aware of an external physical reality, so the latter informs us of an external moral reality. In respect of the external senses there is evidence that Hutcheson embraced a kind of providential occasionalism, whereby our sensations, without necessarily resembling an external reality, are made to serve as reliable signs thereof. I cannot, however, find any vestige of evidence to support Norton's claim that Hutcheson explains our moral perception in much the same way. Although Norton asserts this both in his text[37] and in a footnote, where he says that just as we apprehend external objects by means of non-resembling ideas, so also "it is only by means of another set of non-resembling ideas, or affections (feelings of approbation and disapprobation) that we apprehend moral objects or moral reality",[38] he does not supply any quotations or any references where Hutcheson himself says this. Indeed, Norton's exposition and explication from page 82 to the end of the section on page 86 depend all too heavily on artful editing and rambling paraphrases into which he surreptitiously inserts unwarrantable assumptions in order to be able to make out his case. Some points are stated ambiguously, and in one instance Hutcheson's text is wantonly misrepresented. For example, Norton says that our

> "Moral Perceptions" [of approbation and dislike] are as real and natural and as necessary a part of our experience as any other sensations, and they are quite as unavoidable and unalterable.[39]

This claim needs qualifying. I believe there are two senses in which our moral experience may, according to Hutcheson, be said to be necessary, but a third and crucially important one in which it is certainly not necessary: (i) Our moral sentiments are necessary in that they are not subject to the determinations of our will. We cannot give or withhold our moral approval according as we might find it convenient to do so. On this point Hutcheson is most insistent. (ii) Our being endowed with the moral constitution we actually have may, in some sense, be a necessary consequence of God's goodness: because God is himself benevolent he has given us a moral sense which approves benevolence and thus fits us tolerably well to live in the world. (iii) It could, however, conceivably have been otherwise.

He could have given us a "contrary determination of mind"; just as the relationship between our sense of beauty and the objects which exite it is, in Hutcheson's view, purely contingent and subject to God's pleasure[40]. Hutcheson actually says:

> If it be here inquir'd, "Could not the Deity have given us a *different* or *contrary Determination of Mind, viz.* to *approve* Actions upon another Foundation than *Benevolence*?" There seems nothing in this surpassing the natural Power of the Deity. But, as in the first Treatise, we resolv'd the Constitution of our present *Sense* of *Beauty* into the *divine Goodness*, so with much more obvious Reason may we ascribe the present Constitution of our *moral Sense* to his *Goodness*. For if the Deity be really *benevolent*, and desires the Happiness of others, he could not *rationally* act otherwise, or give us a *moral Sense* upon another Foundation, without counteracting his own *benevolent Intentions.*[41]

That the determinations of our moral sense are thus dependent on God's will is hardly consistent with any kind of moral realism.

It is in his so-called explication of an important passage from the *Illustrations upon the Moral Sense* that Norton adopts what look like really desperate tactics. Here Hutcheson enumerates three distinguishable stages in the operation of the moral sense: (1) the perception by the external senses of an action with an accompanying awareness of its tendency; (2) the formation of an opinion as to the agent's motive (these first two, Hutcheson says, "represent something *external* to the observer, really existing whether he had perceived it or not...[42]"); (3) the perception of approbation or disapprobation. Norton says:

> It is not to be supposed that our approbation or disapprobation is an "*Image of any thing external*", any more than are our sensible ideas. Neither is it to be thought that "calling the *Ideas of Virtue* and *Vice* Perceptions of a *Sense*, upon apprehending the *Actions* and *Affections* of another," diminishes the "*Reality*" of virtue and vice. On the contrary, these ideas arise upon the occasion of what are clearly independently existing actions or affections of an agent, and they serve as signs of the moral nature of these actions or affections.... If approbation is felt, this will be accompanied by the idea of virtue, an idea that represents the moral character of the agent or action under observation.[43]

The text which Norton is here supposed to be explicating runs as follows:

> This *Approbation* cannot be supposed an *Image of any thing external*, *more than the *Pleasures of Harmony, of Taste, of Smell.** But let none imagine, that calling the *Ideas of Virtue* and *Vice* Perceptions of a *Sense*, upon apprehending the *Actions* and *Affections* of another does diminish their *Reality*, *more than the like *Assertions* concerning all *Pleasure* and *Pain, Happiness* or *Misery.**[44]

It should be noted that the phrases of the above quotation which I have enclosed by asterisks are conspicuously absent both in letter and in spirit from Norton's paraphrase. Since their import conflicts so patently with his vision of Hutcheson as a moral realist, one can understand his reluctance to present the quotation in full. For if anything appertains only to the mental state of an observer rather than to an external reality "pleasure or pain, happiness or misery" certainly do. Conversely, there is nothing in Hutcheson's text which corresponds with or supports the views expressed in the second half of Norton's 'explication' reproduced immediately above. If Norton failed to notice the second terms of Hutcheson's comparisons or to appreciate their significance, he must be amazingly inattentive: if, on the other hand, he realised their unwelcome implications and saw fit to suppress them, he is to be accounted somewhat less than honest.

It is similarly disingenuous on his part to preface his fanciful 'summaries' with remarks such as "Hutcheson might well have said something like this",[45] when in fact Hutcheson never said, or at least never wrote, any such thing as that

> Concomitant with these ideas [feelings of approbation or disapprobation] ...are the moral concomitants, the ideas of virtue and vice, which *are* representative of external or objective moral reality. When we experience these kinds of ideas together...we have an idea of moral objects, or moral knowledge.[46]

Norton alleges (quite unwarrantably) that the traditional interpretation of Hutcheson depends on a misreading of his works: evidently, Norton's interpretation depends on their being virtually rewritten! He has by no means established that Hutcheson believed in a moral reality external to observers. Even if there is some hint in the posthumously published *System of Moral Philosophy* that Hutcheson had begun to embrace some kind of metaphysical realism, this evidence is outweighed by the fact that well after the estimated date of the manuscript's completion and only four years before his death he issued an edition of an earlier work in which such realism is plainly discounted, our moral sentiments being no more representative or indicative of an independent moral reality than our other perceptions of "pleasure or pain, happiness or misery".

V

Most of Norton's pronouncements on Hume's moral ontology, like his exposition of Hutcheson's alleged moral realism, owe more to his capacity for invention and misunderstanding than they do to the author's texts; for again it is only by supplying what he finds wanting and by ignoring or contradicting what he finds unacceptable that he is able to present his thesis as a specious account of Hume's doctrine. His first equivocal exposition is as follows:

> Hume is not an affective subjectivist in morals. He does not claim that morality is merely sentiment, feeling, approbation, or disapprobation. On the contrary, Hume is a moral realist who believes that virtue and vice have objective status...[47]

The passage which, he alleges, has bedazzled readers and prevented them from seeing that Hume is a moral realist is the following:

> ...when you pronounce any action or character to be vicious, you mean nothing, but that from the constitution of your nature you have a feeling or sentiment of blame from the contemplation of it. Vice and virtue, therefore, may be compar'd to sounds, colours, heat and cold, which, according to modern philosophy, are not qualities in objects, but perceptions in the mind: And this discovery in morals, like that other in physics, is to be regarded as a considerable advancement of the speculative sciences; tho', like that too, it has little or no influence on practice.[48]

As Norton admits, this passage is susceptible to an interpretation implying a subjectivist view of morality. However, it must be remembered that Hume is delivered from the possible anarchic consequences of a subjectivism based on private idiosyncracies by his postulate of a basic uniformity of moral response. This is why he can claim that the doctrine of ethical sentimentalism, while being a great speculative step forward, has little influence on practice; for since mankind's moral sentiments are, in Hume's view, uniform, it does not matter that there is no ulterior moral reality: this very uniformity constitutes the standard of moral propriety. It is nevertheless an absolutely inescapable implication of the foregoing quotation that Hume's primary characterisation of morality is in terms of feeling. Even more emphatic assertions to this effect – Hume actually calls them definitions – are to be found in the second *Enquiry*.

> It is the nature and, indeed, the definition of virtue, that it is *a quality of the mind agreeable to or approved of by every one who considers or contemplates it.*[49]

> The hypothesis which we embrace is plain. It maintains that morality is determined by sentiment. It defines virtue to be *whatever mental action or quality gives to a spectator the pleasing sentiment of approbation*; and vice the contrary.[50]

Since this work was published more than a decade later than the *Treatise*, during which interval Hume had been accused of "sapping the foundations of morality, by denying the natural and essential difference betwixt right and wrong"[51], we must conclude from these unqualified reiterations of his doctrine that his conviction was undiminished, and that he had absolutely no desire to amend it or to recant. It is not, therefore, twenty-four decades of Hume's readers who have been bedazzled by any hyperbole in Hume's words, but Norton who has failed to take account of the notoriously careless way in which Hume sometimes uses language.[52] For while Norton is right to point out that there is something odd about the sentence immediately following the quotation from the *Treatise* cited above, he is quite at a loss to offer an explanation which accords with the general tenor of Hume's writings. Hume continues:

> Nothing can be more real, or concern us more, than our own sentiments of pleasure and uneasiness; and if these be favourable to virtue, and unfavourable to vice, no more can be requisite to the regulation of our conduct and behaviour.[53]

All Norton says of this sentence is that it suggests "that virtue and vice are not simply the sentiments of approbation and disapprobation that he [Hume] has just claimed them to be, and even that they are not sentiments at all."[54] Strictly speaking, Hume has not said that virtue and vice *are* sentiments: he says that they are features of our experience which *excite* our moral sentiments, and that these features are personal qualities and modes of conduct which are useful or agreeable to ourselves and others[55], and their contraries. Accordingly, an unambiguous rendering of the sentence in question would run: "If our moral sentiments be favourable to socially useful conduct and unfavourable to anti-social conduct, no more can be requisite to the regulation of our behaviour." There are other equally striking instances where one needs to be on one's guard against Hume's careless use of language; for he makes assertions which, in view of his own definitions, ought to be tautologies, and yet they are stated in such a way that they cannot be so intended. Just one page later in the *Treatise*, for example:

> ...we.... must pronounce the impression arising from virtue [i.e. useful conduct], to be agreeable, and that proceeding from vice [i.e. harmful conduct] to be uneasy. Every moment's experience must convince us of this.[56]

VI

An interesting and important corollary of the fact that Hume's primary characterisation of morality is in terms of sentiment is that the meta-ethical part of Hume's theory is itself morally neutral. The features of our experience which excite our moral sentiments are only contingently related to them. It is this contingent relationship which is above all else the subject of Hume's second *Enquiry*: what do we in fact approve and disapprove of, and why? The neutrality of Hume's definition of virtue and vice enables him, moreover, to accommodate intelligibly, albeit disparagingly, what he might call 'moral perversions', i.e. instances where people accord moral approval to what is useless or even harmful, such a "monkish virtues"[57] or "particular regards to meats, days, places, postures, [and] apparel"[58]. That we can profitably undertake an inquiry into the relationship between our moral sentiments and their objects surely indicates that the connection between the two is both weaker and incomparably more complex than that between our perceptions of secondary qualities and the features of the world which give rise to them. The analogy which is often drawn between these two susceptibilities is therefore a limited one. It would, for instance, seem odd to ask, "What objects do we perceive as red, and why?" For to say the least, there is far more agreement about which objects are red and which hot than about which actions are virtuous and which vicious. There are, moreover, standard independent ways of measuring heat and colour, but not of measuring virtue and vice. In the face of general consensus about the colour of objects it can plausibly be contended that those unable to make the usual discriminations have defective colour vision, which deficiency can be accounted for in terms of particular receptors in the eyes. However, it is much less plausible to plead that (analogously) of two antagonistic parties in a moral controversy one party must have defective moral faculties.

While the diversity of morals is something which Hume tries to explain away[59], Norton, not surprisingly, tends to overlook it. This is apparent when he is arguing that the objective status of virtues and vices is in some way guaranteed by their relationship to the indirect passions of pride and humility, love and hatred[60] – a relationship expressly noted by Hume himself:[61] namely, that whatever is a cause of moral approbation is also a cause of pride or love, and conversely, whatever is a cause of moral disapprobation is also a cause of humility or hatred. In Norton's discussion of this topic, the word 'objective' is used ambiguously, and this ambiguity is exploited: as if two distinct senses (a weak, existential sense – 'having an independent existence' and a strong, ethical sense – 'having an independent virtuousness or viciousness) were equivalent. Contrary to what Norton supposes, this relationship will not serve as a guarantor of the objectivity of morality: and this because, while it is true that the passions in question are excited by an objective (in the weak sense of "publicly accessible") state of affairs, the range of stimuli of these indirect passions and of moral sentiment is not in fact circumscribed by some absolute moral standard but is to a large extent culturally determined. Thus, in a savage society a man may feel proud and be acclaimed as a model of virtue for having amassed an impressive collection of scalps; even today one hears tell of conservative Roman Catholics who admire and approve of those who mortify their flesh by fasting and self-flagellation; during the Third Reich perpetrators of barbarous deeds were publicly honoured for, and no doubt felt proud of, the services they had rendered to their Führer. None of these candidates for the appelation 'virtuous' would have appealed to Hume, nor, I suspect, would they make a favourable impression on many of his modern commentators. There is indeed an *existentially* objective state of affairs in each of the examples I have given which might satisfy all formal conditions and give rise to pride, esteem, or even moral approval, but this by no means implies that there is present an objective virtuousness.

VII

What Hume says as to the independent existence of moral qualities contrasts sharply with what Norton says. In the *Treatise* Hume asks:

> ...can there be any difficulty in proving, that vice and virtue are not matters of fact, whose existence we can infer by reason [i.e. by the operations of the

> understanding]? Take any action allow'd to be vicious: Wilful murder, for instance. Examine it in all lights, and see if you can find that matter of fact, or real existence, which you call *vice*. In which-ever way you take it, you find only certain passions, motives, volitions and thoughts. There is no other matter of fact in the case. The vice entirely escapes you, as long as you consider the object. You never can find it, till you turn your reflection into your own breast, and find a sentiment of disapprobation, which arises in you, towards this action. Here is a matter of fact; but 'tis the object of feeling, not of reason. It lies in yourself, not in the object.[62]

In the *Enquiry* the identical doctrine is more eloquently enunciated:

> ...attend to Cicero, while he paints the crimes of a Verres or a Catiline. You must acknowledge that the moral turpitude results...from the contemplation of the whole, when presented to a being whose organs have such a particular structure and formation. The orator may paint rage, insolence, barbarity on the one side; meekness, suffering, sorrow, innocence on the other. But if you feel no indignation or compassion arise in you from this complication of circumstances, you would in vain ask him, in what consists the crime or villainy, which he so vehemently exclaims against: At what time, or on what subject it first began to exist? And what has a few months afterwards become of it, when every disposition and thought of all the actors is totally altered or annihilated? No satisfactory answer can be given to any of these questions, upon the abstract hypothesis of morals; and we must at last acknowledge, that the crime or immorality is no particular fact or relation, which can be the object of the understanding, but arises entirely from the sentiment of disapprobation, which, by the structure of human nature, we unavoidably feel on the apprehension of barbarity or treachery.[63]

Thus while virtuous and vicious actions take place in the public world, Hume states quite unequivocally that their specifically moral aspects depend entirely upon, and have no existence independent of, the sentiments of those who appraise them.

This, however, will not satisfy Norton, who maintains that virtue and vice are the "objective correlates" of our moral sentiments.[64] In a more than usually copious footnote he expounds a luxuriantly inflated ontology whose only relation to Hume's is that of contrariety. He asks "what transforms natural entities into moral ones?" and chides Hume with failing to explain "how moral qualities can be genuinely different from the material out of which they apparently arise, or how they can have a unique ontological status".[65] That Norton can pose such questions at all serves only to reveal the extent to which he has misunderstood Hume, and to indicate how little sympathy he has with Hume's comparatively austere views. For clearly, Hume did not accept that there are any moral entities, and cannot reasonably be expected to have explained what he himself did not believe, namely that moral qualities are essentially different from natural ones and that they have a unique ontological status. While Norton is right to say at the close of the footnote that Hume did not always describe matters accurately and unambiguously, Hume's shortcomings in this particular are certainly not due, as Norton alleges, to his not having developed a "complex ontological terminology" of the kind that appeals to Norton. (In fact much of what Norton says both about Hume's moral realism and about the ontology which might support it is undermined by his admission in the very last paragraph of the book that Hume does *not* think that the standard of morality was independent of human beings or that the rectitude of moral judgments depended on any correspondence with extra-human reality.) Hume's moral theory is an attempt – and in many respects a successful one – to show why any such complex ontological terminology and the fanciful commitment which goes with it are superfluous, since the phenomena of morality can be adequately explained without recourse to any such philosophical fictions. Of course, not everyone finds palatable such a thorough-going naturalistic account of morality, just as not everyone can accept materialistic accounts of the nature of man; but questions as to the adequacy of such explanations are quite external to the theories themselves, since they involve presuppositions of a more general kind. It is a commitment to such a presupposition (his conviction that moral scepticism can be effectively opposed only by some kind of moral realism) which hinders Norton from explaining in simpler fashion the apparent inconsistency (noted in section V) in Hume's use of the words 'virtue' and 'vice'. Norton consequently becomes embroiled in a metaphysical morass that is both profoundly alien to the philosopher whose ideas he claims to be expounding and so unintelligible that Norton is himself unsure just where he stands and therefore unable to make this clear to his readers. For while denying both that virtue and vice are physical objects and also that they exist transcendentally[66], he yet wants to posit for them some kind of independent ontological status as objective correlates of affective states. Evidently, these objective correlates must be non-natural for otherwise there would be no substantial divergence on this issue between Norton's and the more usual interpretations of Hume; nor would he need to posit on their behalf any special kind of ontological status. He says: "...the character of our feeling serves to reveal the moral character of an objective (publicly available) situation."[67] This may well be Norton's view; but we have no good reason to suppose that it was Hume's, who thought not that our feelings *reveal* the moral character of situations, but rather that they *constitute* their moral character – a much weaker but a much more defensible claim.

VIII

The antepenultimate section of Norton's chapter on 'Hume's common sense moral theory'[68] incorporates a fairly detailed enumeration of instances in which Hume appeals to the authority of the general sentiments of mankind both against moral scepticism and against paradoxical or subversive innovation in political theory. Norton affirms very confidently:

> That Hume maintains that any conflicts between moral theories and our common-sensical views of morality are always to be resolved in favor of the common-sense view cannot be seriously doubted.[69]

He subsequently poses what to him is a crucial question in view of his commitment to the thesis that Hume is essentially a common sense moral philosopher: namely, why is such an appeal to common sense justified? Now the phrase 'common-sensical views of morality' is ambiguous. If it means that common sense views *as to the nature of morality* must always override revisionary theories, then Norton's remark is false; for Hume's own moral theory is quite innovatory (Hume himself called it "a considerable advancement of the speculative sciences"[70]) and, as to the nature of morality, it is in clear conflict with the common sense views of his own time, which supposed some kind of moral realism rather than psychological naturalism. Indeed, if Hume had been – and had been seen to be – what Norton imagines he was, he would not have been so often vilified by zealous bigots. If, on the other hand, Norton means that Hume maintained that *on particular moral issues* the dictates of common sense are always to be preferred to the prescriptions of a moral theory, again he is wrong, but less obviously so. I cannot help thinking that appeals to common sense on Hume's part are made more out of convenience than out of conviction. Although Hume's account of the nature of morality is radical, the actual moral content of his writings was, in general, conservative and well attuned to the age in which he lived.[71] On most concrete moral issues then, he was able to appeal to the unreflective sentiments current among contemporary Europeans of learning or rank, since these sentiments were likely to accord with his own prescriptions. When, on the other hand, common sentiments ran counter to his own, he was not averse to dismissing them as the product of error and superstition. The essay 'On Suicide', for example, opens by extolling philosophy for the "sovereign antidote which it affords"[72] when our moral sentiments have been perverted by superstition and false religion. In view of his readiness always in principle and on occasion in practice to revise common sense morality in the light of philosophy, I would not concede that Hume is a common sense moralist. Moreover, in so calling him there is a real danger of assimilating his moral theory to that of Thomas Reid and his successors, whose pronouncements on the nature of morality were designedly in stark contradiction to Hume's. But while Hume's appeals to common *sense* are incidental, his appeals to common *sentiment* are crucial to his moral theory; for he persevered in maintaining – in my submission most implausibly[73] – that, despite appearances to the contrary, the moral sentiments of mankind are in all places and ages uniform. As far as Hume was concerned, this uniformity constituted an ultimate justification of morality and a quasi-logical barrier to quests for any ulterior one. As he himself says in the first appendix to the *Enquiry*:

> ..the ultimate ends of human actions...recommend themselves entirely to the sentiments and affections of mankind...It is impossible there can be a progress *in infinitum*; and that one thing can always be a reason why another is desired. Something must be desirable on its own account, and because of its immediate accord or agreement with human sentiment and affection.[74]

Norton's question as to why Hume thought that an appeal to the common moral sentiments of mankind is justified is very simply answered by the above quotation. The answer proposed by Norton is, characteristically, far more devious. He refers again to the passage in the *Treatise* where Hume says:

> The distinction of moral good and evil is founded on the pleasure or pain, which results from the view of any sentiment, or character; and as that pleasure or pain cannot be unknown to the person who feels it, it follows, that there is just so much vice or virtue in any character, as every one places in it, and that 'tis impossible in this particular we can ever be mistaken.[75]

But instead of taking this passage at its face value (which would be incongruous with the Procrustean bed of moral realism on which he is determined to make Hume lie) he proposes the following 'amplification' of Hume's argument:

> The argument underlying this justification consists of three premises, only two of which does Hume make sufficiently explicit:
> 1. Moral distinctions are founded on the pleasure and pain which arise from the morally proper observation of character or motive (a fixed principle of mind).
> 2. These pleasures and pains (as well as others, of course) must be known to those who feel them.
>
> To these explicit premises Hume should have added a third:
> 3. When one has a pleasure or pain of the sort specified (arising from the observation of character), one *attributes* virtue or vice to the character observed, and, further, there is an exact correlation between the pleasure or pain felt and the virtue or vice which gives rise to them.
>
> With this premise made explicit, Hume's objectivist conclusion does follow:
> 4. "There is just so much vice or virtue in any character, as every one places in it," which is to say that we have direct access to the pleasures and pains produced in ourselves upon the morally proper observation of a character, and as there is an exact correlation between these feelings and the moral qualities of the character giving rise to them, "'tis impossible in this particular we can ever be mistaken...." If one does in fact notice a *moral* distinction, one cannot be mistaken about it, for the pleasure or pain that give notice of the distinction are, under these conditions, infallible signs of virtue or vice.[76]

To the additional premise which Norton has here supplied I would object that it incorporates the false assumption that has always bedevilled Benthamite utilitarians: namely, that pleasures and pains can be precisely quantified. (As Reid quizzically remarks in the early lines of his *Essay on Quantity*, "Pain and pleasure admit of various degrees, but who can pretend to measure them?"[77]) Moreover, since *ex hypothesi* the virtue and vice are supposed to be inaccessible to our ordinary senses and can therefore never be perceived directly (in which respect they are even worse off than the beetle in Wittgenstein's matchbox[78]) how could one even *begin* to establish the accuracy of the correlation which Norton postulates between them and the pleasures and pains which alone are the objects of awareness?

All this would be a very far cry from Hume's "attempt to introduce the experimental method of reasoning into moral subjects"[79]. But in any case, what Norton's additional premise claims (that there is an exact correlation between the pleasure or pain of our moral sentiments and the degree of esteem that we accord) is expressly denied by Hume, who points out that though the qualities of those remote from us (either temporally or spacially) do *not* affect us with such lively pleasures and pains as those close by, we rate the former no differently from the latter on this account because we are able to compensate for the distortion caused by proximity or remoteness.[80] That Norton is himself well aware of Hume's pronouncement to this effect[81] makes it the more surprising – and the more reprehensible – that he presumes to introduce his spurious premise.

IX

To conclude, I agree that Hutcheson and Hume were opposed to nihilistic scepticism, but maintain that their conception of morality was essentially a psychological one, free from metaphysical postulates of any suprasensory or non-natural moral reality. I think, therefore, that to call them moral realists is misleading. In view of the misunderstandings, misrepresentations, ambiguities, and contradictions which pervade Norton's arguments, his attempt to establish that they *were* moral realists must be accounted unsuccessful. Indeed, I submit that Norton's enterprise in seeking to reinterpret Hutcheson and Hume in this most extraordinary manner is, at best, overweeningly ambitious, or, to deploy one of Norton's own phrases, "an exercise of pretentious fancy".[82] Perhaps his book heralds a whole new kind of philosophical scholarship, in which case perhaps we can look forward to the appearance of volumes in which Locke's *Essay* will be interpreted as an elaborate defence of innate ideas, or Karl Marx presented as an apologist for capitalism. For when commentators have the temerity to ignore entirely the consensus of earlier scholarship and allow themselves the liberty to disregard at their pleasure the contents of the very works they purport to be expounding, the possibilities must be truly unbounded.

NOTES

1. David Fate Norton *David Hume – Common Sense Moralist, Sceptical Metaphysician* (Princeton U.P., 1982). Hereafter referred to as N. 116, 150.
2. See my "Hume, Spencer and the Standard of Morals", *Philosophy* 58 (1983):39–55.
3. I am using *naturalistic* in the sense of 'not postulating suprasensory, non-natural qualities', not in the sense of 'involving the complete subordination of reason to feeling'.
4. N. 59.
5. In D.D. Raphael (Ed.), *British Moralists*, 2 vols. (Oxford: Clarendon Press, 1969), II, p. 132.
6. Dugald Stewart, *Collected Works*, edited by Sir William Hamilton, 11 vols. (Edinburgh: Thomas Constable & Co., 1854–60), V, pp. 81–82.

7. James McCosh, *The Scottish Philosophy* (London: Macmillan, 1875) p. 80.
8. Thomas Fowler, *Shaftesbury and Hutcheson* (London: Sampson, Low, Marston, Searle & Rivington, 1882), p. 196.
9. L.A. Selby-Bigge (Ed.), *British Moralists*, 2 vols. (Oxford: Clarendon Press, 1897). Hereafter referred to as BM I 1.
10. T.H. Green and T.H. Grose (Eds.), *The Philosophical Works of David Hume*, 4 vols. (London: Longman, Green & Co., 1874–1875), II, p. 31.
11. T.H. Huxley, *Hume* (London: Macmillan, 1879).
12. W.R. Scott, *Francis Hutcheson* (Cambridge U.P., 1900; repr. New York: Augustus M. Kelley, 1966), pp. 187, 194, 208.
13. John Laird, *Hume's Philosophy of Human Nature* (London: Methuen, 1932).
14. N. 43–48.
15. N. 12 n. 26.
16. N. 284.
17. BM I xli.
18. N. 27.
19. N. 49.
20. N. 72 n. 29.
21. BM I li.
22. N. 72–73.
23. N. 77.
24. Francis Hutcheson, *An Inquiry into the Original of our Ideas of Beauty and Virtue*, fourth edition (London, 1738; repr. Farnborough: Gregg International Publishers, 1969). Hereafter referred to as *Inquiry* 135.
25. *Inquiry* 201.
26. Francis Hutcheson, *An Essay on the Nature and Conduct of the Passions and Affections with Illustrations on the Moral Sense* (London, 1742). Hereafter referred to as EPMS 89.
27. Cf. Anthony Kenny, *Action, Emotion and Will* (London: Routledge & Kegan Paul, 1963), p. 191. Whereas Kenny maintains that the relationship between emotions and their formal objects is *logically* necessary, Hutcheson would maintain that it was *empirically* necessary.
28. N. 85 n. 49.
29. *Inquiry* 130–131.
30. Hutcheson, like Hume, is not entirely consistent on this point. See Scott (note 12 above) 190–191, and note 55 below.
31. I.e. in a class of their own, quite unlike anything perceptible by ordinary senses.
32. *Inquiry* 115.
33. *Inquiry* 129.
34. Francis Hutcheson, *A System of Moral Philosophy* 2 vols. (Glasgow: R. & R. Foulis, 1755; repr. New York: Augustus M. Kelley, 1968), I, p. 58; italics mine.
35. W.R. Scott estimates that it was completed by November, 1737. See his *Francis Hutcheson* (note 12), pp. 113 and 210.
36. See Scott 222–223 for an account of Hutcheson's oscillation between incompatible tenets in *A System of Moral Philosophy*.
37. N. 81.
38. N. 80 n. 44.
39. N. 82.
40. *Inquiry* 100.
41. *Inquiry* 301–302.
42. EPMS 288.
43. N. 84–85.
44. EPMS 288.
45. N. 85.
46. N. 86.
47. N. 109.

48. David Hume, *A Treatise of Human Nature*, edited by L.A. Selby-Bigge, revised by P.H. Nidditch (Oxford: Clarendon Press, 1978). Hereafter referred to as T. 469.
49. David Hume, *Enquiries...*, edited by L.A. Selby-Bigge, revised by P.H. Nidditch (Oxford: Clarendon Press, 1975). Hereafter referred to as E. 261.
50. E. 289.
51. David Hume, *A Letter from a Gentleman to his Friend in Edinburgh*, edited by E.C. Mossner and J.V. Price (Edinburgh U.P., 1967), p. 18.
52. See Selby-Bigge's *Introduction*, E. vii.
53. T. 469.
54. N. 111.
55. Whereas in the postscript of a letter to Hutcheson (*Letters of David Hume*, edited by J.Y.T. Greig, 2 vols. [Oxford: Clarendon Press, 1932], I, 34–35). Hume had laid stress on motives, as indicating durable principles of an agent's character, by the time he wrote the second *Enquiry* he appeared to think that it was the consequences of actions that matter most. See E. 180–181.
56. T. 470.
57. E. 270.
58. E. 198.
59. See "A Dialogue", E. 324–343.
60. N. 113–116.
61. T. 575.
62. T. 468–469.
63. E. 292–293.
64. N. 111.
65. N. 116.
66. N. 111 n. 15.
67. N. 120.
68. N. 133–147.
69. N. 135.
70. T. 469.
71. See David Miller, *Philosophy and Ideology in Hume's Political Thought* (Oxford: Clarendon Press, 1981).
72. David Hume, *Philosophical Works* (see note 10), IV, p. 406.
73. See my "Hume, Spencer and the Standard of Morals", especially pages 45–48 (see note 2).
74. E. 293.
75. T. 546–547.
76. N. 142–143.
77. Thomas Reid, *Works*, edited by Sir William Hamilton, 2 vols. (Edinburgh: Machlachlan and Stewart, 1863), p. 715a.
78. Ludwig Wittgenstein, *Philosophical Investigations*, translated by G.E.M. Anscombe (Oxford: Blackwell, 1963), § 293.
79. T. xi.
80. T. 581–582, E. 227–228.
81. N. 119.
82. N. 302.

Hume, Spencer and the Standard of Morals

J. MARTIN STAFFORD

Philosophy has often been represented by its detractors, and even sometimes by its practitioners, as a subject which, unlike the natural sciences, exhibits a degree of progress far from commensurate with its long history. Many of the questions entertained by the ancients are still very much alive: answers proffered are put forward very tentatively, seldom meet with universal acceptance, and frequently give rise to controversy even more prolific than that which they were intended to lay low.

One area of enquiry which might plausibly be defended against any imputation of failure to make progress is naturalistic ethics, which during the eighteenth and nineteenth centuries underwent an improvement perhaps less striking but no less real than the scientific and industrial innovations of those times. There is no shortage of literature[1] discussing the transition from Francis Hutcheson's theory, in which is postulated an inherent and unanalysable moral sense, by which God-given faculty certain characters and deeds are *felt* to be good or evil, to Hume's more explanatory theory of moral sentiment, in which approval and disapproval are accounted for by the operations of sympathy and benevolence.[2] On the other hand, the more obscure relationship between the ethical writings of Hume and those of Herbert Spencer seems almost entirely to have eluded the attention of scholars. This discrepancy of treatment is no doubt due to the fact that whereas Hutcheson and Hume were partly contemporary and actually corresponded about their common interest, forty-four years elapsed between the death of Hume and the birth of Spencer, who, moreover, despite his awareness of Hume's existence, makes no allusions to his work. The fact that these two enjoyed no contiguity in time or space and that Spencer was not consciously influenced

[1] See especially N. Kemp Smith, *The Philosophy of David Hume* (London: Macmillan, 1941); also J. Laird, *Hume's Philosophy of Human Nature* (London: Methuen, 1932); W. T. Blackstone, *Francis Hutcheson and Contemporary Ethical Theory* (Athens: University of Georgia Press, 1965) and Henning Jensen, *Motivation and Moral Sense in Francis Hutcheson's Ethical Theory* (The Hague: Martinus Nijhoff, 1971).

[2] In the *Treatise*, but not in the *Enquiry*, sympathy is reduced to more general psychological principles. Compare page 317 of the *Treatise* ('When any affection . . .') to the end of page 318 with the note on page 219 of the *Enquiry*. For details of editions see 7 and 21 below.

by Hume has, abetted by Spencer's unduly low posthumous reputation, no doubt deflected Hume scholars from examining the seemingly tenuous connection between their respective theories.

Within recent years, however, Professor Flew has made at least two pertinent but somewhat cryptic remarks, without apparently pursuing their implications. In a short monograph published in 1967 he observed that

> [certain] approaches to moral questions and accounts of their nature—those of Hume, for instance—can accommodate themselves very comfortably with the fact of general and moral evolution; and indeed some—Hume again provides an example—might almost seem to demand an evolutionary background.[3]

More recently Flew has remarked that 'Hume's approach to the origin of social institutions is . . . evolutionary as opposed to creationist . . .'[4] In this paper I shall aim to show: (1) that Hume's pronouncements on moral and social evolution[5] are more equivocal than has hitherto been made clear, and that his moral theory is marred by both internal contradictions and conflicts with evidence available to him; (2) that these defects could have been made good by a more thorough-going evolutionary approach such as that of Spencer; and (3) that Spencer's writings are worthy of both more protracted and more sympathetic consideration than they receive from Professor Flew in his *Evolutionary Ethics*.

I

Despite the high regard in which Hume held his second *Enquiry*,[6] it is in the *Treatise* that some of his most pregnant and far-sighted observations are made, particularly in his treatment of the origin of the artificial virtues. By calling other virtues natural, he effectively denies the need to account for their origin or propagation. As far as Hume is concerned, virtues such

[3] A. G. N. Flew, *Evolutionary Ethics* (London: Macmillan, 1967), 59. Hereafter referred to as Flew. If the hardback collected edition is consulted, all page numbers should be increased by 216.

[4] Antony Flew, 'Three Questions About Justice in the *Treatise*', *Philosophical Quarterly* **26**, No. 102 (1976), 7.

[5] The term 'evolutionary', when applied to Hume's writings should not be understood in a full-blooded Darwinian sense with all its connotations of natural selection. It is none the less appropriate if used simply to suggest that a phenomenon is undergoing development.

[6] In his brief autobiography, frequently reprinted in editions of and selections from his works, he expressed the view that it is ' . . . of all my writings, historical, philosophical, or literary, incomparably the best . . .'.

as kindness to the distressed and care of offspring stand in no need of explanation: they are inherent in human nature. I shall later argue that this nativistic account of the natural virtues and of the benevolence or humanity on which all moral approval ultimately depends poses problems quite unresolved until the advent of evolutionary ethics. Hume's treatment of the artificial virtues, however, is more penetrating in that an attempt is made to explain their origin and development.

The first paragraph of the section entitled 'Of the origin of justice and property' poses two questions

> *concerning the manner, in which the rules of justice are establish'd by the artifice of men;* and *concerning the reasons, which determine us to attribute to the observance or neglect of these rules a moral beauty and deformity.*[7]

Briefly, Hume's account of the origin of society and of justice runs as follows. Man in a solitary state would be unable to support himself; only in society can he supply his intrinsic defects:

> By the conjunction of forces, our power is augmented: By the partition of employments, our ability encreases: And by mutual succour we are less expos'd to fortune and accidents. 'Tis by this additional *force*, *ability*, and *security*, that society becomes advantageous.[8]

He then candidly points out an impediment to social confederation:

> But in order to form society, 'tis requisite not only that it be advantageous, but also that men be sensible of its advantages; and 'tis impossible, in their wild uncultivated state, that by study and reflexion alone, they should ever be able to attain this knowledge.[9]

He then assumes that the family is a pre-social institution out of which a larger confederacy develops. Quite apart from the over-simplicity of this assumption,[10] we might ask why the advantages of social living should be so much more apparent to wild, uncultivated families than to wild, uncultivated individuals. However, this assumption led Hume to envisage no truly pre-social state in human history, and only a very brief period before rules of property were formulated.[11] Having remarked on the

[7] David Hume, *A Treatise of Human Nature*, P. H. Nidditch (ed.) (Oxford: Clarendon Press, 1978), 484. Hereafter referred to as T.

[8] T 485.

[9] T 486.

[10] Over-simple in that while the biological family must have preceded the development of society, it is hardly plausible that pre-social families were as structured as socialized ones.

[11] In this respect, those who postulated a pre-social state of nature were closer to the truth than Hume; though it was not as they imagined, nor was it terminated by a contract.

shortage of natural resources and on man's partiality to himself and his kin, Hume observes:

> ... when men, from their early education in society, have become sensible of the infinite advantages that result from it, and have besides acquir'd a new affection to company and conversation; and when they have observ'd, that the principal disturbance in society arises from those goods, which we call external, and from their looseness and easy transition from one person to another; they must seek for a remedy, by putting these goods, as far as possible, on the same footing with the fix'd and constant advantages of the mind and body. This can be done after no other manner, than by a convention enter'd into by all the members of the society to bestow stability on the possession of those external goods, and leave every one in the peaceable enjoyment of what he may acquire by his fortune and industry.[12]

Now Hume is very vague about the nature of this convention. It cannot be a promise, because the institution of promising is itself dependent on an anterior convention. He does observe, nevertheless:

> Nor is the rule concerning the stability of possession the less deriv'd from human conventions, *that it arises gradually, and acquires force by a slow progression*, and by our repeated experience of the inconveniences of transgressing it.[13]

However, a subsequent remark conflicts with this quasi-evolutionary account of the origin of property. According to Hume, general benevolence is too weak to inhibit men from purloining the property of others. The incentive to restraint was initially one of enlightened self-interest. Men saw that their appetites were ultimately better gratified by their practising some restraint than by unbridled indulgence, for that would have brought about the dissolution of society and a return to the inconveniences of solitary living. Hume says:

> Now as 'tis by establishing the rule for the stability of possession, that this passion [self-interest] restrains itself; if that rule be very abstruse, and of difficult invention; society must be esteem'd, in a manner, accidental, and the effect of many ages. But if it be found, that nothing can be more simple and obvious than that rule; that every parent, in order to preserve peace among his children, must establish it; and that these first rudiments of justice must every day be improv'd, as the society enlarges: If all this appear evident, as it certainly must, we may conclude, that 'tis utterly impossible for man to remain any considerable time in

[12] T 489.
[13] T 490, italics mine.

> that savage condition, which precedes society; but that his very first state and situation may justly be esteem'd social.[14]

Now the point of conflict which arises from this is not so much that Hume was mistaken in attributing the origin of society solely to the prior existence of the family, but that by postulating the family as a more natural entity which precedes society, he is led to contradict his earlier suggestion that 'the rule concerning stability of possession . . . arises gradually, and acquires force by a slow progression'. He now denies that society must be 'the effect of many ages', and asserts rather that the first state of man must have been social. Hume seems, then, to have been in two minds as to whether society and the rules which support it evolved slowly or arose quite suddenly. To us who live after the formulation of evolutionary theory it is easy to appreciate that society is indeed 'the effect of many ages'. Hume's equivocations can be understood, and he can be credited for his perceptive genius in realizing and intimating that perhaps society did evolve; though it is obviously difficult for him to reconcile an evolutionary account of society with the very static view of human nature which he undoubtedly embraced.

I come now to consider Hume's doctrine of the catholicity of moral sentiment. He maintained fairly consistently that there was underlying the apparent differences in moral response a more basic unanimity. This he attributed to the uniform benevolence of human nature—a postulate which he goes to great lengths to defend. I shall try to show that if he had anticipated the evolutionary theory of *human* development even as vaguely as he intimated the possibility of social evolution, some of the difficulties which he candidly presents but unconvincingly eliminates in the short *Dialogue* appended to the second *Enquiry* might have been obviated. I shall also argue later that had he been far-sighted enough to embrace an evolutionary view of human nature, the dichotomy between natural and artificial virtues, of which so much is made in the *Treatise*, would not have appeared so clear-cut. However, since the degree of far-sightedness requisite to this end would have been little short of clairvoyance, Hume's failing in this particular is hardly a very culpable one.

There is clearly a strong case for arguing that the artificial virtues are more deliberately established and promoted than are the natural ones, not merely because it is only when viewed comprehensively that their perpetration is beneficial, but also because reflection confirms that they are indeed less internalized than the natural ones, which in most people receive immediate and instinctive acceptance:

> [Since] every particular act of generosity, or relief of the industrious and indigent, is beneficial; and is beneficial to a particular person,

[14] T 492–493.

> who is not undeserving of it, 'tis more natural . . . to think that the tendencies of the latter virtue will affect our sentiments, and command our approbation, than those of [justice].[15]

However, Hume's determination to assert that some virtues are instinctive is partly a reaction against the egoistic psychology propounded by Hobbes and, more especially, Mandeville, at whom the following paragraph is obviously aimed:

> That many of the natural virtues have this tendency to the good of society, no one can doubt of. Meekness, beneficence, charity, generosity, clemency, moderation, equity, bear the greatest figure among the moral qualities, and are commonly denominated the *social* virtues, to mark their tendency to the good of society. This goes so far, that some philosophers have represented all moral distinctions as the effect of artifice and education, when skilful politicians endeavour'd to restrain the turbulent passions of men, and make them operate to the public good, by the notions of honour and shame. This system, however, is not consistent with experience. For, *first*, there are other virtues and vices besides those which have this tendency to the public advantage and loss. *Secondly*, had not men a natural sentiment of approbation and blame, it cou'd never be excited by politicians; nor wou'd the words *laudable* and *praise-worthy*, *blameable* and *odious*, be any more intelligible, than if they were a language perfectly unknown to us, as we have already observ'd.[16]

The same point is also made more briefly in the conclusion of Book III of the *Treatise*:

> It requires but very little knowledge of human affairs to perceive, that a sense of morals is a principle inherent in the soul, and one of the most powerful that enters into the composition.[17]

The need to maintain a natural sentiment of approbation as the basis of all morality would have been obviated to some extent by an evolutionary explanation, which would have accounted for this feeling by a process of gradual development. As it is, Hume postulated an intrinsic benevolence or humanity common to all men. In the introduction to his selection of Hume's political writings Frederick Watkins remarks:

> Hume had the advantage . . . of living in a period when the detailed historical and anthropological information available to Western scholars was still largely confined to the experience of the Western world itself.

[15] T 580, punctuation slightly amended.
[16] T 578–579. The earlier passage here alluded to is on page 500, and the same point is made on page 214 of the second *Enquiry* (see 21 below).
[17] T 619.

This made it possible to credit historical experience with a degree of uniformity which would hardly bear the scrutiny of modern scientists.[18]

While there is obviously much truth in what Watkins says, we should not overestimate the extent to which the evidence was univocal. Hume and such of his contemporaries as Adam Smith[19] and Thomas Reid[20] were well aware of the barbarous practices of antiquity as well as those of North American Indians. The dissonance between these practices and the sentiments of eighteenth-century Europe could hardly have failed to embarrass writers such as Reid, who professed to believe that all men are endowed with a God-given conscience, or even Hume, who, notwithstanding the evidence to the contrary, persevered in maintaining that human nature is uniformly philanthropic:

> The notion of morals implies some sentiment common to all mankind, which recommends the same object to general approbation, and makes every man, or most men, agree in the same opinion or decision concerning it. It also implies some sentiment, so universal and comprehensive as to extend to all mankind, and render the actions and conduct, even of the persons the most remote, an object of applause or censure, according as they agree or disagree with that rule of right which is established. These two requisite circumstances belong alone to the sentiment of humanity here insisted on.[21]

However, Hume does make concessions which tend to undermine his theory in two less studied works—the essay on the 'The Sceptic' and the *Dialogue* appended to the second *Enquiry*. In the former, while delivering an extreme sentimentalist account of aesthetics and morals, he observes:

> We may push the same observation further, and may conclude, that, even when the mind operates alone, and feeling the sentiment of blame or approbation, pronounces one object deformed and odious, another beautiful and amiable; I say, that, even in this case, those qualities are not really in the objects, but belong entirely to the sentiment of that mind which blames or praises. I grant, that it will be more difficult to make this proposition evident, and as it were, palpable, to negligent thinkers; because nature is more uniform in the sentiments of the mind than in most feelings of the body, and produces a nearer resemb-

18 Frederick Watkins, *Hume's Theory of Politics* (Edinburgh: Nelson, 1951), xv.

19 See Adam Smith, *The Theory of Moral Sentiments*, D. D. Raphael and A. L. Macfie (eds) (Oxford: Clarendon Press, 1976), 205–211.

20 See Thomas Reid, *Works*, 6th edn, Sir William Hamilton (ed.), 2 vols (Edinburgh: 1863), 596.

21 David Hume, *Enquiries* . . . , 3rd edn, revised by P. H. Nidditch (Oxford: Clarendon Press, 1975), 272. Hereafter referred to as E. Universal philanthropy is claimed also on pages 227, 230, 271 and 273.

> lance in the inward than in the outward part of human kind. There is something approaching to principles in mental tastes; and critics can reason and dispute more plausibly than cooks or perfumers. We may observe, however, that this uniformity among human kind, hinders not, but that there is a considerable diversity in the sentiments of beauty and worth, and that education, custom, prejudice, caprice, and humour, frequently vary our taste of this kind.[22]

Although this is a denial of uniformity in matters of taste rather than in morals, the close similarity in their underlying epistemology suggests that techniques which were able to produce variation in one might also be employed to secure change in the other. It is just such diversity which is discussed in the *Dialogue* appended to the second *Enquiry*. This purports to be a conversation between Hume and an imaginary friend, Palamades, who begins thus:

> There is a country in the world, called Fourli, . . . whose inhabitants have ways of thinking, in many things, particularly in morals, diametrically opposite to ours.[23]

He proceeds to describe a period which he spent there, and how he was surprised to find that the following practices were there considered not merely acceptable, but positively laudable: pederasty, incestuous marriage, infanticide, assassination, submission to violence without retaliation, and suicide. Prevailing notions of good manners were also at variance with his own. When Hume disbelieves the story, alleging that 'such barbarous and savage manners are not only incompatible with a civilised, intelligent people, such as you say these were; but are scarcely compatible with human nature',[24] Palamades retorts that the characters he described were in fact the ancient Greeks, disguised by false names, and points out how all the characteristics listed in his narrative are indeed instantiated by the ancients.

Hume replies that his friend has misrepresented the Greeks, and should view with indulgence the customs of a different age, rather than judge them by a standard unknown to themselves. He points out that the Athenians would have deplored the facility with which a certain people countenance adultery, their servile obedience to an absolute monarch, the excesses of gallantry manifest in duelling, and the useless austerities of convents and monasteries. Palamades recognizes the description as one of the French, and pleads that he meant only 'to represent the uncertainty of all these

[22] David Hume, *Philosophical Works*, T. H. Green and T. H. Grose (eds), 4 vols (London: Longmans, Green & Co., 1874–75; reprinted Aalen: Scientia Verlag, 1964), Vol. III, 216–217.

[23] E 324.

[24] E 328.

judgments concerning characters; and to convince you, that fashion, vogue, custom, and law, were the chief foundation of all moral determinations'.[25] For though both the French and the Athenians be a civilized and intelligent people, a character who was esteemed among the one would be contemned by the other. And yet these two peoples are usually thought to be similar in national character:

> What wide difference, therefore, in the sentiments of morals, must be found between civilized nations and Barbarians, or between nations whose characters have little in common? How shall we pretend to fix a standard for judgments of this nature?[25]

Hume seeks to secure his theory by recourse to greater generality of formulation. The conflict is to be resolved

> By tracing matters a little higher, and examining the first principles, which each nation establishes, of blame or censure. The Rhine flows north, the Rhone south; yet both spring from the *same* mountain, and are also actuated, in their opposite directions, by the *same* principle of gravity. The different inclinations of the ground, on which they run, cause all the difference of their courses.
>
> In how many circumstances would an Athenian and a French man of merit certainly resemble each other? Good sense, knowledge, wit, eloquence, humanity, fidelity, truth, justice, courage, temperance, constancy, dignity of mind: These you have all omitted; in order to insist only on the points, in which they may, by accident, differ.[25]

This seems a fairly desperate attempt to reconcile the conflict. The cardinal virtues allegedly common to both French and Greeks are here expressed in too general terms. Palamades could easily reply that there is considerable diversity of opinion as to what constitutes 'humanity, justice, courage, dignity of mind', and in the face of this, Hume's assertion of unanimity is rather empty. Indeed, Hume is best confounded on this point by his own observations in the early paragraphs of the dissertation 'On the Standard of Taste'—one of the four published in 1757, only six years after the *Dialogue*:

> There are certain terms in every language, which import blame, and others praise; and all men, who use the same tongue, must agree in their application of them. Every voice is united in applauding elegance, propriety, simplicity, spirit in writing; and in blaming fustian, affectation, coldness, and a false brilliancy: But when critics come to particulars, this seeming unanimity vanishes; and it is found, that they had affixed a very different meaning to their expressions. . . . Those who found morality on sentiment, more than on reason, are inclined to comprehend ethics under the former observation, and to maintain, that, in all

[25] E 333.

> questions, which regard conduct and manners, the difference among men is really greater than at first sight it appears. It is indeed obvious, that writers of all nations and all ages concur in applauding justice, humanity, magnanimity, prudence, veracity; and in blaming the opposite qualities. . . . This great unanimity is usually ascribed to the influence of plain reason; which, in all these cases, maintains similar sentiments in all men, and prevents those controversies, to which the abstract sciences are so much exposed. So far as the unanimity is real, this account may be admitted as satisfactory: But we must also allow that some part of the seeming harmony in morals may be accounted for from the very nature of language. The word *virtue*, with its equivalent in every tongue, implies praise; as that of *vice* does, blame: And no one, without the most obvious and grossest impropriety, could affix reproach to a term, which in general acceptation is understood in a good sense; or bestow applause, where the idiom requires disapprobation.[26]

Now surely Hume's demonstration of unanimity in the *Dialogue* is merely verbal, since even the words which denote particular virtues are sufficiently indefinite that they can be applied by different people to quite dissimilar situations. When it comes to particulars, there is not the unanimity which Hume liked to believe there was—not even latently.

The diversity of moral response which mankind undoubtedly displays constitutes an important weakness in Hume's moral philosophy. For if human nature fails to exhibit the kind of uniformity which Hume thought can provide a standard for moral judgment, where is that standard to be sought? Where there is real and deep-rooted conflict of moral sentiment, how—if at all—can it be resolved?

II

The writings of Herbert Spencer go some way towards solving this problem, which clearly perplexed Hume, but to which he was able to give only unsatisfactory answers. Moreover, although Spencer was by no means as radical an empiricist as Hume is sometimes represented as being, his speculations were usually supported by a vast quantity of empirical data. In view both of the partial affinity between their respective methods of enquiry and of their shared interests, it is not inappropriate to acclaim Spencer as one of Hume's intellectual successors.[27] I shall here restrict

[26] David Hume, *Philosophical Works* (see n. 22 above), Vol. III, 266–267.

[27] Or, conversely, to see Hume as a precursor of evolutionary theorists. According to Duncan Forbes, Comte saluted Hume as the founder of the law of the Temporal or Active Evolution. See his 'Hume and the Scottish Enlightenment', in S. C. Brown (ed.), *Philosophers of the Enlightenment* (Sussex: Harvester Press, 1979), 108, note 2.

myself to considering only those portions of Spencer's copious writings which bear on the topics I have so far considered.

In *The Data of Ethics* of 1879—part of his great ten-volume *System of Synthetic Philosophy*—Spencer considers the evolution of conduct and of character under three aspects: as it affects (i) self-preservation; (ii) the rearing of offspring; and thence (iii) the maintenance of the race, observing that advances in these kinds of conduct are interdependent. He envisaged an as yet unrealized state of affairs where all conduct would be perfectly evolved—that is to say, where all creatures would be so perfectly adjusted to their environment that the ends pursued by each would be consistent with the well-being of all the others. He also hinted at the development from mere peaceful co-existence to universal co-operation. Why, in Spencer's view, is such active co-operation necessary, and under what conditions is its development possible?

As man becomes more advanced, his requirements become increasingly multifarious—so much so that each individual could not possibly aspire to provide them all for himself. The more advanced his state of development, the more heterogeneous must be the co-operation which takes place; that is to say, a larger number of people must collaborate; they must have different functions, and thus make diverse contributions to the corporate effort. This social process is in fact a particular instance of Spencer's general law of evolution, namely that it is '. . . a change from an incoherent homogeneity to a coherent heterogeneity . . .'.[28] Advances in civilization and co-operation take place concomitantly, the latter making possible the former; the former making necessary the latter. Co-operative action and the adjustments made to favour it are indeed as necessary as the social developments promoted by convention which Hume had in mind when treating of the artificial virtues. Spencer was making a claim for 'evolved' conduct comparable with, but much stronger than, that made by Hume when he observed: 'Tho' the rules of justice are artificial, they are not arbitrary'.[29]

Obviously, co-operation can take place only in social units where internal aggression has been largely eliminated and trust established. Accordingly, civilized societies will tend to be characterized by those norms and sentiments which are conducive to internal harmony and interpersonal confidence. Practices which operate directly against such stability will always be severely censured. Those whose ill-effects are more remote and therefore less evident may, however, be tolerated. Thus while murder, larceny, and untruthfulness are invariably proscribed among civilized people as being wholly incompatible with a highly organized social life,

[28] Herbert Spencer, *First Principles*, 5th edn (London: Williams and Norgate, 1893), 360.

[29] T 484.

various forms of intemperance and unchastity may be regarded with more indulgence, since the harm which they immediately occasion accrues primarily to the participants, while the social ill-effects are more remote:

> ... the social consciousness, not distinctly awakened to the social results, does not always generate consistent social sentiments.[30]

Now certain characteristics of human nature and certain standards of conduct do undoubtedly seem to have been favoured by the evolutionary process, and to have been so favoured inasmuch as they are conducive to the co-operation which advances civilisation, and as they are predictive of that further development which Spencer envisaged. The evolutionary process, therefore, has tended to vindicate these standards as pragmatic. Accordingly, the doctrine of evolution not only explains the diversity of morals, by postulating different stages of moral and social development, but also suggests how we might adjudicate between conflicting moral sentiments. For according to Spencer's theory, those moral sentiments would be counted privileged which empirical evidence suggests are favourable to the co-operation necessary in a civilized society, or which could be deductively shown to be requisite for such further development as Spencer thought to be highly probable.

There are at least two aspects of evolutionary ethical theory which are salient to Hume's account of ethics. Firstly, as has already been intimated, the confutation of Hume's presupposition that human nature is uniform—an assumption which, as we saw in section I, he had great difficulty in defending. Human nature is, even at any one time, at various stages of development. Any comparison between primitive savages and civilized man suggests not only the intellectual but also the moral superiority generally manifested by the latter:

> ... still more strikingly does the change become manifest when we compare undeveloped with developed humanity in respect of the conduct prompted by fellow feeling. Cruelty rather than kindness is characteristic of the savage, and is in many cases a source of marked gratification to him; but though among the civilized are some in whom this trait of the savage survives, yet a love of inflicting pain is not general, and besides numbers who show benevolence, there are those who devote their whole time and much of their money to philanthropic ends, without thought of reward either here or hereafter.[31]

[30] Herbert Spencer, *The Principles of Ethics*, 2 vols (London: Williams and Norgate, 1897–1900), Vol. I, 466. Hereafter referred to as P. of E.

[31] P. of E. Vol. I, 185. Cf. Edward Westermarck, *The Origin and Development of the Moral Ideas*, 2nd edn (London: Macmillan, 1912–17), Vol. II, 743, where in summary of his observations he remarks on the far greater scope of altruism among civilized races than among savages.

Secondly, the distinction between natural and artificial virtues must become blurred, since it is a tenet of Spencer's theory that the incentives to all requisite conduct will ultimately be internalized; that is to say, that all virtues will become natural:

> . . . the remoulding of human nature into fitness for the requirements of social life, must eventually make all needful activities pleasurable, while it makes displeasurable all activities at variance with these requirements.[32]

So that ultimately

> . . . the things now done with dislike from a sense of obligation will be done with immediate liking, and the things desisted from as a matter of duty will be desisted from because they are repugnant.[33]

Spencer supported this view by observing that precisely those adaptations which are consistent with his theory have been effected during the development of civilized man from his former savage state, and insisted that it is irrational not to suppose that there will be further adaptations such as are necessary to harmonise human nature with its conditions. In effect, he foresaw a time at which would be fulfilled *both* the conditions postulated by Hume as singly sufficient to render the notion of justice redundant—namely, the natural abundance of the necessities of life and the flowering of a spontaneous and unbounded altruism.[34] For if the external conditions did not change so as to provide all men with an abundance of what was needful for their welfare, man would himself undergo such changes as would render the environment so adequate. Simultaneously, altruism would become so extensive that we should entertain the same concern for all our fellow-creatures as we do for ourselves.

The similarity between Hume and Spencer on these points is striking, the most significant difference being that whereas Hume considered such a state of affairs only as an extremely remote hypothesis, neither realized in the past nor to be hoped for in the future, Spencer regarded it as an almost inevitable development which would see fruition in time to come. Spencer's remarks are rendered more complicated than Hume's by the more serious consideration which he gave to the idea, by the fact that the state of affairs he described is changing rather than static, and because he postulated the conjunction of environmental adequacy and ever-increasing benevolence, and speculated on their interaction. Hume, on the other hand, merely considered these conditions as alternatives, the fulfilment of either of which would have precluded the need to establish rules of property. After remarking how conflicts between the welfare of children

[32] P. of E. Vol. I, 183.
[33] P. of E. Vol. I, 184.
[34] See E 183–185 and T 491–493.

and that of parents have been reconciled by the development of parental altruism, Spencer observes:

> Now though altruism of a social kind, lacking certain elements of parental altruism, can never attain the same level; yet it may be expected to attain a level at which it will be like parental altruism in spontaneity—a level such that ministration to others' happiness will become a daily need—a level such that the lower egoistic satisfactions will be continually subordinated to this higher egoistic satisfaction, not by any effort to subordinate them, but by the preference for this higher egoistic satisfaction whenever it can be obtained.
>
> Let us consider how the development of sympathy, which must advance as fast as conditions permit, will bring about this state.[35]

Spencer's account of the conditions in which sympathy can develop is well worth summarizing. Since the extent to which sympathy yields pleasure or pain is determined by the frequency with which pleasurable and painful feelings are experienced by those around us, and by our sensitivity towards these people, and since faculties can develop only in conditions where their exercise yields a surplus of pleasure over pain, it follows that sympathy will develop only when we are accustomed to witnessing more pleasure than pain. Accordingly, it cannot develop significantly in a militant society, since its development must be arrested by frequent confrontation with the suffering brought about by aggression. Even in a peaceful society its development is retarded by the fact that imperfect adjustment to productive tasks renders them disagreeable and a source of misery; suffering is occasioned also by improvidence and by means of subsistence inadequate to the expansion of population. These problems will ultimately be solved by perfected adaptation, but this is a protracted process:

> ... as the moulding and re-moulding of man and society into mutual fitness progresses, and as the pains caused by unfitness decrease, sympathy can increase in presence of the pleasures that come from fitness. The two changes are indeed so related that each furthers the other. Such growth of sympathy as conditions permit, itself aids in lessening pain and augmenting pleasure; and the greater surplus of pleasure that results makes possible further growth of sympathy.[36]

III

At the beginning of this paper I claimed that Spencer is worthy of more sympathetic consideration than he receives from Professor Flew in his

[35] P. of E. Vol. I, 243–244.
[36] P. of E. Vol. I, 246.

monograph *Evolutionary Ethics*. I hope that the foregoing pages are alone sufficient to counter Flew's claim that 'such primary sources as Spencer's *The Principles of Ethics* . . . generally make protracted and unrewarding reading'.[37] I would also respectfully challenge, for reasons which should be obvious, Flew's assertion that 'there has been no spokesman for an evolutionary ethic of sufficient stature as a moral thinker to warrant the full individual treatment required by an Aristotle, a Hume, or a Kant'.[38]

One consequence of Flew's refusal to treat separately each of the writers he mentions is that a particular author can by association be tainted with the stain of misdeeds of which he is not guilty. Since Flew points out that in the context of *Darwin's* theory *Spencer's* phrase 'the survival of the fittest' becomes tautological, in that there is no criterion of fitness other than survival,[39] and reproves Joseph Needham for his statement that 'the evolutionary process itself supplies us with a criterion of the good',[40] it is important to emphasize that Spencer's evolutionary ethical theory is neither so trivial nor so uncritical. For Spencer it was the ideal of compatibility and co-operation—or at least their decreasingly imperfect manifestations—not the course of evolution considered as such, which constituted the criterion of morality; and by this criterion an organism's fitness to survive or even the course of evolution itself can be appraised. There can be no doubt that in many respects Spencer deprecated the trend of social evolution during the latter half of his own lifetime; for he declaimed with implacable vehemence against the socialistic legislation which was being enacted ever more and more voluminously. (For this reason alone, one might have expected that Flew, of all people, would regard Spencer with some measure of deference.) Indeed, Spencer fervently believed that increasing governmental interference was certain to promote the survival of types whom he thought decidedly unfit to survive.[41] Spencer did *not* say, then, that whatever was, is, and will be is right; nor, I suspect, did Needham mean this when he (carelessly?) wrote that 'the evolutionary process itself supplies us with a criterion of the good'.[42] Anyone who made so blind a profession of faith would surely be abandoning himself unreservedly as a hostage to fortune. What Spencer did believe was that the course of evolution has satisfied a moral criterion which quite independently of

37 Flew, 65 (see n. 3 above).

38 Flew, 2.

39 Flew, 13–14.

40 Flew, 48.

41 See for example *The Man v. the State* (London: Williams and Norgate, 1884); Vol. III of the *Essays Scientific, Political and Speculative* (London: Williams and Norgate, 1891) and relevant chapters (easily identified by their titles) of *The Principles of Ethics* (see 30 above).

42 Joseph Needham, *Time: the Refreshing River* (London: Allen & Unwin, 1943), 56.

evolutionary considerations we are happy to embrace, and that it will almost certainly continue along the same felicitous path. And inasmuch as the evolutionary process has proved favourable to certain moral characteristics, we can feel assured that they are thus far vindicated.

More problematic aspects of the theory are the dubiously founded confidence with which it encourages us to regard the future, and its limited potency to afford practical guidance. In respect of the latter it is vulnerable because of the difficulty of applying abstract and sometimes conflicting principles to concrete situations—a problem which Spencer himself clearly acknowledged by distinguishing between *absolute ethics* (which is concerned with idealized generalizations about how perfect men would behave in perfect situations—a study he believed to be analogous to the idealized laws of natural science) and *relative ethics* (which is concerned with human nature and society as they actually are).[43] In respect of the former it is vulnerable because of the uncertain continuation of trends hitherto observed. On this issue Flew appears deliberately to conflate Spencer's theory with Darwin's; for he criticizes Spencer's optimistic prognostications by remarking that 'Darwin's theory provides no basis for concluding that there is any such law of progress as Spencer seems to be proclaiming . . . '.[44] Now as Flew is well aware, Spencer's work in part pre-dates Darwin's, and is certainly not dependent on it; and even though Darwin may have postulated no general law of progress, Spencer certainly did. His views were published two and a half years before Darwin's *Origin of Species* in an article in the *Westminster Review* for April 1857 entitled 'Progress: its Law and Cause'. He there set out and defended the view that progress,

> whether it be in the development of the Earth, in the development of Life upon its surface, in the development of Society, of Government, of Manufactures, of Commerce, of Language, Literature, Science, Art, [consists of an increase in heterogeneity which] . . . is still going on and must continue to go on; and . . . thus progress is not an accident . . . but a beneficent necessity.[45]

Clearly, the truth or falsity of this law is not affected by any deficiency in Darwin's work, and if it is to be conclusively overturned, or persuasively supported, it requires treatment in its own right far more extensive than Flew could have devoted to it or than I have occasion to afford here.

1903—the year of Spencer's death—saw the publication of G. E. Moore's *Principia Ethica*, whose main theme is that the concepts with which ethics is concerned, and especially the 'Good', denote non-natural

[43] See especially Chs XV and XVI of *The Data of Ethics* in Vol. I of *The Principles of Ethics*.

[44] Flew, 43–44.

[45] Spencer, *Essays* . . . (see n. 41 above), Vol. I, 10 and 60.

qualities which in some obscure sense really subsist in certain objects, characters, and actions. Any view of the world which fails to take account of these supra-sensory qualities and supposes that the words which denote them can be defined in natural terms is, in Moore's view, fallacious. The self-confident naturalist would, of course, retort that he had not failed to take account of non-natural qualities, but rather that there are no such qualities to take account of. For several decades, however, Moore's book exerted an influence out of all proportion to its slender merits, and certainly one strong enough to put out of countenance ethical theories as blatantly naturalistic as those of Spencer and Hume. The demise of evolutionary ethics was further accelerated by the Great War of 1914–18. All the evolutionary writers had been vociferous in proclaiming their confidence in human progress and perfectibility. This unforeseen cataclysm did more to deflate the residual optimism of the late nineteenth century than any other series of events. Spencer did not survive to witness these less sanguine times, but the despondent reaction of a fellow evolutionary moralist is recorded in a prefatory note to a post-war edition of one of his works:

> . . . the account of . . . the whole development of the humanitarian ideal was based on the period preceding that catastrophe . . . [The years between 1915 and 1923] have unfortunately served only to darken the clouds which hang over our whole civilisation.[46]

Though evolutionary theories have never waxed strong since Hobhouse wrote in this melancholy vein, their importance in the history of ethics should not be underestimated nor their role in the development of naturalistic thought ignored. It is now over 100 years since the publication of Spencer's *The Data of Ethics*, and appropriate that the contribution of this most versatile and original thinker should be rescued from traducement and neglect.

[46] L. T. Hobhouse, *Morals in Evolution*, 4th edn (London: Chapman and Hall, 1923), viii.

HERBERT SPENCER,
from a photograph taken in 1855.

EGOISM AND RIGORISM: SPENCER'S RESOLUTION OF A MORAL PARADOX

The question of how people are induced to behave appropriately has ever been a pre-occupation of moralists and even to this day remains an issue of great practical importance. My aim in this article is to examine the responses to two doctrines espoused by some eighteenth century philosophers: namely psychological egoism - that all human action is fundamentally selfish; and ethical rigorism - that no action can be virtuous which proceeds from or tends to gratify a natural impulse; or, as Bernard Mandeville says in the opening paragraph of *A Search into the Nature of Society*, that there can be no virtue without self-denial. Each thesis considered separately may seem unattractive. However, when they are conjoined, they give rise to the quasi-paradoxical conclusion that human beings are incapable of virtuous action. I shall begin by looking at Mandeville, who professed both these doctrines [1]; I shall then consider several responses, contemporary and subsequent, which his views elicited; finally, I shall present an exposition of Herbert Spencer's more dynamic challenge to these doctrines and to the resolution of the aforementioned paradox which he proposed.

Mandeville was born in Holland in 1670. He was educated in medicine and by 1699 had moved to London, where he enjoyed a successful career as a doctor and eventually died in 1733. Little is known of his life, but he is now best remembered as the author of *The Fable of the Bees*, a book which for most of the eighteenth century lay under the shadow of considerable infamy [2]. *The Grumbling Hive*, the verse allegory on which it is based, first appeared as a pamphlet in 1705. In 1714 two editions were published in which this poem was supplemented by twenty discursive *Remarks* and *An Enquiry into the Origin of Moral Virtue*. In the so-called second edition of 1723 the *Remarks* were further expanded and there were added *An Essay on Charity and Charity Schools* (a vehement attack on proposals to educate the children of the poor) and *A Search into the Nature of Society*. In 1729 he published Part II, consisting of six dialogues in which the doctrines of the earlier volume were further elaborated and defended.

By the mid-1720s, after being presented as a public nuisance by the Grand Jury of the County of Middlesex, the book became notorious and began to provoke numerous replies and objections. On the title page of the first edition of Francis Hutcheson's seminal *Inquiry into the Original of our Ideas of Beauty and Virtue* (1725) it is specifically named as the main target of Hutcheson's criticism. For the next century the paradoxical and shocking doctrines which Mandeville had propagated continued to engage the attention of such distinguished moralists as David Hume and Adam Smith. In the two places where Hume mentions Mandeville by name it is as one of "some late philosophers in England, who have begun to put the science of man on a new footing" namely "the solid foundation [of] experience and observation". [3] Yet Mandeville's psychological egoism is based on no such solid foundation; for it is presented not as an induction derived from experience but as a dogma which no experience could overturn. It therefore fails to satisfy the criterion of falsifiability which is the hallmark of genuine empirical enquiry. One may well wonder why Hume should have admired Mandeville at all. The answer is suggested by Adam Smith, who recognized that Mandeville was an acute and perceptive observer of human affairs, his errors and fallacies notwithstanding: "...how destructive soever this system may appear, it could never have imposed on so great a number of persons, nor have occasioned so general an alarm among those who are the friends of better principles, had it not in some respects bordered upon the truth." [4]

An Enquiry into the Origin of Moral Virtue begins thus:

> All untaught Animals are only solicitious of pleasing themselves, and naturally follow the bent of their own Inclinations, without considering the good or harm that from their being pleased will accrue to others. [5]

Similarly, in the Fourth Dialogue Cleomenes asserts:

> ...Man centers every thing in himself, and neither loves nor hates, but for his own Sake. Every Individual is a little World by itself, and all Creatures, as far as their Understanding and Abilities will let them, endeavour to make that Self happy... [6]

Accordingly, even a savage, a highwayman, a housebreaker, or a murderer, on seeing a young child threatened by an overgrown sow, would be prompted by an unreflective compassion to rescue the child [7]. People give alms to beggars. But, according to Mandeville, in all such cases it is not any moral motive which prompts them to act but rather the desire to allay their own uneasy feelings on seeing distress. However, those who have been thoroughly schooled in civilized society can be prevailed upon to overcome their primary nature, but only because politicians have worked upon their pride in such a way as to furnish them with an adequate recompense for any self-denial which they undergo in serving the interests of others. This compensation consists in the esteem of other people. Thus all apparently moral action is prompted either by natural impulses or by the love of praise and fear of blame. In both cases it is fundamentally selfish. Even the determination of well-mannered persons never to appear proud is itself rooted in pride. Is this, as Mandeville' s editor, F.B. Kaye, claims, "an analysis... of extraordinary subtlety and penetration" [8], or is it rather an ingenious piece of sophistry contrived to produce shocking and provocative conclusions? If to shock and provoke were indeed among Mandeville's principal aims, he certainly succeeded.

It is probable that Joseph Butler had Mandeville in his sights in 1726 when he published his *Fifteen Sermons*. It seems unlikely that their selection from the many he must have preached at the Rolls Chapel in the previous eight years was, as he claims, accidental; for the subject matter of several of them is highly relevant to the controversies raging at the time. It is clear from the long footnotes appended to them that the egoism which spurred him to compose them was that of Thomas Hobbes. However, the doctrine which Butler enunciated was a pertinent critique of Mandeville no less than of Hobbes. The very first sermon maintains that genuine benevolence is intrinsic to human nature, which incorporates various complementary principles (viz. particular appetites, self-love, benevolence and conscience), which when properly regulated and proportioned are conducive to both individual and public welfare. There need therefore be no conflict between virtue and inclination. Indeed, in a later sermon he explicitly avowed that natural affections are, in such creatures as human beings, necessary to prompt us to virtuous actions.

> ...our appetites, passions, senses no way imply...deficiency or imperfection of any sort; but only this, that the constitution of nature according to which God has made us, is such as to require them. [9]

Hutcheson's moral philosophy was another response which was designedly contraposed to both Mandeville's egoism and his rigorism in that Hutcheson postulated in man a natural benevolence which is both the motive to moral action and the characteristic object of moral approbation. As already mentioned, Mandeville's thesis of psychological egoism is stated in such a way as to be impossible conclusively to refute; so some of Hutcheson's counter-assertions do little to threaten it: as, for example, when Hutcheson says that "nothing more is necessary than a little Attention to what passes in our own Hearts" [10]; or that writers such as Mandeville "...have treated our *Desires* or *Affections*, making the most generous, kind, and disinterested of them, to proceed from *Self-Love*, by some subtle Trains of Reasoning, to which honest Hearts are often wholly Strangers" [11], Mandeville could well retort that his own account is in fact the right one in that it overcomes the self-deception to which most people fall victim. Some of Hutcheson's arguments do seem, however, to constitute more cogent objections to Mandeville's thesis; as when he contends that if Mandeville were right in maintaining that our only object in relieving the distress of others is to allay the uneasiness which it occasions in ourselves, then:

should the DEITY propose it to our Choice, either to obliterate all Ideas of the Person in Distress, or to harden our Hearts against all feelings of Compassion, on the one hand, while yet the Object continued in Misery; or on the other hand to relieve him from it; should we not upon this Scheme be perfectly indifferent, and chuse the former as soon as the latter? [12]

Also, Hutcheson observes that on Mandeville's hypothesis a person who knew he was about to die would care nothing about the future welfare of his children, friends or country; whereas in fact "any good Man would as strongly desire at his Exit the Happiness of others, as in any part of his Life". [13]

Although in several important respects Hume's moral philosophy is more sophisticated than either Butler's or Hutcheson's, they are unanimous in opposing Mandeville in that all three believed that human nature has an intrinsic benevolence and that human beings are generally disposed to approve of benevolence as virtuous either (according to Butler) by conscience, (according to Hutcheson) by the operations of an unanalyzable moral sense or (according to Hume) by moral sentiments of which a psychological account can be given. Hume's most sustained criticism of Mandeville's thesis is to be found in what became the second appendix to his *Enquiry concerning the Principles of Morals* - 'Of self-love'. In the nine editions published in his lifetime this constituted (perhaps more appropriately) the first part of Section II - 'Of benevolence'. After describing an extremely degenerate account of human nature which maintains that "all *benevolence* is mere hypocrisy, friendship a cheat, public spirit a farce, fidelity a snare to procure trust and confidence..." [14], he outlines a less cynical doctrine, which corresponds broadly to Mandeville's.

There is another principle, somewhat resembling the former; which has been much insisted on by philosophers, and has been the foundation of many a system; that, whatever affection one may feel, or imagine he feels for others, no passion is, or can be disinterested; that the most generous friendship, however sincere, is a modification of self-love; and that, even unknown to ourselves, we seek only our own gratification, while we appear the most deeply engaged in schemes for the liberty and happiness of mankind. By a turn of imagination, by a refinement of reflection, by an enthusiasm of passion, we seem to take part in the interests of others, and imagine ourselves divested of all selfish considerations: but, at bottom, the most generous patriot and most niggardly miser, the bravest hero and most abject coward, have, in every action, an equal regard to their own happinesss and welfare. [15]

Hume goes on to observe that this doctrine need not have the dire practical consequences that one might expect; for many who have espoused it in one form or another seem to have been as much affected by benevolent sentiments as anyone else. They were no strangers to probity and honour and were quite capable of maintaining friendships. The enterprise of attempting to resolve benevolent affection into selfish turns out to be capable of accommodating wide differences of character and personality. The argument here deployed by Hume is closely akin to the argument from the paradigm case much favoured by English linguistic philosophers of the 1950s and parodied by Ernest Gellner in his book *Words and Things*. [16] Just as the reality of free will is established by the existence of a smiling bridegroom marrying the girl of his choice, so the reality of benevolence is proved by correspondingly paradigmatic cases.

> I esteem the man whose self-love, by whatever means, is so directed as to give him a concern for others, and render him serviceable to society: as I hate or dispise him, who has no regard to any thing beyond his own gratifications and enjoyments. In vain would you suggest that these characters, though seemingly opposite, are at bottom the same, and that a very inconsiderable turn of thought forms the whole difference between them. Each character, notwithstanding these inconsiderable differences, appears to me, in practice, pretty durable and untransmutable. And I find not in this more than in other subjects, that the natural sentiments arising from the general appearances of things are easily destroyed by subtile reflections concerning the minute origin of these appearances. [17]

Hume observes that while the question concerning universal or partial selfishness is of less practical importance than is usually imagined, it is nevertheless "...of consequence in the speculative science of human nature, and is a proper object of curiosity and enquiry". [18] He then proceeds to articulate the following arguments against the selfish theory:

(1) It is so contrary to common feeling and our most unprejudiced notions that there is required the highest stretch of philosophy to establish so extraordinary a paradox. Common observation confirms the existence of the benevolent passions, which have their causes, effects and proper objects all of which are marked by ordinary language and plainly distinguished from the selfish passions. All attempts to reduce the former to the latter have so far proved inadequate and, Hume alleges, have proceeded from a love of simplicity which has been the source of much false reasoning in philosophy.

(2) In all enquiries concerning the internal operations of the human mind, the most obvious cause is probably the true one.

(3) While the selfish hypothesis might explain the grief of a man who has lost a patron from whose friendship he derived some advantage, it could not explain the grief of a man who has lost a friend who made demands upon him.

(4) Animals show kindness to their own species and to men. "Shall we account for *their* sentiments, too, from refined deductions of self-interest?"

If we allow that they are capable of disinterested benevolence, why should human beings not be? [19]

(5) Love between the sexes, parental affection, gratitude, friendship and a thousand other instances suggest that human nature is capable of attachment, which is most simply explained by a disinterested benevolence that is as natural to human nature as other mental or bodily appetites. Accordingly,

> from the original frame of our temper, we may feel a desire of another's happiness or good, which, by means of that affection, becomes our own good, and is afterwards pursued, from the combined motives of benevolence and self-enjoyment... what a malignant philosophy must it be, that will not allow to humanity and friendship the same privileges which are undisputably granted to the darker passions of emnity and resentment? [20]

While the claims of psychological egoism are *prima facie* empirical and therefore susceptible of an experiential refutation, the nature of virtue might seem to be an entirely conceptual question. According to Mandeville's editor, F.B.Kaye, in defining virtue as necessarily involving self-denial and the conquest of natural inclination Mandeville was reflecting a common supposition of his own time. For this assertion he claimed the wide support of other moralists and philosophers without actually naming any [21]. Such ethical rigorism is certainly rooted in the traditions of Christianity: virtue cannot be consonant with human nature, which, since the fall of man in the Garden of Eden, is essentially corrupt, but must consist rather in resisting and mortifying natural affections and impulses. This gloomy doctrine was adopted and refined by the rationalistic moralists of the late seventeenth and early eighteenth centuries, who maintained a sharp dichotomy between reason and feeling and emphasised their essentially antithetical character. Richard Price (1723-1791), a later exponent of this thesis whose work appeared in 1758 (twenty-five years after Mandeville's death) expressed the full severity of ethical rigorism in a tone which foreshadows Kant.

> ...instinctive benevolence is no principle of virtue, nor are any actions flowing merely from it virtuous. As far as this influences, so far something else than reason and goodness influence, and so much I think is to be subtracted from the moral worth of any action or character. [...] Wherever the influence of mere natural temper or inclination appears, and a particular conduct is known to proceed from hence, we may, it is true, love the person, as we commonly do the inferior creatures when they discover mildness and tractableness of disposition; but no regard to him as a virtuous agent will arise within us. [22]

Such a conception of virtue was, however, fundamentally alien to the philosophical enterprise of Hutcheson and Hume and even of Butler (who because of his insistence on the cognitive and authoritative nature of conscience is usually deemed to hold a position between the sentimentalist and rationalist schools). Moreover, the conjunction of an egoistic psychology and a rigoristic definition of virtue has the consequnce of annihilating moral rectitude, which is denied alike to the 'natural virtues' which figure so prominently in Hume's *Treatise* and to artificial virtues also. For even where there is some element of self-denial, it is apparent only, there being an exchange of a primary gratification for one which is based on pride. Hume maintains against the rigorists that his own characterization of virtue as consisting not in self-denial but in qualities which are useful or agreeable to the agent or to others is the one which prevails in common life at least where systems and hypotheses have not perverted our natural understanding. [23] His most explicit repudiation of rigorism is in a passage where he claims that his moral theory represents virtue in all her most engaging charms. "The dismal dress falls off, with which many divines, and some philosophers, have covered her... She talks not of useless austerities and rigours, suffering and self-denial." [24]

* * * * *

I come now to consider the contribution which Herbert Spencer made to the discussion of these issues - a contribution which is no less relevant despite not being in direct response to the British eighteenth century debate. It is relevant because it incorportates a discussion of great insight and depth of the conflicting claims of egoism and altruism and because he explains why ethical rigorism is not merely intuitively repugnant but biologically unsound.

Spencer was born in Derby in 1820. After being employed as an engineer on the London and Birmingham Railway and then as sub-editor of *The Economist,* he spent most of his life studying and writing. He died in Brighton in 1903. More than half of his literary output comprises a ten volume *System of Synthetic Philosophy*, which includes biology, psychology, sociology and ethics - a series of subjects which involve a temporal and logical progression and whose study therefore depends on some understanding of earlier members of the series. (There must be life before there can be thought and feeling, thought and feeling before there can be social organisation, and social organisation before there can be moral awareness or ethical institutions.) Although there was only a century and a half between the publication of *The Fable of the Bees* and the appearance of Spencer's *The Data of Ethics* (1879), the intervening period saw enormous advances in scientific knowledge, the most significant being the formulation of evolutionary theory and the advent of conscious and deliberate (as distinct from semi-conscious and groping) attempts to explain social and moral phenomena in terms of evolution.

First and foremost among the points made by Spencer is that egoism preceeds altruism in order of imperativeness. For the acts which make continued life possible must, on average, be more peremptory than all those other acts which life makes possible - including the acts which benefit others. Secondly, the rightful precedence of egoistic claims is suggested by the fact that sentient beings could have progressed from lower to higher types only under conditions which permitted the superior to profit by their superiority and the inferior to suffer by their inferiority. Conformity to this law is still necessary not only for the continuance of life but for the increase of happiness; since the superior are those having faculties which are better adjusted to the requirements of life and which therefore bring in their exercise greater pleasure and less pain. Such egoism as preserves the vigorous and healthy furthers the happiness of their descendants, whose inherited constitution will help to make the labours of life relatively easy and its pleaures keen. Conversely, unhappiness is entailed on posterity by those who bequeath them constitutions injured by self-neglect. [25]

However, by no means all the arguments are on the side of egoism. If altruism is defined as action which, deliberately or otherwise, benefits others rather than the agent, then, from the dawn of life, altruism has been no less essential than egoism. For while a deficiency in egoism entails enfeeblement and loss of life, a deficiency in altruism causes the death or inadequate development of offspring and thus brings about the disappearance from future generations of the nature that is insufficiently altruistic. At first such altruism is instinctive or, in the case of the simplest and most primitive creatures, even merely mechanical; but in the course of time parental altruism has not only increased in consciousness but also developed in scope so as to extend to people outside the family. Indeed, as societies evolve and people become more inter-dependent the range and intensity of social altruism must increase, extending to an insistence at least on just dealings with all other human beings:

> ...this dependence of egoism upon altruism ranges beyond the limits of each society, and tends ever towards universality. That within each society it becomes greater as social evolution, implying increase of mutual dependence, progresses, needs not be shown; and it is a corollary that as fast as the dependence of societies on one another is increased by commercial intercourse, the internal welfare of each becomes a matter of concern to the others... And if each community has the egoistic satisfactions of its members diminished by the aggressions of neighbouring countries on one another, still more does it have them diminished by its own aggressions. One who marks how, in various parts of the world, the unscrupulous greed of conquest cloaked by pretences of spreading the blessings of British rule and British religion, is now reacting to the immense detriment of the industrial classes at home, alike by increasing expenditure and paralyzing trade, may see that these industrial classes,...thinking themselves unconcerned in our doings abroad, are suffering from lack of that wide-ranging altruism which should insist on just dealings with other peoples, civilized or

> savage. And he may also see that beyond these immediate evils, they will for a generation to come suffer the evils that must flow from resuscitating the type of social organization which aggressive activities produce, and from the lowered moral tone which is its accompaniment. [26]

In view of his ambivalence to Christianity and his hostility to the colonialism so prevalent in his lifetime, it is hardly surprising that shortly after his death a petition to have a memorial erected in Westminster Abbey was cursorily dismissed, even though it was supported by nearly sixty distinguished signatories. [27]

Against ethical rigorism Spencer deploys two arguments : the first is that it is highly counter-intuitive and has implications which most people would find at best paradoxical and at worst intolerable; the second is that it is biologically unsound. The first is set out in a trenchant critique of 'The Ethics of Kant', originally published in 1888 and subsequently included in the third volume of *Essays: Scientific, Political, and Speculative*. To preclude any possibility of misrepresenting the theory he is criticising, Spencer reproduces a long quotation from *Fundamental Principles of the Metaphysic of Morals* in which Kant extols as alone having moral worth those actions which proceed purely from a sense of duty. It is, however, the 'remarkable' doctrine embodied in the following passage to which Spencer takes particular exception.

> To be beneficient when we can is a duty; and besides this, there are many minds so sympathetically constituted that without any other motive of vanity or self-interest, they find a pleasure in spreading joy around them, and can take delight in the satisfaction of others so far as it is their own work. But I maintain that in such a case an action of this kind, however proper, however amiable it may be, has nevertheless no true moral worth, but is on a level with other inclinations. [28]

Spencer argues against this doctrine by supposing - in neo-Kantian fashion - that the principle is universalized - that it is exemplified not just by every man but by all the acts of every man.

> When he pays the labourer who has done a week's work for him, it is not because letting a man go without wages would be against his inclination, but solely because he sees it to be a duty to fulfil contracts .... When he gives evidence on behalf of a man whom he knows to have been falsely charged, it is not that he would be hurt by seeing the man wrongly punished, but simply in pursuance of a moral intuition showing him that public duty requires him to testify. When he sees a child in danger of being run over, and steps aside to snatch it away, he does so not because thought of the impending death of the child pains him, but because he knows it is a duty to save life. And so throughout, in all his relations as husband, as friend, as citizen, he thinks always of what the law of right conduct directs, and does it because it is the law of

> right conduct, not because he satisfies his affections or his sympathies by doing it. This is not all however....
>
> If those acts only have moral worth which are done from a sense of duty, we must not only say that the moral worth of a man is greater in proportion as the number of the acts so done is greater. We must also say that his moral worth is greater in proportion as his sense of duty makes him do the right thing not only apart from inclination but against inclination.... the most moral man is the man whose sense of duty is so strong that he refrains from picking a pocket though he is much tempted to do it; who says of another that which is true though he would like to injure him by a falsehood; who lends money to his brother though he would prefer to see him in distress; who fetches the doctor to his sick child though death would remove what he feels to be a burden. What, now, shall we think of a world peopled with [such] typically moral men - men who, in the one case, while doing right by one another, do it with indifference, and severally know one another to be so doing it; and men who, in the other case, do right by one another notwithstanding the promptings of evil passions to do otherwise, and who severally know themselves surrounded by others similarly prompted? Most people will, I think, say that even in the first case life would be hardly bearable, and that in the second case it would be absolutely intolerble. Had such been men's natures, Schopenhauer would indeed have had good reason for urging that the race should bring itself to an end as quickly as possible. [29]

Spencer then proceeds to point out how - conversely - a world which was populated by people whose inclinations always prompt them to act rightly would be delightful.

According to Spencer, it is not just that ethical rigorism is an intuitively repugnant doctrine: it is also biologically unsound; for one of the conditions necessary for the evolution of sentient beings is that, on the whole, actions which are necessary for life are pleasurable while actions which are life-threatening are painful.

> If we substitute for the word Pleasure the equivalent pharse - a feeling which we seek to bring into consciousness and retain there, and if we substitute for the word Pain the equivalent phrase - a feeling which we seek to get out of consciousness and to keep out; we see at once that, if the states of consciousness which a creature endeavours to maintain are the correlatives of injurious actions, and if the states of consciousness which it endeavours to expel are the correlatives of beneficial actions, it must quickly disappear through persistence in the injurious and avoidance of the beneficial. In other words, those races of beings only can have survived in which, on the average, agreeable or desired feelings went along with activities conducive to the maintenance of life, while disagreeble and habitually avoided feelings went along with activities directly or indirectly destructive of life; and there must ever have been,

> other things equal, the most numerous and long-continued survivals among races in which these adjustments of feelings to actions were best, tending ever to bring about perfect adjustment. [30]

Since, according to Spencer, altruistic actions are necessary, and since as human nature and society develop the scope and extent of altruism must increase until beings are so well adapted to the functions they must perform that no beneficial interference is possible, there follows the corollary that altruistic actions must tend to be pleasurable in those whose natures are most perfectly evolved; wherefore rigorism is, on biological grounds, an untenable doctrine - at any rate, as Hume insisted, "...where men judge of things by their natural, unprejudiced reason, without the delusive glosses of superstition and false religion." [31] However, as Spencer too was aware:

> ... the half-avowed belief, very commonly to be met with, that painful actions are beneficial and pleasurable actions detrimental, has been, and still is, upheld by creeds which present for the worship of men a Being who is supposed to be displeased with them if they seek gratifications, and to be propitiated by gratuitous self-denials and even by self-tortures.
>
> Here, however, we accept the inevitable corollary from the general doctrine of Evolution, that pleasures are the incentives to life-supporting acts and pains the deterrents from life-destroying acts. Not only do we see that among inferior sentient creatures this guidance is undeniably efficient, but also that it is undeniably efficient in ourselves, so far as regards the functions on which life immediately depends. And we cannot here suppose that a regulative system efficient for all essential actions has to be reversed for the actions growing out of them. [32]

Spencer' s avowedly teleological doctrine of evolution was inspired by a confidence widely shared in his time but depressingly incongruous with the pessimism of our own. There is much plausibility in his account of the growth of altruism and in his more general thesis that our moral constitution, no less than our other appetities and instincts, needs to be attuned to the conditions in which we live. However, at the end of the twentieth century the accelerating pace of change, both technological and cultural, not only impedes the gradual development of the accord which Spencer envisaged but imperils the moral heritage so far achieved. By no means all experiences alleged to be pleasurable are life-supporting. Some commercially induced habits such as addiction to alcohol, tobacco or narcotics and the libidinous excesses promoted by the 'sexual revolution' of the 1960s and early 1970s often prove fatal to their consenting victims as well as entailing extensive and manifold miseries on the societies in which they are rife. Even more sinister are those developments which threaten not only individual participants and their immediate communities but the world as a whole: such as, for example, the rapacious consumption of natural resources, with all the resultant pollution, to gratify the desire for such frivolous ends as unrestricted personal mobility. For nearly three centuries the principal tenet of British ethical theorists has been that morality is derived from experience. Experience, as Oscar Wilde dryly observed, is the name we give to our mistakes. In our brave new world, science has empowered us to make mistakes from which morality seems increasingly impotent to restrain us; mistakes which may, moreover, prove so calamatous that we never recover from them.

NOTES AND REFERENCES

[1] Whether or not Mandeville was really a rigorist is disputable. His professions of rigorism were dismissed by his contemporaries as patently insincere but have been considered more sympathetically by later scholars such as Selby-Bigge, F.B. Kaye, and Hector Monro, whose book *The Ambivalence of Bernard Mandeville* (Oxford: Clarendon Press, 1975) was the first full length book in English on Mandeville since the first half of the 18th century. For a discussion of Mandeville's rigorism see pages 223-237.

[2] MANDEVILLE, Bernard: *The Fable of the Bees,* edited by F.B. Kaye, 2 vols. (Oxford: Clarendon Press, 1924). Hereafter referred to as FB.

[3] HUME, David: *A Treatise of Human Nature,* Second Edition, revised by P.H. Nidditch (Oxford: Clarendon Press, 1978) xvi-xvii, 646.

[4] SMITH, Adam: *The Theory of Moral Sentiments,* edited by D.D. Raphael and A.L. Macfie (Oxford: Clarendon Press, 1976) 313

[5] FB I 41

[6] FB II 178

[7] FB I 255-6

[8] FB I 1xii

[9] BUTLER, Joseph: *Fifteen Sermons...* with introduction etc. by theVery Rev. W.R. Matthews (London: G. Bell & Sons, 1967) 89.

[10] HUTCHESON, Francis: *An Essay on the Nature and Conduct of the Passions and Affections..,* Third Edition, (London: 1742) v.

[11] *Ibid.* vi (misnumbered vii in my copy).

[12] *Ibid.* 22

[13] *Ibid.* 23

[14] HUME, David: *Enquires...* Third Edition, revised by P.H. Nidditch (Oxford: Clarendon Press, 1975) 295. Hereafter referred to as E

[15] E 296

[16] GELLNER, Ernest: *Words and Things* (London: Victor Gollancz, 1959) 31

[17] E 297

[18] E 297-8

[19] E 300

[20] E 302

[21] FB I 323

[22] PRICE, Richard: *A Review of the Principal Questions in Morals* (1758) reprinted in L.A. Selby-Bigge: *British Moralists* 2 Vols. (Oxford: Clarendon Press, 1897) II 183.

[23] E 268-9

[24] E 279

[25] SPENCER, Herbert: *The Principles of Ethics* 2 vols. (London: Williams & Norgate, 1897 & 1900) Part I *The Data of Ethics*, Chapter XI.

[26] *Ibid.* 217-8

[27] DUNCAN, David: *The Life and Letters of Herbert Spencer* (London: Methuen, 1908) 483-8

[28] SPENCER, Herbert: *Essays: Scientific, Political, & Speculative* 3 vols. (London: Williams & Norgate, 1901) III 210

[29] *Ibid.* 211-2

[30] *The Principles of Ethics* (See [25] above) I 79. The passage is quoted from p. 280 of Vol. I of *The Principles of Psychology*.

[31] E 270

[32] SPENCER, Herbert: *The Principles of Psychology*, Third Edition, 2 vols. (London: Williams & Norgate, 1881) I 284-5.

The Journal of Value Inquiry, Vol. XI No. 4

ON DISTINGUISHING BETWEEN LOVE AND LUST

J. MARTIN STAFFORD

> For such is the power of words, that if we can be brought to the habit of calling two things which are connected, by the same name, we are more easily led to believe them to be one and the same thing.
>
> *Thomas Reid*

Perhaps the main reason why present day philosophical speculation is so seldom productive of definitive results is that it is not merely the failing, but more remarkably the boast, of analytical philosophy that it concentrates exclusively on concepts as they are manifested in daily linguistic usage, and ignores the facts which ordinary usage so often fails to make explicit.

In a recent paper entitled "A Conceptual Investigation of Love,"[1] Mr. W. Newton-Smith declares that one point of view about the nature of philosophy is that it "... presupposes a linguistic practice which it describes and leaves untouched." (pp. 113-4)[2] The very inclusion of his study in Montefiore's admittedly partisan collection is an unequivocal indication that it is to this point of view that Newton-Smith himself subscribes. The extreme modesty of this enterprise, and of the claims of those who engage in it, is, in a superficial way, almost becoming; but when one considers how inimical it is to advances in our understanding and consolidation of our knowledge, one recalls with approval the scathing remark about linguistic philosophy in Russell's introduction to Ernest Gellner's *Words and Things*:[3] "It excludes almost everything that is of genuine interest, and prescribes either ineffable mysticism or dreary exegesis of the nuances of usage." (p. 14)

While Newton-Smith's paper avoids what is worst in both these excesses, in that it incorporates certain points which are at least provocative, he does not

* I should like to express my indebtedness to Professor Peter Nidditch of Sheffield University for his continuing encouragement, and also to Dr. Raymond Plant of Manchester University, with whom on several occasions I discussed this paper while it was being written.

[1] W. Newton-Smith, "A Conceptual Investigation of Love," *Philosophy and Personal Relations*, Montefiore (ed.), London, 1973.

[2] Page numbers refer to the editions listed. In the case of papers originally published in journals, the two numbers refer respectively to the original publication and the collection (sometimes more accessible) in which the paper is reproduced.

[3] Ernest Gellner, *Words and Things*, London, 1959.

succeed in presenting us with anything like a determinate list of the necessary or sufficient conditions for the use of the word *love*. For although he speaks of "the normative aspects of a conception of love" (p. 117), what he says suggests that there is no single condition whose fulfilment is necessary, and that the disjunction of conditions whose fulfilment is sufficient is not very stringent. Of course, since conceptual analysis is envisaged as being a descriptive rather than a normative exercise, such a tidying-up operation as would be involved in stipulating more exacting requirements than those prescribed by ordinary usage would be quite alien to the spirit of his undertaking, since it follows from the very nature of his kind of philosophizing that the concepts with which he is concerned must retain all the confusion and ambiguity with which the corresponding words are normally used.

Even at this point it would be disingenuous on my part not to acknowledge my own very different bias, being convinced that philosophers achieved more when they endeavoured to clarify existing notions by recommending revisionary definitions or by introducing new technical terms for phenomena not adequately catered for by ordinary language. Ordinary language may fulfil quite satisfactorily our more trivial or primitive communicational needs; but it cannot be expected to reflect the more subtle distinctions which elude most people's comprehension. In support of this contention I proffer two examples for consideration. That both are taken from Hume is not of overwhelming significance.

Even those who are antipathetic to the representative theory of perception could perhaps be prevailed upon to concede that there is a distinction between the primary data of perception (impressions) and the secondary data (ideas) sufficient to warrant the difference of nomenclature introduced by Hume. It is surely no disparagement that both terms are used in a special technical sense as opposed to a popular one; for epistemology is probably very seldom a topic of popular discussion. Again, by extending the use of the word *passion* to include the calm as well as the violent states of mind which influence the will, and by restricting the use of *reason* to inductive and deductive operations, Hume was able to establish the primarily non-cognitive nature of motivation and of morality. Contrary to the assertions of both his contemporary and his more recent critics, the revisionary definition is by no means arbitrary, but is introduced to make explicit a real distinction which ordinary language has overlooked.

Aspiring, then, to emulate these fruitful traditions of Scottish Philosophy, and mindful of Mackintosh's grave warning that "...it is never with entire impunity that philosophers borrow vague and inappropriate terms from vulgar use,"[4] I shall attempt to point out certain distinctions not adequately marked either by ordinary language or by Mr Newton-Smith. Although this will not necessitate a detailed appraisal of his study, I cannot entirely forbear to pass comment on some of what I hold to be its shortcomings.

---

[4] Sir James Mackintosh, *Miscellaneous Works*, London, 1846, Vol. I, p. 212.

After prescribing the limits of his enquiry as being a consideration of love in which there is some element of sexuality, Newton-Smith proposes the following list of relations which are, he maintains, "analytically presupposed" in our use of *love*:

1. A knows B (or at least knows something about B)
2. A cares (is concerned) about B
   A likes B
3. A respects B
   A is attracted to B
   A feels affection for B
4. A is committed to B
   A wishes to see B's welfare promoted. (p. 119)

There are several respects in which this list is defective, apart from its obvious incompleteness (which he himself admits). Firstly, some of the expressions are synonyms, or at least are so closely connected that it would be very odd, if not positively absurd, to assert one and deny the other: *e.g. cares about* and *wishes to see the welfare of...promoted*; also *likes* and *feels affection for*. It seems, therefore, quite without justification that the expressions which I have just put into pairs are subsumed by Newton-Smith under different categories, membership of which is intended to indicate some common feature (to my mind far from clear, despite his explanation), and to distinguish them from the members of other subcategories. Secondly, what does he mean when he says these concepts are "analytically presupposed" in our use of *love*? Not that all, or even that most of these relations must obtain in any situation which we are prepared to call love; for he maintains that in certain cases of love some of these relations may not be satisfied at all, and affirms that "there is no contradiction involved in speaking of, say, love without commitment or love without respect"[5] (p.119). If this is allowed, then one is tempted to wonder whether, in his opinion, there can be love without concern or love without affection. (The converse is, of course, quite plausible: *viz.* that there might be respect without love, concern without love, *etc.*) Given that Newton-Smith's analysis is concerned with sexual love, the only relation which would seem to be necessary is that of attraction. To put it mildly, all this evokes the strongest suspicion that he is using *love* in what is essentially a very weak sense.

Now although *love* is used loosely, it has, even in ordinary language, a certain strong sense in which it is contrasted with its weaker senses, even though the diverse ramifications of this strong sense are not usually made explicit. Indeed, if it were possible to remove its emotive connotations, the interests of clarity and precision would be better served if the word *lust* were used for the weaker senses of *love*. *Lust* was traditionally used to denote the natural propensity of human beings and of animals towards sexual activity. It

[5] This assertion seems quite incongruous with remarks made only two pages later, where literary examples are presented expressly to show that "...in the case of love there are tensions, and this displays the extent to which love involves a commitment." (p. 121)

has, however, acquired strongly pejorative connotations, largely as a result of the excessively anti-carnal attitudes of the early Christian church. None the less, I wish here to use the word *lust* – initially at least – in a more dispassionate sense simply to denote a feature of human nature without presuming to pass judgment upon it.

What do we mean when we say that someone entertains feelings of love, or acts in a loving way, as opposed to that he entertains feelings of lust, or acts in a lustful way? It is, I contend, not difficult to demonstrate that there are different phenomena to which the words *love* and *lust* should be discriminatingly assigned. I further suggest that these phenomena can conveniently be subsumed under two main heads: *viz.* the behavioural (*i.e.* conduct openly manifested), and, *pace* Ryle, the phenomenological (*i.e.* states of consciousness known directly to each of us only by introspection).

I am aware that by introducing the phenomenological as a factor not only relevant but vital to the characterization of an emotion I am defending a position which is in stark conflict with that maintained by Anthony Kenny in his book *Action, Emotion and Will.*[6] I shall briefly argue, however, that Kenny's thesis is vulnerable in at least one general respect, and, more particularly, inept as a tool for exposing a distinction between love and lust which I shall later insist on.

It is a central tenet of Kenny's position that an emotion can be characterised only if its object can be characterised independently. This is unequivocally stated both in the chapter entitled "Feelings" and in the one on "Objects":

> . . .it is not in general possible to identify an emotion without identifying also its object. (p. 64)
>
> . . .each of the emotions is appropriate – logically, and not just morally appropriate – only to certain restricted objects. (p. 192)

This characterization of objects depends not on introspection but, as seems to have been maintained by Findlay almost twenty years earlier,[7] on convention. Thus if a man professes to be afraid, his claim will not be acceptable unless the object of the emotion which he calls fear is one that he can represent as fearful both to himself and to others.

> One cannot be afraid of just anything, nor happy about anything whatsoever. If a man says that he is afraid of winning £ 10,000 in the pools, we want to ask him more: does he believe that money corrupts, or does he expect to lose his friends, or to be annoyed by begging letters, or what? If we can elicit from him only descriptions of the good aspects of his situation, then we cannot understand why he reports his emotion as fear and not as hope. (p. 192)

---

[6] Anthony Kenny, *Action, Emotion and Will*, London, 1963.

[7] J. N. Findlay, "Morality by Convention," *Mind* LIII (1944), pp. 142-169 (reprinted in *Language, Mind and Value*, London, 1963, pp. 66-95). In this article Findlay briefly digresses from his discussion of moral sentiment to observe that ". . .even in the case of the most familiar

Kenny maintains (p. 191) that both intentional and non-intentional actions are specified by their formal objects; but whereas the formal objects of material actions can be articulated without having recourse to phenomenological considerations (*e.g.* only what is visible can be seen; only what is dirty can be cleaned), the specifications of the formal objects of intentional verbs must be qualified by reference to the beliefs of the agent. Thus only what is *believed to be good* can be envied; only what is *thought to be fearful* can be feared. Now surely such a qualification must tend to undermine a thoroughgoing conventionalism in favour of the kind of introspectivist position which Kenny is endeavouring to criticise – and this in the case of all emotions, since one might suppose that a fear or desire could be idiosyncratic to the point of absurdity while still being a fear or desire. This is the more general respect in which I believe Kenny's thesis is at fault (his conventionalism places an arbitrary limit on the objects of an emotion), although I readily concede that when he is discussing such paradigm cases as man-eating lions and uncoiling cobras (p. 67) his theory is by no means without plausibility. This speciousness depends, however, on the fact that in these cases the consensus of feeling is well nigh universal and the appropriate behaviour readily manifested. They therefore lend strong support to his claim that

> The concept of each emotion is linked with non-emotional concepts in three ways. The concept, for example, of fear, stands on three struts:
> a. fearful circumstances
> b. symptoms of fear
> c. action taken to avoid what is feared. (p. 67)

Now what I am about to contend is that in the case of love and lust it is not that the emotion cannot be characterised until its object has been characterised, but rather the reverse – that the object cannot be fully characterised until the emotion has been identified. The inadequacy of Kenny's theory at least to deal with love and lust (and such an incapacity renders it less than comprehensive) is further borne out by the fact that it is not possible to draw up two sets of *non-emotional* concepts such as those which he says can be linked with fear which would be sufficiently distinct to differentiate between the two emotions. For plainly, in respect of circumstances (a) they share – superficially at least – a common range of objects, namely human beings; and they have also many symptoms and courses of action in common: namely (b) sexual arousal and (c) the quest for what in the case of love would be called consummation, and in the case of lust gratification. Indeed, if as Kenny

---

and elementary emotions, we find some definite limitation to their possible range of objects, . . ." (148/72). Since he evidently regards moral sentiment as being in this respect akin to other emotions, it is safe to assume that they too are subject to his view that the use of the language associated with them is governed by conventions. So that just as certain conditions must be present before we are prepared to call an attitude an ethical one, so also it is only in a restricted range of circumstances that we should be willing to call an emotion fear or pride.

suggests (p. 70) the symptoms were given a purely physical description, the superficial similarity between certain situations of love and lust would not be open to challenge, since the non-physical (*i.e.* phenomenological) features of the situations, by which alone they could be differentiated, would, *ex hypothesi*, be excluded from consideration.

Since conduct, unlike states of mind, is susceptible to public observation, I shall begin by considering the modes of behaviour which, even in the estimation of the less thoughtful, tend to distinguish love from lust. Firstly, casual associations of a very transitory kind would not usually be called loving, save in the weakest sense of the word. Surely we should look askance on someone who declared with complete equanimity that within a very short space of time he had indulged in a series of intimate associations with a large number of people with whom he was not previously acquainted nor likely ever to see again, and yet that he loved them all. We should be sorely tempted to ask whether he knew what love was, pointing out that such sentiments as are more usually denoted by that word cannot arise and decline within so short a duration, nor be directed towards so many different people either concomitantly or in such rapid succession. We should conclude that he was using the word *love* in an altogether degenerate sense. Our scepticism would be due not only to the discordance of his language with ordinary usage, but also to our realisation that his claims were inconsistent with our knowledge of human nature. For love, in contradistinction to lust, usually includes at least a desire to have a prolonged relationship with another person, and also to promote his or her welfare. In other words, I, unlike Newton-Smith, think that commitment (even if not necessarily one which overrides all other considerations) and concern are necessary rather than contingent features of love.[8]

There are some philosophers and psychologists who are not prepared to admit as an object of study anything which is not publicly observable, but rather confine their attention to overt behaviour, some even going so far as to deny the reality of any underlying mental phenomena. From the point of view

---

[8] I should not wish to be understood as saying here that persistence is a sufficient condition of love in the revisionary sense I am recommending. *Love* is sometimes popularly used to denote enduring attachments based on vigorous and violent passions which are essentially selfish and exploitative. I contend only that the will to make the attachment a lasting one is a necessary condition of love.

In his article "Sexual Experiences," Roger Taylor maintains that constancy of sexual desire may alone be a sufficient condition of love (*Proceedings of The Aristotelian Society*, LXVIII (1968), 87-104.

> If a man's love is to be explained wholly by his sexual desire for someone, then it must be his sexual desire is more constant and demanding than the man who just sexually desires. Surely we would have no hesitation in affirming that the person who constantly sexually craves, and is sexually concerned with another, is in love with the other. (p. 102)

This passage in particular indicates that Taylor does not favour the kind of distinction I am defending (for he seems explicitly to be discounting it) and that he is inclined to be influenced by the vulgar uses of the word *love*.

of these theorists, inclinations could be understood only in terms of reiterated patterns of behaviour. Now I think this is unsatisfactory in that inclinations as ordinarily conceived might never be realised in actual conduct. One can imagine, for example, that there are people who are disposed to seek homosexual relationships but who, because of adverse social pressure, never actually do so. Similarly, one can envisage pious men and women whose vows of chasity require them to abjure all sexual participation; and yet it would certainly be significant, and probably true, to assert that their concupiscent inclinations abide with them. And so, I take it as granted that there are states of mind, some of which touch most closely upon sexuality and emotion, although they may indeed be of secondary importance when conduct is subjected to public assessment. I am encouraged to note that Kenny's views accord substantially with mine in this respect; for while he maintains the spirit of his mentor's dictum that "an inner process stands in need of outward criteria" (Wittgenstein, *Philosophical Investigations*, Oxford, 1953, I 580), he does not discount the reality of inner states nor even the possibility of their subsisting alone in certain instances.

> Emotions, like other mental states, may be manifested or kept to oneself. In denying that they are essentially private states, one is not denying the possibility of keeping them secret. One is rather denying the possibility that there might be a race of men who felt all the emotions that we feel, but never manifested them publicly by word or deed. Only beings who are capable of manifesting a particular emotion are capable of experiencing it.
>
> But though one *can* experience an emotion only if one *can* manifest it, it does not follow that one *does* experience an emotion only if one *does* manifest it. . . .it is clearly possible to be afraid of something, or in love with someone, without telling anybody about it. (pp. 62-3)

As there are certain types of conduct which tend to be characteristic of love rather than lust, so also there are certain states of mind to which these modes of conduct are positively correlated. Of the former the following instances will suffice: with someone we love we are inclined to spend our time, to do for him or her such things as will please, and to manifest our affection by those agreeable familiarities which it would be neither useful nor proper to expound upon here. Of the states of mind characteristic of love I list the following: the contentment which the presence of a loved one brings; the uneasiness or distress occasioned by his or her absence; satisfaction at his or her prosperity; anxiety at the prospect of his or her suffering any harm. Obviously, neither of the above lists is exhaustive.

I submit, then, that relationships of the kind which are commonly called loving in a strong sense are distinguished from those which are lustful by the behavioural and phenomenological characteristics outlined above.

So far I have claimed only that love and lust are distinguishable by differences of conduct and feeling. I shall now proceed to argue that love is characterised also by a difference in the level of conceptual awareness of its object, and that this distinction is, by virtue of its comparative obscurity, the most neglected and the most in need of philosophical attention. The states of mind previously mentioned are all such as concern our *affective* faculties, that is to say such as constitute the way we feel towards people. But love also involves to a far greater extent than does lust the exercise of our *cognitive* faculties. We conceive the objects of our affection in a particular way, and it is this temporally prior conception which most immediately determines our feelings. This was noted quite explicitly as early as 1728 by Francis Hutcheson (1694-1746) in his *Essay on the Nature and Conduct of the Passions and Affections*, (London, 1728) in which he discriminates between *affections*, which depend on an opinion anteriorly formed, and *appetites*, which arise immediately:

> We are so constituted by nature that as soon as we form the idea of certain objects or events, our desire or aversion will arise toward them; and consequently our affections must very much depend upon the opinions we form concerning any thing which occurs to our mind, its qualities, tendencies, or effects.
>
> The government of our passions must then depend much upon our opinions: But we must here observe an obvious difference among our desires, viz. that some of them have a previous painful or uneasy sensation, antecedently to any opinion of good in the object; nay, the object is often chiefly esteemed good only for its allaying this pain or uneasiness; or if the object gives also positive pleasure, yet the uneasy sensation is previous to, and independent of this opinion of good in the object. These desires we may call *appetites*. Other desires and aversions necessarily presuppose an opinion of good and evil in their objects; and the desires or aversions, with their concomitant uneasy sensations, are produced or occasioned by this opinion or apprehension. Of the former kind are hunger and thirst, and the desire between the sexes; to which desires there is an uneasy sensation previous, even in those who have little other notion of the good in the objects than allaying this pain or uneasiness. (pp. 88-90, capitalisation, italicisation, and punctuation freely amended.)

By "the desires between the sexes" Hutcheson evidently means natural lust as opposed to affection, which depends on an "opinion of good in the object."

In one respect, the distinction between love and lust is analogous to, though not instantial of, that between sensation and perception.[9] This distinction was first expounded by the Scottish philosopher Thomas Reid (1710-96), who maintained that there is an important difference between such rather crude and primitive experiences as feeling pains and itches and acts of perception, which involve some sort of judgment about their object. Reid says: "It is impossible to perceive an object without having some notion or conception of that which we perceive." (p. 106/258)[10] Similarly, it seems to be impossible to love someone without having some notion or conception of the person we love. Moreover, this must be a conception of the person integrally considered, not merely an idea of his or her appearance; whereas if it were not possible for

---

[9] It would be fatuous to suggest that objects of lust are sensed rather than perceived. What is here maintained is that there is a qualitative difference, not merely a difference of degree, between the judgment necessary for a person to be an object of affection and that sufficient to render a person an object of lust.

[10] Thomas Reid, *Essays on the Intellectual Powers of Man*, Edinburgh, 1785 (reprinted in *Works*, Sir William Hamilton (ed.), Edinburgh, 1846).

lust to be aroused simply by the prospect of certain physical features, salacious pictures and obscene performances would not generate the slightest interest even in the most depraved, and no great fortunes would ever be amassed by purveying them. We cannot, however, feel affection or emotional warmth towards another unless we first attribute to him or her such personal characteristics as evoke those sentiments within us and will be adequate, other things being equal, to sustain them. Thus the degree of cognitive activity necessarily involved in love certainly exceeds that sufficient to arouse lust. The point I wish to stress here is an epistemological rather than a moral one: namely, that love is more complex than lust on Cartesian grounds; for since its objects are dualistic (*i.e.* persons considered as integrated unions of mind and body), the judgments about these objects are correspondingly more complex. Perhaps it should be made explicit that this higher degree of cognitive activity is a necessary, but not a sufficient condition of love by pointing out that it is possible for a person not to love, and yet to lust after, someone of whom he has a very comprehensive but unendearing conception, as witness some of the poems of Baudelaire.

It is, I think, his total failure to differentiate between the cognitive and the affective elements of love which causes Newton-Smith to treat so misleadingly what he calls after Stendhal the "crystallization" theory of love. According to this view "one never really loves another person but one loves rather some creation of one's imagination based on, but usually bearing little resemblance to, the actual person one appears to love" (Newton-Smith p. 125). In a form modified so as to temper Stendhal's pessimistic observation on the allegedly invariable disparity between the beloved as conceived and the beloved as actually existing, the theory seems to me both plausible and informative in that it emphasises the dual nature of the objects of affection. By this duality I mean that they are both *material* and *intentional* objects.

The intentional objects controversy is concerned mainly with the ontological status of those objects which have no necessarily physical existence, *viz.* the things we imagine, believe in, fear, *etc.* It is not, however, with the mainstream of this issue that I am here concerned; for though it might be relatively common for people to imagine or fear things which do not exist, instances of people claiming to be in love with non-existent individuals are fortunately very rare. The point with which I am here concerned is the consequence of a divergence of the intentional object of affection from the material one.

Newton-Smith considers an example from Lawrence Durrell's novel *Clea*, in which a character called Darley concludes that he was in love not with Justine but with an illusory creation of his own based on Justine. Newton-Smith's assessment of the situation is as follows:

> Darley thinks of himself as loving Justine for a sequence $\phi_1, \ldots, \phi_n$ of features which he takes to apply to Justine. If the following counter-factual is true, the case is easily dealt with. If Darley would feel as strongly about Justine should he come to see that she does not possess the properties in question, he does in fact, all things being equal, love her. He has

> simply been radically mistaken about her. Perhaps when he discovers what she is really like his attraction for her will actually increase. Suppose on the other hand, Darley would not think of himself as loving Justine if he came to realise his mistake. In this case he never loved anyone at all, and to speak of having loved an "illusory creation" is, at best, a metaphorical way of saying that he mistakenly thought of himself as loving someone as a result of radically misunderstanding the sort of person she was. (p. 125)

What is at issue here are the consequences of attributing to a real person qualities which she does not in fact possess, and thereby effecting a situation in which there is a sharp divergence between the person as she is conceived and as she really is.[11] The question as to the propriety of attributing the two term predicate *loves* or *is in love with* to people whose affection depends on such a misapprehension might be thought to be merely verbal, but there seems to me no more reason to deny that A loved B because his feelings changed when he discovered that B was not as he had first supposed than there would be to deny that Raleigh went in search of Eldorado because the land he discovered fell short of his expectations. After all, it is not his feelings about which A is mistaken (if indeed people can be in error about their own feelings) but the nature of the person to whom they were directed.

If due account is taken of the twofold character of love then no such confusion would arise. If "A loves B" is taken as implying that "A believes that ϕB, ψB, . . . and in view of these beliefs feels emotions x, y, and z towards B", then it is highly probable that if or when his beliefs change, so also will his feelings, but that does not affect either the reality of his former emotional state or the sincerity of any professions which resulted from it. Indeed, if the feelings did not change when the beliefs did, then it was never on account of those beliefs that the feelings came to be entertained in the first place. A further consideration which supports the view here propounded is as follows. Suppose that a substitution is made in the schema set out above so that it is a fearing or a hating situation rather than a loving one. Suppose that A believes that B is proud and aloof and consequently dislikes him. He subsequently learns that B is in fact extremely diffident and retiring, and not at all as he had imagined. At once his feelings change when he sees B in this new light. Now

---

[11] In the terminology of the late Professor C. D. Broad, Darley's is an example of a "partially misplaced emotion." C. D. Broad, "Emotion and Sentiment," *Journal of Aesthetics and Art Criticism*, XIII, No. 2 (1954), pp. 203-214 (reprinted in *Broad's Critical Essays in Moral Philosophy*, Cheney (ed.), London, 1971).

> An emotion may be said to be "misplaced" if either (i) it is felt towards an object which is believed to exist but does not really do so, or (ii) it is felt towards an object which really does exist [but] in respect of attributes which do not really belong to it. In the first case it may be said to be *totally* misplaced, in the second *partially* misplaced. (p. 208/291)

> We must notice that all emotions which are felt towards other persons in respect of their supposed mental or moral qualities must be in part conceptual on the cognitive side. For one cannot literally *perceive* another person's mind or his experiences or his dispositions or his motives. One can only *conceive* them, and we are very liable to be mistaken in our beliefs about them, and thus to have misplaced emotions. (p. 209/292-3)

surely we would not say that A never really disliked anyone at all because the object of his aversion *qua* intentional object did not correspond to the real person. We should say that he disliked B formerly, but came to like him when he had an accurate conception of the sort of person he was. Why then does Newton-Smith conclude that if Darley's love for Justine ends when he realises that it was based on a misconception, he did not really love her at all?

I think the answer lies partly at least in the fact that the complexity of love is shrouded by the social and linguistic conventions in which it is enshrined and which endow it with an illusory unity of character. Loving does, after all, play a far more prominent rôle in social life, in the idioms of language, and in the traditions of literature than does hating or fearing. It may be usual for people who have lost another person's affection to allege that this affection was never genuine; but this need not be the case. The social status of loving and all its attendant linguistic conventions must not be allowed to disguise its true phenomenological nature, and thereby engender further confusion in an area already fraught with wilful disregard of significant distinctions.

To revert to the question of how important a condition of love is a thorough acquaintance of the person who is the object of affection: clearly, the better one's acquaintance, the more remote are the chances of misjudging the person's character. Even so, it would be rash to specify a minimum or a maximum period of association which would preclude all possibility of error, if only because the crucial factors are so widely variable: some people are entirely ingenuous while others are quite inscrutable; some are endowed with uncanny perspicacity, whereas others have but little capacity to assess their fellow creatures. People in whom a fertile imagination is conjoined with a warm disposition may be inclined to attribute on the basis of tenuous evidence the characteristics they are looking for. It is certainly a corollary of my theory that affection which is misdirected is no less real than that whose intentional object tallies with the material object, though it is undoubtedly less felicitous. However, while this and related matters are of great interest in themselves, they are of only peripheral relevance to the issues under review.

My main concern has been to show that there are certain phenomena which are distinguishable in three respects (the behavioural, the affective, and the cognitive), and to these I have assigned the names *love* and *lust*. None the less, I am sadly aware of the prevailing willingness to acquiesce in, and even to aggravate the confusion which blurs the distinction upon which I have insisted – a willingness which is, alas, only too representative of the spirit of the age in which we live. Hitherto in this paper I have not made any explicit evaluation of the phenomena under consideration. Since, however, our affections are a matter in which we have, both as individuals and as social beings, a practical as well as a speculative interest, I shall endeavour to supply this defect, even if only in a brief and perfunctory manner.

Quite apart from its serious material consequences of illegitimacy and disease, against which all the resources of our technology have by no means entirely prevailed, selfish and exploitative sexual activity must be highly pernicious in itself, since it must tend to foster and confirm the traits of personality which beget that and similar misconduct. So there are the most cogent pragmatic reasons why lustful sexual attachments are discountenanced by civilised societies, although these reasons may not always be to the forefront of social or of individual consciousness.

A further consideration which might be advanced against the quibbles of those who are either disingenuous or insensitive enough to dispute the superiority of sexual relationships in which tender emotions have place is that these are, by the prerequisites of their own nature, confined to the most highly evolved species, and would seem in a sense to be vindicated by the evolutionary process. However, the merits and alleged weaknesses of systems of evolutionary ethics constitute in themselves a very extensive issue which this is not the place to examine.

Journal of Applied Philosophy, Vol. 5, No. 1, 1988

DISCUSSION ARTICLE

Love and Lust Revisited: intentionality, homosexuality and moral education

J. MARTIN STAFFORD

ABSTRACT *In his book* Sexual Desire, *Roger Scruton wrongly maintains that human sexual experience is essentially intentional. His thesis depends on his highly revisionary definitions of 'sexual arousal' and 'sexual desire', the artificial nature of which I expose and criticise.*

He admits that homosexual desire is capable of the same kind of intentionality as heterosexual desire, and is therefore not intrinsically obscene or perverted, but he advances reasons why homosexuality is morally different from heterosexuality and is therefore an object of disapproval. His arguments presuppose 'an impassable moral divide' between the sexes and are, on his own admission, not very cogent.

Since he allows that homosexual desire is a natural and spontaneous phenomenon and also proposes that moral education should guide us towards a state in which our sexuality is entirely integrated within a life of personal affection and responsibility, consistency requires that he adopt a sexual ideology which does not discriminate against homosexuality. For homosexuals are unlikely to achieve the 'sexual integrity' which Scruton advocates (and which I endorse) if they are constantly encouraged to disparage their own sexual nature and if social institutions make no positive provision for them.

> For such is the power of words, that if we can be brought to the habit of calling two things which are connected, by the same name, we are more easily led to believe them to be one and the same thing [1]. Thomas Reid

Ten years ago I published a paper entitled 'On distinguishing between love and lust' [2], in which I enumerated some of the distinctions between sexual love, which only human beings are capable of experiencing, and lust, an appetite which we share with other animals. What has impelled me to return to this issue after more than a decade is the appearance of Roger Scruton's recent book *Sexual Desire* [3]. I propose to deal here with three issues: (i) the intentionality of our sexual feelings; (ii) the moral status of homosexuality—an issue which Scruton ultimately evades; and (iii) the treatment of homosexuality in moral education and its accommodation within the ideology of sexuality. Notwithstanding the many criticisms I shall make of Scruton's book, it contains much that I agree with. I share his concern "to rescue sexual morality from the morass into which modern ways of thinking have enticed it" (SD 196), and, like Scruton, I write from a philosophical perspective which is conservative rather than revolutionary.

1 Intentionality

> We have to deal with Man as a product of evolution, with Society as a product of evolution, and with Moral Phenomena as products of evolution [4]. Herbert Spencer

In my earlier paper I maintained that whereas the higher manifestations of human sexuality are characterised by their intentionality (which is to say that they are accompanied by mental states which have a clearly focused directedness towards particular objects) our more basic and primary sexual urges are not. Scruton, on the other hand, contends that human sexuality is essentially intentional. I shall endeavour to show that in this he is mistaken: that his thesis depends on a highly revisionary and stipulative definition of 'sexual desire'; and that it entails an account of human sexuality which accords ill with an evolutionary theory of human nature. Right at the outset, Scruton declares his high-minded aim to "argue against the moral and philosophical impulse that leads us to assign sexual desire to the animal part of our nature" (SD 2). Human sexuality, he contends, is essentially characterised by its intentionality. Sexual arousal is always directed towards a particular person (SD 29), and is "not transferable to another, who 'might do just as well' " (SD 30). It can occur only between persons, being an artefact of their social condition (SD 33). Accordingly, "animals are never sexually aroused; they do not feel sexual desire, nor do they have sexual fulfilment" (SD 36).

As Scruton admits, "to put the thesis so starkly is to invite scepticism". Indeed, rather than merely inviting scepticism, Scruton's bold assertions should prompt us very early in his book to realise—his failure to make any candid declaration notwithstanding—that he is using the terms 'sexual arousal' and 'sexual desire' in a radically revisionary way. For anyone who has more than the most superficial acquaintance with animals knows that they, no less than human beings, *are* capable of sexual arousal. Similarly, his characterisation of sexual desire not as an appetitive instinct but as an intentional mental state which is object-directed to a high degree seems to run counter to so much experience of everyday life. Scruton contrasts sexual desire in which we "... attribute an irreplaceable value to those with whom we are brought into relation" (SD 78) with the appetite for food, which is satisfied by any sample of the appropriate type. But many philosophers, not just Kant, whom Scruton mentions (SD 83), have believed that sexual desire, in some of its manifestations at least, is a non-specific appetite analogous to hunger. Francis Hutcheson explicitly says as much [5] as does his contemporary (and on many issues his antagonist) the worldly Bernard Mandeville. In a quaint though somewhat coarse passage, Mandeville appears expressly to deny Scruton's thesis:

> A vicious young Fellow, after having been an Hour or two at Church, a Ball, or any other Assembly, where there is a great parcel of handsome Women dress'd to the best Advantage, will have his Imagination more fired than if he had the same time been Poling at *Guildhall*, or walking in the Country among a Flock of Sheep. The consequence of this is, that he'll strive to satisfy the Appetite that is raised in him; and when he finds honest Women obstinate and uncomatable, 'tis very natural to think, that he'll hasten to others that are more compliable [6].

A case which is discussed by both Scruton and Mandeville is that of sailors returning ashore after a long period of confinement at sea. The ways in which they describe the situation differ markedly.

> Whatever the peculiarities of orgiastic desire, it is no exception to the rule that the other person enters essentially into the aim of desire. Likewise with randiness, the state of the sailor who storms ashore, with the one thought 'woman' in his body. His condition might be described as desire for a woman, but for no particular woman. Such a description, however, seriously misrepresents the transition that occurs when the woman is found and he is set on the path of satisfaction. For now he has found the woman whom he wants, whom he seeks to arouse and upon whom his thoughts and energies are focused. It would be better to say that until that moment, he desired *no* woman. His condition was one of desiring to desire. And such was his need that he took an early opportunity to gratify his longing: to exchange the desire to desire for desire. It is an important feature of sexual desire that it should arise in this way from a generalised impulse. Nevertheless, desire is as distinct from the impulse that compels it as is anger from the excess of adrenalin. One should think of 'sexual hunger' as one thinks of the hunger for conversation, not as an appetite, but as a predisposition towards an individualising response (SD 90).

> Where six or seven Thousand sailors arrive at once, as it often happens at *Amsterdam*, that have seen none but their own Sex for many Months together, how is it to be suppos'd that honest Women should walk the Streets unmolested, if there were no Harlots to be had at reasonable Prices? For which Reason the Wise Rulers of that well-order'd City always tolerate an uncertain number of Houses, in which Women are hired as publickly as Horses at a Livery-Stable [7].

Plainly, Mandeville does not appear to think that the gross kind of sexual desire which finds its outlet in whoring stands in need of the individuating conceptualisation which Scruton thinks is characteristic of human sexual encounters: one hires a woman just as one hires a horse—more or less any woman or any horse would do.

I do not see how the controversy could ever be definitively resolved, since the only sexual feelings of which anyone has immediate experience are his own. But I cannot help thinking that Mandeville is closer to the truth that Scruton. Mandeville's view of human nature is—notoriously—much more debased than is Scruton's; yet he is able to render a straightforward account of a whole range of seamy sexual aspiration and activity, while Scruton's account seems fanciful and strained. Are we to believe that a man who goes curb-crawling in a city's red light district or a homosexual who loiters in a public lavatory seeks anything higher than sexual gratification of an impersonal kind? Neither resembles Prince Charming in his quest for a particular Cinderella. Pornography, striptease clubs, cinemas which show sleazy films: all pander to—and, I suspect, help to encourage—sexual cravings of the lowest kind. In crediting such activities with the kind of intentionality which characterises the higher emotions Scruton is looking at them through rose-tinted spectacles and paying them a tribute to which they have no proper claim. If he were right, prostitutes, strippers and pornographers would be as out of tune with human nature as gas mantles are unfit for use with electricity, and their services would be as little in demand.

That the senses in which he uses the terms 'sexual arousal' and 'sexual desire' are revisionary is implicitly conceded by Scruton as he progresses through the book: firstly, by the introduction of defining adjectives. What he originally denominates 'sexual arousal' and 'sexual desire' *tout court*, he later calls 'true sexual arousal' (SD 31) and 'true sexual desire' (SD 89) or 'developed' forms of sexual desire (SD 93). In this respect Scruton's enunciation of his doctrine savours of the claim made by Marxists that only communism allows mankind to become 'truly human': what is set out ostensibly as a description is in fact a prescription since it incorporates a value-laden element which cannot be derived from the ordinary empirical denotation of its terms. Secondly, by using the term 'sexual desire' in contexts where its meaning is inconsistent with his original characterisation: if desire is specific and non-transferable, it is self-contradictory to speak of "desire roaming freely" (SD 309) and of "the element of generality in desire which tempts us to experiment" (SD 339; see also 359). Only 18 lines later on the same page this is explicitly contradicted by the claim that "sexual desire is inherently 'nuptial': it involves concentration upon the embodied existence of the other..." Clearly, Scruton is talking about two sets of phenomena, one less extensive than the other and included within it. Perhaps he should have called the first 'sexual desire' and the second (that is, the more refined forms of the first) 'Sexual Desire'; for philosophers often resort to upper case initials when they fancy they are proclaiming something portentous! I would maintain, then, that the term 'sexual desire' as it is ordinarily used and understood may incorporate intentionality and conceptualisation, but it need not do so.

In his discussion, Scruton fails to distinguish between *three* levels of awareness: sensation, perception, and conception.

> ... the pleasures of sight are not pleasures of sensation, but pleasures of perception. They have precisely that epistemic dimension which belongs to sexual arousal. To think that pleasure at the sight of a desirable person is 'in the eye'... is to commit a grave philosophical mistake. It is to confuse perception with sensation, and the pleasures of the understanding with the pleasures of the flesh... The eye is the vehicle of sexual arousal, precisely because arousal is an epistemic condition: it is a state of alertness toward the other, based on the perception of his embodied form. But the eye is not, as the vehicle of arousal, a 'zone of pleasure'. It is, rather, a 'channel of communication' through which the intentionality of arousal may begin to flow (SD 206).

Scruton appears here to be conflating perception and *con*ception. Now if this distinction collapses, so also must that between material and intentional objects; for everything that we perceive would be an intentional object. But that an experience is one of perception and has an epistemic dimension surely does not imply that its object is intentional. The chair that I sit on, the painting I look at, and the person I see are—in the first instance—*material* not *intentional* objects; whereas the chair that I remember, the painting I imagine, and the person whom I love *are* intentional objects, though they may also exist materially. Consider a man ogling the picture on page three of a popular daily tabloid: what is before him is really nothing more than a configuration of tiny dots suggesting a certain shape and outline. It is perceived, however, as a picture of a girl posing seductively, and it evokes in our imaginary onlooker lascivious thoughts. Surely his interest is excited merely by the prospect of her appearance. Perceiving a 'body' which you fancy is a more immediate and epistemically less complex procedure than conceiving a person whom you might love [8]. It is, of course, possible that someone might be obsessed by such a picture and attribute to it a fictitious personality, in which case—but only then—his mental state will involve the conceptualising intentionality which Scruton thinks is essential to human sexual experience.

Apart from the incompatibility of Scruton's essentialistic characterisation of sexual desire with ordinary ways of thinking and the contradictions into which he therefore sometimes lapses, it has a further serious disadvantage: it tempts him to invert the natural history of human sexuality, though again, this is not done consistently. Many of his remarks accord perfectly with the sort of naturalistic, evolutionary account of human sexuality which I should favour. For example:

> ... we cannot doubt that desire is rooted in instincts which we share with the animals (SD 179).
>
> ... we develop from animals into social beings (SD 212).

And even:

> ... we are animals, governed by the implacable requirements of the flesh (SD 233).

These remarks seem dubiously consistent with his expressed intention to resist "the impulse that leads us to assign sexual desire to the animal part of our nature" (SD 2). It is, of course, fair to maintain that even though our sexual feelings have grown out of our animality, yet they ".. are not reducible to any aspect of human conduct that is shared with the 'lower' animals" (SD 182–3). For my own part, I cannot see why Scruton should find it so problematical that "one and the same thing [can] be both a person and an animal" (SD 253). To undertake so complete and precise a demarcation of the several features of human nature, denominating some 'animal' and others 'personal' or 'rational' may well be an enterprise which is grossly misconceived. In Scruton's case, it certainly gives rise to much needless agonising. He seems at times anxious expressly to dissociate desire from our animal nature, as when he speaks of "the introduction of sex into desire" (SD 278), rather than—as seems to me more plausible—the converse; as if the intentional features might have had a genesis and evolution quite divorced from anything so 'sordid' as our sexual instincts. Similarly, rather than defining desire (in his revisionary sense) as 'lust plus the intentional features', he defines lust as "genuine sexual desire from which the goal of erotic love has been excluded" (SD 344). If we were doing mathematical equations rather than philosophy, this would not matter, but Scruton's definition constitutes a deliberate suggestion that sexual desire (in his sense) is the primary category while lust is a derivative one. I would maintain that lust (our basic sexual appetite) is both temporally and logically prior to the higher sentiments which have grown out of it, and that Scruton's attempt to maintain otherwise is tantamount to turning natural history on its head. The analogy between the development of human sexuality and the growth of a tree (also employed by Herbert Spencer [9]) seems apposite, but Scruton too easily forgets that there are many people who appear content to rub their noses in the soil rather than contemplate the leaves.

> A tree grows in the soil, from which it takes its nourishment, and without which it would be nothing. And it would be almost nothing *to us* if it did not also spread itself in foliage, flower, and fruit. In a similar way, human sexuality grows from the soil of the reproductive urge, from which it takes its life, and without which it would be nothing. Furthermore, it would be almost nothing *for us*, if it did not flourish in personal form, clothing itself in the flower and foliage of desire. When we understand each other as sexual

> beings, we see, not the soil which lies hidden beneath the leaves, but the leaves themselves, in which the matter of animality is intelligible, only because it has acquired a personal form (SD 254).

If one accepts an evolutionary account of the world and all that is therein, then our sexuality, rationality, and morality (all of which are inter-related) must have a natural history. Though the details are lost in the remoteness of the distant past, such an account is incongruous with any thesis which lays down what is essential to humanity as such; for in the course of time mankind has undergone changes and still continues to change, albeit imperceptibly. The capacity to conceptualise, on which intentionality depends, did not come about suddenly at a specific point in time. It is at least arguable that even now this capacity is not shared equally by all human beings or by all cultures—a possibility which I should expect to occasion no more distress or embarrassment to the editor of the *Salisbury Review* than it does to me, though one which Scruton could easily be suspected of having overlooked. For although the examples he cites bespeak a cultural awareness which is prodigiously wide-ranging, they are culled almost exclusively from the *belles lettres* and grand operas of the western world. One cannot, therefore, help wondering how applicable his speculations are to the sexual lives of primitive savages or of those who live in communities where women are owned in much the same way as horses or camels.

It is not entirely clear whether Scruton believes in evolution, since he says, "The difference between animality and selfhood is one of kind, and admits of no degrees... However, the transition... is built up of certain stages or 'moments'" (SD 331). The two halves of this quotation are to my mind glaringly inconsistent, the first part being difficult to reconcile to evolutionary theory, while the second half admits that the transition must have been accomplished gradually. Apart from its incompatibility with evolutionary theory, such essentialism also incorporates the risk of making our humanity seem more secure than it is; of blinding us to the precariousness and fragility of that thin veneer which civilisation has grafted onto our lower nature. However, I am in complete agreement with Scruton that intentionality is primary among the things which distinguish the more valuable from the less valuable sexual experiences; but the arguments I would use to support my evaluation are evolutionary rather than essentialist [10]. I would also agree that this factor is of paramount importance in the moral assessment of homosexuality, to which I shall now proceed.

2 Homosexuality

> It is surely one of the vital questions of sexual morality, whether homosexual is distinguishable from heterosexual intercourse (SD 254). Roger Scruton

Despite the admitted urgency and importance of this question, Scruton does not come up with any firm answer. In a book that runs to over four hundred pages, shortage of space could not be pleaded as an excuse for this conspicuous omission, which is due rather, I suspect, to the fact that while Scruton would like to conclude that homosexuality and heterosexuality should be differently appraised, much of what he says implies, or at least suggests, the contrary. The moral status of homosexual desire is broached at three or four points in the book, where Scruton tantalises his readers by holding out the prospect of a definitive—and hostile—conclusion. But no such pronouncement is ever made. In this respect, Scruton is like an exotic dancer, who by the deft manipulation of veils, ostrich feathers, or whatever, continually evokes in her audience the frenzied anticipation of what she never actually reveals.

As early as page 15 he promises an exploration of "the important differences between homosexual and heterosexual desire", but the first place where he actually examines the moral status of homosexual relationships is page 282, where there is a paragraph in which homosexual desire is discussed in relation to Kantian feminism—the doctrine that one's sex or gender is irrelevant to one's personality or 'personhood' since 'person' is a unitary category. He says:

> For the Kantian feminist, the *enracinement* of the person in the soil of animal activity is a single phenomenon, exemplified alike by man and woman. One and the same person might have taken root in either soil. If this were so, there can be no moral difference between homosexual and heterosexual desire. The body's sex would be irrelevant to the interpersonal emotions that are displayed in it; just *this* person might have had just *this* desire whatever his sex. Otherwise we must say that desire is not, after all, an interpersonal attitude, but simply a residue of bodily experience, indicating not the person but his biological destiny, in the manner of sensory pleasure and sensory pain. In other words, Kantian feminism has radical moral consequences. Either it denies the moral distinction between homosexual and heterosexual desire—and along with it the idea of a sexual 'normality' answerable to our nature as sexually reproducing beings. Or else it forces us to accept the Platonic view of desire as 'merely animal'. Neither view is acceptable (SD 282).

I am at a loss to know what this passage is intended to accomplish. Scruton is not (nor am I) a Kantian feminist: but from the falsity of Kantian feminism one cannot infer anything about the respective moral natures of heterosexual and homosexual desire—even if the truth of Kantian feminism would entail (as Scruton asserts) that they are equivalent. To derive the negative inference from the falsity of Kantian feminism would involve the fallacy of denying the antecedent [11]. I suppose Scruton may be arguing that since Kantian feminism would commit us either to the moral equivalence of homosexual and heterosexual desire or to the view that desire is 'merely animal', and neither of these alternatives is acceptable, then Kantian feminism must be false. Such an argument would indeed be valid, but would require an independent proof of the alleged distinction between homosexual and heterosexual desire. No such proof is offered.

A further issue raised by this passage is the putative connection between the moral propriety or impropriety of homosexual desire and concepts of sexual normality. The word 'norm' and its cognates are widely and correctly used both descriptively and prescriptively. Acknowledgement of the normality (in the descriptive sense) of heterosexuality is compatible with either approval or disapproval of homosexuality. It is only the *prescriptive* normality of heterosexuality which is undermined by an accommodating attitude to homosexuality; so it must be in this prescriptive sense that Scruton is using the term. In this case he can be called upon to explain how one is to bridge what has come to be called Hume's gap [12]: in particular, how can a description of our function as sexually reproducing beings imply a universal duty to perform heterosexually, especially when so many individuals have no spontaneous desire so to perform?

It is in this same section on 'Sex and Gender' that Scruton first adumbrates a further argument in support of his claim that homosexual and heterosexual desire are essentially different.

> The plain fact is that, because we live in a world structured by gender, the other sex is forever to some extent a mystery to us, with a dimension of experience which we can imagine but never inwardly know. In desiring to unite with it, we are desiring to mingle with something that is deeply—perhaps essentially—not ourselves, and which brings us to experience a character and inwardness that challenge us with their strangeness...
>
> This might imply that there is a distinction between homosexual and heterosexual desire. The heterosexual ventures towards an individual whose gender confines him within another world. The homosexual unites with an individual who does not lie beyond the divide which separates the world of men from the world of women. Hence the homosexual has a peculiar inward familiarity with what his partner feels. His discovery of his partner's sexual nature is the discovery of what he knows (SD 283).

Is not the issue here raised a particular instance of the problem of 'other minds'? How can I know that other people resemble me or that their experiences resemble my own? Now we might just as well argue that *all* other people—not only members of the opposite sex—are 'a mystery to us'; for if our mental states are essentially private, we have no way of knowing, nor any reason to suppose, that members of the opposite sex differ from us mentally more than do members of our own. Even if one accepts as an apposite description Scruton's extremely sexist assumptions (which issue I am content to leave open), I cannot see how speculations which by their very nature are necessarily precarious could be used to support a moral conclusion as contentious as he is trying to establish. It would surely be (to use Scruton's own analogy) to hang too complex a moral argument on too fragile a peg (SD 287–8).

This argument is repeated in the chapter entitled 'Perversion', which incorporates Scruton's most extended discussion (just over five pages) of homosexuality despite the fact that by his own criterion homosexuality does not in itself constitute a perversion.

> The masculine and feminine denote two distinct kinds of person, and the experience of gender plays a significant part in determining the intentional content of desire. Homosexual desire may retain the interpersonal intentionality that is normal to us; but there may yet be a moral difference between homosexual and heterosexual conduct. The correct position, I believe, is this: homosexuality is perhaps not in itself a perversion, although it may exist in perverted forms. But it is *significantly* different from heterosexuality, in a way that partly explains, even if it does not justify, the traditional judgement of homosexuality as a perversion. I say this with extreme tentativeness, and knowing that it may be received as an outrage (SD 305).

How right Scruton is to express these reservations! But again on the next page the prospect of a censorious conclusion is hinted at.

> The question is whether we can distinguish the intentional content of homosexual from that of heterosexual desire, so as to justify the judgement that the first has a distinct moral character, and perhaps also to justify the judgement that it diverges from the norm of interpersonal relations in the direction of obscenity (SD 306).

He once more asserts that there is an 'impassable moral divide' between the sexes, and contends that this gives rise to a morally significant difference between homosexual and heterosexual relationships. I do not propose to devote too much space to refuting an argument which even Scruton himself admits is not very cogent. Its essence is that in a heterosexual relationship, each party sees the other as essentially different. This can give rise to a respect which requires "a peculiar delicacy of negotiation" and "a preparedness to take responsibility for the effects of this unknown thing". This "opening of the self to the mystery of another gender" is "one of the fundamental motives tending towards commitment" (SD 307). But as Scruton concedes, "such an observation is [not] always and everywhere valid." The features he attributes to heterosexual liaisons are by no means a sufficient condition of commitment; nor are they a necessary one: for there are many heterosexual relationships in which such commitment is wanting, just as there are at least some homosexual ones in which it is present. One would never imagine this from the literary examples which he cites (SD 234–5; 307–8). These are—not to overstate the case—heavily biased towards an impression of homosexuality which few people of ordinary moral sensitivities could fail to find repellent. I cannot help feeling that they were chosen for the sake of polemical convenience, and with a wilful disregard for what might have been said on the other side of the argument. The carnal excesses of antiquity and the morbid effusions of Proust and Genet evoke an image of homosexual desire which is at best pathological and at worst downright depraved. But then since homosexuals have only recently begun to emerge from nearly twenty centuries of unremitting oppression, it is hardly to be expected that there should be an imposing corpus of fine literature which depicts homosexuals in a fair—let alone a favourable—light.

Although Scruton is ingenuous enough to admit that any conclusion which might be drawn from a comparison of the works of Proust and Sappho is vitiated by the extreme disparity of their style and meaning, he none the less maintains that the contrast thereby exemplified between male and female sexuality underscores the complementary nature of heterosexual liaisons, the absence of such 'complementarity' being a "*fault* in the content of homosexual desire—an imbalance which, if left uncorrected, threatens the course of love" (SD 310). Even so, he allows that "homosexuality could be shown to be perverted only if the homosexual act were shown to be intrinsically depersonalised or intrinsically obscene" (SD 310). There ensues an argument which purports to explain why people do in fact so perceive homosexual acts, but it seems to be at best a rationalisation and even to "turn out to have a peculiarly tautologous quality" (SD 205). For Scruton says: "the obscenity is seen in the arousal of the flesh by its own sexual kind" (SD 310), whereas...

> ... heterosexual arousal is arousal by something through and through other than oneself, and other as *flesh*. In the heterosexual act, it might be said, I move out *from* my body *towards* the other, whose flesh is unknown to me; while in the homosexual act I remain locked within my body, narcissistically contemplating in the other an excitement that is the mirror of my own (SD 310).

This argument's first contention is tautologous: homosexual acts are perceived as obscene because they are homosexual and not heterosexual. Its second claim depends on the unsupported assumption that they are essentially narcissistic. Clearly, they have such a capacity, while heterosexual acts never could; but this hardly implies that they are characteristically so. As Scruton allows, his suggestion is far from being a proof. I might add that if it did constitute a genuine reason why homosexual acts are thought to be obscene, then its operation would not be so narrowly circumscribed to the people of a few particular cultures. In *The Origin and Development of the Moral Ideas* Edward Westermarck points out that attitudes to homosexuality range from benevolent toleration to severe interdiction, the greatest hostility having been manifested by Zoroastrian, Judaic, and Christian cultures. He argues at some length, moreover, that Judaeo-Christian antipathy towards homosexuality is rooted not in any of its intrinsic features but rather in its association with foreign cults, unbelief, and heresy [13].

Throughout the book much is made of the intentional nature of sexual desire and of the potential of relationships which are so endowed. On Scruton's own admission, homosexuality is not inherently perverted or obscene, nor does he offer any sound justification for the antipathy with which it has until recently been widely regarded in western societies. The conclusion which his work therefore supports—though he himself resists it—is that homosexual and heterosexual desire are on an equal footing, and that whatever factors may be relevant to the moral assessment of sexual activity, its orientation is not. All this has inescapable implications of the first importance for the way in which homosexuality is treated by moral educators. Since none of these is so much as hinted at by Scruton, I shall proceed to supply the deficiencies in what I consider to be the best part of his book—the chapter on 'Sexual Morality'.

3 Moral Education

> The end of all moral speculations is to teach us our duty; and, by proper representations of the deformity of vice and beauty of virtue, beget correspondent habits, and engage us to avoid the one, and embrace the other [14].
> David Hume

The penultimate chapter of Scruton's book is concerned with the scope and purpose of sexual morality, and the objective of moral education in matters sexual. He begins by emphasising the importance of the subject and expresses the hope that those who disagree with his conclusions will find in his supporting arguments a procedure whereby to refute them. Although I have elsewhere deployed an argument of a different kind [10], I am sympathetic, not hostile, to the conclusions that Scruton reaches. I think it would be fair to say that for many practical purposes, he and I would agree. Indeed, I think that this chapter, and in particular its last 11 pages, should be studied with the most assiduous attention by all who are interested in sex education. In it he makes a number of points with which I entirely agree, and of which I here offer a brief summary, using Scruton's own words as much as possible.

Education is concerned not just with a child's actions but also with his feelings and character (SD 325). In trying to develop the potential to be happy, we are concerned not with the immediate gratification of impulses but with the development of dispositions which will bring long-term fulfilment (SD 326). Among these is the ability to control one's sexual impulses (SD 330). A further prerequisite is the adoption of a system of values, and the capacity to see as desirable only those things which are the occasion of true fulfilment (SD 336). Because sexual desire has the most far-reaching consequences for those affected by it, it cannot be morally neutral. Since the capacity to give and receive erotic love is of incomparable value in the process of self-fulfilment, we have reason to acquire this capacity. Some sexual habits are vicious precisely because they destroy it (SD 337–8). Because erotic love is prone to jealousy, which can entail catastrophic consequences for both parties, the occasions of jealousy must be forestalled by the habit of fidelity, which is fostered by a complex process of moral education (SD 339). The task of sexual morality is to unite the personal and the sexual, to sustain thereby the intentionality of desire, and prepare the individual for erotic love. Only by safeguarding the integrity of our embodiment can we inculcate either innocence in the young or fidelity in the adult. Perversion consists precisely in diverting the sexual impulse from its interpersonal goal, or towards some act which is intrinsically destructive of personal relations and the values that we find in them (SD 343). The ideal of virtue remains one of 'sexual integrity', of a sexuality which is entirely integrated into the life of personal affection, and in which the self and its responsibility are centrally involved and indissolubly linked to the pleasures and passions of the body (SD 346).

I shall now proceed to argue that these conclusions, which I am delighted to endorse, have corollaries of a kind which Scruton will almost certainly find alarmingly radical. As he himself admits, "... sexual desire does not occur only between people of different sex; any account of sexual desire that could not be extended to homosexuality would be ludicrous..." (SD 254). By the same token, any ideology of sexuality or programme of moral education which ignores the fact that a significant minority of the population is homosexual must be accounted inadequate. Since many young people will turn out to be so orientated, should not wise and benevolent educators, unfettered by superstition and prejudice, take all practicable care to assist them to have as fulfilled and complete a life as possible? I would emphasise that such a policy is one not of proselytisation but merely of facing squarely up to reality. Although Scruton makes no suggestions either hortatory or censorious about how homosexuality should be treated by moral educators, his discussions both of homosexuality and of the functions of moral education have positive implications. For since, on Scruton's own admission, homosexual desire is capable of the same interpersonal intentionality as heterosexual desire, homosexual relationships have in this respect precisely the same potential. However, homosexuals can hardly be prepared for erotic love and encouraged towards a life-style in which their sexuality is "entirely integrated into the life of personal affection" (SD 346) if, as has traditionally been the case, they are constantly admonished to depreciate themselves and their sexual nature and offered no support by social norms and institutions. For this reason such negative and disparaging pronouncements as the one recently delivered by the Catholic Church are particularly to be deplored [15].

The Catholic Church's teaching on homosexuality and the depravity of some homosexuals afford a striking instance of a paradox expounded by Bernard Mandeville in *The Fable of the Bees* (1714), namely that "Parties directly opposite/Assist each other, as 'twere for spight" [16]. For it is certain that nothing has been more instrumental in driving homosexuals towards a degraded life-style than the indiscriminate censure they have suffered from Christian moralists. At the same time, nothing appears to justify this condemnation more than the professed wantonness of those homosexual 'spokespersons' who are as undiscriminating in their approval as the Catholic Church is in its condemnation. Herbert Spencer once wrote, "The suppression of every error is commonly followed by a temporary ascendency of the contrary one" [17]. It was once thought that *all* homosexual acts were morally reprehensible: some homosexual organisations would have us think that *no* homosexual acts are. There has long been a need to establish between these two equally pernicious extremes a consensus in which homosexual relationships, like heterosexual ones, can be individually appraised on their merits.

One reason why homosexuals are less likely than heterosexuals to have enduring relationships must be that whereas the latter grow up in a cultural climate (what one might call a 'moral community') which even now still guides most of them into relationships which are both personally satisfying and socially useful, the former are not supported by any positive norms or institutions. On the contrary, they are admonished, directly or indirectly, to view negatively their own sexuality. Hitherto, there has been nothing in popular culture to foster in homosexuals the higher manifestations of amorous passion (tenderness, affection, loyalty) to which heterosexuals are encouraged to aspire. Those who gravitate towards the so-called 'gay scene' will find not only a facile endorsement of promiscuity which creates an ethos that is essentially dehumanising and impersonal, but an ideology which provides a spurious theoretical justification for the wanton and irresponsible conduct to which it gives licence. This so-called liberational ideology has been most baneful where its influence has been greatest, and has led in some American cities to such inordinate and brutalising excesses as make the inhabitants of Sodom seem like paradigms of chastity and restraint [18]. It has served badly those who have been foolish enough to espouse it, for it has proved to be a harbinger of debauchery, disease, and death. The ideology of 'sexual integrity' proposed by Scruton, or something closely akin to it, is equally applicable to both heterosexuals and homosexuals and could serve as an antidote to the virulent poison of anarchic liberationism which menaces society.

I have recently championed elsewhere [19] the policy of promoting before young people positive images of caring and humane homosexuals, who are confident and secure in their own sexuality and responsible in the relationships they form. These would both serve as positive rôle models to those who grow up to be homosexual and also help to dispel ignorance and prejudice among those who do not. But I wonder if this is enough. One of the features which vitiate so much radical thinking about sexual morality is the naive contention that because human institutions are in a sense artificial, they are therefore arbitrary. This thesis is countered by Scruton in his final chapter, 'The Politics of Sex', where he maintains (in a manner similar to Hume's account of justice [20]) that some social artifacts are natural and even necessary to human beings since they bring human nature into harmony with the requirements of social living. Scruton in fact goes further than Hume by maintaining that some artifacts actually make human nature what it is. He dismisses recent 'Rousseauist' attempts to create a 'higher' civilisation based on a Utopian state of nature in which people are divested of the restraints imposed by social institutions, arguing rather that "the fate of persons is inseparable from the history of the institutions which form and nurture them" (SD 350).

If this supposition is correct (as I believe it is), then it emphasises how serious is the lack of appropriate institutions as an obstacle to the establishment of stable homosexual relationships; for since such institutions are the products of time, they cannot be created from scratch at short notice, howsoever desirable they might be; which itself is a point of contention. It is possible that as homosexuals are able to live more openly, any stable relationships they form will become objects of public perception and recognition, and this may in time lead to a kind of institutionalisation comparable to marriage. We have, then, an archetypal chicken/egg paradox: for on the one hand such relationships are likely to flourish to a significant degree only if they are nurtured by institutions; and on the other, the necessary institutions will come into being only through the recognition of phenomena which *ex hypothesi* depend on them. Inasmuch as the positive treatment of homosexuality by moral educators will not produce striking results overnight, some might be inclined to dismiss this policy as unequal to the problem it confronts. But perhaps this is all that can be done, and at least it is a step in the right direction. It is also one which Roger Scruton is bound to applaud if he really believes all that he has written.

NOTES

[1] THOMAS REID (1863) *Works*..., p. 228 (Ed. Sir William Hamilton) (Edinburgh, Maclachlan & Stewart).

[2] J. MARTIN STAFFORD (1977) On distinguishing between Love and Lust, *Journal of Value Inquiry*, 11, pp. 292–303.

[3] ROGER SCRUTON (1986) *Sexual Desire* (London, Weidenfeld & Nicolson). Hereafter references are contained within the text as SD + page number.

[4] HERBERT SPENCER (1897) *The Principles of Ethics*, Vol. I, p. 478 (London, Williams & Norgate).

[5] FRANCIS HUTCHESON (1728) *An Essay on the Nature and Conduct of the Passions and Affections*..., pp. 88–90 (London). The relevant passage is quoted by me on p. 299 of [2] above.

[6] BERNARD MANDEVILLE (1924) *The Fable of the Bees* (Ed. F. B. KAYE), 2 vols (Oxford, Clarendon Press), Vol. I, p. 95.(First published 1714.)

[7] Ibid., p. 96.

[8] For a fuller discussion see pages 299–300 of [2].

[9] H. SPENCER (see [4] above) p. 463.

[10] Sexual relationships incorporating intentionality are, by the prerequisites of their own nature, confined to the most highly evolved species, namely man, and seem therefore to be vindicated by the evolutionary process. I have discussed the merits and weaknesses of evolutionary theories of ethics in 'Hume, Spencer and the Standard of Morals', *Philosophy*, 58 (1983), pp. 39–55.

[11] From the propositions: 'If p then q' and 'p', we may validly derive 'q'. But to derive 'not q' from the conjunction of 'if p then q' and 'not p' is to argue fallaciously. It is known as the fallacy of denying the antecedent. Any elementary textbook on propositional logic will expound on this.

[12] DAVID HUME (1978) *A Treatise of Human Nature* revised by P. H. NIDDITCH (Oxford, Clarendon Press). In a famous passage on p. 469, Hume remarks on the problem of deriving normative propositions (such as are about what ought to be) from descriptive ones (such as are about what is). (First published 1739–40.)

[13] EDWARD WESTERMARCK (1917) *The Origin and Development of the Moral Ideas*, Vol. II, p. 486 (London, Macmillan).

[14] DAVID HUME (1975) *Enquiries*... revised by P. H. Nidditch (Oxford, Clarendon Press), p. 172 (First published 1748 and 1751.)

[15] The *Letter to the Bishops of the Catholic Church on the Pastoral Care of Homosexual Persons* (London, Catholic Truth Society, 1986) states unequivocally that all homosexual activity is 'an intrinsic moral evil' and the disposition to it 'an objective disorder'. Any contrary statements made by the 'pro-homosexual movement' are dismissed as 'deceitful propaganda'. Thus the Holy See not only thinks fit to reaffirm the full rigour of its traditional obdurate doctrine, but also does not scruple to impugn the good faith of all who dissent. Now surely, an institution which has in its time, and to suit its convenience, burned heretics, sold indulgences, condoned the persecution of Jews and the systematic pillaging of South America, and to this day discountenances the use of contraceptives even in countries where people are starving to death—surely, I say, such an institution cannot expect to command unquestioning allegiance as an arbiter of morals. Of course, all the usual passages from *Leviticus, Romans,* and *Corinthians* are paraded before us; and yet the authors conveniently overlook the fact that homosexuality is a phenomenon which pervades the whole of the animal creation, not one which is confined to postlapsian man. Perhaps, after all, the intentions of the Creator are more reliably manifest in His works than in the writings of those who lay claim to His inspiration.

[16] B. MANDEVILLE (see note [6]), p. 25.

[17] HERBERT SPENCER (1861) *Education: intellectual, moral, and physical*, p. 60 (London, Manwaring; subsequent editions, Williams & Norgate).

[18] The BBC 1 programme *Panorama* on 26 January 1987 included a report from San Francisco in which one man stated that prior to the AIDS epidemic there had been places to which homosexual men might resort and in the course of a single weekend have as many as *fifty* different sexual partners.

[19] J. MARTIN STAFFORD (1988) In Defence of Gay Lessons, *Journal of Moral Education*, 17, 1, pp. 11–20.

[20] See p. 484 of [12] above.

In Defence of Gay Lessons

J. Martin Stafford

Abstract
The arguments against the positive treatment of homosexuality depend on such false premises as that it is an illness or is socially subversive or that homosexuals are necessarily promiscuous. Since most of the problems are engendered by the intolerance and hostility which flow from unwarranted negative attitudes, these need to be countered by dissemination of correct information and constructive discussion.

The term *positive image* is a relative one without unambiguous denotation. However, many repellent images are projected by homosexuals themselves. Moral educators must not countenance irresponsible and decadent behaviour, but should guide people towards, and foster respect for, caring and committed relationships whether they be homosexual or heterosexual. So temperate and humane a proposal should command the support of all but bigoted and fanatical extremists.

The title of this paper is deliberately provocative and partly ironic. The policies and practices which I shall undertake to defend are not nearly so outrageous as some accounts would suggest. Certain newspapers, more renowned for titillation and scandal-mongering than for their accurate coverage of events, have surmounted their reports of what has been happening in London with such lurid headlines as 'Green Light for Gay Lessons', thereby evoking in the minds of their prurient readers images of flagrant proselytization or even of orgiastic frolicking on the classroom floor. What is being proposed is not nearly so sensational. The professed aim of the Inner London Education Authority and of some of the London boroughs is rather to counteract the propagation of false images of homosexuality and the consequent fostering of discrimination and prejudice. As Ealing's policy statement points out:

> There are pupils who will themselves grow up to be lesbian or gay. It is vital that they are reassured that homosexuality is not a disease or 'perversion' but simply another variation of human sexuality. Many pupils will also be unsure as to their sexuality, and it is important that they are able to decide for themselves

> without being subjected to pressure at school. Education also involves encouraging respect for and acceptance of others. In the course of their lives, children may have friends, relatives, or their own daughters and sons who form lesbian or gay relationships. This is why we need to overcome prejudice against homosexuality. . . . we . . . wish to create an educational atmosphere in which all pupils are able to recognise, with confidence, their developing sexuality. It is also important to dispel the myths built up by the negative and often derogatory images of lesbians and gay men shown in society.[1]

I shall deal first of all with the arguments advanced against the policy of promoting positive images of homosexuality; then I shall offer an analysis of what positive images are, and suggest how some such might be promoted in a manner consistent with the purposes of an educational institution; finally, I shall look in particular at one book which has been used in this way.

I

As one might have expected, an undiscriminating attack on *any* sympathetic discussion in schools of homosexuality has been made by the radical right and by fundamentalist Christians, much of the criticism assuming on the part of its readers the very antipathy and prejudice which it is designed to inflame but yet conspicuously fails to justify. The radical manifesto of the Hillgate Group, *Whose Schools?* deploys emotive phrases such as 'overt preaching on behalf of homosexuality', which is glibly conjoined with 'sexual licence and social indiscipline'[2], and an appendix reproduces the Introduction from the materiography on *Positive Images* compiled and published by ILEA.[3] This is reprinted without comment (and, I am told, without permission) as if the very existence of such a list were a self-evident affront to propriety and as if any criticism directed against it therefore stood in no need of support whatsoever.

In her tendentiously named booklet *Gay Lessons: How Public Funds are used to promote Homosexuality among Children and Young People*[4] Rachel Tingle lists various publications and organizations, carefully recording the subsidies they have received and rendering an account of their aims and activities; but no solid arguments are adduced to support the underlying assumption that all the enterprises she describes are reprehensible. In the very first paragraph of her introduction she refers to the time before the 1967 Sexual Offences Act (when homosexuals and all their wicked works were decorously concealed) as if it was a Golden Age of decency and moral rectitude whose passing is lamented by all right-thinking people. She states with a seemingly callous indifference that 'homosexuals were subject to widespread job discrimination' and that 'children suspected of homosexual tendencies were often referred to some sort of counsellor or medical practitioner'.[5] She does not mention that it was then quite common for these hapless 'patients' to be subjected to aversion therapy involving either electric shock treatment or nauseating drugs. Nor does she mention the tragically high incidence of blackmail and suicide, which, along with the growing realization of the injustice of punishing men just for being homosexual, eventually bestirred public opinion, touched the conscience of all but two of the Christian churches, and prompted a handful of courageous politicians to introduce reforming legislation.

Although the myth that homosexuality is a sickness is now almost entirely discredited, it is one which Tingle tries to perpetuate. It seems to be like the Hydra: each time you lop off one of its ugly heads, it sprouts another; for similarly crude attempts to draw wide-ranging conclusions from limited and unrepresentative data were avidly cited by David Holbrook in 1972[6] and by Mary Whitehouse in

1977.[7] Referring to a single work, Tingle contends that homosexuality is an illness attributable to severe disturbances in the early child-parent relationship when critical maturational changes are taking place.[8] This and all similar arguments can be countered with devastating force by a very general observation made in 1944 by the late Professor C. D. Broad:

> Of all branches of empirical psychology that which is concerned with what goes on in the minds of babies must, from the nature of the case, be one of the most precarious. Babies, whilst they remain such, cannot tell us what their experiences are; and all statements made by grown persons about their own infantile experiences on the basis of ostensible memory are certainly inadequate and probably distorted. The whole of this part of psychology therefore is, and will always remain, a mere mass of speculations about infantile mental processes, put forward to explain certain features in the lives of grown persons and incapable in principle of any independent check or verification. Such speculations are of the weakest kind known to science.[9]

Tingle then proceeds to complain that when the American Psychiatric Association voted to delete homosexuality from the official list of pathologies, it did so under pressure from gay activists rather than as a result of scientific research. Now the pertinent question is surely whether there was ever any scientific warrant for its inclusion in the first place, or whether, as seems far more likely, the facile presumption that homosexuality is an illness was made in all too eager compliance with the prejudice in which Christian culture is steeped. Moreover, it is not unduly cynical to suppose that the American psychiatrists would never willingly have abandoned so lucrative a doctrine had they been able to put forward a remotely plausible defense on its behalf. In fact, it is possible to categorize a condition like homosexuality as a mental illness only by extending the concept of mental illness in such a way as to render it unserviceably contentious or even viciously ideological. Those who are pleased thus to castigate homosexuality would therefore do well to remember that in the USSR it is Christians and other anti-Soviet dissidents who help to fill the mental hospitals. One of the most witty comments on the thesis which equates homosexuality with mental illness was made by Professor Antony Flew in 1971:

> . . . the whole point of talking of any sort of health or disease – as opposed, perhaps, to appealing to moral or other non-medical ideas or norms – must be to press a supposed analogy with the paradigm of physical health or physical disease.
>
> Now in a typical case of physical disease: there is first something organically wrong . . . ; then, second, the symptoms are not under the immediate present control of the patient . . . ; and, third, the patient himself complains (and what he complains of is the disease itself, and not just the disease considered as the cause of whatever social penalties may happen to be imposed on those who have it).
>
> A moment's thought shows that not one of these requirements is generally met by practising homosexuals . . . First, they could not be practising if the apparatus were not in good working order. Second, though homosexuality as a character trait is no more alterable at will – and for the same reason – than is heterosexuality, there is, surely, no reason to believe that the homosexual is any less, or any more, able than the heterosexual to inhibit the expression of his disposition in what – in the old pre-four-letter days – movie publicists used to call 'acts of love'. And, third, though some homosexuals may be disgusted with

> their homosexuality – just as many of the Christian saints were disgusted with their heterosexuality – many others would have no complaints about their condition were it not for the penalties which are still imposed on them by society.[10]

Two charges made by Tingle concern the revolutionary nature of the gay movement[11] and the high incidence of promiscuity among male homosexuals.[12] In spite of what she suggests, revolutionary radicalism and indifference to promiscuity are by no means necessary features of a coherent philosophy of homosexual equality, nor are they attitudes which I endorse. On the contrary, the revolutionary posturings of some gay activists are, in my view, a bizarre and embarrassing sideshow which is largely irrelevant to the problems which affect homosexuals and frequently diverts attention from them; while promiscuity and the fact that it is condoned by some homosexual 'spokespersons' are an onerous millstone round the necks of those who would make out a plausible and responsible case for gay rights. However, I would add by way of mitigation that the indiscriminate censure which homosexuals have suffered from Christian moralists has done much to drive them towards lifestyles which are less than edifying. A recent pronouncement by the Catholic Church has absolutely nothing constructive to say about homosexuality, and even impugns the good faith of all those who dissent from this view.[13] Literature produced by Family and Youth Concern (formerly The Responsible Society) gives the impression that there are no such people as homosexuals, only those who by mistake or from wilful perversity believe that they are. This organization thus refuses to consider what difficulties these non-existent people encounter or how they might best lead their lives. This head-in-the-sand mentality is, I submit, profoundly *ir*responsible and entirely inconsistent with the social concern which the organization professes.

In salutary contrast, the Inner London Education Authority and some of the London boroughs are actively promoting awareness of the hardships which young homosexuals face and adopting policies to obviate them. Research conducted by the London Gay Teenage Group using a sample of over 400[14] mainly between the ages of 16 and 20 indicates that ignorance and hostility give rise to a wide range of problems. A quarter of those responding to the relevant question in the survey complained of verbal abuse, and a sixth of the male respondents had actually been beaten up.[15] I regard it as scandalous that Tingle should condone the intolerance which gives rise to these evils. That she does so is clearly evidenced by her disapproval of attempts to eradicate it.[5] The London Gay Teenage Group researchers point out that . . .

> Despite all the problems involved in meeting other lesbians and gay men, the lack of information and positive role models, and the generally hostile legal and social environment in which homosexual relationships exist, the vast majority of our survey population had had sex with someone of the same sex. Most of these people were happy with their sex lives. Furthermore, well over half of our survey population said that they had, or had had, a long term homosexual lover.
>
> If [our] recommendations . . . were acted upon, these relationships would exist in an amenable and tolerant environment, enjoying the same support as do heterosexual relationships at present.[16]

Fortunately, many of these recommendations are indeed now being implemented by ILEA and other London boroughs, who have resolved to fight ignorance and prejudice by promoting in schools positive images of homosexuality.

II

What is a positive image? Although this term has now gained a certain currency, it has no clear and unambiguous denotation, and it takes but little reflection to realize why; for being 'positive' in this context is not a simple predicate, but implies a relationship between the image projected and the person to whom it is directed. Let us begin by attending to the most extreme and hopeless cases: imagine an ardently bigoted homophobe[17] whose prejudices are sustained by an unshakeable commitment to a system of religious or superstitious beliefs. To such a person *nothing* would count as a positive image of a homosexual, except, perhaps, one who was disgusted by his proclivities and constantly strove to repress them. At the other end of the scale, consider a strident and amoral gay activist, who blindly endorses anything and everything that homosexuals might do. To this person, almost nothing would count as a *negative* image, except a homosexual who did not live out and enjoy his orientation. The acceptance of something as a positive image depends only on its being attuned to the receptive sensibilities and congruous with the preconceptions of the person to whom it is addressed. There is no *logical* restriction on the range of possibilities, and the only psychological limitations are such as affect the establishment and maintenance of the aforementioned congruity. While these afford *some* safeguard, they do not present an insuperable obstacle to the determined and competent propagandist; for the death camps of Auschwitz and Belsen were no doubt positively regarded by those who superintended them, and the task they accomplished seen as an entirely laudable one. Evidently then, it is possible to present anything at all as a positive image to those whose moral sensitivities have been appropriately perverted or annulled. The issues at stake are therefore not quite so simple as Elizabeth Osborne supposed in her article 'Dispelling the myths', wherein she wrote:

> Promoting positive images quite simply means . . . showing that such people [as women bus drivers, bank managers etc.] exist and it means presenting them in a positive light and on equal terms, thereby fostering the acknowledgement and respect that is their due. It is necessary and important that we address ourselves to the issue of homosexuality and lesbianism in this way as well.[18]

Now the terms 'homosexual' and 'homosexuality' are as extensive in their denotation as are 'heterosexual' and 'heterosexuality', and comprehend just as widely divergent a range of people and lifestyles, not all of which by any means are the proper objects of acknowledgement and respect, and it would be a reckless educationalist who tried to maintain that they are. Some of the most negative and damaging images of homosexuality are disseminated by homosexuals themselves, obviously unaware of their capacity to repel and unmindful of the fact that they, like other groups, are more likely to be judged by their deeds than by their propaganda. In December 1986, the Chief Constable of Greater Manchester, Mr James Anderton, hit the headlines by proclaiming that those most at risk from AIDS (promiscuous homosexuals, drug addicts and prostitutes) were 'swirling around in a . . . cesspit of their own making.'[19] Even those who have most reason to regret his remark were quite unable seriously to dispute it. A spokesman for the Terrence Higgins Trust said that it was 'uncaring and unchristian' but, significantly, he did not venture to say that it was untrue. In fact, Mr Anderton's allegation was corroborated only five days later by a caller to a Radio 4 phone-in programme[20], who confessed that the habit of promiscuous sexual indulgence had rendered him incapable of establishing any kind of stable relationship. He went on to admit, with a candour which is the more refreshing for being so unusual, that many in the 'gay scene' are so sated with sexual activity that it means no more to them than blowing their nose. Now Oscar Wilde did suggest that 'whenever one has anything unpleasant to say, one should always be quite candid'[21], and few things could be more unpleasant than what this person admitted, though what follows certainly is. On January 26th 1987, the BBC 1 programme *Panorama* included a report from San Francisco in which one man declared, with very little sign of remorse, that prior to the AIDS epidemic there had been places to which homosexual men might resort and in the course of a single weekend have as many as *fifty* different sexual partners. Such revelations surely make those much-maligned inhabitants of Sodom seem like paradigms of chastity and restraint, and must evoke in people of ordinary sensitivities the most intense and well-founded feelings of disgust. If it were intended to have the perpetrators of these inordinate excesses received as 'positive images', then, as Rachel Tingle alleges, it would indeed be necessary to mount 'a vigorous campaign to revolutionize moral values with regard to homosexuality':[22] for the public would have to be prevailed upon to renounce all the traditional decencies which constitute the common core of existing sexual morality. Neither the methods necessary to realize this barbarous aim, nor the aim itself, would be compatible with the purposes of our educational institutions.

To advocate, or even to condone, promiscuity and decadence under the alluring banner of liberality and emancipation would be not only a wicked and calculating imposture on the credulity of the young, but a policy pregnant with catastrophic social consequences. It would also bring into disrepute more temperate proposals which might be mistakenly associated with it. The following words of George Berkeley, though written in a remote time, are depressingly apposite to our own:

> . . . the present age aboundeth with injudicious patrons of liberty, who, not distinguishing between that and licentiousness, take the surest method to discredit what they would seem to propagate; for, in effect, can there be a greater affront offered to that just freedom of thought and action which is the prerogative of a rational creature, or can anything recommend it less to honest minds, than under colour thereof to obtrude scurrility and profaneness on the world?[23]

However, it is possible to promote images of homosexuality which many can accept not – as some opponents fear – because they have been seduced into moral nihilism, but because their value system is flexible enough to accommodate homosexual relationships which are seen to share the morally significant features of comparable heterosexual relationships. There is no need for any such radical revision of moral values as Tingle so fearfully prognosticates. The London Borough of Ealing is very right to insist that homosexuality, like heterosexuality, should be discussed in the context of love, personal relationships, home life, and respect for others.[1] If these conditions are fulfilled then the resultant practice is invulnerable to the criticism that it involves undermining morality by promoting radical changes of attitude; for it requires only dissemination of awareness that homosexuals, like heterosexuals, are capable of genuinely loving relationships. It also accords with the government's wish that there be 'due regard to moral considerations and the value of family life'[22] and is secure against the charge that the emphasis is on individual gratification rather than an interpersonal act.[24]

This policy requires that young people be exposed to images of caring and humane homosexuals who are, or become, secure and confident in their own sexuality and responsible in the relationships they form. These might be presented in novels, in films, or on television. It is encouraging that the American television industry has already shown itself willing to treat homosexual characters in this way. The 1961 British film *Victim*[25] tells how a homosexual barrister ends a blackmailing racket which is preying on homosexuals. While this film did much to stimulate sympathetic discussion of the problems with which it dealt, its characters are hardly positive ones. They see their own nature as an affliction, and project themselves as objects of pity rather than of condemnation, but not as people worthy of esteem. Moreover, at the end of the film, the principal character is 'redeemed' by resuming his relationship with his wife. In striking contrast with this, a recent American TV movie, *Consenting Adult*,[26] tells how a young student comes to accept his homosexuality, which he is disposed to view positively despite his parents' initial determination to have him 'cured'. In the end he establishes a loving relationship with a fellow student, who eventually receives parental approval. Such a film would have been inconceivable not so long ago. More recently the televising of a programme with a homosexual theme was thwarted. During the summer of 1986, BBC Schools Television made a two-part drama called *Mates* portraying a romantic attachment between two 17-year-old boys. It was intended to be shown in February, 1987 as part of the widely admired series 'Scene', but its screening was cancelled.[27]

III

In his inaugural lecture as Professor of Philosophy at Sheffield University, the late Peter Nidditch made the following pronouncement which bears on the issue now under consideration.

> Educational processes should bequeath to the next generation the totality of a civilized heritage together with a preparation for improving what has so far been attained. These educational processes have six principal aims: 1) the effective employment of the intellectual powers in all the relevant business of life; 2) the transmission of knowledge; 3) an enthusiasm and respect for truth and for the advance of efforts towards finding it; 4) an awareness of the potentialities and interconnections of the different branches of knowledge; 5) the furtherance of humane feelings and ideals; and 6) an appreciation of the aesthetic. Academic institutions of all levels should concern themselves with the achievement of all these purposes, which can be given many different degrees of stress.[28]

Of the above objectives, those which most concern our present enquiry are the general possibility of improving upon our cultural heritage and the furtherance of humane feelings and ideals; for there is surely good reason to try to improve a moral heritage which has done so little to foster in homosexuals the capacity to have loving relationships and so much to drive them to despair.

While researching this paper I read some of the books listed in the ILEA *Positive Images* materiography.[3] Some of them, as its annotations make clear, are hardly suitable for use in schools, since they are pervaded by foul language and disfigured by voyeuristic accounts of sexual activity; but one, it is claimed, has been used as a set book with great success. Timothy Ireland's short novel *Who lies inside* is an extremely unpretentious little book which is yet permeated by the most humane ideals and the most responsible moral values. It tells how Martin Conway, an 18-year-old who is about to leave school and go to a college of education, comes to realize and to accept his homosexuality despite adverse pressure from his contemporaries and his fears of parental disapproval. He is attracted to one of his classmates, Richard, who appears to give him encouraging signs of reciprocity, but Martin is inhibited from developing this relationship, and in compliance with the expressed wishes of his other friends starts dating a girl called Margaret, with whom before long he has sexual intercourse. This experience is predictably unsatisfying, and is immediately viewed with revulsion and remorse – a perception which the reader is strongly induced to share. Even before this event, his aversion to the course of action on which he has embarked is made clear.

> I thought of the number of times I'd heard men boasting about how many girls they'd laid. I'd never heard any man bragging about being in love. Whilst my sexual success with Margaret, despite her hurt, would be admired, my love for Richard would be derided. It made me wonder bitterly just who was perverted, those that used others for sexual gain, or those that genuinely loved.[29]

The book incorporates many valuable lessons, both by commending the virtues of self-awareness, tolerance and respect for the feelings of others, and by depicting the misery and distress which are caused when, in violation of these principles, homosexual pegs are forced into heterosexual holes. Fortunately, Martin Conway is perceptive and strong-minded enough to retrieve himself before any further harm is done. He does not want to live a lie or to hurt anyone, but only to be able to associate freely and unashamedly with the person he truly cares for; as in fact he does in the final chapter of the book.

Since Roger Scruton is one of the five signatories to the radical manifesto *Whose Schools?*,[2] we must suppose that he endorses its implied deprecation of 'gay lessons'. I think we can also suppose that he did not trouble to inquire very carefully into what he was so ready to condemn, in which case he should perhaps be urged to take to heart six wise words of Chairman Mao: 'No investigation, no right to speak'.[30] I certainly think that if he had read Timothy Ireland's novel, he might have thought twice before declaring himself an opponent of such studies; for the ideals enshrined in this book accord so well with the canons of sexual propriety enjoined in his own voluminous tome *Sexual Desire*.[31] In fact, I could hardly imagine a work of modern fiction which promoted them more eloquently. The attachment between Martin and Richard has all the makings of an ideal *Scrutonian relationship*. (I coin this term to mean 'a caring and committed erotic relationship founded on reciprocal sexual desire with full interpersonal intentionality'.) Although Scruton is less than happy about such relationships between persons of the same sex, there is nothing in his book which shows them to be impossible, and much to suggest the contrary. Accordingly, if he really believes all that he has written, he must surely prefer a Scrutonian relationship between two persons of the same sex to a heterosexual relationship which lacks intentionality and is therefore, in his view, 'perverted'.[32] Thus Roger Scruton, Martin Conway, and (presumably) the author who created him are unanimous on this point: whether they be gay or straight, it is those that use others without loving them, not those who genuinely love, who are perverted.

Perhaps Professor Scruton may yet come round to thinking that gay lessons might not be such a bad idea after all. If he does not, then he and others of his persuasion must bear at least some of the responsibility for the evils which will continue to flow from the problems they have so wilfully ignored. Writing of their sample of over 400, Trenchard and Warren point out:

> Over half had been verbally abused, a fifth had been beaten up, one in ten had been thrown out of home and many others sent to a doctor or psychiatrist because they were lesbian or gay. One in five had felt under such intolerable pressure that they had attempted suicide. It is indicative of the strength of these

> young people that they have all survived these crises and are now happy to identify themselves to us as homosexual. [They] have exhibited a strength in coping with society's prejudices, and have celebrated their sexuality in a way that other generations should envy. At 20 or under they have identified themselves positively as lesbian or gay, have formed relationships, made friends and established lifestyles. On the other hand, we have also read or heard about ways in which young homosexuals are discriminated against, the prejudice, ignorance and bigotry which they experience. We have read or heard how those close to them, and society in general, have shunned, rejected, or abused them because they are homosexual.[33]

Those who are so obdurate and callous as to feel no sympathy towards this needless suffering should reflect that they or their friends or relations may well have homosexual children who are similarly at risk. The issues I have discussed desperately require candid and dispassionate treatment: let us hope that fair dealing and honest inquiry will not be displaced by either the uncritical fanaticism of one extreme or the sermonizing bigotry of the other; for both are the bastard offspring of party spirit and opportunism.

Notes and References

1. LONDON BOROUGH OF EALING: Education Committee Policy Statement on Sexual Equality (approved on 20th January, 1987).
2. COX, C. *et al.*, (1986). *Whose Schools? – A Radical Manifesto*. London: The Hillgate Group. p. 4.
3. ILEA LEARNING RESOURCES BRANCH (1986). *Positive Images*, Materiography Series No. 11.
4. TINGLE, R. (1986). *Gay Lessons: How Public Funds are Used to Promote Homosexuality among Children and Young People*. London: Pickwick Books, hereafter refered to as Tingle.
5. TINGLE, p. vii.
6. HOLBROOK, D. (1972). *Sex and Dehumanization*. London: Pitman, pp. 94–111.
7. WHITEHOUSE, M. (1977). *Whatever Happened to Sex?*. Hove: Wayland Publishers, pp. 66–8.
8. TINGLE, p. 3.
9. BROAD, C. D. (1971). *Critical Essays in Moral Philosophy*. Edited by David Cheney. London: Allen & Unwin, p. 169.
10. FLEW, A. (1971). Letter in the *Bulletin of the Campaign for Homosexual Equality*, May 1971.
11. TINGLE, pp. iii and 5. This controversy is in part merely verbal; for if one characterizes the acceptance of homosexuality on equal terms with heterosexuality as a 'revolutionary' change, then that the aims of the gay movement are revolutionary is a tautology. What I would dispute is the contingent thesis that such an accommodation of homosexuality requires or entails other far-reaching changes such as the general renunciation of family life, private property and money.
12. TINGLE, p. 20.
13. *Letter to the Bishops of the Catholic Church on the Pastoral Care of Homosexual Persons* (1986). London: Catholic Truth Society.
14. Although it is not claimed that the sample of 416 is statistically representative, it ought to be much less defective in this respect than the deliberately biased and much smaller groups (some as small as 12 or 8) on which the conclusions cited by Tingle, Holbrook (n6), and Whitehouse (n7) are based.
15. WARREN, H. (1984). *Talking about School.* London: London Gay Teenage Group, p. 12.
16. TRENCHARD, L. and WARREN, H. (1984). *Something to Tell You*. London: London Gay Teenage Group, p. 139.
17. This word has become accepted to mean a person who fears or hates anything concerning homosexuals or homosexuality.
18. OSBORNE, E. (1986). 'Dispelling the myths', *Times Educational Supplement*, 19th December 1986.
19. *Manchester Evening News*, 11th December 1986.
20. *Call Nick Ross*, Radio 4, 16th December 1986.
21. WILDE, O. (1895). *The Importance of Being Earnest*, Act II.
22. TINGLE, p. iii.
23. BERKELEY, G. (1721). *An essay towards preventing the ruin of Great Britain*, reprinted in *The Works of George Berkeley*, Vol. VI, edited by T. E. Jessop. Edinburgh: Thomas Nelson, 1953, p. 70.
24. TINGLE, p. 14.

25. *Victim*, directed by Basil Dearden (Rank/Allied Film Makers/Parkway, 1961).
26. *Consenting Adult*, directed by Gilbert Cates (Norman Horowitz/Vista Organisation, Los Angeles, 1985).
27. A description of *Mates* and a discussion of the decision to withdraw it were printed in the *Times Educational Supplement*, 14th November 1986, pp. 1 and 34.
28. NIDDITCH, P. (1970). *The Intellectual Virtues*. Sheffield: University of Sheffield, Department of Philosophy, p. 4.
29. IRELAND, T. (1984). *Who Lies Inside*. London: Gay Men's Press, p. 94.
30. MAO TSE-TUNG (1966). *Quotations from Chairman Mao*. Peking: Foreign Languages Press, p. 230.
31. SCRUTON, R. (1986). *Sexual Desire*. London: Weidenfeld and Nicolson.
32. *Ibid*., pp. 289–90. For a fuller discussion of Scruton's account of this issue, see my 'Love and lust revisited: intentionality, homosexuality, and moral education', (1988) *Journal of Applied Philosophy*, **5**, 1.
33. TRENCHARD and WARREN (see n16), pp. 151 and 155.

Homosexuality and Education—a reply to Jim Ferguson*

J. MARTIN STAFFORD

Despite two or three material inaccuracies [1], Jim Ferguson's review fairly represents the spirit and tone of my book. However, I should like to challenge some of the points he raises and the alternative proposals which his criticisms imply.

DID 'GAY LIB' REALLY LIBERATE ANYONE?

Mr Ferguson alleges that I "... fail to emphasise ... the most important feature of the liberation movement of the 1970s ... " (Ferguson, 1989). This is because I do not share his convictions about the nature and significance of the events he relates. First, there were homosexuals who were "conscious of themselves as worthwhile ... human beings" long before the Stonewall riots of 1969. The North West Homosexual Law Reform Committee held its first meeting in Manchester in October 1964 (Horsfall, 1988, p. 27), and the homophile movement in Holland and Denmark dates back to the late 1940s. Accordingly, his declaration that the gay movement had its origin in Stonewall may well serve as a stirring act of faith, but the claim is fictitious, not historical. Secondly, the much-vaunted "analyses and interpretations" propagated in the early 1970s were as deceitful as the stereotypes they displaced. Their effect, moreover, was hardly to liberate but rather to impose constraints no less rigorous than those they challenged. The movement forbad monogamous relationships and proclaimed other subversive and revolutionary doctrines; it prescribed extravagant behaviour and ridiculous attire; and it advocated the adoption of gratuitously strident methods of campaigning. All this gave to homosexuality a high but unrepresentative profile which antagonised the public at large and inhibited more sensitive and responsible homosexuals from declaring themselves. I therefore conclude that the transatlantic variety of Gay Liberation which Mr Ferguson extols never liberated anyone.

*Volume 19, No. 2 of the *Cambridge Journal of Education* contained a critical review by Jim Ferguson of J. Martin Stafford's book *Homosexuality and Education.* Mr Stafford asked to be allowed to reply and the Editors were happy to agree to this.

CAN WE CHOOSE OUR SEXUAL ORIENTATION?

While I was writing my book Clause 28 was being hotly debated. It was therefore imperative to dispel the myth that people can be induced to become homosexual by exposure to 'positive images' of homosexuality. At this time actors Ian McKellen and Michael Cashman were also at pains to emphasise that people do not *choose* to be gay. My pronouncements on this matter accord perfectly with theirs. I admit, however, that I was too dismissive of those lesbians who claim to have chosen their sexual orientation. In Michael Ruse's much larger volume (published shortly after my own) there is a detailed survey of speculation and research on the causes of sexuality. One study suggests that more women than men are bisexual and therefore are more likely to be able to function in either mode (Ruse, 1988, p. 110). This would explain how some might indeed 'choose' to be lesbians. Nevertheless, I believe that the majority of people do not have any such choice. I do not dispute that we may choose either to act in accordance with our nature or to violate its dictates; nor do I doubt that more people might elect to 'come out' as homosexual if heterosexism were eradicated; but these tenets are much weaker than the claim which I reject.

AIDS AND PROMISCUITY

I am perfectly aware that AIDS is the result of a virus and did not originate in promiscuity. The view which I espouse is that promiscuity and other forms of misconduct have been responsible for spreading this infection, even to endemic proportions in certain now notorious places. It is therefore naive or disingenuous to pretend that it is just an illness like any other with no moral implications whatsoever. For setting aside cases which involve embryos, rape and the transfusion of infected blood or products derived therefrom, the transmission of HIV infection must always be due to the deliberate actions of those concerned. Thus it is possible for someone to claim with confidence that he has no fear of contracting this disease since the circumstances of its transmission are alien to his own life-style.

I clearly state that not all AIDS victims have been promiscuous; but then their sexual partners (albeit at two or three stages removed) almost certainly have been. Even before the advent of HIV, the sexually promiscuous had frequent recourse to VD clinics: now, unless and until a cure for AIDS is found, the stakes have been dramatically increased and the odds shortened. The contention that all or most people infected are unlucky innocents who have never put a foot (or any other part of the body) out of place is preposterous nonsense. In fact, Mr James Anderton's memorable castigation of people "... swirling around in a cesspit of their own making ..." is probably much closer to the mark (see Stafford, 1988a, pp. 15–16). The carnal excesses of New York and San Francisco in particular have been too well documented and too widely exposed for any whitewash or cover-up to be possible. Only last year there appeared a collection of essays in which one writer blithely admits that during a three month trip to the USA in 1971 he clocked up one thousand sexual encounters—an average of more than ten 'playmates' per day (Dunn, 1988, p. 39). In the face of these paradigms of promiscuity and in the firm belief that such wantonness has been all too common—a conviction which is vindicated by a superabundance of literature in which licentiousness is condoned or even commended and of advertisements pandering to lust—one cannot but conclude that many AIDS sufferers must indeed have sought sexual gratification for its own sake. It is one thing for Mr Ferguson to claim that 'love' need not necessarily be long-term or exclusive (p. 228), but to suggest that within three months one could 'love' a thousand different people would be to abuse both the words he deploys and the patience of his readers (see Stafford, 1988c, p. 18 or 1977 for a fuller discussion). I concede that if people are firmly resolved so to deport themselves then little can be done to deter them. They cannot, however, expect others to approve of their conduct or to see their misdeeds endorsed by the curricular policies of our schools.

RESPECTABILITY AND THE RATIONALE OF 'GAY LESSONS'

I do not accept Mr Ferguson's insinuation that my high moral tone is inappropriate. For inasmuch as we live together in a complex network of interdependence, we all have an interest in the probity of other people's character. I have therefore advanced a coherent rationale for the positive treatment of homosexuality on the grounds that it is a natural and innocuous phenomenon, but that—like heterosexuality—it needs to be directed towards proper objects, namely stable monogamous relationships [2, 3]. Towards the end of his review Mr Ferguson alleges that my book "does not attempt to provide . . . a rationale . . . for including lesbian and gay life-styles, sexualities and other issues within the curriculum" (pp. 228–229). This is inconsistent with his earlier statement that my book's last chapter "looks at lesbian and gay sexualities within the curriculum and argues that schools should equip students for life by discussing [them] . . . and by dispelling fallacies and stereotypes" (pp. 225–226).

What am I to make of this contradiction? Surely, that Mr Ferguson well realises that I do indeed provide a rationale for my proposals but regrets that it is incongruous with his own ideology. Recent legislation imposes the responsibility for sex education on school governors. DES circulars have suggested that due regard be paid to moral considerations and to the values of family life. Any proposals which encouraged debauchery would certainly prove unacceptable—not just to homophobes and bigots but to anyone with a vestige of decency. I therefore submit that a programme such as my own has more to commend it than the naive and discredited radicalism which was in vogue a decade or two ago.

NOTES

[1] The review misquotes me, printing *injurious* for *injudicious*, and *resisting* for *redressing*.

[2] RUSE (1988) also adduces a number of arguments in support of stable rather than promiscuous

relationships (pp. 192–197) and cites evidence which supports the empirical claim that the former are more likely to be truly felicific (pp. 213, 233).

[3] I have established elsewhere (Stafford, 1988b) that support for such a policy is a corollary of Roger Scruton's pronouncements on sexual desire and the purposes of moral education. See also Stafford (1990).

REFERENCES

DUNN, I. (1988) Scotland against the odds, in: B. CANT & S. HEMMINGS (Eds) *Radical Records* (London, Routledge).

FERGUSON, J. (1989) Critical review of J. Martin Stafford's *Homosexuality and Education. Cambridge Journal of Education*, 19, pp. 225–230.

HORSFALL, A. (1988) Battling for Wolfenden, in: B. CANT & S. HEMMINGS (Eds) *Radical Records* (London, Routledge).

RUSE, M. (1988) *Homosexuality—a philosophical inquiry* (Oxford, Blackwell).

SCRUTON, R. (1986) *Sexual Desire* (London, Weidenfeld & Nicolson).

STAFFORD, J.M. (1977) On distinguishing between love and lust, *Journal of Value Inquiry*, 11, pp. 292–303.

STAFFORD, J.M. (1988a) In defence of gay lessons, *Journal of Moral Education*, 17, pp. 11–20.

STAFFORD, J.M. (1988b) Love and lust revisited: intentionality, homosexuality and moral education, *Journal of Applied Philosophy*, 5, pp. 87–100.

STAFFORD, J.M. (1988c) *Homosexuality and Education* (Manchester, J. M. Stafford).

STAFFORD, J.M. (1990) The two minds of Roger Scruton

The Two Minds of Roger Scruton

J. MARTIN STAFFORD

ABSTRACT: In two recent pieces Roger Scruton recommends that we should instil in children feelings of revulsion towards homosexuality; whereas the corollaries of his earlier book *Sexual Desire* contradict this. These inconsistencies are exposed and discussed and the preferability of his earlier stance defended.

KEY WORDS: homosexuality, moral education, sex education

In a contribution to *The Sunday Telegraph* Roger Scruton has unequivocally declared his opposition to the positive treatment of homosexuality and propounded the view that we should "continue to instil in our children feelings of revulsion" towards it. That Scruton should pen a vehement tirade against homosexuality might come as no surprise. If he were merely a journalistic hack who earned his daily bread by scribbling for the popular press, his views might have little claim on our attention. Indeed, we should probably dismiss them as unworthy of a serious refutation. However, not only is he a prominent spokesman on educational issues for the radical right but also he has held the chair of Aesthetics at Birkbeck College London and written several books, including a voluminous work on *Sexual Desire*. That a professional philosopher should write anything so deficient in candour and balance as the *Sunday Telegraph* piece must alarm us; and it should do so all the more since it was evidently no fleeting aberration. The very same homophobic proposal was enunciated at greater length in a lecture which had been delivered the previous month and has since been printed in a collection of his essays entitled *The Philosopher on Dover Beach*. I shall aim first to expose and discuss serious weaknesses in Scruton's argument and then to demonstrate that the educational practice which he recommends is not only exceptionable in itself but also inconsistent with what he said in a book written less than four years earlier.

I

Scruton's thesis may be summarised thus: since homosexuals have no children, they have no interest in society or in the future and therefore indulge their carnal appetites without restraint. Only by completely sublimating their sexuality and directing their energy to socially useful work could they acquire a stake in the community. Wherefore "we should continue to instil in our children feelings of revulsion" towards homosexuality. (Presumably Scruton's *we* includes both parents and professional educators.)

Studies in Philosophy and Education **11:** 187–193, 1991.

I entirely agree with Scruton that morality has a vitally important function in safeguarding social order and whole-heartedly endorse his disapproval of irresponsible sexual activity. However, even before our age of easy contraception and abortion virtually on demand it would have been naive to suppose, and disingenuous to claim, that transient, lustful encounters were the exclusive domain of homosexuals. Both in fact and in fiction, the amorous exploits of such characters as Casanova and Don Juan were imitated, or at least admired, by countless men. Now the "mysterious interdiction exerted by the other sex" on which Scruton relies as an impediment to heterosexual promiscuity has lost much of its mystery and virtually all its restraining force. Many heterosexuals – sometimes for unashamedly selfish reasons – either abstain from begetting children or else discharge their parental duties so carelessly that it would have been better had they never embarked on the enterprise. Accordingly, if Scruton's thesis were sound, it would apply to *all* childless people, not just homosexuals.

However, his argument is seriously defective on three counts: (1) It is not true that all homosexuals are promiscuous. (2) It is not true that all homosexuals are childless. Some – particularly lesbians – have children from marriages contracted under heterosexist social pressures or before they realised that they were homosexual. Moreover, homosexuals do not exist in complete isolation from other people. It is probable that many have brothers and sisters or friends in whose children they take a benevolent interest. (3) Consequently, having children is neither a necessary nor a sufficient condition of a sense of social responsibility. Many childless people are at least as committed as their progenitive peers to the well-being of society, and their concern extends beyond the probable duration of their own lives. Conversely, there are – as Scruton must surely be aware – prolific and irresponsible breeders who have little or no social conscience. Therefore, Scruton's thesis is, to say the least, seriously flawed. Since both the quality and non-fecundity of homosexual relationships are important and interesting issues, which he, of all people, should be capable of discussing sensibly, it is all the more unfortunate that he saw fit to present them in so tendentious and one-sided a manner.

Whereas I pointed out long before Roger Scruton that there is a need to differentiate sexual experiences which are loving and responsible from those which are merely lustful (Stafford, 1977), there has been a concerted attempt in the apologetic writings and pronouncements of some gay activists to characterise as 'loving' or 'caring' relationships *all* sexual encounters which are neither procured by remuneration nor based on duress. For instance, one reviewer of my book *Homosexuality and Education* contended that love need not be long-term or exclusive (Ferguson, p. 228). If taken strictly at face value this claim might be admitted. The attachment between the two principal characters in David Lean's 1945 film *Brief Encounter* is neither long-term nor exclusive, since each is already married and their association lasts only a few weeks; and yet the audience is left in no doubt that they are in love. On the other hand, it would surely be infelicitous to suggest that the term 'loving relationship' could be truly predicated of each of the one thousand sexual encounters which a recent author claims to have clocked up during a three month trip to the USA in the summer of 1971 (Dunn, p. 39). For even at a linguistic level there would be something dubious about such a claim, and one would be justified in disputing on *a priori* grounds the legitimacy of calling such brief (and perhaps even anonymous) assignations 'loving' or 'caring' relationships. Such a usage would certainly involve a more attenuated notion of love and care than these words normally denote; for unless the words were being used sardonically (which in the context here envisaged would be inconsistent with the propagandist aims of those who deploy them), the concepts of love and care thereby denoted must be attenuated almost to the point of vacuity. A meal which consists only of beans on toast may be a snack but it cannot be a banquet; four lines of verse may constitute a vulgar limerick, but not an epic poem; and a dozen or so bars of music, however tuneful, could not include a five-part triple fugue. By the same token, a transient sexual liaision between strangers could not be a loving relationship in anything like the ordinary sense of the term, since loving relationships, whether gay or straight, necessarily have features whose conditions are incongruous with such extremes of ephemerality.

Annette Baier has supported the kind of distinction I am keen to make by maintaining the need for "a way of testing whether one does really care about what one claims to care about" (Baier, p. 94). Love, she concludes, involves a desire for fidelity and permanence (*Ibid.* p. 100); caring is prospective: "love has continued unity and continued mutual enjoyment ... as its telos or objective"; and – most succinctly and pointedly – "One must in *some* way intend the love to continue, for it to be love at all." (*Ibid.* p. 102) I suppose that avowedly promiscuous people who see their dissipation for what it is and make no attempt to misdescribe it are at least being honest; they do not compound their misdeeds by adding to them the sins of self-deception and hypocrisy.

Baier also anticipates Scruton in raising the question as to whether homosexual relationships are in some way less valid because they are non-reproductive; though her tentative objection is not that lack of offspring causes homosexuals to behave irresponsibly but rather that a lifestyle which is exclusively homosexual is, in a significant sense, parasitic on heterosexuality, on whose fecundity the continuance of homosexuality as a phenomenon depends (*Ibid.* pp. 97–8). Baier seems not to think this a fatal objection to the legitimacy of homosexual relationships – a view which I gladly endorse. I might add that if the argument *were* cogent, it could be applied with equal force to monasticism; for the monastic life is quite incompatible with participation in reproductive processes and yet depends on them for its long-term survival, as indeed do all human enterprises.

A possible counter-argument to the charge that homosexuality does not contribute to the propagation of the species is presented at some length by Michael Ruse, the sixth chapter of whose book is entitled 'The Sociobiology of Homosexuality'. In his introductory remarks Ruse says:

> These explanations try to understand homosexuality in a Darwinian mode – as, in

> some sense, a function of adaptation brought about by natural selection, in response to life's struggles for existence and (more importantly) reproduction. (Ruse, p. 130)

In brief, the theories which Ruse here outlines and discusses suggest that homosexually orientated people make to the survival of their species a contribution which is not less real for being indirect – a line of argument which I find both congenial and persuasive. Scruton too, while criticising both the reductivism and the exaggerated claims which it has prompted some sociobiologists to make, is far from dismissive of the viability of evolutionary and functional explanations. He even makes what is surely a concession very damaging to his more recent homophobic stance, namely that "whatever exists exists because it is not dysfunctional" (Scruton, 1986 p. 186). Quite so. One might add that homosexuality has not only survived the processes of natural selection: it has also successfully resisted all culturally inspired attempts to eradicate it.

II

The reason why Scruton had recourse to so fragile an argument as the one outlined at the start of Section I becomes apparent from a study of his book on *Sexual Desire*, which reveals a striking incongruity between the sober reflections of Scruton the philosopher and the demotic rantings of Scruton the man. The principal thesis of this book is that human sexual desire, as distinct from the libidinous propensities which we share with other animals, is characterised by intentionality. This implies a qualitative difference in the level of awareness of objects. The objects of the more refined forms of sexual desire must be *intentional* while those of lust need only be material. Intentional objects are those objects of thought which are *con*ceived rather than merely *per*ceived. Thus the chair that I sit on, the painting I look at and the person I see are – in the first instance at least – *material* objects; whereas the chair that I remember, the painting I imagine, and the person I love are *intentional* objects. They may also exist materially, but they need not do so; for my memory of the chair may not be veridical, and both the painting and the person I love may be no more than figments of my imagination. That objects of love must be intentional is borne out by the fact that it is impossible to love someone without having an integral (albeit possibly erroneous) conception of him; whereas lust can be arroused by the prospect of physical features alone. Where this is not so, pictorial pornography would be as unmarketable as spent matches. I entirely agree with Scruton that in a proper sexual relationship we fully encounter our partner *as a person*, and I concur with him in deprecating transient or impersonal sexual activity in which we merely use someone else's body. Now Scruton admits (albeit reluctantly) that homosexuality is just as susceptible as heterosexuality of interpersonal intentionality and is therefore not intrinsically obscene or perverted, though, as with heterosexuality, some of its manifestations may be (Scruton, 1986 p. 305). That homosexuality and heterosexuality are alike in their capacity for what is essential to a proper relationship ought – as I have argued at length elsewhere (Stafford, 1988a) – to commit Scruton to an ideology which does not discriminate against homosexuals. Unfortunately, he cannot reconcile himself to the clear implications of his own philosophy. Indeed, his most recent pronouncements in the *Sunday Telegraph* and the *Dover Beach* essay are a desperate attempt to contradict them and thereby defend his prejudices.

Since Scruton's various opinings on this subject incorporate such violently antithetical elements, they cannot possibly be viewed as a logically defensible whole. By admitting that homosexual and heterosexual desire are alike in what is for him a crucial respect, he has laid a most unsuitable foundation on which to erect the edifice of ardent heterosexism which he aspires to build. His exhortation that we should "continue to instil in our children feelings of revulsion" towards gay relationships entails the propagation of attitudes which are quite unwarranted even by his own representation of the facts. He castigates "the growth of proselytizing homosexuality, which seeks to enter schools and households with the liberating message that there are rival 'orientations'" (Scruton 1990 p. 263). [Surely, in this context *different* would have been a less inflammatory word than *rival*.] This message, whose truth he does not dispute but whose dissemination he bitterly deplores, Scruton would displace by an 'endarkening' process designed to instil guilt and inhibitions.

> Only if the revulsion is implanted in him, by means which by-pass his reflective powers, could he ever come to see the point of the traditional interdiction. In his formative years, therefore, he must be subject to an educative process which could never be justified from liberal premises. His moral education cannot be a purely 'enlightened' and 'enlightening' one ... It must involve an 'endarkened' and 'endarkening' component, by which he is taught ... to regard certain paths as forbidden ... There is no force like religion, for endarkening the mind in this way. (*Ibid.* p. 271)

Even if this extremely sinister and avowedly indoctrinatory proposal were not utterly repugnant, such a policy would, I suspect, be unworkable in an age so resistant to dogma. There is, moreover, a corpus of empirical evidence which indicates that the consequences of the self-loathing and rampant homophobia which Scruton advocates are far from salutary. Of these inordinately high personal and social costs he takes no account whatsoever. Numerous instances of isolation, despair, and alienation – sometimes leading to eviction from home and even to attempted suicide – have been documented and published by the London Gay Teenage Group. I have myself outlined the problems in the fourth chapter of my book *Homosexuality and Education*. Moreover, on Scruton's own admission it is not realistic to expect people to repress completely their sexuality, and the practice of sublimation which he commends was probably never as widely adopted as he supposes but was rather little more than a sham. For as he has conceded, "... we are animals, governed by the implacable requirements of the flesh" (Scruton, 1986 p. 233). Secondly, because to have a relationship based on erotic love "...is to achieve something of incomparable value in the process of self-fulfilment" (*Ibid.* p. 337), it cannot, in Scruton's view, be reasonable to require a substantial minority of the population to renounce so enhancing a potential.

Neither the *Sunday Telegraph* article nor the *Dover Beach* essay considers the main reasons why many gay relationships fall far short of the standard attained by the best heterosexual unions, but one of them is intimated in *Sexual Desire*: "The fate of persons is inseparable from the history of the institutions which form and nurture them" (*Ibid.* p. 350). The likelihood that homosexuals will develop relationships of the kind that a consistent Scruton would endorse is greatly diminished in a society which encourages them to disparage their own sexual nature and makes little provision for them. Also, of course, within the last two decades there has arisen an ideology – Gay Liberationism of the left-wing, revolutionary kind – contrived to defend (among other things) the wantonness which Scruton rightly deplores. The correct response, however, is not to set up a false dichotomy between 'ordinary decencies' and 'gay rights' but to distinguish homosexual relationships which should be accepted from those which should not be. Such discrimination is of the same kind as should be applied to heterosexuality: it should focus on the quality of relationships but ignore the sex or sexual orientation of the participants. Yet many of those who set – or claim to set – moral standards treat heterosexual lust and infidelity with a tolerance they refuse to monogamous gay relationships.

In *Sexual Desire*, Scruton argues both cogently and eloquently that moral education should guide us towards a state in which our sexuality is fully integrated within a life of personal affection and responsibility (p. 346). Since he allows that homosexual desire is a natural and spontaneous phenomenon, he should be willing to endorse a programme of moral education designed to serve all children equally well irrespective of their sexual orientation. If Scruton really believes what he published only six years ago he should be foremost among those who are pressing for the positive but discerning treatment of homosexuality by moral educators. If he no longer believes it, he should tell us clearly what has prompted him to revise his views. Perhaps he is unsure as to what he thinks or changes his mind from day to day. He would not be the first philosopher to suffer from a kind of intellectual schizophrenia, but his Jekyll and Hyde pronouncements on this important issue constitute a particularly serious case.

REFERENCES

Baier, Annette: 1985, 'Caring about Caring', in *Postures of the Mind*, Methuen, London. This paper was first presented at a conference in October, 1981.

Dunn, Ian: 1988, 'Scotland Against the Odds', in *Radical Records*, ed. by Bob Cant and Susan Hemmings, Routledge, London.

Ferguson, Jim: 1989, Critical review of J. Martin Stafford's *Homosexuality and Education*, *Cambridge Journal of Education* **19**, 225–230.

Ruse, Michael: 1988, *Homosexuality – a Philosophical Inquiry*, Blackwell, Oxford.

Scruton, Roger: 1986, *Sexual Desire*, Weidenfeld & Nicolson, London; Free Press, New York.

Scruton, Roger: 1989, 'Why Heterosexism Is Not a Vice', *Sunday Telegraph*, 24th September.

Scruton, Roger: 1990, 'Sexual Morality and the Liberal Consensus', in *The Philosopher on Dover Beach*, Carcanet Press, Manchester.

Stafford, J. Martin: 1977, 'On Distinguishing Between Love and Lust', *Journal of Value Inquiry* **XI**, 292–303.

Stafford, J. Martin: 1988a, 'Love and Lust Revisited: Intentionality, Homosexuality and Moral Education', *Journal of Applied Philosophy* **5**, 87–100. Reprinted in *Applied Philosophy: Morals and Metaphysics in Contemporary Debate*, ed. by Brenda Almond and Don Hill, Routledge, 1991.

Stafford, J. Martin: 1988b, *Homosexuality and Education*, J.M. Stafford, Manchester.

Trenchard, Lorraine and Warren, Hugh: 1984, *Something to Tell You*, London Gay Teenage Group.

Roger Scruton

Journal of Philosophy of Education, Vol. 19, No. 1, 1985 137 – 141

J. Martin Stafford

Public Schools, Private Privilege and Common Sense

> ... Historians, and even common sense, may inform us, that, however specious these ideas of *perfect* equality may seem, they are really, at bottom, *impracticable;* and were they not so, would be extremely *pernicious* to human society. Render possessions ever so equal, men's different degrees of art, care, and industry will immediately break that equality. Or if you check these virtues, you reduce society to the most extreme indigence; and instead of preventing want and beggary in a few, render it unavoidable to the whole community. The most rigorous inquisition too is requisite to watch every inequality on its first appearance; and the most severe jurisdiction to punish and redress it. [1] (David Hume)

In recent issues of this journal there have been four contributions discussing the moral status of independent education. Since the matter at stake is part of the most profound and irreconcilable ideological divide imaginable, it is to be expected that participants in the debate take up intransigent positions. I shall try to show, however, that an egalitarian conviction such as that of Mr R. J. Royce [2] can be maintained only when it is accompanied by a wilful and perverse refusal to face the facts. The most recent contributor to the debate, John Colbeck [3], chides his immediate predecessor, Beverley Shaw [4], for not directing his argument against ".... the case as it might be made by a reasonable egalitarian, it [being] all too easy to knock down unreasonable dummies" [5]. I do not know whether it was Colbeck's intention to characterise Royce as an 'unreasonable dummy': it is certainly against Royce that Beverley Shaw's article was primarily directed. Whether Royce is an unreasonable dummy or something rather more sinister, I shall criticise his programme for enforced equality and also some of the assumptions on which it is based—assumptions which Colbeck appears to share, though he does not offer any similarly radical prescriptions.

Early in his article Colbeck intimates an analogy between the law and education: just as all men should be deemed equal before the law (".... all accused ought to receive equal (weight of) consideration by the judge, similarly qualified legal representation and equally severe punishment if guilty" [6]), so, for the egalitarian, all children should be esteemed of equal value and accorded equal treatment in respect of educational provision. Now this analogy is at best a weak one; for whereas the law may be seen as a monolithic dispenser of justice to which we all are—or ought to be—equally subject, it is not the case that all children stand in a similarly identical relationship to a single source of educational provision. Since the early years of a child's life are so crucial and the influence of its domestic circumstances so pervasive, nearly all of the factors most significant in promoting or retarding educational achievement are determined not by the state or its impersonal minions but by the child's own parents.

Colbeck appears to deplore the fact that it is " 'natural' (i.e. a common trait not easily changed) for parents to be more concerned about the education of their own children than about the education of others" [7]. In the face of his disparagingly weak definition, I would maintain that 'natural' has much greater and more far-reaching significance than he wants to allow. Addiction to tobacco is 'a common trait not easily changed', but it is hardly natural. On the other hand, the partiality which parents feel towards their own children is a strong instinct shared by man with all the other higher animals, and arguably one which has played a major rôle in furthering his evolutionary advancement. Any parent who did *not* feel a partiality to his/her own offspring would, in most people's estimation, be culpably deficient. In salutary contrast to the attenuated notion of parental affection which commends itself to Mr Colbeck, there can be found in the same issue of the journal David Bridges's account of the equanimity with which he bore the indignities of nursing his own sick child [8].

In similar vein to Colbeck, Royce's paper implicitly supposes a communal responsibility for the education of children, and common ownership is more definitely implied towards the end of his final paragraph by his use of the phrase 'the community's children' [9]. Now although the community does indeed have a legitimate interest in the well-being of children, and rightly intervenes when parents neglect or abuse their progeny, to speak thus of 'the community's children' as if they were a public asset (or a liability, as the case may be) on a par with footpaths, canals, and national parks is to beg a crucial question. For children belong to, or, in the case of adopted and foster children, are entrusted to, particular people who have a natural or assigned right and duty to superintend their welfare. As was pointed out by Brenda Cohen (whose article predates Royce's by four years), "such a position [as that adopted by Royce] is essentially totalitarian in character, and will not commend itself to those who do not share this overwhelming preference for state control" [10]. The rights of parents are further discussed in David Bridges's paper [8]. The bases of parental duties and of the community's duties in the provision of education are set out by Frederick A. Olafson in his paper, 'Rights and Duties in Education' [11]. These issues have been recently examined also by Peter Hobson [12]. Since all of these three sources present arguments which effectively counter the totalitarian assumptions made by Royce, I do not need to say more on this head.

Colbeck points out that state schools would be better endowed if the wealthy, influential and articulate people who now have recourse to private education had to send their own children thither [13]. Fortunately, this plausible supposition has little appeal as an argument for the abolition of private schools except among the fanatically committed to be found in some colleges and departments of education and at Labour Party conferences. The very same considerations have comparable or even (as I shall later show) greater force in respect of the private and public sector of medical care. But why draw the line at health and education? If people could not buy homes on the open market and had to reside in whatever accommodation was allotted to them by the state or by the local authority, there would probably be far more effectively directed concern to improve the stock of council houses. (This would not, of course, eliminate inequality. As a tour of most council estates would reveal, there are those who maintain their homes to a high standard of comfort, while others allow them to degenerate into stinking slums. Equality could be approached only if the slothful were somehow compelled to keep their homes clean or the more industrious were denied the use of cleaning materials.) One could even extend the scope of the argument to the provision of food, in which regard I would venture to affirm that children are more nearly equal in their capacity to enjoy a wholesome meal than they are in their ability to profit from sound teaching. My question as to where we draw the line was not entirely rhetorical. The demarcation is made partly to accord with the requirements of pragmatism, and partly in submission to the dictates of prevailing fashion. Since no one would choose to take all his meals in communal refectories; since most of the population are already owner-occupiers, and many who are not aspire to be, 'equality of nutritional opportunity' or of 'residential opportunity' could never be incorporated into the manifesto of a political party that entertained any serious hopes of coming to power through the ballot box. In recent years, however, equality of educational opportunity has been widely endorsed, and espoused by extremists in politics and opportunists in education who either fail to appreciate or refuse to acknowledge its impracticability. Just as we expect that the children of the wealthy will, with few exceptions, be better housed, better fed, and better dressed than those of less affluent parentage, we should not be surprised that they have greater access to educational opportunities. Indeed, I find it hard to imagine how it could be otherwise. To say that the freedom of the less well off is limited in that they may not avail themselves of the many advantages which are the prerogative of wealth is, of course, true but trivial. It is no more than an acknowledgement that money is the key to most goods and services and the only reason why most people are willing to work. Royce's contention that the ability of parents to pay is not a relevant criterion [14] in determining the education that their children should receive is pure dogma, born of his own political convictions but unsupported by any arguments.

The National Health Service and state schools are often presented as strictly analogous; but between the public provision of health care on the one hand and of education on the other there is an important and instructive difference which is neither as widely nor as thoroughly appreciated as it ought to be. It explains why the demand for private education has increased; why state schools could *never* be so drastically improved as to render private schools no longer attractive; and why, even if private schools were outlawed, there would remain the most enormous disparities in educational provision and achievement. With few exceptions, people who are ill are desirous of being cured, and parents of sick children are anxious that their offspring be restored to health. On the other hand, it is far from true that all children are keen, or even willing, to be instructed, or that all parents are eager that their children learn. My experience of school teaching is sufficiently varied to enable me to pronounce on this matter with confidence and authority, and my impressions are generally endorsed by the many other teachers with whom I have discussed them. I mention, for instance, how at one parents' evening at a comprehensive school where I taught classes in all three streams most parents of top stream children attended, fewer parents of middle stream children, and very few whose children were in the lowest stream. At an inner city school where I worked as a supply teacher I was informed that attendance at parents' evenings was very poor indeed, and one boy's mother actually told me that she thought education was of little importance. In view of the high correlation between parental interest and pupil achievement and the degree of obdurate indifference to be found among some parents, we must conclude that expenditure on improvements to the health service is far more likely to prove effective in relieving sickness and disease than expenditure on education could ever be in eliminating ignorance. If prodigal spending made for good schools, Inner London would be a veritable Mecca in whose direction all lovers of excellence would prostrate themselves.

The assumption that state education could be greatly improved simply by increased expenditure is either expressed or acquiesced in by all the participants to the debate so far. Even Brenda Cohen mentions in passing the aspirations of pre-war socialists to make ".... massive improvements in state schools, which would make them indistinguishable in quality from famous independent schools" [15]. But it is Royce who states the thesis with a degree of clarity and detail commensurate with the extremity of his own attitude:

> If the annual fees for day pupils at Millfield of £1530 in 1979 are necessary to achieve the higher standards, this would require a total educational expenditure of around £14·5 thousand millions pa as opposed to the £7 thousand millions then spent, to achieve equality for all. [16]

Ominously, he goes on to say:

> It may well be that the United Kingdom cannot afford the cost of providing all with the educational standards given to the few .... The remaining alternative is to lower the standards of the best private schools to that of par with all others, or to close them down if they refuse to comply with this directive .... In so far as particular schools or classes of schools favour or disadvantage pupils in general then a case can be made in the name of equality against such schools. [17]

This gives us an unequivocal indication of the extent to which Royce would go in his pursuit of equality. One can envisage that, as in the hypothetical situation described by Hume in the passage which serves as a motto to this paper, inquisitorial commissions might make regular inspections and inflict penalties on those schools (or perhaps even those pupils) which threatened to rise above mediocrity. One school might be ordered to demolish its science laboratory; another to plough up half its sports field. I suspect, however, that if *per accidens*—or even *per invidiam*—a good school did lose some such facilities, the effect on the quality of the education it offered would be fairly marginal. Conversely, no matter what resources were devoted to the improvement of state schools, their ethos—especially since they have become almost exclusively comprehensive—would always be vitiated by the presence of pupils who are at best indifferent and at worst hostile to their aims; who attend school not because either they or their parents have any relish for learning but because the law coerces them to do so. Even when their numbers in a school are relatively small, their influence and the demands they make on staff are disproportionately great. Here private schools are, by their very nature, on a much surer footing: fee-paying parents will have made a very conscious and deliberate choice of a school and must demonstrate their commitment to education by a willingness to part with quite substantial sums of money; in those few cases where a pupil does prove to be incorrigibly recalcitrant, it is easy to expel him. Accordingly, when people elect to send their children to private schools it is not so much that they are paying for better buildings and equipment, or even better qualified and (dare I add?) non-striking teachers, as that they are buying their way into a community which is unanimous in the high value it accords to education. This community of shared values is probably far more important than an imposing edifice or a lush green field in fostering the success of such schools, and it is something which few state schools could now hope to offer. When teachers in the public sector believe firmly in the value of their work, they must often be disheartened by the poor response which their best endeavours meet with. That many send their own children to independent schools is neither surprising nor particularly reprehensible. Expediency may require them to pay lip service to the false god of educational equality, but it does not require them to sacrifice their own children on his altar.

REFERENCES

[1] HUME, DAVID (1975) *Enquiries....*, 3rd edn revised by P.H. Nidditch, p. 194 (Oxford, OUP).

[2] ROYCE, R.J. (1982) Public schools: private privilege—a reply to Brenda Cohen, *Journal Of Philosophy of Education*, 16, pp. 105–113.

[3] COLBECK, JOHN (1984) Private schools in the perspective of a reasonable egalitarian, *Journal of Philosophy of Education*, 18, pp. 129–132.

[4] SHAW, BEVERLEY (1983) Procrustes and private schooling, *Journal of Philosophy of Education*, 17, pp. 131–135.

[5] COLBECK, p. 129, punctuation slightly amended to accord with the syntax of my own sentence.

[6] COLBECK, p. 130.

[7] COLBECK, p. 132.

[8] BRIDGES. DAVID (1984) Non-paternalistic arguments in support of parents' rights, *Journal of Philosophy of Education*, 18, p. 60.

[9] ROYCE, p. 112.

[10] COHEN, BRENDA (1978) Equality, freedom, and independent schools, *Journal of Philosophy of Education*, 12, 121–128, p. 122.

[11] OLAFSON, FREDERICK A. (1973) Rights and duties in education, in: DOYLE, JAMES F. (Ed.) *Educational Judgments* (Henley, Routledge & Kegan Paul).

[12] HOBSON, PETER (1984) Some reflections on parents' rights in the upbringing of their children, *Journal of Philosophy of Education*, 18, pp. 63–74.

[13] COLBECK, p. 132.

[14] ROYCE, p. 107.

[15] COHEN, p. 123.

[16] ROYCE, p. 106.

[17] ROYCE, pp. 106–107.

Bulletin of The British Society for Eighteenth Century Studies No. 38, 1995

Was Hume's *Natural History of Religion* inspired by Mandeville's *Fable of the Bees* Part II ?

I have recently noticed striking similarities between passages in *The Fable of the Bees* Part II and *The Natural History of Religion*. So far as I am aware, these have - surprisingly - not been noted previously.[1] For example, Mandeville is completely ignored by J.C.A. Gaskin, and while F.B. Kaye's long and erudite

[1] I am grateful to Dr Gerardo Lopez Sastre, whose studies in Hume's philosophy of religion are more extensive than my own, for confirming that my suspicion is correct.

introduction to his edition of *The Fable of the Bees* includes a section on Mandeville's influence, it does not allude to theological topics.[2] In the first paragraph of the introduction to his edition of *The Natural History of Religion,* H.E. Root states that the philosophy of religion had little history before Hume. He proceeds, however, to highlight the centrality of 'hope and fear, unknown causes, [and] imagination' to Hume's account of the origin of religious belief - a doctrine which, according to Peter Jones, Hume had adopted from Cicero and which was also shared by French authors such as Fontenelle and Bayle.[3]

I do not discount the possibility that both Hume and Mandeville were inspired by earlier sources. Indeed, it is certain that Mandeville was profoundly indebted to the writings of Pierre Bayle and might even have known him personally.[4] My sole aim in this article is to suggest that in writing the first three chapters of *The Natural History of Religion* Hume was directly influenced by what Mandeville had published three decades earlier. My claim is based primarily on strong thematic parallels and also on similarity of language. That Hume knew Mandeville's works and extended to them a qualified admiration is beyond dispute. He alludes to the *Fable* in the essay 'Of Refinement in the Arts' (originally titled 'Of Luxury') but mentions Mandeville by name only twice in all his published writings, namely in the Introduction to the *Treatise of Human Nature* and in the *Abstract,* where the list of authors from the *Treatise* is simply repeated.[5] He is not mentioned in any of Hume's surviving letters.

However, it is highly probable that Hume was familiar with both parts of Mandeville's best known work. It was *The Fable of the Bees* [Part I] which had provoked his intellectual forebear Francis Hutcheson to write his first book, *An Inquiry into the Original of our Ideas of Beauty and Virtue* (1725). Mandeville was, moreover, at the height of his notoriety when Hume was a young man. By

---

2 J.C.A. Gaskin, *Hume's Philosophy of Religion* (Basingstoke: Macmillan Press, 1978, 2nd ed.1988); Bernard Mandeville, *The Fable of the Bees,* ed. F.B. Kaye, 2 vols (Oxford: Clarendon Press, 1924).
3 David Hume, *The Natural History of Religion,* ed. H.E. Root (London: A & C Black, 1956), 12; Peter Jones, *Hume's Sentiments - Their Ciceronian and French Context* (Edinburgh: Edinburgh University Press, 1982), 77-8.
4 According to Kaye, Bayle was by far the most important of Mandeville's intellectual precursors: see Mandeville ed. Kaye, Vol.I pp. xlii-xliii and ciii-cv.
5 David Hume, *A Treatise of Human Nature,* ed. L.A. Selby-Bigge and revised by P.H. Nidditch (Oxford: Clarendon Press, 1978), xvii, 646.

1735, Part II of the *Fable* (first published in 1729) was in its fourth edition. A work by an author he admired on a subject so germane to his interests would, in all probability, have been among those books that the young Hume was 'secretly devouring'.[6] Also, a more specific indication that Hume already knew Part II of *The Fable of the Bees* by the time he wrote the *Treatise* is afforded by the fact that the Fifth Dialogue opens with a discussion about the singularly distinctive taste of pineapple - one of the examples used by Hume in the first section of the *Treatise* to prove the precedence of impressions to ideas.[7]

The fifth dialogue subsequently includes a digression in which the interlocutors discuss the origin of religious belief. The arguments advanced by Cleomenes are repeated in the very same order in Chapters 2 and 3 of *The Natural History of Religion*. It is, I submit, not improbable that in writing these chapters Hume adapted and elaborated on Mandeville's earlier book. The plausibility of this suggestion is enhanced by the difference in style and content between these first three chapters of *The Natural History of Religion,* which contain only three allusions to other writers and the ensuing ones, in which citations proliferate. Although Hume makes no reference to his indebtedness to Mandeville, no negative conclusions should be drawn from this: first, because failure to give sources was more common in the eighteenth century than it is today; and secondly because Mandeville's considerable infamy might well have inhibited Hume from acknowledging his indebtedness in an enterprise which in any event was sure to prove deeply controversial.

Both authors make the following claims: (i) religion has its origin in fear of the unknown causes of the many calamities which can befall primitive men; (ii) they attribute intelligence and will to inanimate objects around them; (iii) it is harmful rather than beneficent events which excite their interest. Religion therefore is rooted in fear, not gratitude. I reproduce below parallel texts by Mandeville and Hume. Words and phrases given in bold are deployed by both writers either *verbatim,* as cognates, or as synonyms or near synonyms. In the first pair of texts there are a dozen such instances of similarity in passages which contain only about 250 words. All page numbers refer to the editions by F.B.Kaye and H.E. Root already cited.

---

6 David Hume, 'My Own Life' (1776), para.3.

7 Cf. *The Fable of the Bees* II, p.94 and the *Treatise* p.5.

Mandeville

Fear is the Passion, that **first** gives [**Savages**] an Opportunity of entertaining some glimmering Notions of an **invisible Power**...(*FB* II.207). Every Mischief and every Disaster that happens to [them], of which the Cause is not very plain and obvious; excessive Heat and Cold; Wet and Drought, that are offensive; Thunder and Lightning, even when they do no visible Hurt; Noises in the dark, Obscurity itself, and every thing that is frightful and unknown, are all administring and contributing to the Establishment of this Fear. The wildest Man, that can be conceiv'd, by the time that he came to Maturity, would be wise enough to know, that **Fruits and other Eatables** are not to be had, either always, or every where: This would naturally put him upon hoarding, when he had good Store: His Provision might be **spoil'd by the Rain**; he would see that Trees were blasted, and yielded not always the same **Plenty**: He might not always be in **Health**, or his young ones might grow **sick**, and **die**, without any Wounds or external Force to be seen. Some of these Accidents might at first escape his Attention, or only **alarm** his weak Understanding, without occasioning much Reflection for some Time; but as they came often, he would certainly begin to suspect some **invisible Cause**; and, as his Experience encreased, be confirm'd in his Suspicion. It is likewise highly probable, that a **Variety of different Sufferings**, would make him apprehend several such **Causes**; and at last induce him to believe, that there was a great Number of them, which he had to fear (208-9)

Hume

...the **first** ideas of religion arose not from a contemplation of the works of nature, but from a concern with a regard to the events of life, and from the incessant hopes and **fears,** which actuate the human mind...

Storms and tempests ruin what is nourished by the sun. The sun destroys what is fostered by the moisture of dews and rains (*NHR* 27).

No passions...can be supposed to work upon such **barbarians**, but the ordinary affections of human life; the anxious concern for happiness, the dread of future misery, the terror of death, the thirst of revenge, the appetite for **food and other necessaries**. Agitated by hopes and fears of this nature, especially the latter, men scrutinize, with a trembling curiosity, the course of future causes, and examine the **various and contrary events** of human life...We hang in perpetual suspense between **life and death**, **health and sickness, plenty** and want; which are distributed amongst the human species by secret and **unknown causes**, whose operation is oft unexpected, and always, unaccountable. These ***unknown causes***, then, become the constant object of our hope and fear; and while the passions are kept in perpetual **alarm** by an anxious expectation of the events, the imagination is equally employed in forming ideas of those **powers**, on which we have so entire a dependance (28-9).

Mandeville

All young Children seem to imagine, that every thing thinks and feels in the same Manner as they do themselves: And, that they generally have this wrong Opinion of Things inanimate, is evident, from a common Practice among them; whenever they labour under any Misfortune, which their own Wildness and want of Care have drawn upon them. In all such Cases, you see them angry at and strike, a Table, a Chair, the Floor, or any thing else, that can seem to have been accessory to their **hurting** themselves, or the Production of any other Blunder, they have committed... It is not to be imagin'd that this natural Folly should be so easily cured in a Child, that is destitute of all Instruction and Commerce with his own Species, as it is in those that are brought up in Society, and hourly improved by conversing with others, that are wiser than themselves; and I am persuaded, that a wild Man would never get entirely rid of it, whilst he lived... Whence came the *Dryades* and ***Hamadryades*** ? how came it ever to be thought impious, to cut down, or even to wound, large venerable Oaks, or other stately **Trees**; and what Root did the **Divinity** spring from, which the **Vulgar**, amongst the ancient Heathens, apprehended to be in **Rivers** and Fountains ? (209-10).

Hume

There is an universal tendency among mankind to conceive all beings like themselves, and to transfer to every object, those qualities, with which they are familiarly acquainted, and of which they are intimately conscious. We find human faces in the moon, armies in the clouds; and by a natural propensity, if not corrected by experience and reflection, ascribe malice or good will to every thing, that **hurts** or pleases us. Hence the frequency and beauty of the *prosopopoeia* in poetry; where **trees**, mountains and streams are personified, and the inanimate parts of nature acquire sentiment and passion. And though these poetical figures and expressions gain not on the belief, they may serve, at least, to prove a certain tendency in the imagination, without which they could neither be beautiful nor natural. Nor is a **river-god** or **hamadryad** always taken for a mere poetical or imaginary personage; but may sometimes enter the real creed of the ignorant **vulgar**; while each grove or field is represented as possessed of a particular ***genius* or invisible power**, which inhabits and protects it (29).

Mandeville

Man takes every thing to be his own, which he has from Nature: Sowing and Reaping, he thinks, deserve a Crop, and whatever he has the least Hand in, is always reckon'd to be his. Every Art, and every Invention, as soon as we know them, are our Right and Property; and whatever we perform by the Assistance of them, is, by the Courtesy of the Species to itself, deem'd to be our own...In brewing, baking, cooking, and almost every thing we have a Hand in, Nature is the Drudge, that makes all the Alterations, and does the principal Work; yet all, forsooth, is our own. From all which it is manifest; that Man, who is naturally for making every thing centre in himself, must, in his wild State, have a great Tendency, and be very prone to look upon **every thing, he enjoys, as his due**; and every thing he meddles with, as his own Performance...

In all the Labours of Self-Preservation, Man is intent on avoiding what is hurtful to him; but in the Enjoyment of what is pleasant, his Thoughts are relax'd, and he is void of Care: he can swallow a thousand Delights, one after another, without asking Questions; but **the least Evil makes him inquisitive, whence it came**, in order to shun it. It is very material, therefore, to know the Cause of Evil; but to know that of Good, which is always welcome, is of little Use (211-2).

Hume

Any of the human affections may lead us into the notion of invisible, intelligent power; hope as well as fear, gratitude as well as affliction: but if we examine our own hearts, or observe what passes around us, we shall find, that men are much oftener thrown on their knees by the melancholy than by the agreeable passions. **Prosperity is easily received as our due**, and few questions are asked concerning its cause or author. It begets cheerfulness and activity and alacrity and a lively enjoyment of every social and sensual pleasure: And during this state of mind, men have little leisure or inclination to think of the unknown invisible regions. On the other hand, **every disastrous accident alarms us, and sets us on enquiries concerning the principles whence it arose** (31).

Index

FOGGY BOTTOM

A Garden to Share

ADRIAN BLOOM

TEXT AND PHOTOGRAPHS BY ADRIAN BLOOM

Matt, Adrian, Richard, Rosemary and Jason on the bridge in Foggy Bottom, photographed by Robert Bloom in summer, 1986.

Foggy Bottom is the garden of my lifetime. Whilst my dedication in this book goes to all who made it possible, it is primarily given as a thanks and tribute to those who are closest, my late wife Rosemary and our three sons Jason, Matt and Richard. The Foggy Bottom Garden still came second to the family, all grew older and so did the appreciation and understanding of each other.

CONTENTS

Photograph by Richard Bloom

Foreword

Trite, but true, 'gardening is (or can be) for everyone'. With a garden small or large, a terrace, patio or balcony, everyone can grow plants. But if you take fifty or more years creating (with valuable helpers) your own garden, which eventually extends to six acres, where does it end? Human life is finite, even if the final date is unknown. Even a known unknown! The garden lives on, but seldom in the same way.

Most gardeners, perhaps like artists, like (or need) to share. You can sell your art, and maybe have sold ninety percent of your creation before you pass on. The painting or sculpture, once finished, never changes. That's mostly where art and gardens differ, but that's another book!

Perhaps there is another way.

The Concept of Sharing a Garden

My garden is called Foggy Bottom, situated in a meadow on the edge of the small village of Bressingham in Norfolk, England. The story of how it came to be is the second half of this book.

You, as a special guest, in going through this book, are being given a private tour by me, Head Gardener and owner of Foggy Bottom.

If you come as an ordinary visitor, The Bressingham Gardens are open from 10.30am to 5pm and after your journey to get here you can see what there is to see on one day. But as my privileged visitor, you see the six-acre garden not just on one day, but magically at several times of the year in a single visit. You are being made aware, through images and copy, as to what makes this garden work. The best time to really take in the atmosphere of the garden for much of the year is when the gardens are not open, in the early morning and early evening.

This book is your guide, the start if you want, of a journey to learn, think, see and absorb. You can get to know the design, layout, and vistas. You can learn about and understand more about many plants. Enjoy the early morning mists, the autumn colour and the winter light. In close up, see what the photographer sees, imagine yourself behind the lens spotting the spider's web, the frosted foliage, the veins of leaves. You are in the garden, both alone and in company. You might even spot some of the wildlife!

Enjoy this book, its pictures and words. Enjoy the gardens through the seasons and return for enjoyment and inspiration.

Social media wasn't thought of when I started the garden. Now it means from this first book you can follow Foggy Bottom and other gardens and plants at Bressingham.

'The Devil is in the Detail' was a title initially thought of for this book and it is a theme we will come back to time and again. Another trite and sometimes used phrase, 'look and you will discover, seek and you will find' is a good note to finish on.

Enjoy the journey!

Adrian Bloom

Introduction

When Rosemary and I were married in Trumpington church, near Cambridge in October 1966, our house at Bressingham wasn't even completed. Having helped local builders in small ways at weekends since March that year, we were quite happy to move in. Returning from a few days' honeymoon in a very wet Lake District in North West England, we managed for three months with only one bedroom and a kitchen finished. There was no garden. The home was built in the north-east corner of a seven-acre meadow of which below was a wood, and a herd of cattle enjoyed the verdant grass for most of the year.

Adrian and Rosemary Bloom, 1966.

The house (we didn't like the term bungalow) was initially set within one acre, and a barbed wire fence was put up to deter cattle from invading what was to become our family area and garden. During my travels in the United States in 1959 and 1960, I had come across a place called 'Foggy Bottom', and we thought this a great name to give our house and garden.

Such was the beginning of the development of the eventual six-acre Foggy Bottom Garden, which has played such a central role in my own and my family's life, and far beyond. The full story will be revealed in this book, but I feel it is right to start with the Foggy Bottom of today: what it is, and what it means. In later sections of the book, I will reveal its development, decade by decade, since 1966 and the environment in which the garden grew.

Building the house at Foggy Bottom, 1966.

Big Garden, Small Garden, Terrace, Balcony or Patio

This book is about scale, the selections made and the decisions faced. It is about growth; not only of the plants in the garden, but knowledge inevitably learnt over fifty years. Creating such a garden at Foggy Bottom throughout most of my adult life has been a unique and privileged experience.

I had no formal training in horticulture or design so I have learnt and continue to learn through observation, a passion for plants, and a will to create. In many ways I had differences with my father Alan Bloom, however, we both shared a similar nature in wanting to do the best we could in our field. In the case of Foggy Bottom, perhaps field is an apt word to use!

Alan, with helpers, had designed, dug, and planted the six-acre Dell Garden at Bressingham, innovative for its time in creating a new design idea for growing perennials – the 'island beds'. This simple idea was to plant perennials in groups, the shorter plants around the outside with taller in the middle. The staged levels helped to support the taller varieties, and a choice was made of different perennials to flower from spring until autumn. Starting in front of our home, Bressingham Hall, in 1953 he created 'islands' cut into the lawn and had these prepared for planting perennials. I was thirteen years old at that time and more interested in football, but fitting this in as well as managing the nursery, Alan's gradual development proved a success.

In 1957 when he published his first book on plants, *Hardy Perennials*, he was ready to break out into the surrounding meadow. By 1962 with the help of his gardeners, he had created forty-eight island beds within six acres and had over 4,500 species, cultivars and varieties in his collection. In the autumn of 1958 after leaving school, I had gained a little experience and helped in the development of some of the planting.

Travels Abroad

Briefly, since it is covered elsewhere in more detail, in 1958, aged eighteen, I wasn't sure that gardening or our nursery business was for me, so I took out an emigration visa to the United States and left in February 1959. Twenty-two months later, after a period of selling encyclopedias in San Francisco (but not enough to make my fortune!), I returned to give horticulture a try; first in Denmark, then in Switzerland. Planning to work a year in a nursery in Germany and then France, I received a letter from my father whilst in Switzerland asking if I would return to join our family business, Blooms Nurseries Ltd. This was in the summer of 1962, when my elder brother Rob also came back from gaining experience in his chosen career of farming.

This was the beginning and the background to my involvement with the nursery business through nearly sixty years, working with my father and increasingly, my brother. It was inevitable that my brother's role would gradually move towards the burgeoning nursery side and away from the farm as the nursery grew rapidly to meet increasing demand from emerging garden centres and home gardeners. It was an exciting time, but seldom plain sailing.

Being a Part of History

More history and recollection later, but let's jump forward fifty years to look at Foggy Bottom today. As the plants in Foggy Bottom have developed and grown, dominatingly in some cases – more subtly in others, so have changes in the design, combinations, vistas, and close-ups. Light and shade have also become a greater factor. Perhaps now that I have more time available to observe the seasons in the garden, my awareness has also increased.

Viewing plants and combinations with and without a camera has added to my continued efforts to create some striking and memorable plantings for me and for visitors. Memorable in the way of the relative transience of a garden and its plants. They seldom look the same from one year to the next; some grow fast, some flower better one year than the next, some struggle and perhaps a few die. Always changing.

Keeping a Record

This book is a record, largely in photographs, plus commentary, connections, recommendations, and reviews. Overall, I must have taken some 50,000 images of Foggy Bottom and its plants. Nearly every time I am photographing in the garden, going back years, I can but only smile and be reminded of Rosemary's often heard words, "You've taken photos of that view hundreds of times!". Digital cameras have a lot to answer for, in that we are able to take many more photos without changing a film. How wonderful to be able to record the wonders of nature – even if it is mostly man-made!

I want and hope you will feel the Foggy Bottom effect after turning the first pages of the book, and even if you don't, I hope you feel as though you have been here, to absorb the plants, the atmosphere, and the seasons. You may take inspiration from the Foggy Bottom Garden, perhaps learning about plants and ideas might lead you to experiment in your own garden.

There's little doubt, judging by the numbers of reports and surveys appearing regularly in the media, that gardening and plants are good for you. Think of the physical activity, the opportunity to create, the therapeutic or calming effect that plants or a garden can give, let alone the whole aesthetic, the beauty of flowers and plants, the closeness of nature and attraction to wildlife, what's not to embrace and get involved? There is the other many-sided argument largely about reality, time and opportunity – but we needn't go there!

I have always taken photographs; black and white, colour transparencies, and now digital, but I still don't really understand or make use of the camera's technical ability. I am lucky to have an increasingly well-known professional photographer, my youngest son Richard, to help me out on occasion. I have the six-acre Foggy Bottom Garden surrounding our house and other gardens, particularly Adrian's Wood, nearby, so I am ready to take advantage at almost any time of day and in any weather to take my camera out. Firstly to record, but increasingly to try to capture the plants, the mood and the atmosphere of the garden, the details of plants and flowers, and the changing seasons.

The Foggy Bottom Garden Today

Many visitors are hardly aware of the Foggy Bottom house, now nestled behind mature trees and plants, the area including (to younger visitors' chagrin!) a tree house and my private garden. The area north of the Long Bed is also private and for me and our gardeners only.

The beds and areas are numbered to help myself and the gardeners communicate. In fact, Martin and Anja, who then maintained Foggy Bottom, were responsible for putting forward their commonly used names which I've included, such as 'Rhus Corner' and 'Book Bed' – the explanation of the latter comes later!

Designer, Denise Keating, who I commissioned to make a map, had a difficult task in creating one that encompassed the seventeen acres of The Bressingham Gardens, of which Foggy Bottom is one. Her finished artwork has been a considerable help to us and a useful guide to visitors.

The design of Foggy Bottom was always based on the principle of having beds – yes, island beds in some cases – cut out of an existing meadow with a perimeter bed planted for shelter and to encompass the six acres, adjoining the existing Gap Meadow to the east. The principle within the garden was to create long vistas from almost any point, and in the early days, plan new vistas and planting schemes to surprise as each corner appeared. The main north-to-south views were clearly observed from our house, and the broad pathways led to the distant wood. Some years later, when we opened Foggy Bottom more regularly, we were glad our 'garden within a garden' blocked off the view of our private garden and the house from visitors.

Gap Meadow
Entrance
Adrian's Wood
1
2
3
4
4
4
4
5
7
8
10
11
13
16
20
22
23
24
25

Foggy Bottom Map

KEY

1. Entrance Bed
2. Crossways Corner
3. Front of House Bed
4. Mini-Pinetum
5. All Seasons Bed
6. Sad Bed
7. Rhus Corner
8. Pond
9. Rosemary's Wood
10. Book Bed
11. Long Bed
12. Acer Glade
13. TV Bed
14. Vertical Bed
15. Magnolia Jane Bed
16. Snake Bed
17. Foggy Bottom Henge
18. Summer House
19. Rosemary's Spire
20. Redwoods
21. Japanese-style Garden *(under construction)*

PRIVATE

22. House
23. Tree House
24. Kitchen Bed
25. Back of House Bed

This map depicts an illustrator's view of Foggy Bottom as it was in 2020. Constant updates mean that particular areas change and develop. Please note that we have only highlighted particular beds and that many areas of the Garden will evolve year to year.

Getting to Know Foggy Bottom

Though not large by some standards, occasionally visitors will get lost and ask, "How do I get out?". The purpose of these introductory pages is to reveal what lays behind the garden and I would like you to feel you are paying a visit. With the map and photographs, I will try to give you some orientation as to where you are and what you are looking at in the garden. We will look at certain beds and plantings, often in different seasons and from different vantage points, as though you are alongside and receiving a guided tour of Foggy Bottom, from myself, Adrian Bloom, fifty years from when I began planting.

It is an early autumn day and the Gap Meadow on your left is swathed in fog, silhouettes of still, dark-leaved, young oak trees visible.

The entrance to Foggy Bottom, seemingly titled to represent the fog which dramatically drifts into this lower valley several times a year to create an 'otherworld' feeling.

It is 1973…

Imagine you are back in time, back to the future even. You have walked into a meadowland in the lower part of the Waveney Valley, below the Norman church of St John in the small village of Bressingham in Norfolk, England. The large eighteen-acre Gap Meadow to your left, a six-acre meadow to your right, fenced to keep the cattle that were here in the summer. Stopping at a gate, you can see across the smaller, very flat fen meadow to the western perimeter, one or two houses along Church Lane in the far distance. The meadow grass is still very green except for some curious markings. All very rural.

↓

Fifty years later

After passing the entrance sign, you can see a maturing fifty-year garden vista that is now the Foggy Bottom Garden in summer. We are looking towards the centre of Crossways – itself perhaps the central point of the garden and from where the next four photographs are taken.

'Welcome to the Enchanted Garden'.

From Crossways Corner Looking East

From Crossways Corner Looking North

From Crossways Corner Looking South

From Crossways Corner Looking East

So here you are on a rather dull misty day in autumn, looking back at the main entrance to the garden. To the right of the gateway stands a light-yellow foliaged bush *Cornus sanguinea* 'Midwinter Fire'. Leaves have dropped on some trees (the maple to the top left), whilst others are still purple (*Cotinus coggygria* 'Royal Purple', left), grey (the tall specimen of *Sorbus thibetica* 'John Mitchell', right), and shades of green. In the next two or three weeks, they will fall, presaging winter. The highlight, close right, is the unmistakeable large white and brown pompom heads of *Hydrangea arborescens* 'Annabelle', arguably one of the most remarkable and rewarding plants in Foggy Bottom.

From Crossways Corner Looking North

The house used to be in view, but now the focal points are the three blue spruce, *Picea pungens* 'Koster', dominating the distant skyline. Without a reasonably broad pathway, this might have been a conifer-edged woodland. On the right, above a late flowering *Aster* 'Cotswold Gem', is an incense cedar, *Calocedrus decurrens* 'Berrima Gold', and beyond on the same side, determined to outgrow its name is *Picea omorika* 'Nana' ('Nana' meaning dwarf, of course!). Grasses, mostly *Molinias*, line either side, and on the left, the variegated foliage of *Cornus sericea* 'White Gold' contrasts with the massive noble fir behind, *Abies procera* 'Glauca'. Out of view, left of the fluffy white plumes of pampas grass, *Cortaderia selloana* 'Pumila', is a seat which offers a garden-long view down to the summer house, built by my son Matt.

From Crossways Corner Looking South

No sun today, but plenty to see. In the far background are trees planted near and behind the unseen pond, blending into the 'natural' woodland behind. The grass splits into two pathways either side of the All Seasons Bed (which used to be called the Conifer Bed). The gold foliage of *Pinus contorta* 'Frisian Gold' and deciduous yellow-leaved shrubs *Cornus* and *Physocarpus* are highlights, and in the centre foreground stands the tall, striking gold-leaved dawn cypress, the deciduous conifer *Metasequoia glyptostroboides* 'Gold Rush'. Our first planting on Crossways Corner will be on the left, where *H. a.* 'Annabelle' is the most dramatic plant, and looking to the right, behind the bench, are two or three selections of pampas grass, adding an unmistakeable autumn display. And what a difference a bright autumn day will make, sunlight and early morning frost perhaps.

From Crossways Corner Looking West

It may not yet be obvious, but as autumn progresses, evergreens and conifers will soon demand attention with their multiple forms, shapes, sizes and colours. As leaves turn and fall on the *Catalpa bignonioides* 'Aurea', right centre, and *Betula nigra*, the black birch behind, the conifers will show in relief almost from any angle, providing much of the winter structure to the garden. I say much, because the many, now substantial trees play an important role; white bark from several silver birches, striped or coloured bark from many maples, and a strong twiggy framework from beeches and oaks. Three very different conifers show off in the middle distance, from left, a small group of Italian cypress, *Cupressus sempervirens* 'Green Pencil', are going for the sky. It seems as though the weeping giant redwood, *Sequoiadendron giganteum* 'Pendulum', in the front, is in two minds whether to go up or down – or in two directions! The large specimen blue spruce, *Picea pungens* 'Erich Frahm', makes a solid backdrop… and what I know but you can't see is that behind is one of our latest projects, a Japanese-inspired garden.

From Crossways Corner Looking West

Crossways Observations for the Gardener

If you had arrived for your tour of Foggy Bottom any day of the year and at any time of day, you would observe the same plant groupings, the same plants and the same vistas, but almost certainly in very different lights.

On this day, the sunlight will dramatically affect light levels and contrasting shade on all subjects as the sun rises in the east, reaches its midday peak, and sinks out of sight in the west. Few, if any, would have the time or inclination to watch a day's effect of light even in their own garden. Perhaps few gardeners would factor in their planting and design the important and dramatic effect light can add. Yet, I believe it is an important consideration and hope to demonstrate that in this book.

In our guided tour we'll start with my Crossways Corner and span the seasons and time of day from various vantage points…

This is a part of my garden, but please try to imagine it could be part of yours.

PART ONE

A GARDEN TOUR

01
01

Crossways Corner

This corner we call Crossways is like a promontory jutting into a sea of green grass, though still attached to the large island bed on one side. Dramatic as the planting was intended, it was also planned to keep well below head height of even a very short person, so not only could it be overseen from a distance, but viewed as a foreground display, allowing views across to other vistas.

Sometimes you are glad you got up early in the morning! The early mist was soon brushed aside by the late August sun, but there was just enough to show a hazy sunlit background. Much of the *Hydrangea arborescens* 'Annabelle' is still in shade, though notice to the left how the sun has washed out the detail on the inflorescences. *Rudbeckia* and *Agapanthus* are now adding their contrasting flowers and colours. Centre right, in front of a purple-leaved *Cotinus* is *Hydrangea paniculata* 'Limelight', a woodier, taller shrub than *H. arborescens*. Although the mop-headed 'Annabelle' has some heads down, primarily because of the weight of the overnight dew, most will right themselves by midday.

In early days across the flat meadow landscape that was Foggy Bottom, I wanted to create structure. This meant planting trees, conifers and shrubs so that when these were established, you would need to walk to the end of the bed before you could see another vista. The aim was to create a surprise around every corner!

Without thinning out as plants grew into each other, the structure would be very congested. As the height of some trees reached well beyond 10 m (33 ft), a great many large specimens have had to be removed. This is the most difficult decision gardeners have to make; it can be like parting with old friends.

White is one, if not the, strongest visible 'colour' to use as focal points in the garden, so the placing of a bold planting in Crossways Corner was likely to add a special ingredient to a much wider area. This view, again on a summer's morning, was taken with the Sad Bed on the left, the All Seasons Bed on the right, and some magnificent conifers in the distance. The *Hydrangea* 'promontory' gives the impression it is in the same bed as the planting rising above it, purple-leaved *Cotinus coggygria* 'Royal Purple' and *Calocedrus decurrens* 'Berrima Gold' behind. From this point, you wouldn't be aware that there is a broad grass path between.

On the left is the weeping blue Atlas cedar, *Cedrus atlantica* 'Glauca Pendula', following through to the sunlit golden yew, *Taxus baccata* 'Aurea Pendula'. Centre is the magnificent noble fir, *Abies procera* 'Glauca', and way beyond is the deodar cedar, *Cedrus deodara*. At the lower level, the deep blue *Agapanthus* 'Isis' competes with *Eryngium bourgatii* and above, on slender stems, is the short-lived but useful perennial *Verbena bonariensis*. Beyond, scarlet-flowered *Crocosmia* are surrounded by grassy leaves of the later-flowering pampas grass *Cortaderia selloana*. And for the eagle-eyed gardeners, below the noble fir is *Hemerocallis* 'Flasher' and *Hydrangea arborescens* 'Strong Annabelle'. Lastly, to the right of the *Hydrangea arborescens 'Annabelle'* and beneath the *Phlox paniculata* 'Blue Paradise', the planting of *Hakonechloa* almost creates an island of 'Annabelle'!

← A focal point from at least four pathways, *Hydrangea arborescens* 'Annabelle' also dramatically frames the foreground, as you look toward other views and plants. It is about a hundred yards to the summer house near the pond and Rosemary's Wood. The pathway to the left is hardly visible, but you can see the mostly evergreen conifers in the All Seasons Bed which vary in shape, form and colour. The golden *Rudbeckia fulgida* var. *sullivantii* 'Goldsturm' is holding its own, but the *Geranium* 'Rozanne' in the foreground is getting swamped by the robust *Hydrangea*. I make a note that I either must curb the slowly spreading *Hydrangea* or move the *Geranium*. This area has a rich loam soil which holds moisture, the sort of conditions that 'Annabelle' likes.

Foliage and flower paint a colourful yet reasonably balanced picture. 'Wow' plants; *Hydrangea arborescens* 'Annabelle' and crimson *Crocosmia* in the distance, create repetition through three different cultivars. In the foreground is a short wiry-stemmed purple-leaved aster called *Symphyotrichum lateriflorum* 'Prince'. Yet to flower, its dark foliage, compact growth and fine branching contrasts strongly with *H. a.* 'Annabelle' and the grassy foliage of *Hakonechloa macra* 'Albovariegata'. Almost hidden amongst the variegated *Hakonechloa* are a few deep-green mounds of *Pinus heldreichii* 'Smidtii', which are about fifteen years old. This view is looking down towards the summer house.

Principles and Practice to Create a Wow Factor

Take your choice, but thirty, forty or even fifty years is a very long time, and few could or would be able to plan on that timescale. To help illustrate what I was faced with and what I planned for this important central pathway in the garden, we need to go back eight years from the point of writing this, to January 2015. Over the years, the trees and conifers in this four-cornered crossways had grown too large, and too close to each other. Conifers become dead on the side they have shade and competition. Looking south to north at the crossways, I could see some would have to be removed to protect others and keep vistas open. I may have planted them myself some years ago, but I aim to take the longer view and put the garden first above individual plants. Culling is therefore a necessary part of the process if the garden is destined not to become an uncontrolled mess. I consider the many, many trees left in Foggy Bottom to be an important benefit to the environment!

So, the blue Atlas cedar, *Cedrus atlantica* 'Glauca', the tallest tree on the left, would have to come down, together with a blue spruce, *Picea pungens* 'Thomsen'. On the other side, behind the flattish-topped golden Scots pine, *Pinus sylvestris* 'Aurea', the golden beech, *Fagus sylvatica* 'Dawyck Gold'. I was reluctant to dispense with this distinctive tree, which had thrived, but it was too close to others. Eventually the roots would inhibit other plants nearby to grow freely. We often have tree surgeons in to cut down trees, they climb and drop branches in enclosed areas one by one. But in this case, the trees could be felled onto the lawn, limiting damage so that Kenny Roberts – who worked on our farm and woodland – was able and willing to do the deed.

It's sad to see a tree fall. Though in truth, the cedar and the blue spruce had grown into each other, if either was left it would have been a one-sided specimen. It is a lot of work to clear it up – which is one reason why it is a winter job.

From another angle, Kenny is clearing away the last of the beech. The enormous stumps were dragged to the back of the beds with some soil attached and would soon offer some attraction to wildlife whilst they gradually decayed.

A much more open view has been created and the promontory-like planting area, with the surround of grass, can be seen. Some *Hydrangea arborescens* 'Annabelle' on the edge of the bed had been left, and a few *Rhododendrons* were moved to the left; providing colour in early summer and a darker background for the more colourful planting planned. Notice the enduring plumes of pampas grass beyond, likely to get a new lease of life now that the conifers have been cut down.

As trees come into fresh spring growth, so is the view to the summer house. The opened-up Crossways Corner is letting in more light, reducing overcrowding and any feeling of imposing woodland either side. Golden-leaved conifers, trees and shrubs carry the eye through to the distance.

The same day, but a different view. The craggy golden Scots pine (right) is only golden in the winter, and another can be seen in the distance directly behind. It is natural for most conifers, when overcrowded or in dense woodland, to drop their lower branches due to the lack of light.

Only a year later, the beech stump is providing a haven for weeds – and foxgloves. The weeds will be removed, the foxgloves are encouraged to stay.

Year-Round Interest

Letting plants die back naturally, as leaves have long fallen from deciduous trees and shrubs, can still offer a striking winter scene. Taken in January, midwinter with obviously no snow on the ground, the dried heads of *Hydrangea arborescens* 'Annabelle', now a pleasant light brown, still stand on the one-year stems, the weight they bear now much lighter than in summer. *Cornus sanguinea* 'Magic Flame', similar to 'Midwinter Fire', displays the only strong colour, but the eye is still drawn to the distant tall plumes of *Cortaderia selloana* 'Sunningdale Silver'.

Now in Foggy Bottom I have been able to open up pathways, thin plants to get partial views through to distant beds and create equally arresting plantings at a lower level. This has been a constant theme now for the past twenty years, winter thinning and pruning, preparation for planting in late winter, early spring, then planting. It has taken two years to establish what maintenance is required and, apart from some weeding, an area such as Crossways Corner will reward over a long seasonal period for a few years with little attention.

The garden value of *Hydrangea arborescens* 'Annabelle' can hardly be in doubt when the February sun filters through the trees behind the Crossways Corner bed. The planting creates such drama, the rays of sunlight briefly focussing on the flowerheads in front of a perimeter of frosted grass.

1971, the Front of House Bed is protected by a fence from the meadow beyond, which in 1976 became an extension of the garden.

01
02

The Front of House Bed

The 'Front of House Bed'… I can hear you asking, "What sort of name is that?"

Well, Foggy Bottom is not a grand house, and when first built in 1966, the garden I planned was a relatively small area around our home, fenced from and overlooking the five-acre meadow to the south. At this stage, I hadn't considered creating a larger garden that would eventually encompass the meadow or develop a garden that would be open to the public.

In 1976 prior to the long hot summer, the fence came down and I started to open up the garden beyond. Gradually, we carved out beds in the field, leaving long broad sweeps of meadow grass north to south and east to west. I planned to have the house slowly disappear as the plants developed in the long and quite narrow 'Front of House Bed'. As plants, conifers, shrubs and trees grew, the house would come to be largely hidden from garden visitors, but the term 'Front of House' might still need some explaining.

To re-iterate, the 'Back of House', 'Front of House' and 'Kitchen' beds in Foggy Bottom are all part of my private garden and this is not open to the public. It might be argued that 'front' of the house could literally mean any part of the Foggy Bottom Garden, all of which are to the front, that is south of the house. Perhaps a look at the map of the garden will clarify. These are the beds which stretch from near the tree house on the left (east), along to the right (west). I will give the garden tour from a visitor's point of view, though you will get to see some special views only offered to the special people allowed into my private garden… so a somewhat privileged tour then!

It's early morning in mid-October and we are looking north-east towards the giant redwoods I planted in Adrian's Wood back in 1964, now towering above the garden. But it is the sunlit tree house, built by my son Matt in 2010, that catches the eye. This (often to the chagrin of young visitors) is in our private garden, but in front of it is where the Front of House Bed begins, continuing from east to west. In front of the tree house, plumes of white fluffy flowers of the pampas grass *Cortaderia selloana* 'Pumila' are vibrant even at a distance. Silver birch leaves are turning to gold and are soon to fall. From those two trees, look left to two conical-shaped conifers. The blue needled fir is *Abies procera* 'Glauca', and close to it a form of the deodar cedar with golden yellow foliage, *Cedrus deodara* 'Nana Aurea' (though it is not exactly 'Nana', which means dwarf). In the foreground, making a carpet close to the green grass is the striking silver-blue autumn flowering *Aster novi-belgii* 'Silberteppich', and left are two tightly conical Alberta spruce, *Picea glauca* var. *albertiana* 'J.W. Daisy's White', whose dramatic transformation happens in spring – always something to look forward to!

The Tree House Area

With the tree house on our left and daffodils in flower near the silver birch, we are looking from my private garden to the south. Had I not planted conifers and shrubs in the Front of House Bed some years ago, we would have got a long uninterrupted view to the pond in the distance, where you can glimpse the white blossoms of *Prunus incisa* 'Pendula'. Of course, this bed, and to the right where you get another view into the garden, was intended as an informal barrier between the otherwise singular Foggy Bottom Garden. The main plants are *Abies procera* 'Glauca' and *Cedrus deodara* 'Nana Aurea', both of which are pruned every year to keep their shape and to prevent them getting too large. Yet to come into leaf is the orange-stemmed maple, *Acer* × *conspicuum* 'Phoenix' – one of my favourites for winter colour.

← Often, if not almost always, atmospheric images come by surprise and with a certain amount of luck. Up in the tree house one slightly misty spring morning, I looked through the branches of a silver birch, *Betula papyrifera*, and saw the light catching on the waving catkins. The bluish grey of *Picea pungens* 'Thomsen' was itself highlighted in front of the brilliant white, densely packed flowers of *Magnolia* 'Ballerina' ...and again, behind it are more high-rise conifers. Not a matter of "here's one I produced earlier", perhaps more "here's one I started fifty years ago".

Spring glory! We are now just beyond the threat of spring frosts and both the *Rhododendron yakushimanum* 'Koichiro Wada' and *Acer palmatum* 'Fireglow' have escaped damage. The purple leaves are as intense as they will get all year and contrast well with the blue spruce, *Picea pungens* 'Globosa', and the fresh green foliage of *Prunus incisa* 'Kojo-no-mai' behind. Hiding in the next part of the Front of House Bed are the bright yellow tips of *Cytisus scoparius* 'Golden Sunlight'. ↓

Fast forward five months and *Cornus kousa* 'Wolf Eyes' (is that meant to be a complimentary name?) is in flower. Kousa dogwood is not too exciting a common name and another, Chinese dogwood, is somewhat misleading since the origins of this species are mostly from Japan and Korea. In recent years, this group of large shrubs or small trees have become quite popular, with several recent selections becoming available. 'Wolf Eyes' is one of the best with variegated foliage and usually flowers well each summer in Foggy Bottom. They grow best in reasonable light, a good loam, but are less successful on poorer, chalky soils. Here you get a view of the brightly variegated *Cornus* close to a very slim, columnar *Thuja occidentalis* 'Foggy Bottom Sentinel', contrasting with the dark blue fir, *Abies procera* 'Glauca'. Quite a landmark in the distant Mini-Pinetum bed is the distinctive purple-leaved Japanese maple, *Acer palmatum* 'Crimson Queen'.

Almost a white-out as the snow settles and we look down across the garden, a few dark-looking conifers standing out from the more ephemeral deciduous trees. All is very quiet, no sound of distant traffic and no birds. This photograph was taken from near the tree house, close to the *Cortaderia selloana* 'Pumila', to its right is the starkly outlined branches of *Cornus kousa* 'Wolf Eyes' highlighted by the snow.

The Phoenix Area

You can see we had a thorough clear out and pruning away → the lower branches on the *Picea pungens* 'Globosa' had given them much more character, if a little scrawny. The tall maple on the right with orange bark is *Acer* × *conspicuum* 'Phoenix'. I was just starting the planting, and with the quite heavy soil prepared, I used a board to spread my weight as I went. I had planned a colourful combination of *Crocosmia*, purple-leaved *Heuchera* and *Rudbeckia* which had been there already. Amongst the snowdrops are plants of *Geranium* 'Rozanne' which are yet to appear.

Just four months later, the steel blue, new growth on the → central group of *Picea pungens* 'Globosa' dominates a mixture of perennials yet to come into flower. But it is early enough for us to distinguish several green foliage colours and forms of these and spiky grasses. The tallest grass on the left is *Panicum virgatum* 'Northwind', in the centre *Geranium* 'Azure Rush' with the first flower of *Crocosmia* 'Spitfire'. Opening yellow *Rudbeckia* in the foreground and *Geranium* 'Rozanne' to the right.

I can certainly claim that this *Hosta* 'Shade Fanfare' was one I ↓ had planted earlier, as it was fully established and not disturbed by the pruning of the *Picea*. It is now exposed to more light and we get a different perspective of the garden as the sunlight is shed beyond and beneath the blue spruce.

On a late summer's morning, two years after planting, I was now quite pleased with the transformation. The rather static conifers which were past their best have gone and now the group of *Picea pungens* 'Globosa' allow seasonal vibrancy to highlight their boldness and character. Rather too comfortable at the front is *Rudbeckia fulgida* var. *sullivantii* 'Goldsturm' with orange flowers of *Crocosmia* 'Spitfire', a strong contrast. And of course by chance (and getting up early on a sunny summer's morning), I had managed to capture the glorifying effect the sun's filtered rays can bestow, highlighting the stems of *Acer* × *conspicuum* 'Phoenix'.

The Spruce and Pine Area

Let's start viewing this area in the Front of House Bed in November, just before the last of the leaves fall in Foggy Bottom. This is the time of year when you can observe conifers, trees and shrubs more distinctly than in any other season. See if you can follow my eye as it goes from left to right and bottom to top. The group of *Spiraea japonica* 'Magic Carpet' curves around silver needled *Picea sitchensis* 'Tenas', almost matching the colour of the slightly prehistoric-looking arch of *Picea omorika* 'Pendula Bruns'. In front of it is a golden-leaved Jasmine, *Jasminum officinale* 'Fiona Sunrise'. Above are the last rusty-red leaves of *Hamamelis* × *intermedia* 'Feuerzauber' before winter branches are exposed.

Behind this scene are the white trunks of *Betula utilis* var. *jacquemontii* 'Jermyns' in front of a sweetgum, *Liquidambar styraciflua*, a yellowish *Cryptomeria japonica* 'Sekkan-sugi' nestling up to an imposing, evenly branched blue spruce, *Picea pungens* 'Hoto'. To the right from the ground there is *Ageratina altissima* 'Chocolate', the leaf colour faded, chocolatey foliage now topped with late creamy white flowers. Pruned back hard immediately after flowering is the deep green *Cytisus scoparius* 'Golden Sunlight', which contrasts with both the golden thread cypress, *Chamaecyparis pisifera* 'Filifera Aurea', and the silver blue *Picea pungens* 'Thomsen'.

↑
Late spring merges into early summer, a time of flower for many outstanding shrubs and new foliage. Looking at the previous image taken in autumn but from a slightly different angle, we will note a similar positioning in the Front of House Bed with the two *Picea* in the centre. Though relatively brief, the golden broom, *Cytisus scoparius* 'Golden Sunlight', lights up in front of the blue spruce, *Picea pungens* 'Thomsen', to the right. Move to the left and you can see a striking combination of background shrubs, the early blue flowers of *Nepeta racemosa* 'Walker's Low' setting them all off. The tree to the left, of which you can only see a half, is *Robinia pseudoacacia* 'Lace Lady' and from the right of it is an old specimen of *Rhododendron* 'Olga' with its striking annual display of salmon orange flowers. In front, is a much younger plant of *Cornus kousa* 'Venus', a recent introduction with almost the largest flower bracts of any dogwood. Lastly, the seldom seen dwarf purple beech, *Fagus sylvatica* 'Purpurea Nana', makes a dark contrast to all other plants in this area.

A month later and now more plants in the foreground are in flower, including three different roses. Some visitors are puzzled why there are not more roses in Foggy Bottom since there are so many shrubs. I could use more, just as I could use more *Clematis*. The latter is another story, but I'm happy to use roses where they do well in the garden and if they don't need a lot of attention – i.e. pruning or spraying against pests and diseases. We also have deer, mostly roe or Chinese muntjac, and they seem to snack on most roses as well as many other things. We have tried various preventions, one of which was to suspend a piece of soap above their favourite plants. This seemed to work for a while until our local crows took a liking to eating the soap and wrecked our plans!

← *Picea omorika* 'Pendula Bruns', the weeping blue-green conifer in the centre, looks morose if not downright grumpy, perhaps because of the lightness of all the plants and colours around it. This is a summer's evening as the sun gets lower in the sky and shines through the twisted leaves of *Robinia pseudoacacia* 'Lace Lady'. Scarlet crimson *Crocosmia* 'Lucifer' can be seen against the dark *Picea*, and from this angle the view in front looks like a small meadow or cottage garden. You can't see the broad grass path that runs between the far side and the more frontal planting which shows a Shasta daisy seedling, *Leucanthemum maximum*, and the glowing maroon *Lychnis coronaria,* also a seedling. A flowing, low growing grass, *Stipa tenuissima,* catches the light as it moves in the breeze.

↑
This pine arose as a witches' broom on a Scots pine, *Pinus sylvestris,* and was propagated by Don Hatch who discovered it in Surrey, England around 1975. That's more than we need to know in realising that a 'dwarf conifer' may be only a temporary description, but in relative terms my plant, *Pinus sylvestris* 'Lodge Hill', now forty years old and about 4 m high, is still dwarf in comparison to its parent, *P. sylvestris,* which at the same age might be 15 m (50 ft).

Without pruning 'Lodge Hill', the branches and foliage would touch the ground, block any view, and take up twice as much garden space. Therefore, in most gardens, it would probably have had to be removed. Pruning changes nearly all those negative points to positive ones. By pruning (see p.275), you create an arresting specimen, add character where there was little and expose the attractive, light brown, slightly peeling bark. You can now see through the lower area to garden vistas and plants beyond and finally, you can plant beneath it – though select plants that will grow in very dry conditions.

← The original plant was multi-stemmed and most of these stronger stems were left, leaving enough distance between those remaining to get an unusual view through to *Acer palmatum* 'Crimson Queen' in the Mini-Pinetum.

Conifers on the left create a barrier to my private garden, interspersed with the single specimens of late flowering pampas grass, *Cortaderia selloana* 'Pumila'. In the foreground, *Pinus contorta* 'Frisian Gold' is lit by the unusual November sun after a frosty start to the day. The distant *Pinus sylvestris* 'Lodge Hill' now makes a strong focal point, and this specimen is now one of my most striking of all the conifers in Foggy Bottom.
↓

01
03

The Mini-Pinetum

This is one of the most varied plantings in Foggy Bottom which interact with each other and the rest of the surrounding garden. No formality, no 'rooms' to enter or exit, and from the centre, beneath the oldest trees, you can turn a full circle of 360 degrees to get an interesting view from every vantage point. We had positioned a circular bench beneath the golden Scots pine, but the pigeons loved sitting on the branches at night, which inevitably meant covering and uncovering the bench each day, with a slight risk that a tame pigeon might one day settle on a branch above an unsuspecting visitor. We removed the bench before we received our first indignant complaint...

From positions outside this area comprising three slightly raised island beds, a few mature conifers dominate. These beds were planted back in 1976, and it is the central bed that I called the 'Mini-Pinetum' some years ago. 'Pinetum' refers to a collection of coniferous trees, as opposed to 'Arboretum' which means all trees. The two largest conifers here are *Picea pungens* 'Thomsen', a Colorado blue spruce, and close to it on the central island is *Pinus sylvestris* 'Aurea', the golden Scots pine. I have gradually removed the lower branches so now you can stand beneath them and get views into other parts of the garden. The full story from first planting is revealed in later pages, but inevitably, many conifers and other plants nearby got too large and had to be removed. An opportunity was then created to feature some new and relatively dwarf, slow growing pines. Hence the name of Mini-Pinetum seemed appropriate.

As far as the other beds are concerned, these too, as you might expect, have changed over fifty years as plants have matured. Often, the planting is allied or reflected in plantings nearby in other beds. Let me take you around the area called the Mini-Pinetum to see how it looks today.

A wall of mature conifers creates a dramatic background in this spring view. Only gold in winter, the Scots pine, *Pinus sylvestris* 'Aurea', sits beside the taller blue spruce, *Picea pungens* 'Thomsen'. As the sun disperses the ground frost, it also highlights (from the right) *Picea pungens* 'Glauca Prostrata', several narrow green conifers, *Thuja occidentalis* 'Degroot's Spire', and two orange *Berberis darwinii*.

Location, location, location. Not a photograph taken by a guided drone, but from our (private) tree house in November. On the far left side you can locate with the previous photograph by spotting the *Picea pungens* 'Glauca Prostrata', and *Pinus sylvestris* 'Aurea' centre right, minus a few branches. These were mostly affected by its closeness to another pine in earlier years. For the observant, there are many other plants of note, but getting a glimpse of the sunlit pampas grass plumes in the distance shows how this area fits in, almost the whole Mini-Pinetum is captured in one take.

Insider's View

Here follows some insight into the design and planting of a few areas in the Mini-Pinetum, most linking and shown in different seasons. In most cases, as time passed plants grew and either had to be accommodated for or they had to be moved (increasingly difficult as plants got bigger). If we want to achieve an interesting and balanced garden, this must be part of the process. We don't all want, or are able, to move house and start gardening elsewhere, but as plants get older, so do we and difficulties increase for both with age. I'm not sure I have an answer for that one, but here are some renewed plantings retaining older specimen plants.

↑

Small vistas, big vistas …as you may have gathered, all are part of my garden ethos. Foggy Bottom has many large vistas, mostly following contours of grass pathways – the 'green river' that joins all the garden together. Here, we look through the Mini-Pinetum; a tall conifer on the left, *Allium*, *Spiraea*, *Geraniums* and *Bergenia* in the foreground, and centre stage is a forty-year-old weeping hemlock, *Tsuga canadensis* 'Pendula'. Behind, you see the deep green foliage of a Japanese maple, *Acer palmatum* 'Shishi-gashira' close to the purple *Cotinus coggygria* 'Royal Purple'. Somewhere left of centre is a small section of lawn…

← …where we are now standing, on the grass pathway in early summer. Right of the *Tsuga canadensis* 'Pendula', a drift of *Hosta* 'Buckshaw Blue' contrasts with the smaller-leaved *H.* 'Golden Tiara'. *Campanula poscharskyana* and dwarf fern, *Adiantum aleuticum* 'Subpumilum' in the foreground. The slow growing pine on the right is *Pinus densiflora* 'Pendula', and by removing the lower branches of *Acer griseum* and *Pinus sylvestris*, it has opened up a view through to the garden beyond.

↑

Looking east from beneath *Pinus sylvestris* 'Aurea', the golden Scots pine planted in 1978, the camera is shielded from the early morning sun, which highlights the low grass *Stipa tenuissima*. Silhouettes of smaller pines and *Acer palmatum* 'Crimson Queen' dominate the background.

A moment in time, since this line of cone shaped conifers now could not be replicated. The reason? Unfortunately, the bluish needled noble fir, *Abies procera* 'Glauca', had to be removed because of disease, some of which you can see in the dark patch of foliage halfway up the forty-year-old specimen. The two compact plants in the foreground are *Picea glauca* 'J. W. Daisy's White', showing their creamy-white new shoots. These have not been pruned, unlike the golden foliaged cedar behind in the Front of House Bed which is pruned or sheared every spring. Both this and the *Abies* would have been twice as tall if they had not been pruned. →

Snow can, and does, dramatically transform a garden and the plants within it. The three *Picea glauca* var. *albertiana* 'J.W. Daisy's White' (even whiter than usual) now seem to resemble the Daleks from the TV programme *Dr Who*. In recent years, we have had less snow in winter, and seldom the 'right' kind of snow – that is the lighter, powder-like snow that settles gently on branches and foliage – with the air cold enough to prevent immediate thawing. I was lucky enough to be at home during this brief snowfall to record its effect.

Who could imagine that an *Agapanthus* would survive, let alone flower so freely, in such a dry semi-shady position as this *Agapanthus inapertus* subsp. *pendulus* – that's quite a name to grapple with! Taken on a misty autumn morning, the dark pendulous flowers stand out dramatically amid wispy grasses *Stipa* and *Molinia*. On the left is the trunk of the blue spruce (one I planted earlier!), *Picea pungens* 'Thomsen'.

A Perfect Place for Conifers

The colour green is dominant in this view across to the south of the Mini-Pinetum and drives home the importance of structure and repetition. Whichever angle you see this planting from, the specimens of *Thuja occidentalis* 'Degroot's Spire' complement each other and connect the planting in a casual, yet structured way. This has proved to be a good selection but there are many upright conifers which would do equally well. Soon to provide a blaze of colour are the clumps of erect, emerald bladed leaves of *Crocosmia* 'Lucifer's Match?'.

↓

All of a sudden, attention moves from the *Thujas* to the crimson scarlet *Crocosmia* 'Lucifer's Match?', now in full flower in mid-July. Aside from the stunning, almost exotic flowers, the *Crocosmia* now unites the whole planting. *C.* 'Lucifer's Match?' is a more compact form of *C.* 'Lucifer', the popular cultivar raised in the early 1960s at Bressingham by my father Alan Bloom and his helper Percy Piper. 'Lucifer's Match?', trialled over ten years, is shorter and less prone to collapse after summer wind and rain. →

↑

The green pillars of *Thuja occidentalis* 'Degroot's Spire' offer a vista through to the strikingly grey-blue foliage of *Picea pungens* 'Glauca Prostrata' in the middle distance. (In case you were curious, the smoky-looking plume above the *Picea* is a jet of water from an irrigation sprinkler!). Now in late summer, the *Crocosmia* has finished flowering, but colour and interest continue with the golden yellow flowers of *Rudbeckia fulgida* 'Viette's Little Suzy', and *Sedums* beyond amongst bottlebrush flower heads of *Pennisetum orientale*.

The wider view makes it obvious that this must be late → autumn and from the grass edging and pendulous plumes of *Pennisetum orientale,* a frosty morning. Weather starts to provide more dramatic effects on plants in autumn and winter, whilst the emerging growth in spring sets it aside as a season of life's affirmation. Autumn can be moody and glorious in its displays of colour, but there is something melancholic about the seasonal shutdown into winter. Here, our tall *Thujas* still provide structure and permanency amidst transformation that is happening around them. The startling white heads of *Hydrangea paniculata* 'Limelight' are fading, background foliage on deciduous trees and shrubs highlights conifers that will soon come into their own. The aptly named *Sorbus* 'Autumn Spire' adds to the seasonal theme with its bronzed leaves and orange-tinged fruits.

Year-Round Interest

Not all the conifers in the Mini-Pinetum are pines. In fact, in this autumn view on a moist dewy morning with signs of spider activity, there is only a glimpse of a dark green *Pinus heldreichii* on the right. In the foreground are the bluish needles of *Larix kaempferi* 'Dwarf Blue', immediately behind is another larch, the compact pendulous *Larix decidua* 'Puli'. Although it looks like a *Taxus*, the erect stems of golden tipped needles are the closely related *Cephalotaxus harringtonia* 'Korean Gold'. Effective once again is the purple form of the Japanese maple, *Acer palmatum* 'Crimson Queen'.

It is not often known, nor recognised, that the *Cornus sanguinea* species and cultivars retain their leaves much longer in autumn than most others like *C. alba* and *C. sericea*. This means that they add more value as a reliable shrub for autumn interest. The foliage transitions from butter yellow to tinges of orange and red, as you can see here with *C. s.* 'Magic Flame'. Although sparse, the late deep blue flowers of *Geranium* 'Rozanne' make a good contrast.

Less visible when in leaf, plants with attractive bark come into their own in winter, though this was taken on a frosty morning in November on the edge of the Mini-Pinetum. We are looking at the shady north side of *Acer* × *conspicuum* 'Candy Stripe' living up to its (less than glorious) name, to the orange and red stems of *Cornus sanguinea* 'Magic Flame' beyond. From this date on, until the *Cornus* is pruned in late March, colour and interest will remain whatever the weather.

A view from the north side of the Mini-Pinetum taken in early morning towards the end of November. The hoar frost adds to the beauty and drama as it clings to branches of *Acer palmatum* 'Crimson Queen' and Young's weeping birch, *Betula pendula subsp. pendula* 'Youngii'. The conifers on the right can now be fully seen. Adding attraction on the left are the plumes of *Cortaderia selloana* 'Pumila'. There is much to enjoy now and look forward to in the garden.

↑

Another season, another view. From beneath the mature blue spruce and Scots pine, the *Hamamelis* coming into flower in the distance is revealed, alongside droplets on the needles from three different *Pinus* cultivars in the Mini-Pinetum. From left to right, there are the long bluish needles of *Pinus x schwerinii* 'Wiethorst', *Pinus sylvestris* 'Vargguld' (Wolf Gold) and *Pinus wallichiana* 'Nana'. All three are in line for pruning so that they don't grow into each other.

Few beds in Foggy Bottom stand completely alone and from each there are several views or vistas 'borrowed' from other plantings – which to my mind, enhances the whole. This is taken from the centre of the Mini-Pinetum looking south to Crossways Corner and beyond; the fluffy white plumes of pampas grass, *Cortaderia selloana* highlighted in the distance. Working backwards, omitting the grasses, the most distinctive colour is provided by the large leathery leaves of *Bergenia* 'Bressingham Ruby'. Slightly hidden, and revealed better from a different angle, are the orange-red stems of *Cornus sanguinea* 'Magic Flame'.

Arguably, the dried winter heads of *Hydrangea paniculata* 'Limelight' are as valuable in the garden in early winter as they are in summer at their spectacular best. There is now a great choice of cultivars of this useful hardy shrub, and although they can be left unpruned, there are many advantages in pruning as we will see.

The *Hydrangea paniculata* 'Limelight' could have been pruned a month earlier. But with young green shoots already showing, it was time to individually prune away last year's panicles and weaker shoots in preparation for another striking performance in only a few short months.

From this, with no one in a red jacket to distract, you can clearly see the woody structure that remains after pruning; leaving strong shoots and an evenly balanced outline. Behind is the rather ungainly outline of the deciduous *Cotinus coggygria* 'Royal Purple'.

Fast forward three months and *Hydrangea paniculata* 'Limelight' is enjoying a moment shaded by the *Cotinus coggygria* 'Royal Purple', as the early evening sun picks out the wispy plumes of *Pennisetum orientale* and succulent *Sedums*.

↓

← Again, in the rays of evening sun is another specimen of *Hydrangea paniculata* 'Limelight', which I planted a few years ago on the other side of the *Cotinus*. A ground covering of *Anaphalis triplinervis* 'Sommerschnee' (Summer Snow) beneath and a hint of blue *Agapanthus* in the background. It is only a matter of preference, but unlike many other selections of *Hydrangea paniculata*, the panicles of 'Limelight' don't turn a vivid pink or red in the autumn.

However, here's one that does. Raised in France, *Hydrangea paniculata* 'Vanille Fraise' tinges pink and deepens colour into autumn. This is also located in the Mini-Pinetum with one of my favourite *Agapanthus*, the pale blue *A. inapertus* 'Summer Blue Bells'.

↓

0104

The All Seasons Bed

This bed, a true island, surrounded by grass pathways is centrally placed at the lower half of the garden. Earlier photographs will reveal that this used to be called the 'Conifer Bed'. Why? Because all the plants planted there were conifers... and if I wasn't sure where a new conifer accession was going, it ended up in the Conifer Bed. There was not much design, except form, texture and colour. The soil was good, medium and well-drained; therefore, it was more or less perfect for conifers. A few that had not spoilt each other and fitted the new design remain today.

From a distance, the Conifer Bed had form and seasonal colour, but up close it was an overgrown mass of trees, most of which had grown into each other. In 1999, I finally decided that if I were to make something of it, I would have to be ruthless. That meant a complete clear out of ninety percent of the conifers. Some were able to be moved and assimilated elsewhere, but most had to be dug up and removed. I wanted the bed to reflect a connection of using fewer conifers combined with other types of plants. Through the next group of images, you can see how this worked out... though as plants grow and time doesn't stand still, I will again need to re-design.

"Heaven! What a joy to walk barefoot on the soft green grass. I love this place to bits."

Views From the North

Let's then view this, the onetime Conifer Bed, which became the 'All Seasons Bed' when it was re-planted in 2000. A wider range of plants would be used and still provide year-round interest. Initially, we'll look at this bed from a distance and from different vantage points, before looking at the ten different areas in detail. From the north end, the All Seasons Bed clearly represents an island with lengthy grass pathways each side. The distant summer house is an obvious focal point to the right, and *Miscanthus* plumes in the Snake Bed to the left. It's a rather dull, late autumn day with the fading *Hydrangea arborescens* 'Annabelle' on our left at Crossways Corner and pampas grass brightly waving on the right. The taller is *Cortaderia selloana* 'Sunningdale Silver' and the two shorter-stemmed cultivars are *Cortaderia selloana* 'Pumila' (the very short one was only planted this year).

Although cloud can be seen, the spring light is still bright and reflects most strongly on the early growth of gold or yellow deciduous trees and shrubs. On the north side of the All Seasons Bed, one of the few deciduous conifers,

Metasequoia glyptostroboides 'Gold Rush', towers above other slower growing conifers. I had intended to move it at one time, but 'it got away'! Both left and right in the distance are selections I made of a golden alder, one of which I named *Alnus glutinosa* 'Foggy Bottom Sunshine'. Different shaped and sized conifers are tucked into temporary spaces. Very brightly showing up in the foreground, centre right, is the early foliage of *Physocarpus opulifolius* 'Angel Gold'.

↑

Views From the South

In early summer, shades of green and yellow are dominant. The red spring colour of *Acer cappadocicum* 'Rubrum' (left) has now faded to green, the showy purple-leaved beech, *Fagus sylvatica* 'Rohanii', stands out in front of a large specimen of *Liriodendron tulipifera* 'Aureomarginatum', the variegated tulip tree. On the right, the yellow-green shrubs are *Cornus sericea* subsp. *occidentalis* 'Sunshine'; brighter leaves and perhaps more vigorous than the similar *Cornus alba* 'Aurea'. Directly behind the *Cornus* is the broadly columnar *Metasequoia glyptostroboides* 'Gold Rush', and in the far distance is the slightly golden-topped conifer *Calocedrus decurrens* 'Berrima Gold'. As you will see as we continue to tour Foggy Bottom, I am rather fond of using geographical descriptive terms… and here perhaps imagine that the finely cut grass 'flowing' into the distance and around the 'island' is a green 'river'. Of course, informal flowing grass surrounds and sets off all parts of the garden. Does that mean we, with imagination, are walking on green water?

It's now late summer and vibrant colours light up the All Seasons Bed. This view is taken from the southwest and includes part of the Magnolia Jane Bed where the purple-leaved *Heuchera* 'Prince' is at the front, accompanied by the bronze-leaved form of *Carex comans*. *Salvia pratensis* and the dwarf yellow flowers of *Hemerocallis* 'Stella de Oro' are dotted in the foreground planting and the golden cut-leaf plant in the centre of this bed is *Rhus typhina* 'Tiger Eyes'. Beyond in the All Seasons Bed is a group of the stunning orange-flowered *Crocosmia* 'Bright Eyes', low enough to highlight *Agapanthus* 'Loch Hope' and the yellow mounds of *Cornus sericea* subsp. *occidentalis* 'Sunshine' either side. The limbs of *Betula davurica* have been taken away to reveal a distant view through to the grey-bronze inflorescences of *Cotinus coggygria* 'Young Lady'. →

Here, the foreground grouping relies on two outstanding perennials, colour contrast, texture and timing, all combining to create a tremendous impact from a distance as well as close up. A well established clump of the tall late flowering *Agapanthus* 'Loch Hope' rises above the closely packed flowers of *Crocosmia* 'Bright Eyes'. You can see why the name was given, as each open flower has an intense red centre. The All Seasons Bed continues on the right into the distance, whilst on the left approaching the Sad Bed, the *Crocosmia* and *Agapanthus* are repeated and joined by larger heads of *Agapanthus* 'Windsor Grey'. In the early morning, there is a slight mist in the air which partially blurs the heads of *Hydrangea arborescens* 'Annabelle' in the planting beyond.

There's no doubt that the most colourful times of year for the All Seasons Bed is late summer and autumn; colour that is always backed by or mingled amongst conifers. This view of the All Seasons Bed is from the eastern side. Since replanting in 2000, many conifers have had to go and even now, as I write this, I am approaching another dilemma. The main, bluish green conifer in the centre of this photograph is the slow growing *Pinus koraiensis* 'Winton'. When I bought a small plant, 30 x 30 cm (12 x 12 in), from Hillier Nurseries in 1978, I was told the maximum height it would grow to was 2 m (6 ft 6 in), by twice as wide. Over forty years later it is 4 m (13 ft) high by 6 m (20 ft) wide. If I had not cut away the bottom branches there would not have been room for any other plants in this area. In doing this, I needed to create a tree with character, allow planting near and below, and lastly, create views through from all angles by exposing the branches to head height.

Various perennials and grasses are in the foreground of *P. k.* 'Winton'. Next to the green path is a blue fescue, *Festuca glauca* 'Elijah Blue', the light green shrubby *Nandina domestica* 'Firepower', a crimson tipped *Imperata cylindrica* 'Rubra' (the beginning or end of the river of Japanese blood grass), above which are the unruly-looking bottlebrush heads of *Pennisetum villosum*.

↑

The other side of the All Seasons Bed, now looking from west to east, is almost in full shadow. Several conifers clearly reveal their outline, some quite dwarf or prostrate, some tall like the *Metasequoia glyptostroboides* 'Gold Rush' on the immediate left. The sun lights up the Rhus Corner beyond and as we look through, throws into relief the lower branches of *Pinus koraiensis* 'Winton'. I intend to cut one or two more branches off this imposing pine, to open up the vista beyond even more clearly. On the right of our pine is the tightly conical *Picea glauca* 'Alberta Blue', near the broader-leaved golden-tinged shrub *Physocarpus opulifolius* 'Angel Gold'. Mounded above is a forty-year-old specimen of *Chamaecyparis lawsoniana* 'Globus', a little known but worthwhile Lawson's cypress raised in Hungary.

← Now in autumn, it's back to foliage with only the small red poker heads of *Persicaria amplexicaulis* 'Taurus' in flower (centre left). Leaves are turning colour and are shortly to fall. From this vantage point, you can quietly absorb the view – the shapes, forms, colours and textures – that completely captures a man-made scene. "If only he had left it as a meadow", did I hear someone say?

Taken directly from the south and the closest point to the Snake Bed, this is a good example of the impact that conifers can have once leaves of deciduous plants have fallen. Conifers remain resolute throughout the autumn and winter. The only two shrubs with leaves still remaining here are the bright yellow *Cornus sericea* subsp. *occidentalis* 'Sunshine' in the centre, and the deep orange yellow of *Spiraea japonica* 'Magic Carpet' in front of the birch. The All Seasons Bed has several conifers, whilst taller forms tower behind. From left to right, starting with the broad yellow-green fir, *Abies nordmanniana* 'Golden Spreader' (since it eventually makes a pyramid up to 6 m (20 ft) high, the name of it somewhat of a misnomer), comes into its own in late winter when the needles turn a deep golden yellow. In the foreground is a rather dumpy *Pinus mugo* 'Glendale' which will need pruning from the base. Next, the only deciduous tree at this end of the All Seasons Bed is the striking *Betula davurica*, a smaller growing birch from Siberia with finely flaking bark. A combination of conifers; the golden yellow *Chamaecyparis obtusa* 'Fernspray Gold' and light green *Chamaecyparis lawsoniana* 'Globus', which for various reasons I've allowed to grow into each other. In front, *Pinus sylvestris* 'Foggy Bottom Pillar', a seedling that arose by chance in the garden, contrasting in colour and form with an old specimen of *Pinus mugo* 'Ophir', the needles gradually turning to winter gold.

← A closer view reveals the deepening ruby-red leaves of *Nandina domestica* 'Firepower' in the foreground, now outshining the *Imperata* as it starts to die back for winter. *Pinus mugo* 'Ophir', which has been pruned at the base, completes the picture together with silver *Stachys*, orange-yellow leaves of *Spiraea* and a *Miscanthus* in the Snake Bed.

↑
This is a day when you would probably not wish to venture out into any garden, the wind blowing and snow still falling. But year-round interest needs to be captured in all sorts of weather. Whilst the green grass has been turned into a white snowy covering, branches of deciduous trees are highlighted by snow-laden branches and conifers blend into the scenery.

The River of *Imperata cylindrica* 'Rubra'

We first planted the All Seasons Bed with a river of Japanese blood grass, *Imperata cylindrica* 'Rubra', in 2000, weaving its way through the centre, 35 m (114 ft) in length. I had seen this striking grass used as a river in the US where it was very effective, although the plant of course originates from Japan. It can be a delicate plant and doesn't succeed everywhere, preferring moisture during the growing season. Growing to about 45 cm (18 in), it has small spreading rhizomes as opposed to clumps. The green-leaved species is considered invasive, though it is seldom seen or grown; in some states in the US, the ornamental 'Rubra', like the species, is prohibited from distribution. Whilst hot summers, akin to those in Japan, occur in much of the US, I would say based on my twenty-five years of growing it, *Imperata cylindrica* 'Rubra' is spreading but not invasive. It is easily controlled from going places you don't want it to. We regularly supply our nursery with any surplus after curbing our river... lifting, planting and potting is best done in mid-spring.

The red-tipped *Imperata* is prominent in the foreground, as seen through the spreading branches of *Pinus koraiensis* 'Winton'. To the right are the soft yellow leaves of *Cotinus coggygria* 'Golden Spirit' and to the left are the pink, soon deepening to crimson, inflorescences of *Hydrangea paniculata* 'Vanille Fraise'. *Pennisetum villosum* is fully in flower and will continue until the frosts. The perfect late flowering grass? Almost, but it's not fully hardy in colder parts of the UK, but still worth considering as an annual.

Now to the conifers, filling the photograph on the left is the fascinating and unusual *Picea glauca* 'Alberta Blue', a bright powder blue sport or mutation, which without attention is gradually recovering back to green. The rounded form of *Platycladus orientalis* 'Franky Boy' has finely threaded yellow foliage (I've yet to make up my mind as to whether I want it in the garden), and beyond is the main plant featured in the Sad Bed, *Cedrus atlantica* 'Glauca Pendula'. More on that great conifer later...

← From inside the All Seasons Bed, close to the *Pinus koraiensis* 'Winton', we look left from beneath the pine to a view out towards the Rhus Corner planting. Believe it or not, I had been delaying the removal of the two-pronged branch until we recorded it on a television programme. Most gardeners are apprehensive about pruning conifers (they obviously haven't read my book *Gardening with Conifers* yet!), and we hope to cover some of this in the programme. Although there is a view, it will certainly be more open and dramatic when this branch is gone. Letting in more light will suit the *Erica vagans* in the foreground, as well as the *Imperata*. *Acer campestre* 'Pulverulentum', which has creamy white leaves in spring, is on the right.

↑
To have a plant, shrub, perennial or grass offering this colour in late summer and well into autumn is a real bonus for gardeners. From my experience, the *Imperata*, which deepens in colour from spring to autumn, needs a mainly sunny position in reasonably moist soil, or where it could be watered if dry. I have been told, "It isn't hardy with me" many times, but classed as Zone 6 in the US, this is seldom true in most areas. When my father first received this from Japan many years ago it was planted in sun, but on fairly light soil where it didn't thrive. I was more than happy, before we gave up on it, to discover the conditions *Imperata* prefers, as this plant brings great pleasure to me and to the garden's visitors. Although the description has been used, I have resisted the urge to call my Foggy Bottom planting 'The River of Blood'!

Foggy Bottom Henge

"It's nice to have space to create interesting and seasonally dramatic designs in the garden ...but what relevance can they have in my small garden?" – this is the sort of question some might pose after visiting larger gardens like Foggy Bottom. The more positive view is, "What can I learn that might be helpful to me?". Answering, I would say firstly, enjoy the visit. Secondly, make notes of some of the plants you see and like that might fit into your garden, and thirdly, ask yourself, "What am I seeing?".

You are looking at a view of Foggy Bottom Henge, with vertical oak posts hewn from a storm-felled oak in our woodland, serving as a see-through perimeter to this planting. Even such a small, implied barrier produces an inclusive feel to this area, rather than a mere section of the whole bed. Although lesser known than its celebrity sister (or mother?) *Geranium* 'Rozanne', *G.* 'Azure Rush' is similar in its impact and long flowering period. Slightly paler in colour and lower growing, it is equally vigorous, making a carpet of blue flowers until autumn frosts. The waving bronze-leaved grasses are *Chionochloa rubra*, a native of New Zealand, which drift into the further side of the All Seasons Bed, connecting the distant planting. Right of the foreground is the mounded *Hydrangea paniculata* 'Bombshell'.

The devil is in the detail, and it helps to have the ability to walk into the bed to take a closer look. A cool, still morning has brought in a damp, misty start to the day and once again, it's the weather conditions that help create magic in the garden. Foreground plants such as *Agapanthus* 'Loch Hope' would take all the attention if they were in focus but add to this 'peeking through' effect. The attention goes directly to the shiny long stems of the grass, *Chionochloa rubra*, a few crimson flowers on *Rosa* 'Knock Out' hidden behind the dull green needled *Pinus mugo* 'Ophir'. Here is the magic that happens only late in the summer and early autumn… the spun silk of spiders' webs, whose traps are set for insects that will be flying around later in the day. Right now, we can enjoy the results of their industry.

Plants and Combinations

This warm, well-drained spot in front of *Pinus mugo* 'Ophir' is ideal for this combination of plants. To the left, the pink flat-headed flowers of the golden-leaved *Spiraea japonica* 'Magic Carpet', next to the cobalt blue stems of *Eryngium* × *zabelii* 'Big Blue', topped with similarly coloured thistly bracts. The subdued silvery grey, woolly foliage of *Stachys byzantina* 'Big Ears', right, completes the planned planting scheme, but an open space has allowed a pinkish-white seedling of *Astrantia* to insert its presence. A case where despite the name 'Big' attached to two of the plants, this is an association that could suit a small garden too.

↑

A late summer medley of pastel shrubs and conifers is connected by the crimson river of Japanese blood grass, *Imperata cylindrica* 'Rubra', flowing through the centre of the All Seasons Bed. The slightly blurred subjects give this scene a painterly look (or is that just my observation?). The narrow pyramidal conifer showing patches of foliage reverting to green is *Picea glauca* 'Alberta Blue'. *Cotinus coggygria* 'Golden Spirit' is highlighted in the distance from white and pink-tinged *Hydrangea paniculata* forms.

I don't care for the name much, even though it might be → memorable, but *Hydrangea paniculata* 'Pinky Winky' is one of an increasing range of late flowering, shrubby *Hydrangeas*. Its imposing flowerheads transform from white to pink, to a deep glowing crimson in autumn. The great thing is that they are hardy and flower on new seasons' growth. So, if you prune branches back in late winter, plants will be in flower soon after midsummer. Here is an example of 'Pinky Winky' in the All Seasons Bed taken in August, with pink bracts showing on older flowers, and the same plant six weeks later at the end of September. Best position in sun or half shade, where not too dry.

You don't often see them in the daytime, but it's obvious that web making spiders also appreciate conifers, seemingly able to 'fly' or jump from one conifer to another. All the better to catch something during the day but leaving their silken activity to be enjoyed on a dewy early morning in autumn. This is where my priority isn't to name the conifer varieties for you.

Few would be able to identify the round-topped pine as *Pinus koraiensis* 'Winton', since from this position, it is only the outline against the early morning sun rising in the east which can be seen. Of course, the conifer name hardly matters, but the fact that I have pruned away the lower branches – the lifted canopy is the reason that this view is revealed. I was almost at ground level looking up to get this dramatic moment in the All Seasons Bed on a bright Christmas morning. This time of year, and over several months in winter, the sun in low light, snow, frost and mist add immeasurably to this often dull season, when more static and dormant landscapes are the norm.

↑

Is this the winter wow factor for real? A conifer? Well, it was exactly that feeling that came to me as I excitedly set up the camera. In my experience, *Pinus mugo* 'Dezember Gold' (raised in Germany) is the brightest yellow in winter of any of the remarkable mugo pines, closely followed by *P. m.* 'Carsten'. Brightest colour will occur to plants during cold winter weather when positioned in full sun. It's amazing that these bright yellow needles will be green in a few months' time. The conifer behind is *P. contorta* 'Frisian Gold', whose needles are shades of yellow all year. The tips may get scorched by freezing winds, frost in winter and hot sun in summer, so place carefully. Lastly, note the bare twigged shrub on the left, between the two conifers. It is *Magnolia stellata* 'Jane Platt' and will be shown in flower in just over a couple of months' time. Every plant should be given a chance to shine.

At about the same time as I took the previous photograph, elsewhere in the All Seasons Bed the snowdrop *Galanthus* 'S. Arnott' was at its peak in full flower. This superb snowdrop is a big feature in many places and situations in Foggy Bottom, and here robust multi-stemmed clumps with pure white, green-tipped flowers contrast with the deep purple winter flowering heather, *Erica* × *darleyensis* 'Kramer's Rote'. →

After fragrant winter flowering shrubs such as *Hamamelis*, *Viburnum*, *Chimonanthus*, *Lonicera*, *Sarcococca* and *Daphne* have flowered, along come the *Magnolias* – most with outstanding flowers on bare stems. Fingers crossed that there is no spring frost to singe the unfolding double pink flowers of *Magnolia stellata* 'Jane Platt' here in the All Seasons Bed. Behind is *Acer palmatum* 'Shishi-gashira', the emerging yellow-orange leaves lit by the rising sun, disconcertingly sparkling as though threads of gold.

And then there was one... this single specimen of *Erica erigena* f. *alba* 'W.T. Rackliff', shown in late spring, is about forty years old. Though a member of a species which used to be under the name *Erica mediterranea*, it is considered on the borderline of hardiness in our climate. It has, in a relatively sheltered position, survived harsh winters and sometimes very wet conditions. Now 1.5 m (5 ft) high with only an occasional light pruning, you can hardly see a space without flowers and as soon as the sun warms the day the bees will find it. Summer foliage is a rich green.

The Sad Bed

For a bed with a name like this, there must be an explanation. Always looking at the quirky side, I called this the 'Sad Bed' since all the plants in it are weeping (did I hear a groan?). The name has stuck, and I'm only occasionally asked why. There are two main pendulous plants which dominate the bed; a beech, *Fagus sylvatica* 'Purpurea Pendula', and blue cedar, *Cedrus atlantica* 'Glauca Pendula'. As with all parts of Foggy Bottom, this area has changed considerably over many years. Today, the Sad Bed starts just opposite the All Seasons Bed and heads north to opposite Crossways Corner. Like most island beds it can be viewed from many different angles, encompassing a woodland to the west and a broad grass pathway on the eastern side, which only gets the sun in the morning and early afternoon. The soil is good fertile loam above a sandy base, well-drained, but due to its position and tree roots it does dry out.

Apart from creating some interesting plantings, this pathway forms the longest view in the garden, from an oak bench close to the house, all the way to Matt's summer house – about 200 m in total. When you create a long vista, you need some highlights along the way. At the halfway point, Crossways Corner stands boldly in the middle, often in the foreground when looking south or in the background when looking north.

"We can't think of enough adjectives to describe this wonderful place! Fantastic, beautiful, idyllic. Simply the best."

Stark and sharp in winter, this shows the weeping blue cedar and close to it on the right, the tight weeping habit of the beech. Left foreground is the deciduous *Cotoneaster horizontalis* 'Variegatus', hummocks of blue fescue, *Festuca glauca*, and to the right, still from the autumn, the erect plumes of *Cortaderia selloana* 'Pumila'. At this time of year, the mix of shrubs and trees add an interesting backdrop. The prime attraction is the white-stemmed *Betula utilis* var. *jacquemontii*. To the right, the foliage tips of a variegated *Elaeagnus*, a trunk of a leaning American oak, *Quercus rubra*, and the large deep evergreen bush *Prunus laurocerasus* 'Magnoliifolia'.

Cedrus atlantica 'Glauca Pendula' is no ordinary conifer, as you might gather seeing it here in Foggy Bottom. But it should be said that it also needs human intervention if it is to become a notable and attractive garden plant. Introduced around 1900, it is a pendulous form of the massive and erect blue Atlas cedar, *Cedrus atlantica* 'Glauca', from the Atlas Mountains in Morocco. Without pruning or training, this would make a sprawling, ungainly plant with seemingly no purpose in life except to exist. Train it up a post or over an arch and let it cascade naturally. Pruning in early years will create more shoots and improve density. The main plant spreading widely here is between the two trees, but I planted another in a drier position to the left, which has now joined up to make an impressive curtain of foliage. A living, growing statue, still at liberty, but needs help to keep in shape. But how to make the most of it?

All trees have a past to reveal and here is our Sad Bed cedar being moved with the help of some nursery staff in 1994. I was doing my best by holding the tree up to prevent branches from being broken. Our weeping cedar survived – and thrived.

Now in late spring, with new growth on all plants and more intense blue shoots on the cedar, this area is now transformed. Purple *Aquilegia*, a different purple *Allium* and purple-leaved *Heuchera* form a line to the weeping purple beech, *Fagus sylvatica* 'Purpurea Pendula'. The background will take a back seat for some months as the show goes on.

Papaver orientale 'Patty's Plum' has been in this well-drained position for years and makes a striking combination with *Heuchera* 'Prince' and *Allium hollandicum* 'Purple Sensation' nearby.

The static blue-grey foliage of the cedar is there to be shown off, and what better than to combine it with an orange eruption of one of Alan Bloom's and Percy Piper's best *Crocosmias*, *C.* 'Spitfire'. This perennial will not overcrowd the foliage of the cedar and will die back naturally. In Bressingham, England in 1966, *C.* 'Lucifer' was introduced at the same time as *C.* 'Spitfire'; though almost as vibrant, *C.* 'Spitfire' reaches half the height at 60 cm (2 ft).

A full-frontal view of the two plants of *Cedrus atlantica* 'Glauca Pendula', set off by *Crocosmias* and *Agapanthus*. The bright yellow leaves of *Cornus sericea* subsp. *occidentalis* 'Sunshine' unsuccessfully trying to hide in the background. Compare this with the first photograph of the Sad Bed in winter.

↑
Late in summer and close to the Crossways Corner planting, the pampas grasses are about to have their moment of glory as they come into flower. Here in early September, as the sun's rays filter through the trees, an established clump of *Cortaderia selloana* 'Pumila' pushes up strong stems and starts to open its silver-white plumes.

Over two months later, the *Cortaderia* plumes are fully open and play a significant role in this combination. Stems still erect with plumes of fluffy off-white, the grass is distinctly different to the rounded forms of the bright crimson *Berberis*, copper-purple beech, and metallic blue cedar. →

Another, much larger, perspective from the north of the Sad Bed with the pampas grass starkly contrasting with red, orange, and bronze foliage of deciduous trees in Foggy Bottom. The taller, clearer, white-plumed cultivar is *Cortaderia selloana* 'Sunningdale Silver'; more spectacular than the shorter, denser-plumed *Cortaderia selloana* 'Pumila'. These plants have been in situ for over forty years and were, over time, getting drawn into the shade from nearby fast growing conifers; with whom they were competing for moisture and gradually losing out. Drastic, but necessary for other reasons, a large cedar and a blue spruce were cut down and removed. This soon offered a new lease of life for the *Cortaderias*, which have rewarded with an increasingly confident annual display.

"Truly wonderful and so peaceful. Thinking of my mum who loved this place too."

From Crossways Corner, a last overview of the Sad Bed in the distance shortly before leaf fall. Standout late colour comes from the crimson patch of *Berberis*, the pampas grass plumes, and the rich deep green mounds of *Pinus heldreichii* 'Smidtii' rising above the wavy pale-yellow foliage of *Hakonechloa macra* 'Albovariegata'. Winter is coming, to be much enjoyed in this garden.

Rhus Corner

Whilst our tour of Foggy Bottom began with distinct plantings, each area has a part to play in the six-acre garden, either as a focal point from different angles or as a seasonal change or attraction. Each area has its own aspect and its own type of soil in which plants suited to it thrive, and those tried and less successful obviously haven't.

Aspect and Soil

South-facing, but also open to the east and west at the front, Rhus Corner stands like a promontory edging into the lawn. Slightly raised, it is generally well-drained, medium alluvial soil above sand – one of the best areas to plant sun-loving plants. Like many other parts of Foggy Bottom, the planting has evolved. Many plants – particularly conifers, but also trees – have gone, and other woody plants put in as part of the design. This large bed is an island and includes Crossways Corner at the northern end and the Book Bed adjoining Rhus Corner, divided by split rail fencing.

Rhus Corner doesn't sound tremendously interesting, let alone inspiring, but let me take you through the seasons and see if you can understand why it has become one of my favourite plantings.

↑
Aptly named *Eryngium* × *zabelii* 'Big Blue', this is a stunning plant when in flower as both flowers and stems are deeply coloured. Behind are the spiked flowers of *Dictamnus fraxinella*.

The long view. In April it's time for spring, leaves are about to burst and plants surge into growth. All is cut back as necessary and ready to go. But still at the lower end of Foggy Bottom, next to the pond, we are in a bit of a 'frost pocket'. South of the pond, we are given a sharp, clear view towards the Snake Bed and across to Rhus Corner, small hummocks of *Stipa tenuissima* clearly visible in the distant right. This is a view where you can get a sense of the structured conifers and trees which are the bones of the garden and providers of year-round interest. Were it not for these, we would have a flat open meadow, or perhaps plantings of cut back perennials and grasses waiting for a new season to start.

On what promises to be a sunny spring day, we are looking at one of the main views of Rhus Corner. Few early spring or winter interest plants display, except a few clumps of *Primula* near the dark green *Pinus thunbergii* 'Sayonara' in the foreground. There could certainly be more spring bulbs, but there is also some benefit in anticipation now, with the *Stipa tenuissima* cut back and weeding done, all we are waiting for is the warmth of the sun. →

Just over a month later, growth is very evident (as should be expected). Note on the right at the front of the bed, an older plant of *Stipa tenuissima* is rather sparsely clothed in green stems, whilst younger seedlings to the left are fully green and starting to form inflorescences. In between the *Stipa* are early flowering perennials, foxgloves, *Digitalis purpurea* 'Alba', oriental poppies, *Papaver orientale*, and spiky stems of soft blue *Nepeta*. In contrast is the bronze-purple foliage of *Physocarpus opulifolius* 'Diabolo', its arching branches in full flower. The other shrubs on the left providing structure and height are yet to shine, *Euonymus alatus* 'Compactus' and the always late to shoot *Cotinus coggygria* 'Young Lady'. Prepare to be amazed!
↓

Still time to plant!

Whilst the right side of Rhus Corner is well established, a large *Buddleja* has been replaced, in part, by a slow growing Japanese pine, *Pinus thunbergii* 'Sayonara'. Although this is midsummer, there's still time to put some plants in. Firstly, the creeping thistle in the planting area which has become established needs to be dug up carefully by hand. The creeping thistle, in the black pot, has been dug out with a fork, following the roots to (hopefully) get all of them out. The pine will need some dwarf plants around it so that it will not be swamped or hidden.

Festuca glauca, dwarf *Agapanthus* and *Hylotelephium* are plants to fill these gaps, looking reasonably natural and with a long period of interest. Watering plants in thoroughly then mulching with composted bark helps plants get off to a good start.

There are a few new weeds among the *Stachys byzantina* 'Big Ears', but the purple-leaved *Hylotelephium telephium* 'Xenox' has made up well in two months and is already in flower. The *Festuca* will take longer, but you can see how much the planting has highlighted *Pinus thunbergii* 'Sayonara' and created a foreground contrast to the *Agapanthus* 'Loch Hope' behind.

Rhus Corner from this viewpoint is set against another feature in the background, the All Seasons Bed; unseen is the broad grass path that divides them. In front, *Stipa tenuissima* creates a dramatic carpet of green topped by wispy beige inflorescences. The background continues to be an integral feature of this planting as we go through the seasons, so from left to right, here are some of the main plants. The birch, *Betula davurica*, is hardly silver but a slow growing species from Siberia which has attractively peeling bark. The narrow pillar-like conifer is a seedling of *Pinus sylvestris* which arose by chance in Foggy Bottom, named *Pinus sylvestris* 'Foggy Bottom Pillar', the other larger round-shaped pine is

a forty-year-old *Pinus koraiensis* 'Winton'. Standing out amongst the greens is a golden-leaved dawn redwood, *Metasequoia glyptostroboides* 'Gold Rush', striking and one of the few deciduous conifers. Lastly, notice the *Cotinus* in the right foreground ready to soon amaze.

The fluffy plumes of emerging *Stipa tenuissima* provide an attractive foil in early midsummer to colourful seedlings of the oriental poppy, *Papaver orientale*, a single foxglove, *Nepeta* and *Geranium*. As they die back, other 'hidden' plants will emerge.

An image taken on the same day from the east aspect of Rhus Corner shows how the two narrow erect Japanese pines, *Pinus nigra* 'Green Tower', serve as a focal point and backdrop to plantings in front. From this viewpoint, they also frame a view into the garden beyond. The striking early summer display of *Geranium* 'Eureka Blue' in the foreground is carpeted against the green blade-like leaves of *Crocosmia* 'Lucifer', and beyond, the grass *Stipa tenuissima*.

To get the best images, you often must be prepared to get up early on a summer's morning when you know it's supposed to be a nice day. Cool damp evenings can often be followed by morning mist and fog. As the sun comes up on a June morning, a scene like this on Rhus Corner is as dramatic as it comes. We'll see it again and again how much the light affects the appearance of our plants. Each wisp-like head of *Stipa tenuissima* bears tiny droplets of water weighing down on the arching inflorescences, some sparkling in the slanted early sunlight. It reminds me of frothy ocean spray as a wave breaks onto the shore, but in this, as with many other cases in a garden, an atmospheric image can portray a mood much better than any attempted flowery words!

Wreaths of delicate *Stipa tenuissima* surround this clump of a bright yellow succulent, the hardy *Sedum aizoon* 'Euphorbioides', whose crimson stems can hardly be seen. It is a striking summer flowering *Sedum* which needs careful placing, but can also seed around and is easily removed if not wanted. →

↑

Spot the *Pinus nigra* 'Green Tower' in the background left of *Cotinus coggygria* 'Young Lady', itself now in full bloom. The wavy, wispy *Stipa* now fully forms the carpet through which other perennials can shine. Silvery grey-leaved *Stachys byzantina* 'Big Ears' fronts the overlapping cut leaves of *Acanthus* 'Hollande du Nort', its early summer spikes showing above the foliage. Glimpsed to the right is *Rhus typhina* 'Tiger Eyes', a golden-leaved form of the sometimes invasive North American native.

↑

White on white. In early summer, *Campanula lactiflora* 'Avalanche' rises through filigree strands of *Stipa tenuissima*, linking with the early flowers of the enormous bushy perennial *Persicaria polymorpha*. The latter can reach 2.4 m (8 ft) and is not spreading or invasive. The species originates from the Himalayas and is a recent introduction to our gardens. Large, pointed leafy foliage makes quick growth in early summer and has successive spikes of white flowers for weeks. Recommended, but probably not for the smaller garden.

The imposing spikes of *Acanthus* 'Hollande du Nort' with finely cut mid-green leaves, stiffly erect stems and distinctive flowers and bracts. The white flowers are almost outdone by their protective maroon bract, creating an extraordinary effect as 1.2 m (3 ft) stems rise above the *Stipa tenuissima*, flowers continuing for most of the summer.

← The most commonly used smoke bushes are usually those with purple foliage, offering colour, contrast and a long season of interest. They are perhaps not so reliable in producing an annual display as this selection, *Cotinus coggygria* 'Young Lady'. It has fresh green foliage and both surprises and delights when flowers open to frothy heads of pinkish white, lasting for some weeks. Like the *Stipa tenuissima* around it, it can be highlighted by other contrasting plants such as the vibrant *Crocosmia* 'Vulcan', itself fronted by the lilac-blue *Nepeta racemosa* 'Walker's Low' – all about to be lit by the early morning sun.

Take a close look at the candyfloss heads of this remarkable smoke bush and you can see why the name seems applicable. The fine, down-covered filaments make a fluffy ball, reminiscent of a puff of smoke. *Cotinus* are best placed in full sun and tend to flower on the previous year's growth, so hard pruning is not advised. This is where, for most gardeners, a dwarf form like 'Young Lady' is preferable since it is slow growing enough to seldom need spring pruning.

White is the linking colour between the All Seasons Bed (foreground), Rhus Corner (centre) and the Snake Bed (behind). *Agapanthus* 'Bressingham White' with its angled spreading stems and white flowers is matched by the same plant across the pathway. Daisy-like flowers of *Leucanthemum maximum* 'Flying Saucers' are to the left and earlier *Campanula lactiflora* 'Avalanche' provided a link to the large bold *Persicaria polymorpha* in the Snake Bed behind. *Buddleja davidii* 'Butterfly Heaven' shows dying flower heads as well as new ones, intensely fragrant and beloved by bees (and yes, butterflies).

One of the best *Agapanthus* for a long late summer and early autumn display must be 'Loch Hope'. Strange that a distinctly South African plant should be named after a lake in Scotland. Here you can see how striking a plant this is on Rhus Corner, the tall, angled stems bearing large heads of small deep blue flowers, dominating the planting. A good fertile soil in a sunny spot that doesn't get too dry is ideal. Hardy to Zone 7 in North America, this has thrived after thirty winters with no protection in Foggy Bottom.

In the foreground of Rhus Corner is a broad patch of the sun loving *Stachys byzantina* 'Big Ears'. Far in the background is the eastern edge of the garden and the Gap Meadow beyond.

Whilst the *Stipa* loses its height of summer glory, it still serves a purpose as an attractive ground cover. Now into early autumn, the golden-leaved *Rhus typhina* 'Tiger Eyes' makes a central foil to the taller pale blue *Symphyotrichum* 'Little Carlow', and the deeper blue heads of *Agapanthus* 'Loch Hope'. Behind is the early changing leaf colour on *Euonymus alatus* 'Compactus'.

← Autumn shows a balance of attraction between late flowers, dead flowerheads, and evergreen and deciduous foliage. The star of this show is *Euonymus alatus* 'Compactus', where rather dull green foliage has turned to a glorious short-lived display of glowing scarlet. Dead heads of *Agapanthus* and *Acanthus* are offset by the clear blue flowers of *Symphyotrichum* 'Little Carlow'. In front of the dark green *Pinus thunbergii* 'Sayonara' is *Hylotelephium telephium* 'Xenox' and a silver-grey carpet of *Stachys byzantina* 'Big Ears'.

Approaching October, colours are definitely changing. In Foggy Bottom, the first birch to change colour and for leaves to fall is *Betula davurica*, shown on the left. Conifers of various shapes and forms in the All Seasons Bed are behind as the eye is drawn to *Euonymus alatus* 'Compactus' and *Cotinus* 'Grace' on the right.

↓

↑

Leaves are falling off all over and already in early November the *Betula davurica* is without leaves. Instead, you can see the intricate branching system and grey peeling bark. In the background, a variegated tulip tree, *Liriodendron tulipifera* 'Aureomarginatum', shows clear gold. The structure of conifers will soon be the most visible side of the garden as autumn leads into winter.

Capturing the moment is always important whether it be → humans, animals, insects or plants – and with the latter, the weather. *Cotinus* 'Grace' is a vigorous shrub, making erect but somewhat unstable shoots in summer clothed in large maroon leaves. The young growth holds onto its leaves well into autumn as days shorten and light is an increasingly valuable commodity. With the camera pointed to a somewhat bright but shrouded sky, the *Cotinus* is captured!

↑

Often in midwinter, before snowfall and hopefully few gales or hurricanes, grasses can be brought to dramatic life again by a hoar frost such as this. The view looks across Rhus Corner, the *Stipa tenuissima* still effective in covering the ground and frost highlights a clump of *Miscanthus sinensis* 'Ferner Osten' in the foreground. Taller cultivars can be seen in the Snake Bed beyond, behind which are the rounded heads of *Eupatorium maculatum* 'Gateway'.

↑

Frost helps to dramatise views, plantings and close-up portraits of plants. Even if relatively brief, the contrast between the wispy *Stipa tenuissima* and the green-yellow stems of *Agapanthus* 'Loch Hope' forms an arresting picture.

↑
The midwinter view shows only some foliage of grasses and perennials beneath the snow in Rhus Corner. In a month or two it will be time to cut them back, but in the meantime the various shapes, sizes and colours of the conifers provide structure and interest. You can just about spot in the All Seasons Bed beyond, the golden mound of *Pinus mugo* 'Ophir' which turns from green to a bright gold in winter. Now that does seem miraculous, doesn't it?

01
07

The Pond

Midwinter, but no frost or snow – the occurrence of which seems to be becoming a rarity in England. Though you might glimpse the flash of white from distant snowdrops at the top of this scene, you may be as amazed as I was at the clarity of the reflection of trees near the pond. This picture is all about 'knees'. Look at the island and close to the edge are some knobbly-looking aerial roots belonging to the swamp cypress, *Taxodium distichum*. I have been watching these slowly growing over some years and am delighted at how natural they appear as they do in the wild in southeast North America, from Florida to Virginia.

A large garden needs a feature like a pond, or at least that is what I felt from the beginning as I developed the Foggy Bottom Garden from 1967. Explained in more detail later in the book, a natural pond was not practical. So, I had to find a way to create a pond, situating it at the lower (but not by much) southern end of the garden and furthest from our home. This was in 1978, twelve years after Rosemary and I moved in.

Ironically, this lower end, probably only a metre lower than our newly built home, could often flood in winter when the water table was high. Even dug to a depth of 1.2 m (4 ft), it dried out completely the following summer. Despite me marking out an awkward shape, the contractors managed to cleverly merge sheets of butyl liner to place on the sunken dry bed of the large indentation, dug earlier with a large digger. It took some time to fill with water, but the pond, looking somewhat incongruous, was now part of the garden. Some images of this development can be seen on p.322.

We can now fast forward to the present day and look at what the pond has added to Foggy Bottom, and how it has become an integral part of the six-acre garden. So integral, that it is come by as a surprise to most visitors, who are not able to view it from the entrance nor for most of the year, until they are within twenty metres. As with each feature we are highlighting, none of them are planned to entirely stand alone… one area blends and connects with others and views are shared. This is not a garden of 'rooms' or a series of separate gardens, but planned as an informal, natural-looking space where views and vistas encourage the visitor to explore features glimpsed in the distance. Once there, other views open up. And if we've done our job right, there will be close-up combinations and individual plants that make it happen.

Positioning The Foggy Bottom Pond

By referring to our map you can see where the pond is situated, on the south side of the Foggy Bottom Garden. Looking north is the maturing garden created from an open meadow. The following images will gradually bring you into the planting around the pond and the magic that water can create. Peace, wildlife, seasonal reflection and drama.

Gardener turns to photographer, getting up early on a spring morning to capture a moment before the sun fully floods into the garden. The water in the pond is, for a while, warmer than the air after a brief ground frost, leading to a faint rising mist above the surface. The freshness of spring still shows in the new leaves and emerging growth. Foreground reflections are balanced by forms above ground and the distant giant redwoods, *Sequoiadendron giganteum*, can be seen faintly above it all.

"Beautiful — almost beyond words. You are closer to God in a garden than anywhere else on Earth!"

A view from the summer house in summer shows the long vista with the pond on the right, the water surface mostly hidden by the rush-like *Carex pendula*. Behind foreground vegetation, the outlines of trees and shrubs in the All Seasons Bed can be seen, including the tall golden dawn cypress, *Metasequoia glyptostroboides* 'Gold Rush'. Taller conifers are visible in the background.

As the seasons change, so do the plants around the pond. Now clearly reflecting an autumnal atmosphere, the water is like a mirror offering a double bonus above and below the water line with *Cornus sanguinea* 'Midwinter Fire' on the island and *C. s.* 'Green Light' almost hiding the summer house behind. The rusty-coloured leaves above *C. s.* 'Midwinter Fire' belong to the swamp cypress, *Taxodium distichum*. Both *Cornus* had been pruned the previous spring.

A simple wooden bridge becomes something special when given a slightly more rounded shape. From here, the visitor can look down and across the pond. We are looking at the bridge in autumn from beneath the swamp cypress, *Taxodium distichum*, catching a glimpse of the main area of water beyond. As part of developing Rosemary's Wood, we created a smaller pond, shown in the foreground, and inserted a leak proof membrane; the sides built with old railway sleepers. This is the feeding pond, kept at a slightly higher level to provide a constant recycling of water. We are not quite there yet, but like many things, it is 'in our programme'.

Mid-November, the first frosts have already brought down some autumn leaves on several trees including the river birch in the foreground and the golden-leaved *Alnus glutinosa* on the left. Beyond the pond surface is the Snake Bed which includes many ornamental grasses, mostly *Miscanthus sinensis* cultivars, which stand out alongside the fluffy flowerheads of a Joe-Pye weed, *Eupatorium maculatum* 'Gateway'. Beside the pond, to the right, is the bamboo-like *Arundo donax*, the blue leaves retaining their colour a little longer. What draws the eye is the hint of sunlight on distant trees, reflecting autumnal leaf hues before they too fall to the ground.

This view approaching the pond from the east shows the woodland path entering Rosemary's Wood on the left, the decking and bridge in the centre, and the pond and summer house beyond. What may not be noticed are the young silver birch arranged in a circle on the frosted grass, and logs laid on the ground near them. The logs are the remains of a large birch, *Betula nigra* 'Heritage', which gradually died and had to be removed. I replaced them with another form of American native birch, *Betula papyrifera* 'Saint George'. These should make a strong feature in this part of the garden with white bark all year, good autumn colour and a delicate tracery of branches and twigs in winter.

The Bigger Picture

The Foggy Bottom pond is just a man-made body of water. As a statement this is not incorrect, but of course to us as individuals and to the garden, it is so much more. Beauty, romance, movement; it has the capacity to evoke mood, both from visual and atmospheric reaction. Here, we see seasonal changes, taking in wide vistas.

Although there is much gardening to be done, it would be a pity not to enjoy and be inspired by first walking around the garden on a clear day in spring, the light sharp and the air crisp after a cool night. This is where a camera enables you to capture special moments that can be re-visited time and again (if we make the time). Catkins hang on the birch and the alders, the deciduous swamp cypress, *Taxodium distichum*, displays an intricacy of seemingly tangled branches on the island. All of the perennials and grasses are cut back in the Snake Bed, now for a short time, allowing a view to evergreens beyond. Spot the forty-year-old specimen of the white-flowered *Erica erigena* f. *alba* 'W.T. Rackliff' in front of a golden conifer.

For a gardener, snow can be quite a nuisance, but in most of the UK, we get it so seldom. When we do, it generally only stays for a few days, so it is best to enjoy what it offers. Enjoy the tranquillity that happens as snow lands on all plants in the garden, framing branches of trees and shrubs, and clothing the ground with a homogenous white blanket. In this morning scene, look at the decking and the bridge as the sun's rays strike the handrails. Across the semi-frozen pond are the snow laden rails of a more rustic fence and the eye, as so often, follows upwards to the majestic giant redwoods in the nearby Adrian's Wood.

Reflecting On Reflections

As it grows and develops, the possibilities of a garden grow with it. Of course, I have been very fortunate to have had the opportunity to create a six-acre garden, to which later the pond was added. Did I foresee the drama that our stretch of water could eventually provide? The water, the trees, the reflections and how big a part light could play? The sun blocked and dispersed by a pine tree? That I might be out early one morning with my digital camera to capture a moment? Not specifically yes, to any of those questions, but I felt some awe and emotion created by all these factors outside of my control. Now, in a photograph, I can look at the detail and reflect on the reflections.

Exochorda × *macrantha* 'The Bride' is seldom noticed in the garden until it erupts into flower in spring. Though pruned, this specimen has been in its present position in Foggy Bottom for many years and becomes a dramatic focal point from distant views in the garden. Whilst the golden twigged willow, *Salix alba* 'Hutchinson's Yellow', on the left is in full growth, to the right on the pond's edge, the *Nyssa sylvatica* 'Pendula' is yet to come into leaf – this leaves a worthy *Exochorda* to take centre stage. Although ten metres from the water, 'The Bride' and *Pinus flexilis* 'Vanderwolf's Pyramid' behind seem to have a clearer presence under water than above.

↑
The bridge over very calm water on a spring morning in Foggy Bottom. There is almost more interest and clarity in the water's reflection than the real bridge above. The sun's glare in the distance is masked by the bridge and the bright green spring foliage in the water is more vivid and intricately dappled. A Monet bridge and a work of art it is not, but as a feature it fits the garden very well. As seen in other images, it is enhanced by being part of a seamless path to the decking. The clump of bronzed leaves to the right of the bridge belong to *Rodgersia podophylla*.

Prone to scorch in the sun, *Fagus sylvatica* 'Aurea Pendula' →
must be placed carefully. It needs to be shaded from full sun but exposed enough to catch the light in the morning or at the end of the day. Although it will eventually become a large tree, it can be regularly pruned to smaller proportions. In this spot, it makes a stunning and graceful specimen, now perhaps thirty years old and big enough to have its own reflection in the nearby pond.

Darmera peltata flowering in spring with golden flowered kingcup, *Caltha palustris*, at the pond's edge.

By the waterside, when the water is clear and still, a reflection can give you double value. A large-leaved waterside plant such as *Darmera peltata* (formerly *Peltiphyllum peltatum*), makes a showy subject with its leaves in various stages of decay, a patchwork of autumnal hues. Its creeping stubby rhizomes and sparse spring flowers on 60–75 cm (2 ft 6 in) stems, the *Darmera* seems almost pre-historic.

We are always pleased to see wild mallard ducks land on our pond in late winter, and even more delighted when they start to nest on our ready-made island. The Canada geese outrank the ducks, if only in size, but they can be aggressive too and usually force the ducks to nest elsewhere. Nonetheless, the geese are not unattractive and, as is mostly the case, there are only two of them. They are relatively unobtrusive, particularly as the female is tied to sitting on her eggs for some weeks, hidden behind a *Cornus*. Here is the male distancing himself from the camera, whilst maintaining a watchful eye for his partner. The caption for this reflection of 'Double Goose' doesn't have quite the same ring that 'Double Duck' might have had…

Some Plants from Around the Pond

Osmunda regalis 'Purpurascens' is a fine and vigorous form of the royal fern, which loves its spot near the pond where I planted it years ago. The multitude of purple-tinged fronds could be likened to a nest of snakes struggling for air! There is no doubt that this quickly emerging spring growth is dramatic, and in summer, the fern becomes a fully-fledged imposing plant with lighter green fronds reaching 150 cm (5 ft) in moist conditions. Though perfect as a waterside plant, it is also suitable in other areas of the garden which are not too dry.

Strong contrast is provided from two very different plants. Undoubtedly, the bronze, finely ribbed and crinkled leaves of *Rodgersia podophylla*, broad and spreading, take the eye. The golden-leaved form of one of our native European sedges, *Carex elata*, was found by chance in the Norfolk Broads in England by plantsman Edward Augustus Bowles. The correct botanical name is *Carex elata* 'Aurea', though to Bowles it was (and still is) commonly known as Bowles's golden sedge. This is a plant that, in shade where not too dry or beside the water, cannot be missed for its bright yellow foliage in spring, contrasting with slender spikes of deep chocolate brown flowers in early summer.

← Between the decked pathway and the pond, we planted a mix of moisture-loving perennials with the aim to provide a long season of appeal. Here shown in late summer, foliage is as important as flower. It helps to have an interesting background, and in front of the green-leaved woodland is the lichen-covered summer house roof and the graceful weeping golden beech, *Fagus sylvatica* 'Aurea Pendula'. In the foreground, the showy coneflower, *Rudbeckia fulgida* var. *sullivantii* 'Goldsturm', contrasts the slightly tarnished, bronze-leaved *Rodgersia podophylla* and the large plate-sized, cupped leaves of *Darmera peltata* to the far right. The clump of outstanding black-purple foliage with long white bottlebrush flowers is *Actaea simplex* 'Brunette'. For those still looking to identify other plants, the blue-leaved *Hosta* left of centre is 'Krossa Regal', and the slow growing variegated shrub with congested foliage is the fine, if understated, dogwood, *Cornus alternifolia* 'Argentea'. Lastly, spotted beneath the dark green weeping *Picea breweriana* (top left) is the hummock-shaped *Berberis thunbergii* 'Aurea'.

Once again after a ground frost in autumn, the pond water is warmer than the early morning air, so the sun's rays filtering between the trees highlights the rising steam. The aerial roots of *Taxodium distichum* are protruding from the surface of the small island in the centre of the pond.
↓

This short and long view from the pond to the giant redwoods → was recorded on a typical English late autumn day with a long winter ahead. Another calendar year soon to close, but we will have sunny days, the leaves will turn and fall, the low sun will sharpen the visibility, frost will appear on the ground and foliage, and maybe snow on trees. The garden goes quiet. We don't have to be in it during inclement weather or worry about the work or the weeds. If the garden can chill, so can we, and we can prepare some great ideas and plans for another year. Well, perhaps I'll just clear those leaves…

Two weeks later, I recorded a much more positive picture as the morning sun made all the difference. Sunlight is a real boon in late autumn and positively creates a golden glow as it strikes the leaves of *Cornus sanguinea* 'Midwinter Fire' to the right of the bridge. The bark of the young birch tree reflects a brilliant white. The detail stands out in the shadier parts behind, including the summer house, and leaves are being gradually shed from the *Taxodium* near the bridge.

↓

The bench beside the pond looks rather lonely in the early morning November sunlight, but it has been occupied many times by visitors relaxing as they overlook the water. We too have seen the seasons change around the pond, though I rarely think of sitting down to enjoy the peace and tranquillity that this area of the garden offers. Perhaps... well almost certainly... I should.

The island was a challenge to the contractor who laid down the butyl liner back in 1978, but I wanted an island for the purpose of planting a swamp cypress, the distinctive North American native *Taxodium distichum*. It is not evident, but whilst the liner holds the water in the pond, it also cuts off the pond water from the now isolated roots of the *Taxodium*. It would be true to say "not many people know that" when visitors view the natural looking island, with hopefully very little of the black liner showing. The water table is normally high enough for the roots within to access moisture, but over a very long dry period in 2019, it was evident from the stressed look of the tree that it was not getting enough water. So, we had to run a water sprinkler beneath its canopy for two days. This image was taken in late autumn as leaves start to change from green to brown to bronze before falling to create a carpet below.

All the leaves have gone from the swamp cypress on the island, leaving bare branches to be silhouetted against the winter sky until new leaves appear in late spring. The opportunity to catch an image of snow settled on branches and twigs seldom happens, but now the full specimen of *Taxodium distichum* can be seen against a pale blue sky and the outline of the island defined by the snow at its base.

↑
The term 'the bare bones of winter' might apply to the foreground, the dormant perennials and woodland plants waiting for their turn to shine. But structure and colour show in distant conifers, particularly in the higher branches of the golden Scots pine, *Pinus sylvestris* 'Aurea' (centre), and the landmark giant redwoods towering in the distance. Snow, even such a thin covering as this, is lifted by the weak winter sun, and the decking and bridge too. I have skated on our pond, but it's certainly not thick enough to be safe this morning.

Here is a full picture of the pond, decking, bridge and distant summer house. A touch of ice on the pond with snowdrops nearly in full bloom. A varied collection of trees on the left form a backdrop to Rosemary's Wood, which is described in its own chapter. Just note the whiteness of the bark on the small silver birch, *Betula papyrifera* 'Saint George', and the trunk of a previous birch at its base. →

01
08

Rosemary's Wood

Matt Bloom created this natural looking spire from curved English oak, which was erected in memory of his mother. This was a wonderful tribute which Matt, a skilled timber framer, created (on behalf of himself and his brothers, Jason and Richard) as a memorial to complement the planting in Rosemary's Wood. It stands, now more weathered and less conspicuous, in a position formerly occupied by a giant North American silver maple, *Acer saccharinum*, which had shown signs of disease and had to be removed.

There was, and is, a well established wood at the southern end of Foggy Bottom, probably planted over 150 years ago. It used to be well maintained as a woodland for autumn pheasant shooting, its paths or 'drives' kept clear for the gentleman farmer and his family to walk on a summer evening. This was prior to my father purchasing the land belonging to the owner of Bressingham Hall in 1946. Now with established oak trees and scrubby willow, ash and alders, it is no place of beauty, but it still serves as a backdrop to the new woodland I planted from 1978, which only in recent years has become part of the Foggy Bottom Garden.

Foggy Bottom had started initially around the house we built in 1967. By 1974, I began to take in the empty meadow to the south, gradually marking out beds, arriving at the lower quarter in 1977. It needed a water feature… a pond rather than a grand lake, so this was dug out and we waited for it to fill up in its first winter – which it did. However, with no water holding lining, it promptly dried out almost completely the following summer. So, a digger dug out the soft sand which lay beneath a light alluvial soil, which allowed us to create a broad mounded bank to the south. This brought the soil level at least 45 cm (18 in) higher than the eventual pond water level and here, I planted a mixture of trees to eventually form the 'wood' for our woodland.

There was room initially to plant some *Rhododendrons*, ferns, and ground cover perennials like *Epimediums* between – and eventually beneath – the trees. Impressed by its bold display at Cambridge Botanic Garden, I was given some Bithynian squill, *Scilla bithynica*, and planted this in a moist shady spot in the wood. Earlier flowering and more compact than our native bluebell, *Hyacinthoides non-scripta*, this beautiful *Scilla* has made carpets of blue year after year and have

The evening sun bathes the west side of Rosemary's Wood in a soft light, highlighting the golden-leaved weeping beech, *Fagus sylvatica* 'Aurea Pendula', and the sparkling white stems of *Betula utilis* var. *jacquemontii* behind. Between the birch and the sturdy Hungarian oak I planted in 1978 is a cluster of pink and yellow *Rhododendrons*. Between them and the summer house, you can peer into the borrowed landscape of the older, established woodland behind. Late to come into leaf is *Betula nigra* (left), a typical river birch with rough fissured bark, and beyond is the decked pathway with a sign warning visitors 'Decking Slippery When Wet'.

spread to dramatic effect. Because she loved the bluebell and woodland such as it was, I had intended to develop this area and when finished, name it after my wife Rosemary. Sadly, she died after a short illness in May 2014, but hopefully would have been pleased at how the woodland garden, that bears her name, has developed. In the photographs, and seen by visitors to Foggy Bottom, is an oak spiral created by our son Matt, in memory of his mother.

Positioning Rosemary's Wood

Once again, looking at the Foggy Bottom map, you can't miss the pond… the only blue area of planned water in the garden. Immediately south of it is Rosemary's Wood, which now extends and includes the timber framed summer house, or as we sometimes say, 'The House That Matt Built'. The water, decking, bridge and summer house are all integral parts of this garden area, apart from the plants of course. The following images will take you through the wood, giving vistas out and views in, through all the seasons. And as I always hope, there will be some plants or ideas that might fit into your garden too.

As trees come into leaf we know summer can't be far away... but let's enjoy the spring for all that it can give. In this view along the main pathway in Rosemary's Wood, emerging foliage is new, allowing light to filter through, but soon the leaf cover will become dense. Back in 1978, along with bigger trees, I planted some Japanese maples. Some have not done well where it has become too dry, but the purple-leaved *Acer palmatum* 'Bloodgood', though not a perfect shape, helps immeasurably to create a more diverse and attractive woodland. We have already removed some trees to let more light in, but I wanted to add more summer light by using shrubs with coloured or variegated foliage. In shade, most yellow or golden foliage will turn to a darker colour, even to green. The *Physocarpus opulifolius* 'Angel Gold' on the left is an example of when maturing tree leaves reduce the light. Variegated shrubs and perennials with white foliage, rather than yellow, are more likely to keep their brightness.

It's all about the timing and the behaviour of plants… Even the weeping golden beech has its top branches spread so I could get it in the picture! It's late spring and we are looking toward the summer house, which with its roof covered in moss seems as though it might have been there forever… Matt built it only in 2000, the deep maroon-red *Rhododendron* beside it is already then twenty years old. The shrub amongst the perennials in the foreground, which may eventually make a small tree, is a dogwood of distinction with curled and delicately variegated leaves, *Cornus alternifolia* 'Argentea'. The moist bed around is planted with large-leaved *Rodgersia podophylla*, *Astilboides tabularis* (formerly *Rodgersia tabularis*), *Darmera peltata*, dark purple-leaved *Actaea simplex* 'Brunette', and pink flowers belonging to *Persicaria bistorta* 'Superbum'.

The Year-Round Bergenia

← As the water level after recent rains has led to flooding in the foreground of this early April view and the height of the pond beyond, the decking is not only a pleasing visual feature, but a necessary one. The snowdrops have finished flowering for another year and colour is provided by the large, intensely purple leaves of *Bergenia* 'Eroica', contrasting with a group of cheerful golden daffodils, *Narcissus* 'Tête-à-tête', and three young white-stemmed birch, *Betula papyrifera* 'Saint George'. Wet conditions in summer the year before led to the demise of a *Cornus controversa* 'Variegata' – the dead trunk and roots should have been removed. Well, you can't get round to everything…

← As the *Bergenia* 'Eroica' comes into flower, startling with its intensity of deep pink pendulous heads, it rises above the early spring foliage of a mixture of other plants. Foreground left are the silver marbled leaves of *Brunnera macrophylla* 'Mister Morse', an unusual white flowered form, but less striking than the more widely known bright blue of *B. m.* 'Jack Frost'. Nestled between the *Bergenia* are the emerging leaves of *Aconitum* and a hardy *Geranium*, *G. phaeum* 'Springtime', with variegated leaves.

Fast forward to autumn and a few, now green, *Bergenia* leaves can be seen beneath this strikingly bold *Aconitum carmichaelii* 'Foggy Bottom Blue', now the dominant foreground perennial on the edge of Rosemary's Wood. *Aconitum*, commonly known as monk's hood are poisonous (though as my father used to say, "only if eaten"), most gardeners would be happy just to judge them on their value as garden plants… →

Woodland Plants...

The good thing about a woodland garden is that it should look natural, therefore leaves and twigs can be left for authenticity! Evergreen sedges such as *Luzula sylvatica* 'Aurea' and *Carex morrowii* 'Variegata' (out of focus behind) will not have looked much different throughout the winter, but then when the new year arrives, up come the golden aconites, *Eranthis hyemalis*, and the snowdrops, *Galanthus* 'S. Arnott'.

Helleborus hybrids have come a long way in recent years. From very few, single flowered forms available to gardeners, now both single and double flowered forms are offered in garden centres in late winter and spring. Many offer *Helleborus orientalis* selections in a range of colours from black, purple, red, cream, yellow and green, as well as selections with marked and mottled flowers – these (almost) come true from seed. Some are more floriferous and vigorous, some are much weaker, but they are generally reliable plants for sun or shade where not too dry or wet. These three selections shown in Rosemary's Wood are all Harvington hybrids, a strain developed by Hugh Nunn at his nursery in Worcestershire, England.

If only the Virginian bluebell, *Mertensia virginica*, were as easy to please as our own native bluebell, *Hyacinthoides non-scripta*, which spreads quite rapidly in woodland where not too dry. These belong to different families, and both are valuable woodland plants, but whilst the native bluebell is spreading, even aggressive, the *Mertensia* comes from North America and is considered a choice plant which requires moist but well-drained soil. It rapidly comes into leaf and soon has clusters of exquisite blue flowers above soft blue-green leaves which, after flowering, die back almost as quickly as they emerged.

Around the base of a silver birch trunk is a medley of spring flowering and foliage plants. Despite being positioned in a shady woodland spot, which is normally quite dry in summer, *Scilla bithynica* is thriving, gradually spreading by root and seed. The evergreen *Pachysandra terminalis* is common and an excellent ground cover, even in very dry shade. Early wispy white flowers show above the foliage. In front, in this shady position *Luzula sylvatica* 'Aurea' still has soft yellow green leaves, which in sun would be much brighter. However, this golden-leaved form of the European native greater woodrush thrives in semi-shade and may scorch in too sunny a position.

↑

Carex morrowii 'Fisher's Form' is a more robust and clearly variegated selection of the similar *Carex morrowii* 'Variegata'. Both sedges make reliable evergreen ground cover and do surprisingly well in dry shade. It might look a little scruffy after winter, but this is still a great contrast to one of the earliest flowering lungworts, the cheery blue *Pulmonaria angustifolia* 'Azurea'. *Pulmonarias* generally prefer some moisture in the soil if they are to be long-lived.

↑

You might gather that I rather like *Luzula sylvatica* 'Aurea' since I feature it so often in Foggy Bottom, in combination with other contrasting perennials. In winter and very early spring, there is a dearth of colour in a woodland garden, so when such a colour breakthrough comes along, I like to experiment with some pleasing companion plants such as this deep blue flowered, green-leaved *Pulmonaria* 'Blue Ensign'. Are they equal partners? I suspect the *Luzula* might submerge the *Pulmonaria* in time, so best not to plant too close. Keep an eye open so that either can be moved to a new spot if necessary.

Another colourful, understated collection of woodland plants between the trunk of a forty-year-old Himalayan birch, *Betula utilis* var. *jacquemontii*, and the main pathway in Rosemary's Wood. Only planted three years earlier, the pale yellow-white flowers of the common primrose, *Primula vulgaris*, sit next to the deep blue flowered periwinkle, *Vinca minor* 'Bowles's Variety'. Rising above are the strikingly marbled leaves of *Arum italicum* 'Pictum' and to the right of the trunk, a wood anemone, *Anemone nemorosa*.

One of the first bulbous perennials to poke its rich green leaves above the soil, often in January, is *Leucojum aestivum* 'Gravetye Giant'. It flowers later in spring when leaves are nearly 60 cm (2 ft) tall. Deep rooted and adaptable to most – except very dry – soils, the hanging white bells invite close examination, their curving petals prettily marked with green. Here, the light catches the foliage and its almost luminous flowers.

This little known but charming spring flowering perennial, *Cardamine heptaphylla*, comes in various colours; lilac pink (as shown), deep purple and white. Some (mostly European) species are similar, *C. pentaphylla* and *C. enneaphylla*… and with previous botanical name changes (when I first started gardening, they were mostly under the generic name *Dentaria*), it is confusing, which probably hasn't helped their popularity. All prefer shade and some moisture, and since the plants are dormant for many months, they have the capacity to surprise us in spring – unless your plants are rigorously labelled!

Nature in action. From a bed of Hungarian oak leaves that fell last autumn, new shoots push their way into the daylight. The leaves act as an excellent mulch, keeping moisture in the soil and preventing annual weeds from growing. The sharper points of a blue-leaved *Hosta* 'Big Daddy' catch the light less than the golden-leaved lily of the valley, *Convallaria majalis* 'Mary Brooks'. Recently planted, it is hoped (and planned) that the *Convallaria* will spread to surround the clump forming large-leaved *Hosta*.

Discovered in Germany and formerly called *Brunnera macrophylla* 'Variegata' (which describes the plant well), this was later renamed 'Dawson's White' by an English plantsman named… Dawson. There's a story and an opinion behind this, but even if slightly variable, it is a plant that can light up a shady spot as seen here in Rosemary's Wood. The pretty blue forget-me-not flowers are a bonus in spring and the leaves are brightly variegated all summer.

Good ground cover plants that are happy in dry shade are few and far between. Not all can provide much in the way of flower, and some flowers, as with *Asarum europaeum,* are largely hidden from view beneath the leaves. But all that said, the heart-shaped leaves have a glossy sheen brought to life when sun filters onto them. As so often, the devil (and the beauty) is in the detail, here shown in their leaf form which is cupped and the surface faintly lined or marbled. Almost fully evergreen and spreading where happy, you are permitted to search for the unusual flowers found beneath the leaves in spring.

The common name barrenwort as *Epimediums* are known seems hardly a compliment to this group of wonderful, mostly evergreen perennials. They are useful for shade and often succeed where few plants will thrive. Some, like *Epimedium × versicolor* 'Sulphureum', have coppery spring foliage which follows attractive pale-yellow flowers. More vigorous spreading forms such as *Epimedium × perralchicum* 'Fröhnleiten' are planted in drier positions beneath the trees in Rosemary's Wood.

A Sense of Spring

About a month earlier to flower than our commonly grown → English bluebell, *Hyacinthoides non-scripta*, the Bithynian squill, *Scilla bithynica*, has now happily established itself in Rosemary's Wood. The early flowers are deep blue in bud and gradually lighten as they fully open. On their own en masse they make a cheerful show, but here amongst the emerging fronds of the shuttlecock fern they look very much at home.

Prepare to be amazed! This photograph of the same planting was taken only three days later, the shuttlecocks still unfurling and now 60 cm (2 ft) tall. Although the *Scillas* are soon to be past their best, a pink *Dicentra* is in flower in the foreground and the *Rhododendron* behind is starting to bloom.
↓

↑
A month later, the fern has now fully taken the limelight. The bluebells, not seen, have finished flowering and are naturally dying back. *Matteuccia struthiopteris* has vigorously spreading growth in moist situations, losing its early season shuttlecocks to much broader arching fronds. Large-leaved perennials and the fern either side of the path make the area look smaller. The eye is led towards the bridge, framed by the trunk of a large-leaved maple *Acer* × *conspicuum* 'Silver Vein'.

← The dark purple-black leaves which have been this perennial's main attraction are now somewhat eclipsed by the bottlebrush heads of fragrant white, tinged pink flowers borne on long purple spikes. This is still early in the flowering season for *Actaea simplex* 'Brunette', as you can see when you look at the numerous side shoots still to flower.

↑

I must admit, I haven't managed to keep labels on all the woody plants in the Foggy Bottom Garden. Labelling isn't so important in design, but it is when wanting to share information with other gardeners. Most of the established *Rhododendrons* in Rosemary's Wood were from trials at the Bruns nursery in Germany, so were delivered with a number instead of a name thirty years ago. What I do know, is that on my slightly acidic soil they grow well and make quite an impact as they come into flower in the wood and around the summer house. Up close they can be quite stunning, like many *Camellias*, providing a wow factor to visitors… if they manage to escape damage from the Foggy Bottom spring frosts!

Capturing a moment… Summer is surely over, and autumn is yet to begin. The first cold night in mid-September has produced an atmospheric mist over the warmer water in the pond as we look at the wooden bridge and its reflection. The large, green-leaved perennial also reflected in the water is *Darmera peltata*. Both reflections could create the impression that the pond is pretty deep!

↓

The early spring marbled leaves of *Arum italicum* 'Pictum' are attractive, if understated. But the plant really shows off later in the year when it produces striking orange fruits in early autumn. An attraction to birds who, after digestion, assist in a potentially wide distribution of seeds. The succulent orange fruits do suggest 'beware' and are indeed considered poisonous to humans.

↓

Autumn Colour

We are now into late autumn and many trees and shrubs have shed their leaves, including *Quercus frainetto*, the Hungarian oak. Whole leaves are slowly drifting to the woodland floor. This is almost the last week of combined colour in this group of trees, as a sharp frost or strong wind will result in more leaves deciding they've hung on long enough for this year. From left to right, the golden autumn leaves of *Acer* × *conspicuum* 'Silver Vein', the deep crimson *Acer palmatum* 'Bloodgood', the pendulous dark green conifer *Picea breweriana* and the brown-leaved golden weeping beech, *Fagus sylvatica* 'Aurea Pendula'. On the sheltered side and close to a silver birch, *Betula utilis* var. *jacquemontii*, some beech leaves are still yellow.

↑

Sometimes you just have to stare at the wonder of plants and nature. I have been lucky enough to see more than one New England 'fall', and autumn colour in Japan's landscapes and gardens. Both are a long way to go when you can create such colour in your own garden (even if it takes a long time to achieve it). Green turning to a rich yellow, *Acer* × *conspicuum* 'Silver Vein' is a hybrid between the North American *A. pennsylvanicum* and *A. davidii* from China. The Japanese maple behind is a forty-year-old specimen of *A. palmatum* 'Bloodgood'. Of course, as with autumn colour elsewhere, some seasons are better than others, both the weather and the timing of leaf abscission being factors.

Three *Juniperus* create structure and continuity in the background, whilst from left to right golden flowered *Rudbeckia fulgida* var. *sullivantii* 'Goldsturm' makes a river behind *Cornus sanguinea* 'Midwinter Fire' and a clump of the dark-leaved *Ageratina altissima* 'Chocolate'. *Geranium* 'Rozanne' is in full flower in between the *Ageratina*, and just coming into flower are the pink heads of *Sedum* 'Matrona'. On the right is the narrow-leaved variegated *Miscanthus sinensis* 'Morning Light' and the golden yellow grass *Hakonechloa macra* 'Alboaurea'. These are all plant combinations which could fit into smaller spaces in smaller gardens.

01
09

The Book Bed

The Book Bed was previously called the 'Take Twelve Bed' (no this is not the start of a puzzle), both names occurred only after 2010 when the planting in this area in Foggy Bottom was almost completely re-done. 'Take Twelve Plants' was a chapter in my book *Bloom's Best Perennials and Grasses*. The purpose was to select twelve distinct and garden worthy (from my experience) perennials and grasses and show how a garden with year-round interest could be created in a relatively small area. After all, not everyone has a six-acre garden! Of course, in most cases I used more than one of each of the twelve varieties and included a few shrubs for structure, interest and year-round colour ...and one little known conifer which has been a favourite of mine over many years, *Juniperus chinensis* 'Aurea'.

Early on, the Take Twelve Bed was signposted to visitors to encourage them to seek more information about the plants in my new book. Somehow, the Foggy Bottom gardeners, Martin and Anja, started to call it the 'Book Bed' when discussing jobs to be done etc. It made sense for us all to use the same name, so outnumbered (I joke), the Book Bed it has remained. And if you are still with me, I had plants for sun and plants for some shade to consider in my twelve. Rather than list them, we'll look at them through the seasons and in combination with each other.

A year earlier, the initial planting shows the spacing of perennials, grasses and other plants, which becomes less visible as plants grow into each other. Having just trimmed the columnar *Juniperus chinensis* 'Aurea', these conifers are yet to display their golden foliage. They will become more important later in the year, but now is the time for perennials and grasses to come into their own. You can see where the removal of a large conifer has left adjoining tree trunks bare on one side.

Crocosmia 'Lucifer' has always had wow factor since its introduction by our nursery in 1966. It was one of many bred by Percy Piper and selected by my father Alan Bloom. I think we used the term 'scarlet vermilion' to describe the vibrant colour of the flowers. 'Lucifer' now adorns gardens throughout the world. It is among the earliest *Crocosmias* to flower in the summer and one of the hardiest. It is also very attractive for its early bright green, sword-like foliage. Ever truthful, even if it was raised by our family, 'Lucifer' eventually makes a dense clump and can be prone to top heavy collapse after heavy summer rains and strong winds. *Geranium* 'Rozanne' makes an excellent partner, as does *Miscanthus sinensis* 'Morning Light' and *Ageratina altissima* 'Chocolate'. The imposing *Buddleja davidii* is one I selected and named 'Butterfly Heaven'.

The semi-shady pathway leads out to the lawn, from where you can view the main planting to your right. The early autumn morning is slightly misty, softening colours and outlines, but look left and you notice the bronze-leaved form of *Carex comans*. Nestling behind is the green foliage of several *Helleborus*. Single clumps of *Hakonechloa macra* 'Alboaurea' line each side of the path, contrasting with the broad green leaves of *Bergenia* 'Bressingham Ruby'. Planted more recently for winter colour and seemingly in the centre of the path is a large single specimen of *Cornus sanguinea*. At this time of year, the most spectacular plant from this position at the back of the Book Bed (right) is the large pinkish inflorescences of *Hydrangea paniculata* 'Phantom'.

Only the blue flowering *Geranium* 'Rozanne' is going to make a major contribution as a flowering perennial to this association of foliage plants, but the whole grouping will not lack interest from mid-spring to midwinter. The aptly named *Stachys byzantina* 'Silver Carpet' is perfect at the front of a border where it thrives in full sunlight and grows to less than 15 cm (6 in). The golden variegated foliage of *Hakonechloa macra* 'Alboaurea' contrasts brightly with the *Stachys*, the purple of *Ageratina altissima* 'Chocolate' behind and *G.* 'Rozanne' below *Miscanthus sinensis* 'Morning Light'. Again, this is an association which I feel those with much smaller gardens could replicate.

It's a great plant for a long period of stunning flowers and that's a prime reason *Rudbeckia fulgida* var. *sullivantii* 'Goldsturm' is one of my top ten perennials. I planned this as a short river, and in this reasonably moist soil 'Goldsturm' has excelled itself, producing masses of golden petalled flowers with a central black cone. Often called 'black-eyed Susan', which correctly belongs to another species (*Rudbeckia hirta*), the correct common name is coneflower. Whatever the name… 'Goldsturm' is a great perennial! We shouldn't overlook the brilliant, white-flowered shrub *Hydrangea paniculata* 'Phantom' making a striking display in the background. Over the next few weeks these panicles will gradually turn pink. →

← Frost, though no sun to enhance the effect of *Cornus sanguinea* 'Midwinter Fire' in the centre, perennials and grasses surrounding. The two *Miscanthus sinensis* 'Morning Light' in the foreground will generally stand up throughout the winter.

↑

Snow can change everything in the garden and here, it is still snowing. There is certainly drama and beauty when snow is fresh and powdery, less so when it starts to melt. Two plants to note in the foreground; *Cornus sanguinea* 'Midwinter Fire' is subdued in impact, but branches are picked out as they support layers of snow. Left of the *Cornus* is a clump of *Miscanthus sinensis* 'Morning Light' standing up to an increasing load of the white stuff, whilst evergreens and deciduous trees create a magical backdrop.

↑

This willow has been transformed by fine and intermittent snowfall, gentle enough to land on its tortuous branches and so far, not disturbed by wind. A moment when you are glad to be there with a camera. *Salix* × *sepulcralis* 'Erythroflexuosa' has a difficult name and apparently originated in Argentina. It is a good idea to pollard it (cut back hard) each year once it has built a framework. This results in strong twisting branches which turn a deep golden yellow in winter.

This photograph was taken only three weeks later, the snow gone and snowdrops making a show on the grass in Foggy Bottom. The Book Bed is centre left behind the stretch of rustic sweet chestnut fencing, the orange-red stems of *Cornus sanguinea* 'Midwinter Fire' clearly visible. Left is the rather untidy-looking *Salix* × *sepulcralis* 'Erythroflexuosa'. Established conifers and trees clearly show the 'bones' of the garden in late winter, the tree house almost hidden. →

Forward to last winter nearly ten years after planting. Though still attractive, it is obvious that it's now time to plan to thin out and possibly re-organise this planting scheme. This is really how Foggy Bottom has evolved over many years within the overall design, enabling change and development. Trying out new plants and combinations that should work in a changed environment, generally leaving the larger plants – though by no means always. So, what needs doing? The now lone conifer, *Juniperus chinensis* 'Aurea', has made a good specimen and so has the *Hydrangea paniculata* 'Phantom' behind. On this dull winter's day, *Cornus sanguinea* 'Midwinter Fire' is showy, surrounded by snowdrops, *Ophiopogon* and *Bergenia*, but it is beginning to put out runners. These will need digging up and soon the stems will need a hard pruning. The *Rudbeckia* is running into other plants so should at least be curbed to a narrower river… or possibly dug up and re-planted… a big job. The *Ageratina* and *Miscanthus* together on the right will need digging up and splitting to restrict their size and growth. If it's looking okay and largely looking after itself, you might be happy to put this work off for two or three years. I will sort the Book Bed out, but I presently have other priorities…

Some Plants in the Book Bed

I've shared some of the combinations and overall design of the Book Bed with you, but here are some other notable plants, not already seen.

The *Helleborus* hybrids have largely enjoyed their position → in half shade and reasonably moist soil, and nearly ten years since planting, they have made sizeable clumps. These are some of the Ashwood Garden hybrids which I selected in flower at John Massey's Ashwood Nurseries. Although several selections almost come true from seed, if you do get a chance to see what you buy whilst in flower at a specialist nursery or garden centre, you may still be able to pick out better selections… both for flower and apparent vigour. They are rewarding plants, offering flowers for several weeks in the new year when few other perennials or bulbs are evident, and carry on into the spring.

↑

As so often in winter and early spring, it is light that makes a difference, often to a common plant like *Bergenia* known as elephant's ears (I wonder why?). There are now several selections that have distinctly purple or maroon winter leaves, and 'Bressingham Ruby' is one of them. Notice that this clump, now several years old, has foliage forced upwards, revealing the reddish leaf veining below and marbled markings above. Severe and prolonged frost may damage leaves, but otherwise cold weather brings out the most intense colour. On the verge of spring, leaves start to lighten, then new bright green growth emerges as the flower spikes start to flower. For 'Bressingham Ruby' the flowers are a deep pink, whereas others like 'Overture' and 'Eroica' are closer to red. The best colour is achieved in full sun where good drainage exists.

There are some trees or shrubs which you find yourself reluctant to part with, even if they are disappointing most years. You hold on, since you know when you get the best performance it is worth the wait, as so with *Cornus florida* 'Cherokee Chief'. Having seen the impressive North American species in flower in Washington DC in the spring of 1958, it was on my list to try in Foggy Bottom. I planted a small plant of 'Cherokee Chief' in 1978 in a sunny, well-drained position. I waited for it to grow and flower, but it seemed reluctant to do either. It grew very slowly and flowered infrequently, but after taking out a tree that had begun to shade it, 'Cherokee Chief' started to grow. Finally in May 2018, it rewarded with a mass of small pink flowers. Here is the spring sunshine catching some of the flowers, or bracts, at the back of the Book Bed.

Hidden amongst the *Helleborus* and surrounded by the black-leaved *Ophiopogon planiscapus* 'Nigrescens', the brightly variegated leaves of *Hosta* 'Francee' make a startling appearance with the creeping, fresh green fronds of the shuttlecock fern, *Matteuccia struthiopteris*. The latter likes reasonably moist soil, though given it, it can become invasive.

Here looking across the Book Bed, it's already the first week of June. Nothing yet in flower, but there is plenty of variety in foliage type, height and colour. It's a good time to look across at the shrubs and the trees in the background. Starting from left to right, you can see the rounded broadleaved shrub, *Hydrangea paniculata* 'Phantom', with flowers yet to come. Above and behind is the smaller-leaved shrub, *Cornus florida* 'Cherokee Chief', which has just finished flowering. Look now to the dark purple 'hole' filled by *Cotinus coggygria* 'Royal Purple', above that is a green Katsura tree, *Cercidiphyllum japonicum*, and rather squeezed in, a golden-leaved silver birch, *Betula pendula* 'Golden Cloud'. Now we come to the lilac *Syringa emodi* 'Variegata', though you can hardly see the leaves for the multitude of pale off-white, lightly fragrant flowers. Lastly, to the right is *Platycladus orientalis* 'Flame' bright yellow with new growth, though this conifer was given its name because of its burnished bronze colour in winter.

PART TWO

THE TREASURY OF PLANTS

Spring in Rosemary's Wood. *Scilla bithynica* make a perfect contrast to *Matteuccia struthiopteris*.

02
01

Love or Hate – Hostas can be Great in the Garden

On a dewy morning in June, the leaves of *Hosta* 'Big Daddy' are fully open and is almost living up to its name, the large scalloped and ribbed leaves and two-toned foliage tumbling over each other trying to find space. This group has been in this spot beneath trees for more than ten years and now might benefit from being divided. Individual leaves can get smaller when *Hostas* get congested and are in competition with themselves. As with much that we are seeing, there is more to most plants than often meets the eye… which light and shade cleverly reveal. The *Hosta* certainly forms a dramatic foreground to the garden view behind.

Most *Hosta* species originate from Japan, China and Korea. Many were first seen in Japan where their adaptability, structure of foliage, and long period of interest suited the design style of Japanese gardens.

Here was a potential treasure trove waiting to be explored and though initially plant collectors introduced the species to Europe, it wasn't until the 1860s that many were imported to North America. The fact that *Hostas*, like the daylilies, were suited to most climatic regions of the US was a prime reason for their increasing popularity.

When I first joined our nursery in 1962, the range of *Hosta* varieties was extremely limited. This soon changed, led by the wide interest in the US. Breeding and selection from enthusiasts led to an increasing range of cultivars. Both small and large leafed forms were developed with strikingly attractive foliage, the emphasis increasingly on ornamental cultivars with blue to grey and variegated leaves. Paul Aden was an outstanding breeder who selected and introduced varieties such as 'Big Daddy', 'Big Mama' and 'Sum and Substance'. With such brash and maybe unforgettable names, it seemed obvious these had to be from an American breeder! However, I was happy to plant many of these in Foggy Bottom and you can see them in the following photographs. I drew the line on another of Paul's introductions which he named 'High Fat Cream' …there's still no place for it in Foggy Bottom!

Formed in 1968, the American Hosta Society now has over 3,000 members, and it wasn't long after that a British Hosta and Hemerocallis Society was formed. I should also pay tribute to British *Hosta* breeding too and mention Eric Smith in particular, a true plantsman from Dorset, who worked on *Hostas* for many years. He is responsible for some of the best medium leaf sized plants adorning gardens across the world.

Less flamboyant in look and name, but equally garden worthy are 'Buckshaw Blue', 'Halcyon', 'Hadspen Blue' and the larger-leaved 'Snowden'. And it fell to English enthusiast and nurserywoman Diana Grenfell to write the ultimate internationally acclaimed book on *Hostas*.

And so, after the brief 'potted history', how useful are *Hostas* as garden plants? At this point, anyone who has gardened with these potentially stunning perennials will bring up their No. 1 enemies... slugs and snails. Whether you live in Europe or North America, both can cause havoc to your prize *Hostas*... and other plants too of course. Go to one of the *Hosta* societies for more detailed advice, but I can tell you that being vigilant, as we try to be in Foggy Bottom, can help prevent unsightly damage. As soon as warm or wet weather arrives in spring, we are out with our organic pellets scattering them round the base of our *Hostas*. Catch them early and, if necessary, repeat until the *Hosta* leaves mature. Depending on your local climate this may be enough, though wet periods in summer can encourage slugs and snails to mount marauding raids from their hiding places. Diana Grenfell in the chapter of her book on *Hosta* pests and diseases says in her extensive review, "the real enemies of *Hostas* are the little black and brown slugs that eat both shoots and roots".

With that positive introduction and less positive cultural questions, I can only show you how I have used *Hostas* in Foggy Bottom and why fifty years later I still think they have a role to play.

Hosta 'Big Daddy'

From fully closed and sharp pointed shoots (to break through the soil surface unscathed), to cigar-shaped rolled leaves, this photograph of early growth of *Hosta* 'Big Daddy' records nature's marvel. Not a slug to be seen in this quite dry area... Infront you will notice the shoots of the golden-leaved grass *Hakonechloa macra* 'Alboaurea' and out of focus behind, the light blue flowers of *Pulmonaria* 'Opal' and white *Narcissus* 'Actaea'. Obvious to me and to keen-eyed gardeners is a young seedling willow weed in front of 'Big Daddy' (adding a touch of realism?) that I should have removed before taking the photograph.

↑ Big-leaved *Hostas* can make a dramatic impact in any garden with the intensity of the colour, varying according to the cultivar and possibly in relation to soil and positioning. Though *Hosta* 'Big Daddy' doesn't include blue in its name (and there are more than fifty *Hostas* which do), it is one of the best blues, holding its colour until late in the season. As I often suggest, two or more plants can transform the relatively ordinary to extraordinary, hopefully clearly demonstrated here less than a month after the previous photograph was taken. The golden striped leaves of *Hakonechloa macra* 'Alboaurea' is a contrast to *H.* 'Big Daddy' in colour as well as texture. And yes, we obviously didn't get every slug, nor weed.

Hosta 'Sagae'

← *Hosta* 'Sagae' (formerly given the botanical name *Hosta fluctuans* 'Variegated'), is one of my favourite *Hostas*, partly because it eventually makes a single bold architectural specimen and is great in a container on a patio or terrace. I say 'eventually' as from a small plant 'Sagae' takes a few years to become an imposing specimen – as you can see from my plants in Foggy Bottom. Here three years ago in spring, new leaves appear above ground at the same time as a ruby red *Helleborus* still in flower.

Sun and shade. Generally, *Hostas* perform better and for a longer period if grown in shade where not too dry. Most, including those with variegated leaves, maintain their leaves better in shade than in sun. In climates with hotter summers, leaves can be scorched. In Newfoundland, Wales, Scotland and similar climates, more open positions would be fine. Here, the specimen in fairly dense shade, seen earlier with the *Helleborus*, now has a fairly natural blend of plants around it and is maintaining a good colour. The other 'Sagae' in Foggy Bottom which I planted in a sunnier position next to a bronze-leaved *Rodgersia podophylla* contrasts in form, texture and foliage colour, making an eye-catching combination. A shuttlecock fern and pink *Rhododendron* behind.

This is one I took earlier in 1996 before I managed to get → it out of the pot, which is almost hidden by the graceful wavy and overlapping leaves. In a way, it is remarkable that this specimen which had been on our terrace still looks so luxuriant and healthy. No slug or snail damage (I can't be sure that I didn't remove a few leaves!), but ideally to keep the plant in good condition it needs to be fed (slow-release pellets applied in early spring), watered, and put in shade not too close to a wall. Why? The shape needs to be maintained on all sides and snails can easily navigate walls! There is room to cut out some leaves at the base to create a more artistic impression, as some Japanese gardeners might do, but to me this plant was close to perfection at this stage. It had come to a point of congestion, needing either to grow on in a larger pot intact or be planted in the garden.

More *Hostas* and More Combinations

Before starting this feature on *Hostas*, which are blended into the gardens and not planted as standalone collections, I made a few quick notes. *Hostas* can and often are a collector's dream. With over 4,000 (and I suspect there are more) species and varieties in cultivation, societies to join and learn about them, and specialist nurseries who only grow *Hostas*, you could create your own Hosterie (or should it be Hostery?) fairly quickly. The latter is a term first used, as far as I know, by Alan Titchmarsh back in 1980 or so when on a visit he saw my burgeoning collection at Foggy Bottom.

We are not going to describe all these points, but will look at the options you might have as a collector or gardener:

- **Size:** Mammoth, large, medium, small or miniature.
- **Special characteristics:** Foliage, flower, fragrance or stem colour. Many are considered and used as edible plants in Japan.
- **Leaf colour:** Blue, grey, green, gold or yellow. Matt or glossy, variegated.
- **Leaf shape:** Round, cup-shaped to narrow, pointed.
- **Cultivation:** Single specimen, group, river, a collection or with other plants.
- **Seasonal interest:** Prominent and colourful new shoots, autumn colours and tones.

The following photographs taken in Foggy Bottom show aspects of these elements described.

Hosta 'Golden Tiara', described by one expert as "among the most important *Hostas* ever introduced" is some accolade, and in my experience too this cultivar is a very garden worthy selection. 'Golden Tiara' soon makes a showy plant in the garden and for a small-leaved *Hosta* it has a long season of interest and is attractive in flower. Slightly undulating leaves are finely edged with creamy yellow. Brighter variegation occurs where exposed to more light. Here, I've planted in a more natural fashion, spaced so that each plant is an individual and so that there is room for other plants to mix in and enhance one another.

A fine balance is achieved, at least for a few years, with these three dwarf plants. 'Golden Tiara' has attractive lily-like flowers which are deep blue fading to lilac purple. In front are the bronze leaves of the rather slow growing *Tellima grandiflora* 'Purpurteppich'. These plants are on a slight slope beneath a specimen of *Tsuga canadensis* 'Pendula', where the finely cut fronds of a miniature fern *Adiantum aleuticum* 'Subpumilum' creates diversity within the combination.

You need a fairly robust grower as well as contrasting foliage to make a long-lasting plant partnership. In a moist shady spot in Foggy Bottom, the bright, white-edged leaves of *Hosta* 'Francee' are planted amongst black mondo grass, *Ophiopogon planiscapus* 'Nigrescens'.

In midsummer in this shady spot, *Hosta* 'Halcyon' is retaining its blue-grey leaf colour, accentuated by *Campanula poscharskyana* 'Purple Fountain' which I selected from seedlings many years ago.

We try not to (completely) hide our faults. It's late summer and beyond the ferns is *Hosta* 'Sagae', a few spikes long finished flowering, and though *H.* 'Halcyon' in the foreground has lost its bloom on the leaves and signs of snail damage is evident, the fading flowers still draw the eye.

↓

↑

You can hardly not notice the brightly variegated leaves of *Hosta* 'Patriot' in the foreground, nor the pink *Rhododendron* in the far distance. But in between are plants that complete the picture; bright green fronds of *Matteuccia struthiopteris*, the reddish pink of *Geranium macrorrhizum*, and purple-black fern-like leaves of *Actaea simplex* 'Brunette'.

← Another large-leaved *Hosta* and closely allied to *Hosta* 'Big Daddy' – both cultivars were selected and introduced in the US by Paul Aden – this is *H.* 'Big Mama'. Leaves are a softer texture and more open than 'Big Daddy', shown here in vivid contrast to the bronzed foliage and orange flowers of *Euphorbia griffithii* 'Fireglow'. The *Euphorbia* is enjoying the moist soil and though spreading and attractive, it will need to be kept from invading the clump forming *Hosta*.

Considered slug resistant and one of the largest-leaved *Hostas* available, *H.* 'Sum and Substance' certainly can make an impact in the garden. However, it is a bit of a chameleon... in full sun it is likely to have bright golden leaves, whilst in shade it will colour a rather undistinguished dull green. This plant in Foggy Bottom gets sun for only half of the day. ↓

For a deer, this new foliage must be tasty, and you can see half a leaf has been snacked. But so far, local Bressingham deer are mostly happy enough with other plants. This is another I use in Foggy Bottom called *Hosta* 'Krossa Regal', it's a good blue with long narrow leaves on tall upright stems. A note to myself as I write this… space out the clumps more widely and plant in between with *Ophiopogon planiscapus* 'Nigrescens' or a low growing pink hardy *Geranium*.

Even in late autumn, the slowly decaying *Hosta* 'Krossa Regal' leaves can light up a combination. This is the same group, but from this vantage point you can glimpse the mass of *Symphyotrichum lateriflorum* 'Prince' flowers. Through the narrow-stemmed grass *Molinia caerulea* subsp. *caerulea* 'Moorhexe' is a blue *Aconitum* and pink *Persicaria amplexicaulis* 'Taurus'.

02
02

Gardening with Hardy Ferns

I have always liked ferns, but as a gardener I don't feel I have come to grips with them. Perhaps it is the names and relative similarity to each other... As my knowledge has increased, I have realised how much variety exists in this fascinating group of plants.

I have been collecting and trialling ever since I started the garden to find out which ferns like moisture, which will grow on drier soils, which prefer shade, and lastly, which are evergreen. I didn't want to create a fernery; it was more a case of choosing ferns to fit in with other plants and creating situations that they might thrive in. Ferns add their own distinctive element to Foggy Bottom. Here are some that I have used and the conditions that they seem to like (or not like).

The Language of Ferns

Perhaps the mystery of ferns lies in the descriptive terms generally and uniquely applied to this wide range of plants. Latin words such as 'stipe', 'rachis' and 'pinnae' are seldom terms most would come across in descriptions of most garden plants. But perhaps ferns are not just any garden plant...

So, whilst I generally avoid words that I and most gardeners are not familiar with, in my attempt to treat ferns as any other garden plant, I feel obliged to pass on a few terms you might come across.

These I hasten to add are only a fraction of the terms applied to this ancient group of plants. My selection is but a brief introduction and recommendation to include some ferns in your garden plantings.

- **Crosier:** Which came first, the bishop's staff or the description of tightly furled fronds? See *Polystichum*, *Osmunda* and *Dryopteris*.
- **Frond:** The complete stem and leaf, also known as the rachis.
- **Stipe:** The section of the rachis below the leaf and the blade is the leafy section above.
- **Pinnae:** The side leaves of the main leaf, whist pinnule are the smaller side leaves.

Taken in Rosemary's Wood in early May, this photograph shows two of my favourite ferns, the tall, bright green fronds of the shuttlecock fern *Matteuccia struthiopteris*, and in front surrounding the base of a Japanese maple, the dainty maidenhair fern *Adiantum venustum*. *Matteuccia* is a great and showy fern in the right place, quickly colonising in moist soils and good next to streams or ponds. In spring, fronds rapidly unfurl to resemble shuttlecocks before widening to a bright green. As the foliage dies back in autumn it leaves erect fertile fronds to carry through winter. The spreading habit can be curtailed by cutting shallow creeping roots away.

Adiantum venustum with *Hosta* 'Shade Fanfare'. *Adiantum* spreads gently once established, growing happily on drier well-drained soils where some shade is available. Hardier than it looks, it is very useful beneath trees and in milder climates it is semi-evergreen.

What could be stranger and more dramatic than the new spring growth of the royal fern *Osmunda regalis*. A frosty morning near the pond in Foggy Bottom, as the sun rises the unfurling heads look like Catherine wheels. In the right conditions, this fern eventually makes an imposing specimen 1.2 m (4 ft) to as much as 1.8 m (6 ft). It is particularly striking next to, or even in, water. The cultivar 'Purpurascens' which is similar but has purplish stems in spring is also worth considering. In my experience, they will grow in sun or semi-shade where not too dry in summer.

I can never understand why this spectacular yet understated Japanese maiden fern isn't better known. Perhaps the name is one reason, since *Adiantum aleuticum* 'Japonicum' gives no clue that this is no ordinary green fern. Shrimp pink shoots deepening to rosy red in spring, it is something a bit special. Here, I have planted it next to a blue-leaved *Hosta*, the fern creating a colourful yet delicate effect against a contrasting background. Enjoy it while it lasts as the foliage changes to a mid-green for the rest of the growing season.

In my mind, this is one of the best ferns for creating a striking foliage effect. As with many others it comes with an unforgettable name… *Athyrium otophorum* var. *okanum* (often listed simply as *A. otophorum*). Its distinctive fronds are late to emerge, dark reddish stems highlight the creamy-green, finely divided foliage. Native to Japan, China and Korea, it needs some shade and is best in moist soil, not overcrowded by other plants. Height 30–45 cm (12–18 in).

This feathery soft shield fern, *Polystichum setiferum*, nestles comfortably between an *Ajuga* in the foreground and *Hosta* 'Big Mama' behind. The strangely compelling emerging fronds here are semi-mature, though tip growth is still unfurling. Colour and texture are quite different to surrounding plants. As growth matures, fronds become dark green and more spreading. In milder climates it is semi-evergreen. To my mind, most ferns are generally much more effective as individuals and groups amongst different plants than with other ferns.

The papery looking fronds of this hart's tongue fern, *Asplenium scolopendrium* 'Crispum', are lit up by the sun in early morning, the fresh lettuce green fronds finely crisped and curled at the edges. Native to Europe, *Asplenium scolopendrium* come in all sorts of variations with equally tortuous names. I think they are much underused in gardens. They provide a distinct contrast to other low growing flowering and foliage plants, grasses, perennials and bulbs. Best in part shade where not too dry, it is a fern that prefers an alkaline soil, but seems to do well enough elsewhere too.

If I were to recommend a fern that should be in every garden, this is it – *Dryopteris erythrosora*. Looking at the name, you can envision it being around at the time of the dinosaurs, the truth is much more basic. Simply translated from Latin, the name means 'having red spore cases'. The upside is that this is an adaptable fern for sun or shade and should be treated as the star it is. It works well with contrasting plants such as silver-leaved *Pulmonaria* 'Diana Clare', or near a blue flowered plant such as *Geranium* 'Rozanne'. The evergreen fern looks good all year, even against snowdrops in winter. Best colour is achieved in a sunny spot.

↑

A compact and colourful selection of the Japanese painted fern, *Athyrium niponicum* 'Burgundy Lace', an apt description when you study the beautifully marked foliage. There are various selections of the silver fronded *A. niponicum* and maybe several names for rather similar plants, but most are worthy of a place in the garden. Access to moist soils and some shade will give success. Each year, just as you are about to wonder whether it has survived, up come the spindly shoots, soon to fill out as a carpet of slowly spreading foliage. There is no mistaking the red wine stems suffusing into the exquisitely formed pinnae (side shoots), which merit a closer look.

Frost and early morning sun combine to create magical fronds in Rosemary's Wood. → As the leaves fall and perennials die back, one of the most striking of larger ferns, *Dryopteris wallichiana*, will continue to dominate the woodland floor throughout winter. This, perhaps like *Osmunda regalis*, is a fern best treated as a specimen where it can stand out and be highlighted by lower growing plants with broader leaves; *Brunnera macrophylla* 'Jack Frost', *Pulmonaria* 'Diana Clare', or a blue, gold, or variegated *Hosta*.

← As for many plants, frost adds sparkle to foliage and leaves exposed to it, evident from this showy low growing Japanese native *Polystichum polyblepharum*. Its spreading, glossy, finely divided fronds are attractive all summer. Again, in milder climates it is evergreen, as shown here in winter at Foggy Bottom. Best in semi-shade where not too dry.

Dividing Ferns

← Many of us want to increase our fern population and though not achieved without some effort, the best time for most is in the early spring just as they are about to come into growth. This is an unassuming but useful evergreen fern, *Polystichum acrostichoides*, commonly known as the Christmas fern. But like most described as evergreen, their least showy time is as they ready themselves for a new season each spring. This procedure covers most evergreen and many other ferns. Firstly, as shown, use sharp secateurs to cut away the full length of the previous year's fronds.

A certain amount of brute force might be required to divide a mature fern, but some effort can be alleviated by first cutting around the clump with a sharp spade. Then, carefully position two forks (okay so you don't have two forks… borrow one from a neighbour or gardener friend who also might help you if needed) so as not to damage emerging fronds. The forks need to be set in tightly back-to-back to allow maximum leverage, then once the division starts to happen, the forks can be adjusted to complete the task. This must be done in situ, but subsequent divisions are also best done in the same place where the fork can go into the ground, bearing in mind that the best leverage is at the base of the handle. Separate and replant as soon as possible.

↓

Bark

As my family know only too well, I am inclined to look for puns in many levels of conversation… and hopefully my captions are of a conversational nature. So how to resist 'bark'? 'His bark is worse than his bite' doesn't apply here, but 'barking up the wrong tree' is better and much more appropriate if slightly altered to 'barking up the right tree'.

I started planting trees in Foggy Bottom as early as 1966. One of the first being a silver birch, then about 2 m (6 ft) tall, which I had dug out of our woods. That multi-stemmed tree is now at least 15 m (50 ft) high and is seen every day within sight of our kitchen window. One of the most pleasing descriptive names for this European native birch, *Betula pendula*, is 'lady of the woods' and observing its elegant outline you can understand why.

The now substantial trunk is a silvery white, tinged by green algae (which is normal) as this tree is providing its own shade. Giving the trunk an occasional 'winter wash' to keep the bark white, if not sparkling, is now not considered eccentric. Because of their winter interest and contribution to the garden, I continued to plant trees that have attractive bark, knowing of course that time would be needed for these plants to develop to produce an eye-catching display. The devil is truly in the detail when getting a camera up close to bark.

Birches are worth growing for their bark and often have other attributes too. Some are vigorous and make large trees, but although they may vary, the Siberian birch, *Betula davurica*, is a relatively small tree with good autumn foliage colour and very attractive papery, curling bark. This photograph was taken in bright sun, but as you go round the tree, the light on the bark and colours will differ. This tree is shown in its entirety on p.78.

↑

The benefits of a tree, grown as much for its bark as anything else, is surely enhanced when it has several stems. This ten-year-old multi-stemmed Japanese birch with four strikingly white stems creates much more impact than if single. The original tree, a selection of *Betula apoiensis,* was found on the slopes of Mount Apoi on the northern island of Hokkaidō and consequently named *B. a.* 'Mount Apoi'. I have used 'Mount Apoi' in several places at Bressingham, the Winter Garden and Foggy Bottom, as it seems to tick all the boxes: a small tree, good autumn colour and exceedingly attractive bark. In Foggy Bottom, the dark foliage of *Taxus baccata* 'Repandens' in the background is a perfect contrast to the brightness of the bark.

→

On a sunny late January day a few years ago, I was visiting the Minnesota Landscape Arboretum, not knowing how much I was going to be able to see as the garden and arboretum were blanketed with 60 cm (2 ft) of snow. The trees of course rise well above the snow and the bark really stands out, for me none more so than a specimen *Betula davurica* coded 783961. This was a large birch which, in an expanse of snow, was stunning. A weak sun was enough to light up the peeling and colourful bark. The full story will have to be told elsewhere, but back in England I was kindly sent some propagating scion wood. After successful grafting, two years after my visit a small tree was planted in the Snake Bed in Foggy Bottom. Some years later, the duckling became a swan and the winter bark on the specimen is now nearly as impressive as its parent in Minneapolis!

This shrub or small tree was only introduced from China in 1980 and given the uncommon common name 'seven son flower of Zhejiang'. This is one that I would highly recommend for the smaller garden. *Heptacodium miconioides* is a bit of a mouthful, but think about how impressed your gardening friends might be if you asked them, in perfect Latin of course, whether they have this plant. By this time of course, you will have planted yours and would say "it has large leaves and clusters of fragrant flowers in late summer and autumn". You could also say that one of the reasons why you grow it is because "it has attractive peeling bark when larger". And though for bark it may not compete with the best, how many small trees have fragrant flowers at the end of the summer season? I initially pruned this plant as a shrub, hence the five stems showing their worth in the winter sunshine.

If I had to choose one tree for my garden it would probably be this one... *Acer griseum*, the paperbark maple. And I mean this multi-stemmed tree in the photograph which I was lucky enough to find at a local nursery. The species originates from Central China and is grown almost exclusively from seed, so there is some variation in habit and bark. It is widely recommended as a relatively small tree for the smaller garden, but no large garden should be without it either. I now have several in Foggy Bottom, some of which I have grown from seed collected from older specimens in the garden. This selection, with an even well-branched form, is likely to be featured more with new planting around it and is a real treat as sunlight shines on the glossy stems and the curling papery bark creates a glowing living presence.

Considering leaf fall has mostly happened by the end of October and leaves seldom appear until April, that gives any shrub or tree known for winter interest six months to perform. And this one, *Acer* × *conspicuum* 'Phoenix', truly does. From all sides, the orange bark is simply outstanding throughout winter. This specimen is now about thirty years old and in full sun from mid-morning. If you could make the time, watching the sun cast its light onto this maple throughout a day would hardly be a chore! I now have a smaller plant and I will have a bit more courage to cut that back to increase the number of stems, knowing now that this plant readily breaks from older wood.

From Bark to Stems

When does a stem become a trunk? My answer: when it gets thicker! In my understanding, bark appears on older stems whether described as a branch or a trunk of a tree. The trunk and branches of the *Acer griseum* on the right have typically peeling bark, whilst the Japanese maple, *Acer palmatum* 'Sango-Kaku' (formerly known as *A. p.* 'Senkaki'), has less interesting bark on the lower branches or stems of the tree, but is renowned for striking coral red stems at the top. Here, the stems are highlighted by the background of blue foliage from *Abies procera* 'Glauca', the noble fir. Dark stems to the right belong to a *Physocarpus*. All add interest to Foggy Bottom in midwinter.

← One reason to explore and experiment with plant associations is to give each individual plant a greater opportunity to reveal their full qualities. A plant of *Cornus sanguinea* in the wild would probably struggle to exist amongst its close neighbours, perhaps in a hedgerow. Bring it into 'captivity', breed something more 'cultivated' and then offer it to a gardener. As gardeners, we should be thankful that we now have several selections of European dogwood to choose from to brighten our winter days. This is *C. s.* 'Midwinter Fire' which appears to have captured the little group of snowdrops, *Galanthus* 'S. Arnott', which I planted with it and alongside the black-leaved *Ophiopogon planiscapus* 'Nigrescens' (so dark you can hardly see it). This grouping, visible from our kitchen window, has been providing pleasure for over ten years with little maintenance beyond cutting back the stems of the *Cornus* in late spring.

Fallen Leaves

Mid-November in Foggy Bottom and leaves are still falling – although *Sorbus thibetica* 'John Mitchell' is one of the last. We are usually in no rush to clear them from the grass as they remain attractive for some time. Leaves tumble down in a haphazard fashion, some more showy displaying their silver-grey undersides, even more so when frosted. Some have fallen on ferns, grasses and perennials. In a week or two, the leaves will be raked off the grass, a few picked off foliage, and be made into leaf mould which can later be used as a mulch or compost.

As the years passed and the plants in Foggy Bottom grew, they gradually formed a whole world devoted to nature and the beauty of plants. If one can make an analogy, the owner, with the help of gardeners, becomes the conductor. In my own case, I hope to continue to be a gardener too. To many gardeners, leaves are a nuisance, untidy and an interruption to gardening activities. They fall as autumn becomes winter, darker and shorter days sometimes interrupted by the whine of leaf sweepers or the blasting of leaf blowers. All this makes for an antipathy to leaves when perhaps we should consider their interest and potential benefits.

First there are the aesthetics, the interest and beauty of some leaves as they fall from the tree. We are inclined to take deciduous shrubs and trees for granted in their season of prime interest for foliage or flower. But for a short while, before leaves start to decay, they retain or even enhance the plant's appearance. To demonstrate the impact of a few different leaves, I will share those that I look forward to each autumn.

Of course, leaves can be a nuisance. They can blow into corners, bury some treasured plants, and spoil the grass on the lawn. But almost whatever age you are, the exercise and satisfaction from collecting leaves to make into composted leaf mould has that double benefit. In other words, you are left with having created a worthwhile and natural product to benefit your soil and your plants.

The autumn spectacle from the sweet gums, *Liquidambar styraciflua*, is impressive each year... but some years are better than others. Some named selections are more reliable than others. Being a North American native, the sweet gums are used to hotter summers and warmer autumns than those in Britain and Northern Europe. So, it was a welcome occurrence when *L. s.* 'Worplesdon' was introduced from Surrey, England, as the autumn display of crimson leaves could be relied upon in a cooler climate. It was given the Royal Horticultural Society's Award of Garden Merit in 1987. When leaves fall they can still be enjoyed as a carpet on the ground, particularly if lit by the late autumn or early winter sun.

Looking like giant paddles, the leaves of *Magnolia macrophylla* are magnificent and seemingly quite exotic. The undersides of the leaves are silver-grey and ribbed, matching the now brown surface. This *Magnolia* originates from the American Southeast and whilst not suitable for the average garden, it is one that is very satisfying to grow, with white fragrant flowers marked purple in the centre. Closely allied is a shrubbier form, *M. m.* subsp. *ashei*, which flowers at a younger age.

↑

The Hungarian oaks, *Quercus frainetto*, are big trees as I discovered, having planted them myself only in 1980. Straight of trunk and limb, these are handsome trees which in the spring and summer you must look up to study the glossy surfaced, finely lobed leaves. When they fall, they cover a wide area including the grass lawn, so we can't leave them too long without clearing them. But they make a pleasing picture as the distinct light brown leaves temporarily carpet the ground.

↑

Often in woodland conditions it is best just to let nature take care of itself, leaves provide a natural mulch all winter and into the next season. Of course unless carefully labelled or marked, you will have a job to remember where everything has been planted until there are signs of growth in spring. Here at the end of April, tentative new shoots of *Hosta* 'Big Daddy' poke through the covering of Hungarian oak leaves.

02
05

Using Spring and Summer Flowering Shrubs in the Garden

Spot the bee! Seeing such an abundance of early flowers on *Prunus incisa* 'Kojo-no-mai', it is hardly surprising that bees are attracted to the pollen that exists in every small flower (that said, I can't see one in this photograph!). Flowering usually lasts for two or three weeks, the flowers gradually shading to pink.

From my experience and for my greater enjoyment of the garden, there must be flowering shrubs in the mix. Foggy Bottom is of course a large six-acre garden and without trees and shrubs… not forgetting conifers, it would not be able to offer the same experience, structure and diversity as it does. It is to some extent an antidote to my father's garden, which is primarily devoted to his speciality of perennials and in later years, grasses. I planted a different type of garden partly because I (like many sons perhaps) wanted to be different and add something of my own to our gardens and business.

From the early stages of developing Foggy Bottom, I started planting many shrubs as a testing ground for new selections which we were growing on our nursery. It was here where *Potentilla fruticosa* 'Red Ace', for example, was introduced to the world – that's another story. Now for various reasons, I don't have a single *Potentilla* in the garden. With the soil being on the acid side, I was able to grow *Rhododendrons*, winter and summer flowering heathers, *Camellias* and *Magnolias*, as well as some more unusual plants. These were shrubs that I fitted into my designs and used amongst the wide range of conifers I was collecting and trialling in the garden.

Trees, shrubs and taller conifers eventually bring shade, which suited many plants, and I could add those that enjoyed woodland conditions. Looking at the long period of developing and planting Foggy Bottom in the third part of this book, you will see how important thinning out some larger trees, conifers and shrubs became to allow the garden to avoid becoming an overgrown mess!

From the images I have selected, all taken in the past five years, you will get an idea as to what role shrubs can play and how important they are to enlivening the garden with vivid splashes of colour, primarily from spring to midsummer. Of course in Foggy Bottom, few plants remain in isolation and each ideally needs to serve a role that leads to year-round colour and vibrancy in parts of the garden.

Lastly in this brief overview, I have selected some flowering shrubs shown as part of the garden and some that are worth looking at in close-up… a role that the camera can play almost better than the human eye.

Spring Breaks

When daffodils start to come into flower, they herald to most people that spring has arrived. Exactly when that happens is determined by your local climate and even that may vary to a certain extent each year. This photograph is taken from near the house at Foggy Bottom at the end of March. The scattering of daffodils beneath the silver birch, *Betula pendula*, have been flowering every spring for over fifty years since planted. No leaves are yet on the trees, so the forms, shapes and colours of conifers are clearly defined. In the centre are two pyramidal conifers, the blue is a noble fir, *Abies procera* 'Glauca', next to a golden deodar cedar, *Cedrus deodara* 'Nana Aurea', both of which are trimmed each year to prevent them getting too large and dominant to their surroundings. Stems of white-barked silver birch show from some distance and help provide the year-round structure of the garden. So finally having set the scene, I realise the most striking white-flowered shrubs have yet to be mentioned. Tight pink buds seem to explode into a mass of small white flowers, which invite swarms of hungry bees. The two shrubs on the right are *Prunus incisa* 'Kojo-no-mai', and in the distance a hundred metres away is *Prunus incisa* 'Shidare'. A recurrent theme is to use flowering shrubs to help light up the garden, generally contrasting with surrounding plants.

This graceful Japanese cherry, *Prunus incisa* 'Shidare', sits quietly on the edge of the garden, hardly noticed by summer visitors who often sit on the simple wooden seat behind. But suddenly in spring its moment of glory arrives. Now over forty years old, the solid framework of stems support pendulous branches festooned with masses of pure white flowers. Now in its prime season, its presence draws the eye from distant parts of the garden.

Note: Should you look for this attractive shrub for your garden, please note I obtained my plant years ago from a nursery in Japan under the name 'Shidare', which translates as 'weeping' or 'pendulous'. It might be the same as *P. i.* 'Pendula', though I suspect there may be more than one selection offered under that name.

Closely sheltered from the eastern rays of early morning sun by evergreen conifers (left), *Camellia* 'Donation' is about to begin its long period of flowering. One of the best, most reliable and free blooming *Camellias*, this plant – with occasional pruning – has been in its present position in Foggy Bottom for over forty years. One year, I counted out a hundred flowers one at a time and gave up... Up close, the double, somewhat exotic, blooms are a work of nature. Quite compact and bushy, the glossy leaves make a pleasing evergreen year-round. Prune soon after flowering has finished.

Strikingly colourful new shoots emerge crimson from a leafy canopy fading to pink, just → as lightly fragrant bell-like flowers appear. This is a combination on the aptly named *Pieris* 'Forest Flame', which has been a feature in Foggy Bottom for several years. Spectacular and rewarding when in flower like many early flowering shrubs such as *Rhododendrons*, *Magnolias* and *Camellias*, it is also prone to spring frost damage. If you can, place carefully in your garden where it can't be reached by the early morning sun.

Few evergreens are more adaptable for → a shady position than *Skimmia* × *confusa* 'Kew Green'. Here it is growing close to the trunk of a silver birch in a shady, dry position, yet this male form still makes an annual display of fragrant creamy petalled flowers. The scent is particularly noticeable during a quiet evening stroll round the garden. A few vibrant blue forget-me-not-like flowers of *Brunnera macrophylla* appear beneath.

← This shrub, commonly called dwarf fothergilla, needs acid soil and is frustratingly slow growing in its early years. But ultimately, you may decide as I have that it is one of the most worthwhile shrubs in your garden. *Fothergilla gardenii* flowers as a young plant but becomes more impressive year on year, making an abundant display of rounded, fragrant bottlebrush flowers – a marvel of nature in close-up. Small wispy yellow-green heads develop to pure white flowers in spring, starting before the leaves which generally turn to a wonderful golden orange in autumn. Although my plant is in half shade, *F. gardenii* will do well in full sun if not too dry.

↑ 'Magic of nature' might be a phrase you will see me use more than once! Here the *Rhododendron* 'Baden-Baden' acts as a colourful background to *Viburnum plicatum* 'Grandiflorum' in its early stage when both leaves and clusters of young flowers are bright green.

Spring Glory

A bright spring morning walk in the garden can be a delight, even the air itself seems fresh and sharp, and flowering shrubs and trees stand out from their surroundings. Later, once flowering is over, these plants largely blend into and become part of the background. Enjoy the moment for every day is different, weather changes and so do plants in the garden. Here, looking from the Acer Glade through a gap close to the coarse papery bark of *Betula nigra* 'Little King', is a view which highlights the strange but appealing, narrow yet vertical *Sequoiadendron giganteum* 'Pendulum', the weeping giant redwood. In flower on the left is the white rounded form of *Magnolia stellata* 'Water Lily', and on the right, a much more compact, scarlet-flowered *Rhododendron* 'Baden-Baden'. Both shrubs have been in their present positions in Foggy Bottom for over thirty years, but *Prunus* 'Tai Haku', the great white cherry to the right of the *Rhododendron,* was only planted ten years ago and will get much bigger in time.
↓

Unfortunately, all good things come to an end for *Rhododendron* 'Baden-Baden' which has nearly finished flowering for this year, as has the *Magnolia stellata* 'Water Lily' in the background. Star of the moment is the *Viburnum plicatum* 'Grandiflorum', now transformed from green to much larger white snowball flowers. The *Viburnum* will benefit from pruning after flowering, then we wait for next year… But plenty is still going on elsewhere in the garden.

Rhododendron Spring

Both in their diverse natural environments across the world and through years of selection and breeding, *Rhododendrons*, if you can grow them, can play an important role in your garden. Whilst they need placing with care, their often-vivid flowers can almost jump out at you, so brazen can some seem, though you don't want them to gain all the attention. It is often not understood that there are different species and cultivars of *Rhododendrons* (and this includes *Azaleas*) which between them flower from early spring to early summer. The early ones, often flowering before the leaves appear, are inevitably more prone to spring frosts, as we know to our cost in Foggy Bottom which is in a 'frost pocket'. This term applies mostly to lower elevations where frost 'drains' from higher land into lower valleys or areas. A certain amount of protecting can be done in situ with materials such as fleece or coverings, though this is laborious and time consuming. If you have a choice, it's best to plant your frost susceptible plants where they will not be caught by the morning sun, at least until mid-morning. Here are a few *Rhododendrons* photographed in Foggy Bottom.

One of the most desirable *Rhododendrons*, which best represents the distinctive Japanese species originating from Yakushima Island, is the exquisitely flowered *R. yakushimanum* 'Koichiro Wada'. It is named after the plantsman and nurseryman who discovered it on the southern island in 1934. Here it is in Foggy Bottom in mid-spring.

"Extraordinary and beautiful. Good for the eyes and for the soul."

The unusual orange-pink flowers of *Rhododendron* 'Olga' is one of my favourites. Here in late spring, it is toning in well with a purple-leaved *Berberis thunbergii* f. *atropurpurea* 'Dart's Red Lady' and the brightly foliaged shrub *Cornus mas* 'Variegata'.

← This Knap Hill hybrid blazes with colour so my thought was to place it where it counts in its flowering season. Unfortunately, (as sometimes happens) I've long lost the label, but if I suggest it's probably *Rhododendron* 'Glowing Embers' will anyone complain? After several years, because of its cramped position, it has become a somewhat scrawny shrub, but in late spring it comes into bloom. The large flowers contrast brilliantly with purple-leaved *Cotinus coggygria* 'Royal Purple' and the golden yellow foliage of *Cornus mas* 'Aurea' behind.

I have somewhat of a passion for *Rhododendrons* with 'blue' flowers, and one of the closest to that colour is the dwarf *R.* 'Songbird'. Described as violet, the colour depends on the light and the camera… but I'm calling this blue!

Magnolia Spring

A wide spreading *Magnolia* × *soulangeana* bursting into bloom from naked branches, looking from the south. An early morning mist rises in the background above and amongst trees, shrubs and conifers. On the right, the trunk of a silver birch and fresh golden yellow shoots on *Philadelphus coronarius* 'Aureus', a golden-leaved mock orange.

What you don't see… Many years before, this *Magnolia* was planted where I thought it had room to grow – a familiar thought had by many gardeners as they plant a new addition. Of course, other surrounding plants were also going to grow, and did. Left to their own devices, plants generally adapt, as did the *Magnolia* – one long branch extending more each year into the light whilst the other side of the shrub has gradually died back due to lack of light and moisture. Now, a little careful pruning is enough to maintain this distinctive annual display.

Apart from the colour, this lives up to its name 'Black Tulip' and is a stunning *Magnolia*. Fairly upright in habit and easier to fit into a small garden than the larger wider-spreading varieties, it can also be pruned to keep its shape. Tulip or goblet-shaped burgundy flowers (black they are not!) will make a bold show in any garden.

More shrubby and delicate-looking than the other two *Magnolias*, this slower growing and more compact selection of the star magnolia, *Magnolia stellata* 'Water Lily', has lightly fragrant flowers and has been a regular in Foggy Bottom for over forty years.

A Spring Medley

Though distinctive, *Sophora* 'Sun King' seems too exotic a shrub to flower in early spring. But here it is in Foggy Bottom, a vigorous grower in sun and on well-drained soil, making some impact with clusters of bright golden yellow bell-like flowers amongst the evergreen leaves.

The vivid orange flowers of a *Berberis* × *stenophylla* seedling in Foggy Bottom and many other *Berberis* with such vibrantly coloured flowers can be difficult to place in the garden. That said, the glowing orange can light up your spring garden. Though often held in low regard, *Berberis* are accommodating and easy growing plants.

↑
The evergreen *Choisya* are reliable plants for almost any size of garden, adaptable to sun and some shade if they have good drainage. They respond well to pruning if their eventual size becomes an issue. This plant of *Choisya* 'Aztec Pearl' is pruned annually after its main spring flowering period and always responds with a superb display of fragrant dazzling white flowers. Place it close to a pathway that's used regularly to enjoy both fragrance and flower.

↑
Like many spring flowering shrubs and small trees, flowers are often fleeting, affected by possible frost and fluctuations in temperature. *Berberis* can be one, *Amelanchier* another, but ideally you want your plants to have more than one season of interest. *Amelanchiers*, known as the serviceberry, are recognised for their autumn colour. Here in Foggy Bottom, *A.* 'La Paloma' has coppery leaves in spring to contrast with pendulous racemes of sparkling white flowers.

The brooms may be relatively short-lived, but amongst them are some with the brightest of flowers. I have always had space for a few in Foggy Bottom, placing them for maximum impact as they come into flower in late spring. The compact *Cytisus* 'Lena' is one of the most colourful – and it might have been even more outstanding had I planted it in front of a blue spruce (*Picea pungens*). That said, it's very striking here in front of *Picea glauca* var. *albertiana* 'J.W. Daisy's White'. →

Whilst it may be a somewhat ungainly shrub, few could deny that *Cornus kousa* 'Miss Satomi' is rather special. Here it is planted in full sun in the Mini-Pinetum surrounded by ferns and perennials, the saucer-like pink bracts on short stems almost weigh down the branches. The intensity of colour may vary each spring. Prune after flowering to improve the shape.

The Dogwoods of Spring

I could hardly cover the subject of spring flowering shrubs and small trees without including the *Cornus* which feature so much in Foggy Bottom, and perhaps deserve to be better known and planted more widely. I am of course not referring to the equally valuable *Cornus* species and cultivars like *C. sanguinea* 'Midwinter Fire' grown for their coloured winter stems. Below are a few selections from the garden.

A more recent introduction is *C. kousa* 'Venus', a five-year-old plant rising above ferns and perennials which has been pruned to form a better shape. Though impressive, I'm not sure the large bracts look entirely natural.

I rescued this specimen of *Cornus kousa* var. *chinensis* from a rather inhospitable position some years ago. Now established, it seems to have thanked me every year with a magnificent display of flowers, so massed that you can hardly find space between them. The flowers are actually raised buds in the middle of the bract which in warm autumns become edible, looking very like a strawberry.

Late for Spring, Early for Summer

Having spent a couple of springs working on a nursery in the US many years ago and seeing certain plants in the wild, I was inspired to try them in Foggy Bottom when I got the opportunity. These are two of them and every time I observe them in flower in late spring, I wonder at the beauty and diversity of nature. The first is the North American fringe tree, *Chionanthus virginicus*, which I would hardly want to give space to as a deciduous foliage shrub, but when the wispy white strap-like petals come out you have to take notice and enjoy the moment. ↑

Somewhat dull as an evergreen shrub, there's no mistaking the brilliant scarlet buds of this mountain laurel, *Kalmia latifolia* 'Ostbo Red'. There are several selections with mostly red, pink or white flowers, often prettily 'painted' as they open to reveal their delicate markings. Like most *Rhododendrons*, *Kalmia latifolia*, also known as the calico bush, needs an acid soil to thrive. →

You won't find many roses in Foggy Bottom for two main reasons. Firstly, our local deer like them too much and secondly, they need to be trouble free from pests and disease. Those two reasons might cancel each other out, but the photograph here is a case in point where a rose can be the ideal shrub. *Rosa* 'Knock Out' here is creating a vibrant summer long display as a single plant in an otherwise mostly evergreen backdrop. It wasn't really planned at the time (but of course, I can claim it is evident now!) that there is a sort of symmetry to the rounded evergreens behind the bright cherry red rose. The light-coloured conifer immediately behind is *Sequoia sempervirens* 'Adpressa' and being pruned each spring results in new fresh creamy white shoots shimmering like fallen snow. Without pruning, this form of the coastal redwood might be close to 10 m (33 ft) or more by now. The dark green bush behind is a fifty-year-old *Pinus sylvestris* 'Moseri'. Further back, the purple leaves of *Cotinus coggygria* 'Royal Purple' contrasts in turn with a pyramidal blue spruce, *Picea pungens* 'Hoto'. The rose, perhaps too close to the house for the deer, happily flowers on and off all summer.

02
06

Gardening with Grasses

This is a classic combination, entire opposites in colour and foliage type. *Hosta* 'Halcyon' is one of the best blue-leaved *Hostas*, which in half shade holds its colour well and is notable for its flowering performance. The variegated Hakone grass, *Hakonechloa macra* 'Alboaurea', with narrow gold and green striped leaves intermingles with the *Hosta* creating an arresting foliage partnership. Although this planting was completed at least twenty years earlier when the plants were separate, the natural spreading habit of the *Hakonechloa* has resulted in them growing together... and it could be that without intervention it will eventually overrun the *Hosta*. Nothing stays the same, so after so many years, lifting and replanting may now be necessary.

This indispensable group of plants were initially listed in most books or catalogues as 'Ornamental Grasses' to bring them to the attention of gardeners, who until then, largely considered grass as what made a lawn! How things have changed...

Again, I refer to their early days in the 1960s and 70s when groups or collections of ornamental grasses were planted as a standalone feature, almost as though they might infect the rest of the garden if allowed to mingle with other plants. Creating an early bed in Foggy Bottom primarily using grasses, I quickly realised this wasn't the best way to display them and that they would be more effective combined with different textured and flowering perennials, conifers and shrubs. Now their wider role in gardens and landscapes has been fully accepted and their considerable diversity has allowed their use in a wide range of situations.

As with perennials, there are grasses suitable for all sizes and types of gardens, which shouldn't be a surprise if you consider how widely they are dispersed in nature across the world. Natural is the effect that they offer to a garden, where drifts can be used in a prime or supporting role and single specimens can be the centre of attention given careful companion planting.

Although you will already have seen the use and effect of grasses in Foggy Bottom, here are a few selections with my comments.

"Very tranquil and lush.
Feels like an oasis of calm."

I value this grass highly for the stature it offers amongst perennials and the contrast it provides to different types of foliage and flower. It has come a long way since the species is a native of New Zealand, widespread on both North and South Islands where it is often dominant in grasslands. In this example in Foggy Bottom, the *Chionochloa* is central to the grouping. It fronts the variegated *Cornus sericea* 'White Gold' and subdues, or perhaps helps to absorb, the vivid cerise flowers of rose campion, *Lychnis coronaria*. Whilst the plants around it have changed, the red tussock grass has been in this position for over fifteen years. *Salvia nemorosa* 'East Friesland' is on the left.

Sometimes to really 'discover' your plants, you have to get up early on a summer's morning just before sunrise and spend the next hour or so wondering at the glory of nature. This indispensable grass, *Stipa tenuissima*, is a case in point. A combination of a happily healthy plant growing in an open sunny situation with dew following a cooler night. Tiny droplets which weigh lightly on delicate feathery plumes create an amazingly intricate and dramatic effect. You then can't take photographs quickly enough to record this seemingly magical scene.

As gardeners, and particularly in Britain, we often tend to be attracted to plants with more colourful flowers or foliage, as with the Hakone grasses, so named for the species that is found in the region of Mount Hakone in Japan. But green is also a colour and this drift of *Hakonechloa macra* at Foggy Bottom shows how ornamental and striking it can be, catching the sun and the wind. The band of flowing green frames the bottom of this view in late summer with the contrasting *Rudbeckia fulgida* var. *sullivantii* 'Goldsturm' between and the brilliant white mound of *Hydrangea arborescens* 'Annabelle' behind.

Two grasses, the glowing crimson-leaved *Imperata cylindrica* 'Rubra' and brilliant white bottlebrush inflorescences of *Pennisetum villosum*, have timed it perfectly to make a memorable combination in late summer. Both do better on moist soils but need good drainage. The *Imperata* is aptly called the Japanese blood grass whilst the *Pennisetum* is called the feathertop grass. Originating in Africa and on the borderline of hardiness (Zone 8 in the US perhaps), but even as an annual it is worth a permanent spot in the garden as it flowers until the autumn frosts.

← In the shade of Rosemary's Wood in early winter, the subdued yellow foliage of a ground covering greater woodrush, *Luzula sylvatica* 'Aurea', contrasts well with the dark glossy green leaves of *Mahonia japonica* 'Bealei'. Given a sunny position the *Luzula* leaves will turn a bright gold but are prone to scorching from summer sun.

↑
When leaves of any *Hakonechloa* die back in autumn, the last thing in my mind to do is to cut them back, since in their dormant state there are still several months to enjoy. Light, sunlight, wind, frost and even wet days will change the dying foliage. Here in January, you can get a feeling of how attractive *Hakonechloa macra* 'Albovariegata' (or any other cultivar) can be at this time of year, meandering, perhaps as a river, between the dark evergreen *Pinus heldreichii* 'Smidtii'. Leave the cutting back until mid-spring, just as new season growth begins.

↑
Ground frost on the foliage of grasses is transformed to water droplets by the warmth of the sun, highlighting the subdued Japanese blood grass. This *Imperata cylindrica* 'Rubra' in the foreground, whose foliage is now light brown in late winter, is quite different in habit to the red tussock grass from New Zealand, *Chionochloa rubra*, more ever-brown than evergreen. I have used this imposing and useful grass in several locations at Bressingham, where it has survived nearly all winters.

Three Aspects of *Miscanthus*

The increasing range of *Miscanthus* cultivars now offer a real choice to gardeners and landscapers. Most of the twenty or so species originate from Japan and the Far East, the most common being *M. sinensis*, which has innumerable cultivars of varying heights, inflorescences and foliage. Whilst few are invasive via a spreading habit, in hotter climates earlier flowering selections seed freely. Clump forming selections can get large and difficult to manage… but that still gives a wide selection. Here are some distinct cultivars shown in Foggy Bottom.

A close-up of the horizontal stripes; creamy white bands are vividly marked on the green vertical stems of *Miscanthus sinensis* 'Gold Bar' making a dazzling contrast. At around 90 cm (3 ft), this is the most dwarf of this type which makes it a good container plant. It seldom flowers with me. Also recommended for the garden is the taller *M. s.* 'Strictus', 180 cm (6 ft).

The clue is in the name *Miscanthus nepalensis*, a distinct species from the Himalayas which has a charm of its own. It deserves a sunny, well-drained spot where it can make a stunning display of elegant pendulous plumes from late summer to midwinter. With good drainage it survives winters in the UK, though it is probably Zone 8 in North America.

Although this *Miscanthus sinensis* 'Kaskade' has died back for winter, the previous year's growth is still making a bold show in the garden. In autumn, some *Miscanthus* (particularly the taller ones) may be damaged by wind, and if unsightly could be cut to the ground. Others like 'Kaskade', introduced by German plantsman Ernst Pagels, is still garden worthy in midwinter as the pendulous plumes are dramatically enhanced by jewel-like frost.

In Praise of Pampas

You may have noticed from earlier pages that I have used the (often considered overused) pampas grass in several ways in Foggy Bottom. Why? Because it is a dramatic late interest plant that in milder temperate zones and countries looks good all winter. It is clump forming, so in similar climates (but not like California where it seeds freely) it is long-lived and performs year after year with little maintenance. However, perhaps in a small garden even the best and so called 'dwarf' *Cortaderia selloana* 'Pumila' may eventually dominate, so it should be a considered decision. The following images may inform that decision more.

Most of the pampas grasses don't 'flower' until autumn, but few gardeners may be aware that for some years there has been an early flowering cultivar in cultivation. Discovered in Chile by American nursery owner Kurt Bluemel, *Cortaderia selloana* 'Patagonia' not only flowers two months earlier than most other cultivars of this species but is also hardier. Here is a clump in Foggy Bottom with plumes rising above surrounding perennials in late summer, drawing attention to the large golden-leaved *Catalpa bignonioides* 'Aurea' behind.

Pampas grasses come into their own in autumn and seem designed to contrast with autumn colours. Imposing from a distance with their white plumage, they are equally impressive up close. There is no doubting which of these might be *Cortaderia selloana* 'Pumila', but even this can reach 2 m (6 ft) or more. The other cultivar *C. s.* 'Sunningdale Silver' is almost more showy, long stems topped by fluffy heads reach 3 m (10 ft) but will be prone to early damage if exposed to strong winds. ↓

A sunny morning in late November (unusual in England!) is responsible for creating an uplifting spectacle, the light filters through *Cortaderia selloana* 'Pumila' behind the leafless stems of *Cornus alba* 'Baton Rouge'. The full power of the sun's light blanches the plumes on the right, blurring the definition of the delicate fluffy inflorescences. ↓

The Snake Bed in late January. Some might suggest it's time to cut and tidy the plants, including the grasses… but although that time is near, there is still some drama to be had as frost and morning sun light up grasses and perennials.

02
07

Conifers and their Place in Foggy Bottom

One of a few selections of Norway spruce discovered in the wild, *Picea abies* 'Rydal' was found in a forest in Sweden. This seemingly dark green pyramidal conifer is transformed for a short period in spring by spectacular new growth, a crimson-purple foliage that quickly dulls and goes back to green. It is best kept pruned as a compact pyramid immediately after new growth has faded, so that new buds can develop.

My father Alan Bloom had a passion for perennials and his innovative 'island beds' was his way of displaying them. By 1962 his six-acre Dell Garden contained about 4,500 varieties of hardy perennials, ferns and grasses, planted in forty-eight beds. Now, maintained much as they were, Alan's son-in-law, Jaime Blake, has kept them in immaculate condition (except ironically with much more damage from deer and rabbits than there was in 1962).

I began my conifer collection, growing them to sell on our nursery along with perennials. Foggy Bottom expanded to six acres as I brought in more conifers to 'trial', so I could recommend their diversity from experience. And diversity there certainly is. In the early days since starting to plant in 1966, conifers were classed as Tall, Slow Growing and Dwarf. You will get much more of an idea of this when you see the development of Foggy Bottom in the latter half of this book.

Size Matters

Unlike the Dell Garden, where perennials are cut to the ground each winter, Foggy Bottom has changed dramatically. Many of the original conifers are now of tree size, and the trees… well, have become trees. It's what they do, given a chance. Now the combination of plants in Foggy Bottom, once an empty meadow devoid of trees, has a structure that adds to the overall definition and drama of the garden. Thinning and pruning must be done of course and for most gardeners, this is perhaps the least understood aspect of growing conifers as garden plants. As you look at them, individually or with other plants, hopefully this book will provide some helpful ideas.

The Big Picture

This view of the Mini-Pinetum encompasses the many aspects of conifers. Taken in November, it should dispel the myths that "conifers are all the same" and that "conifers lack colour compared with other plants". Here, the taller ones planted before 1980 are reaching for the sky; tall blue in the centre is a noble fir, *Abies procera* 'Glauca'. Just in front to the right, now 10 m (33 ft) tall, is the seemingly misnamed dwarf Serbian spruce, *Picea omorika* 'Nana', contrasting with the bright golden yellow *Pinus contorta* 'Chief Joseph'. The latter may be the largest specimen in Britain and is now about twenty years old. It has green foliage in summer, but when most of us need uplifting as we enter the darker days of winter, 'Chief Joseph' obligingly transforms into a brilliant winter colour. The taller specimen to the right is a Colorado blue spruce, *Picea pungens* 'Thomsen', itself next to a half-hidden golden Scots pine, *Pinus sylvestris* 'Aurea', which also only colours in winter. Behind the columns of green *Thuja occidentalis* 'Degroot's Spire' to the left, there are still leaves to fall from deciduous plants. From left to right; *Cotinus coggygria* 'Royal Purple', *Acer palmatum* 'Shishi-gashira', and the orange red *Sorbus* 'Autumn Spire'. The taller conifers have not been pruned, though lower branches have been removed. The two conifers in the front centre, *Picea pungens* 'Glauca Prostrata' and *Juniperus squamata* 'Holger', are pruned annually.

"This is truly one of the, if not the, most magnificent gardens we have ever visited."

Get your bearings by spotting the tallest conifer, *Abies procera* 'Glauca', the same fir as in the previous November view of the Mini-Pinetum. Now from the south, morning frost in late January clings to grass and plants until the sun rises and creates some transformational magic. Conifers provide important structure as well as colour in Foggy Bottom. Of course, not many could look back as I can to this view when it was a flat meadow in 1966.

← Looking across Rhus Corner from this vantage point, you don't see the broad grass pathway dividing it from the All Seasons Bed behind. Year-round this offers a taller backdrop to grasses (mostly *Stipa tenuissima*) and perennials in front, soon to make a spectacular display. In Foggy Bottom I have been able to design the planting to take advantage of 'borrowed' views, with vistas always in mind. On the same theme, taller trees beyond are in yet a further bed. Intended to be planted in a temporary position since I knew it would become a large tree, *Metasequoia glyptostroboides* 'Gold Rush', the tall golden foliaged conifer to the right is a striking selection of the deciduous dawn cypress. Temporary became permanent as 'Gold Rush' eventually became too big to move!

Conifers By Design

This photograph illustrates how imposing a conifer can be → when it is planted to rise well above its surroundings as a lone specimen. This remarkable form of the Serbian spruce is not in Foggy Bottom but planted by myself and a few colleagues in 1995 in the Dell Garden as a memorial for my brother Robert. *Picea omorika* 'Pendula Bruns' has certainly been a special tree, becoming more outstanding year by year, and has developed a character of its own… visible from a considerable distance, akin to *Jack and the Beanstalk*. The Serbian spruce in its natural habit is now classed as an endangered species.

Fronting two beds, but very much combining their effect is a ↓ grouping of deep green columnar conifers, *Thuja occidentalis* 'Degroot's Spire', interplanted with crimson red flowers of *Crocosmia* 'Lucifer's Match?' and *Helenium* 'Sahin's Early Flowerer' in the foreground. The narrow sentinel-like conifers offer structure and year-round colour – more bronze in winter – and whilst not taking too much space, create opportunities for plant combinations.

On a misty spring morning, *Pinus thunbergii* 'Sayonara' becomes a plant of substance. Late winter and new early spring shoots are white – a distinct feature on this Japanese species – but are now losing contrast and will soon develop into green needles. Central to the lower planting around it is a blue fescue, *Festuca glauca* 'Elijah Blue'. If there is a lesson here, it is that a conifer can be the focal point of a year-round plant association. Selections of more temporary plants can vary as the conifer grows so it remains in scale with the plants around it and are mutually complimentary.

Chameleon Conifers

← It seems a pity, perhaps a lost opportunity, when a new conifer (or any plant for that matter) is given a rather dull non-descriptive name. This plant in my view deserves better than *Picea abies* 'Pusch', until you understand that it was named after the person who discovered it in Germany, Herr Pusch. No doubt it started as a collector's plant, but to get wider recognition you might need to call it 'Pusch's Spring Surprise'... Anyway, it is a dwarf form which has a startling display of red cones in spring, even on young plants. Though the vibrant colours soon fade, 'Pusch' retains its cones for a long period, the main point of interest on such a small conifer.

Knowing that this Austrian pine would become a large, somewhat ungainly tree without pruning, I decided to keep it pruned in as natural a manner as possible. The process continues each year, and the black pot containing a few trimmings and a pair of red handled secateurs might lead you to see some of the cuts I have made. No ordinary Austrian pine, this is *Pinus nigra* 'Aurea' with pale golden-yellow new shoots in spring lightening up the whole plant.

↓

↑

What makes a conifer turn from green in summer to gold in winter? There is a scientific explanation which is to do with temperature and light, but it is to our advantage as gardeners that this happens. Green is a good background for other colours in summer, but when this mountain pine, *Pinus mugo* 'Carsten', turns to gold in winter you don't need another colour to go with it. This plant is thirty years old; its best colour is achieved in full sun. Here I have pruned the front part, but not the shoots and stems to the upper left, so you can see without pruning it would soon become too large and untidy.

Conifers That Grow On You

One of the most eye-catching conifers in spring, when most people visit garden centres, is *Picea glauca* var. *albertiana* 'J.W. Daisy's White'. You might even find it irresistible! Many of us might be tempted to buy on impulse and I am no different... but we won't pursue that here. It seems a confusing name, but the initials J.W. are those of the man who discovered it in Belgium and he named it after his granddaughter Daisy... not many people know that. But how fast will it grow and where to put it? You are looking at three plants of the *Picea*, almost hugging each other, that I planted in Foggy Bottom about twenty years ago. They are now over 2 m (6 ft 6 in) tall and have started growing into each other, but I am happy to leave them as they still make a great feature in the garden. But something has to give. On the right is a prostrate yew with variegated leaves, *Taxus baccata*, growing upwards but also sideways. If allowed to continue, it will grow into the *Picea* and spoil it. Pruning back the *Taxus* is only a temporary solution, so eventually it had to be removed. This area will be completely changed, but the *Picea* remains for at least a few more years. In fact, I have nicknamed (in jest) the snow-capped spruces Jungfrau, Eiger and Mönch after the iconic Swiss mountains which I have often visited!

↑

Looking at the All Seasons Bed in Foggy Bottom, the conifers themselves underline their diversity. Diversity in form, colour and size. Looking at the smaller conifers in front, you will be able to spot a five-year-old *Picea glauca* var. *albertiana* 'J.W. Daisy's White'. To gauge an idea of age and size, the tall scrawny looking pine in the distant left is a golden Scots pine, *Pinus sylvestris* 'Aurea', planted more than forty years ago and has typically lost its lower branches. The conifers in the centre of the bed are about thirty years old and those recently planted in the foreground are aged around five years. In a more mature garden, small conifers would look out of place and out of scale, so this tends to be used as my 'garden nursery' to trial but also to grow until big enough to fit the 'big' garden.

Conifers Up Close

← The delicate new leaves …or needles on the deciduous conifer *Metasequoia glyptostroboides* 'Gold Rush' look almost pre-historic. And of course, it is. Named the dawn cypress, it was only seen in fossils and considered extinct until it was discovered in China in 1941. You are looking at the leaves of a 'fossil tree', the other common name, whose ancestors go back fifty million years.

↑

There is an amazing brightness to this recent selection of the Korean fir, *Abies koreana* 'Kohout's Ice Breaker', which has green needles that are silver beneath. Natural mutations have brought us forms like *A. k.* 'Silberlocke' (Silver Curls), the parent of *A. k.* 'Kohout's Ice Breaker'. A very descriptive name for an interesting plant which you see here. It may try to revert to a tree, so any strong upward shoots need to be cut away if your evergreen silvery *Abies* is to maintain its identity.

↑

Most conifers don't have cones until they reach a certain maturity. Both male and female 'flowers' often appear on the same plant in close proximity and the wind does the rest. It is female cones that develop, hold, and eventually disperse the seed as the cones open. That is about as much as I know, and probably as much as the average gardener wants to know! But cones can be quite an attraction, as can be seen on this Japanese white pine, *Pinus parviflora* 'Negishi', a free coning and handsome selection. Captured in early summer, the cones are tightly formed and held in clusters near the new branch tips and clear of the needles. They are often quite resinous and sticky to the touch. Not noticeable here are less attractive, more open cones from previous years.

You never know what lies beneath… These somewhat strange wooden shapes look like something from Tolkien's *The Hobbit* or perhaps sleeping toads peeking above the soil for a look as to what is going on. Imagination need go no further as, perhaps equally strangely, these are aerial roots belonging to a swamp cypress, *Taxodium distichum*, on the island in the Foggy Bottom pond. I was delighted when I first saw these emerge a few years ago and have watched them slowly developing. The roots are largely hollow and have been best described as 'respiratory knees' which assist the plant in breathing, no doubt a considerable benefit when in a swamp.

02
08

Indispensable Foliage

What is foliage? The Oxford Dictionary simply states – leaves, leafage. In the plant world that covers a very wide range. Size, colour, shape and form. In the garden, we are likely to only notice foliage when it stands out from other plants. On the other hand, we grow many plants primarily because of their striking foliage. It seems to me that we should also consider foliage as something alive and on a plant, not fallen leaves on the ground nor specimen leaves, dried or preserved. Whether that is correct or not, my coverage on this subject is shown in photographs taken at Foggy Bottom. Let the images speak for themselves, though not entirely (since I might be doing myself out of a job). My captions are intended to give more depth and understanding than a picture would do on its own. But you won't, I am sure, have any doubt as to how important I believe foliage is in Foggy Bottom – and for that matter, any garden.

Morning dew is not uncommon in Foggy Bottom, particularly on cooler nights in autumn. Look at this dramatic contrast between the golden autumn leaves of *Cornus sanguinea* 'Magic Flame' and *Cotinus coggygria* 'Royal Purple'. The dew glistens on the leaves of the *Cotinus*, and if you look hard to the lower right you will spot the blue flowers of *Geranium* 'Rozanne' which has been flowering since June.

The Colour Purple

Not a flower to be seen. In the Vertical Bed in Foggy Bottom, a spring view of foliage contrasts at different heights, in colour and size of leaves. The tall, most dominant shrub on the left is the deep purple-leaved *Corylus maxima* 'Purpurea', which is pruned at least twice a year to keep the plant bushy and maintain its rounded shape. In front are two dwarf *Berberis* cultivars contrasting with the *Corylus* and with each other; bright green-leaved *B. thunbergii* 'Kobold' and *B. t.* 'Bonanza Gold'. Directly behind these is a columnar (partly because it has been pruned) *Cupressus arizonica* var. *glabra* 'Blue Ice', and *B. t.* 'Golden Torch' near the birch. The *Berberis thunbergii* species and cultivars are not considered much for their flowering performance but offer a lot of choice for shape and foliage colour and take well to pruning. Seldom pruned are two rigidly upright specimens of purple-leaved *Berberis*, *B. t.* f. *atropurpurea* 'Helmond Pillar', on either side of this image. As a contrast, the front is planted with the low grey-leaved *Lavandula angustifolia* 'Blue Cushion', soon to splash the scene with lilac-blue fragrant flowers.

Ageratina altissima 'Chocolate' – the name best describes this excellent clump forming perennial which offers striking purple spring and summer leaves until it flowers (if you let it) in late autumn. It is a great foliage contrast to many different perennials and grasses. Here in one of many groupings in Foggy Bottom, it has been planted between the now finished flowering *Crocosmia* 'Lucifer', and the truly gold petals of the hardy coneflower, *Rudbeckia fulgida* var. *sullivantii* 'Goldsturm'. Behind and close enough to contrast are the white panicles of *Hydrangea paniculata* 'Phantom'. I usually cut back the *Ageratina* in midsummer to ensure the longevity of the purple foliage. Without pruning, your plants might grow to 1.5 m (5 ft) before delicate panicles of white flowers appear.

Another first-class perennial which seems to have everything going for it. *Actaea simplex* 'Brunette' is one of a few cultivars of this bugbane (not the most complimentary of common names) with dark purple, finely cut foliage. Attractive grown as a single specimen or in a group where not too dry, in shade or sun (where summers are not too hot and prolonged). In late summer, there is usually a good show of white bottlebrush, fragrant flowers. 'Brunette' and other cultivars are great foliage plants to use in combinations in a prime or supporting role. Here, I planted 'Brunette' close to a free flowering scarlet rose, *Rosa* 'Knock Out', now in its second flowering. Whether it be a shrub or perennial, bold purple leaves make a striking contrast to red, orange or blue flowers. These make for distinct combinations which I have used a lot in Foggy Bottom. Consider planting *A. s.* 'Brunette' in half shade with *Geranium* 'Rozanne' and *Hakonechloa macra* 'Alboaurea'. Such a combination can be created in a small garden and makes an impact for three seasons of the year.

Although not always the easiest of shrubs to grow, few can match the impact *Cercis canadensis* 'Forest Pansy' has with its large, heart-shaped purple leaves. The underside of the leaf is wine-coloured, often revealed by the wind. Only the foliage is seen from an established plant in Foggy Bottom, positioned in half shade and maintaining a strong colour against nearby conifers in late summer. In another planting in the Summer Garden at Bressingham, a large group of scarlet vermilion *Crocosmia* 'Lucifer' in front of 'Forest Pansy' makes a much more dramatic impact than if either were planted on their own.

Gold or Yellow, or Golden Yellow?

You need to be down at ground level to fully appreciate the beauty of this hardy *Geranium* 'Blue Sunrise'. Although here it makes a startling contrast with leaves emerging from a carpet of purple-leaved free flowering *Ajuga*, the latter will eventually smother the golden foliage. 'Blue Sunrise' is best in half shade and has a good show of blue flowers in early summer.

↓

Pink and yellow? Pink and yellow may not be an ideal colour match, though this is less obvious among plants and particularly softer coloured ones. Earlier in the summer, the *Hydrangea paniculata* 'Dart's Little Dot' had white flower panicles, now they shade to pink in late summer, deepening to maroon as autumn arrives. *Cotinus coggygria* 'Golden Spirit' is brighter yellow in full sun, but still stands out against a shady background. Though effective and easily pruned, it is not as vigorous as the purple-leaved forms. In the foreground, the free flowering *Pennisetum villosum* contrasts with another grass, the Japanese *Imperata cylindrica* 'Rubra'.

There's no doubt as to the dominant plant in this part of Foggy Bottom! Creating a sense of drama is relatively easy with a tree like *Catalpa bignonioides* 'Aurea'. The species is commonly known as the Indian bean tree, originating not from India but the American Southeast. In warm climates it will make a large tree with enormous leaves; the green form considered an excellent shade tree. Spring frosts tend to do the pruning for me and keep my plant quite small, but the *Catalpas* are quite easy to prune in early spring when branches are leafless. In this planting I have made it a 'star' amongst the lower, less obviously coloured surrounding plants. This is in a sheltered spot in full sun, and if we miss a severe winter, it flowers and fruits freely.

This is one of many holly seedlings I have found in Foggy Bottom over the years, but the → only one with golden leaves. This arose from *Ilex aquifolium* 'Flavescens' and seemed to be more compact with pricklier leaves and distinctive reddish bronze spring shoots. Rather unimaginatively, I called it *I. a.* 'Foggy Bottom Gold'. Although golden-leaved plants can be attractive in the right position in the garden, they are not always so easy to produce on a nursery, as I found out. The soft leaves lacking chlorophyll are prone to scorching. Placing them in a garden can be challenging too. In exposed situations foliage can also get damaged. Too much sun and maybe leaves will burn. Too little sun and leaves turn green. Well, some plants are more of a challenge than others but 'Foggy Bottom Gold' in the right place makes a great garden shrub!

Green Is a Colour Too

One of the strangest perennials is this large-leaved *Darmera peltata* (formerly named *Peltiphyllum peltatum*). The giant scalloped leaves die back in autumn, usually turning to golden green before a long period of dormancy. In early spring well before the leaves emerge, several 60–75 cm (2–2.5 ft) spikes arise, snake-like as if testing the air, terminating with small clusters of pink flowers. The leaves, waiting their turn, slowly unfurl to form upturned umbrella-like scalloped canopies. This group is very happy planted down near the pond in Foggy Bottom.

Another spectacular plant is the North American skunk cabbage, *Lysichiton americanus*. Skunks are rather clever animals who have the ability when threatened to literally make a stink, exuding an ammonia like gas that you don't want to get on your gardening clothes (or any others!). If you are downwind of a *Lysichiton* in the spring, you might catch a similar (but wholly natural) smell. Now to the good points... The *Lysichiton* has early exotic 'flowers' on a cone-like head hidden amongst deep golden yellow spathes, long before the enormous glossy and finely veined leaves develop. In moist areas, they reach around 2 m (6 ft) in height. The central cone seen in the centre of the photograph develops seeds, which when ripe can spread far and wide, usually by water in streams and rivers.

↑

These seriously large leaves belong to *Astilboides tabularis*, a very hardy perennial from China and Korea, but probably still better known among gardeners as *Rodgersia tabularis*. The latter name, translated as 'table-like', is quite apt. Looking closer (as often we don't), you can see the intricate veins and structure of the leaf. Best in part shade where not too dry, *A. tabularis* has a scattering of fluffy white plumes in midsummer.

← A change of colour is provided by this plant raised at Bressingham, the leaves, bright green in summer, are transformed by shorter days and cooler nights. This is *Bergenia* 'Bressingham Ruby' named for the winter leaf colour. It would be much less noticeable were it not for the sparkling white flowers of *Galanthus* 'S. Arnott' planted nearby. The *Bergenia* is a tough plant and good for winter interest and ground cover, even at the base of a tree. The leaves turn back to green in late spring just as deep pink flowers emerge… a truly year-round plant.

Colour Up Close

← The glorious spring display of this Eastern European perennial, *Euphorbia epithymoides*, seems to be sunshine itself. In the garden we mostly observe it from a distance of a few feet, not a few inches, so we get a splash of vibrant yellow. Yet, look more closely and although you can notice the small yellow flowers in the centre, it is the underlying layers of yellow leaves that give *Euphorbia* impact. This selection was found in the wild in Romania, but there are several similar selections with *E. e.* 'Sonnengold' considered the brightest. Best in sun where not too dry.

What's the difference between the leaf of a *Hosta* and a *Pulmonaria*? Well, one aspect is that a *Hosta* develops its leaves in spring, well ahead of its summer flowers. As gardeners, we are all aware that without a lot of love and care, the leaves of *Hostas* can be shredded by snails and slugs almost before the flowers arrive. On the other hand, *Pulmonarias* flower for weeks in spring before the foliage comes into its own. According to the variety, I consider that the foliage of many, mostly slug free, *Pulmonarias* are at least equal to some of the best *Hostas*. This striking seedling of *P. longifolia* from Foggy Bottom, captured in midsummer, continues to look good for several months well into the autumn.

↓

There are *Heucheras* and then there are *Heucheras*. What do I mean by that? Well, there are so many varieties available now, such is their popularity for planting in containers and window boxes, it is inevitable that some have been introduced before being fully trialled as garden plants. So, I approach every new selection with a certain amount of suspicion until it has successfully come through three winters with me in Foggy Bottom. I am keeping my fingers crossed on *Heuchera* 'Boysenberry', now impossibly colourful, seen here in its third summer season. Catch the light and you can almost warm your hands beside the glowing leaves. *Hosta* 'Halcyon' behind makes a good contrast.

Considered on the borderline of hardy (Zone 8 US), the South African *Melianthus major* is certainly worth garden space alone for its distinctive summer foliage. That said, this photograph was taken in Foggy Bottom in late October and has survived several winters since planting. There is nothing quite like the soft blue, jagged-edged leaves which can associate with a wide range of perennials or shrubs.

The Autumn Leaves

I'm more impressed each year by this less common variety of *Cornus sanguinea*. We are probably more familiar with *C. s.* 'Midwinter Fire' than this later selection from Holland, *C. s.* 'Magic Flame'. Both varieties retain their soft golden yellow leaves for weeks, but given some sun and reasonable drainage, 'Magic Flame' seems to start colouring earlier and hangs onto leaves a bit later. You can also see the crimson stems which will give a winter long show once leaves have gone. Prune back hard in mid-spring for a strong autumn display.

Parrotia persica, commonly known as Persian ironwood, makes a slow growing broad spreading shrub or small tree. In an open position it is likely to have tinges of gold and red autumn leaves – a bit hit and miss compared with *P. p.* 'Bella'; a more recent introduction shown here. The autumn colour gets more intense and leaves seem to last on the tree for some time. It may well be that we will have to move this plant as it is rather close to another valued shrub. Note the crimson spikes of *Persicaria amplexicaulis* 'Taurus' which flowers until the frost.

The 'stag's horn sumach' would not, on the face of it, be one to recommend for the smaller garden nor for many gardens. Rather ungainly and coarse in appearance, once established it is a vigorous spreading, usually suckering plant and the sap is poisonous. But in the right place it makes a stunning show in autumn. *Rhus typhina* 'Dissecta' has finely cut leaves, but the variety shown here in Foggy Bottom is a selection called *R. t.* 'Radiance'… and who can argue with that? →

This was a holding of breath moment as the early morning sun filtered through the scarlet crimson leaves of 'my' *Acer palmatum* 'Bloodgood' in Rosemary's Wood. You can try to tell people of such a glorious memory, but having a photo to prove it long after the leaves have fallen means you can not only share with others, but relive the moment. That's the main reason for this whole book, to portray and record the glory of the garden…and pass it on to others.

02
09

The Japanese Maples – Full of Eastern Promise

A sense of place, looking from the north. Nearly all these trees were planted within two or three years of each other, so you can get a feeling of scale and the rate of growth. The mounded *Acer palmatum* 'Crimson Queen' in the foreground has been touched by spring frost – a scourge of Japanese maples, particularly if you garden in a 'frost pocket' – but it will recover. Colour changes in the background; from the dark green *A. p.* 'Shishi-gashira' to the silver-leaved *Sorbus thibetica* 'John Mitchell'. Almost hidden is the lime tree, *Tilia × europaea* 'Wratislaviensis', framing the back with golden foliage which turns green in summer.

Nearly all gardeners will have been tempted to grow, or have grown, a Japanese maple at one time. You can see them for sale as very young plants in supermarkets, as Bonsai plants, and as large specimen plants in garden centres. Recommended for pots and containers for a patio or terrace, and for a special place in the garden. Being on neutral to acid soil at Foggy Bottom, I know that if I can give them the right conditions they will add much to the garden, whether Japanese orientated or not. After several years of growing many different varieties in many different situations, I know more about what they don't like than their ideal situation. I'll share my findings alongside the photographs, but suffice to say, as garden plants they must be considered 'unpredictable'.

But all that said, such is the beauty, the drama and their diversity, that even if I do lose a few, I would still accept the challenge of growing them in Foggy Bottom. To underpin that statement, I am embarking on the creation of a Japanese-style garden in which Japanese maples figure prominently. One of the oldest and most treasured Japanese maples in Foggy Bottom is *Acer palmatum* 'Crimson Queen', now about fifty years old. Let's start with this dependable and outstanding cultivar.

"An inspirational garden that makes your heart sing."

Early summer, new growth and no frost damage… *Acer palmatum* 'Crimson Queen' is making a perfect performance fronting this view from the Mini-Pinetum. I had planted *Hakonechloa macra* 'Albovariegata' (almost looking like a cushion) around the base of the maple to 'set it off', and in front of that, *Campanula poscharskyana* 'Blue Waterfall'. Unlike many purple-leaved Japanese maples, 'Crimson Queen' maintains its deep purple colour through most summers.

A Queen for All Seasons

↑ The first ground frost of the autumn shades grey onto the green grass, leaving the colour combination of gold and purple to take all the attention. And yet, timing is everything as *Acer palmatum* 'Crimson Queen' will have lost its leaves within a month as Foggy Bottom goes into winter. A month earlier and the needles of *Pinus mugo* 'Carsten' would still be green. Remarkably, the dwarf pine (formerly called 'Carsten's Wintergold') along with some others makes this dramatic change each year, the colour remaining until the following spring.

← A week later, from a distance among some trees, I caught a glimpse of *Acer palmatum* 'Crimson Queen' as the sun shone through the late autumn foliage. The intricate branching structure developed over fifty years partly revealed.

In early winter, there are still signs of autumn. Some leaves still cling onto our *Acer palmatum* 'Crimson Queen', but the autumn glory days are over. The *Hakonechloa* now provides a calmer tone whilst the variegated leaves die back, beige when moist, pale sand when dry.

In a way, this winter photograph of *Acer palmatum* 'Crimson Queen', is a prime example of what plants mean and can be. As demonstrated, the maple along with other plants grow and change through each season. The light and the weather can create additional drama, and if it can be recorded, that drama can be fully appreciated and remembered. A moment of time is captured. Grasses have died back but remain an interest. Conifers in the background portray their diversity and create a structure of both form and colour.

The garden has changed over fifty years and so has the weather. A snowfall like this has become a rarity in Foggy Bottom, which means if I am lucky enough to be at home it is absolutely vital to get out with the camera to record the drama and transformation that snow brings. Highlighting the branching stems, the three plants featured are different sizes but similar ages; *Acer palmatum* 'Crimson Queen' is in the foreground, left *Prunus incisa* 'Kojo-no-mai', and immediately behind *Betula pendula* subsp. *pendula* 'Youngii'. Another big advantage of snow is that you can believe that there are no weeds!

Successes and Failures

From my experience of growing Japanese maples in Foggy Bottom, to succeed in growing them they prefer an acid or neutral soil. In other words, they don't much like alkaline soils whether clay or chalk. They prefer a humus-rich soil, which can mean adding copious amounts of well-rotted leaf mould or composted pine bark. They dislike poorly drained soils particularly in winter and do not like dry soils. They prefer a position sheltered from strong and cold desiccating winds. They are also susceptible to spring frosts. With all that stacked against them you'd think we'd say, "they are too much of a problem to grow". Then you visit gardens, look at photographs, and see wonderful specimens in pots… you might then decide as I have that even with those problems, and with perhaps some losses, they are worth persevering with.

Too dry? Now perhaps 10 m high, planted in 1978, this is one of the original Japanese maples planted in the woodland area below the pond in Foggy Bottom. The maple was well established by the time my son Matt built the summer house in 2000. Unfortunately, the spreading roots of other trees have made this area much drier, so the maple is struggling to receive enough water in summer and is dying back. So, I either watch it die or try to move it. My preference would be the latter and though I will have to prune it quite severely, there is every chance that it will break out with new growth.

This *Acer palmatum* 'Dissectum Garnet' was happy for some years after planting until roots from a nearby beech tree denied it enough water to thrive. It was gradually dying back to the stump. I made the decision to remove the beech and then the half dead maple remarkably came to life, sprouting from old wood. →

This is the much happier *Acer palmatum* 'Dissectum Garnet' two years later, making a contrast to *Brunnera macrophylla* 'Jack Frost', the red tipped fern *Adiantum aleuticum* 'Japonicum', *Hosta* 'Krossa Regal' and a large-flowered *Rhododendron* hybrid beyond. ↓

More Japanese Maples

Acer palmatum 'Shishi-gashira', introduced as long ago as 1882, is a reliable and distinctive maple that makes a bushy shrub and eventually a tree. This specimen in Foggy Bottom is reaching that stature forty years after planting and has a quiet presence throughout the year. The erect stems are greenish in winter, clusters of leaves are bright green in spring as seen here and darker green in summer and early autumn. The leaves turn to a cinnamon brown much later than most other Japanese maples, though this may vary year to year.

↑

Since getting a further collection of Japanese maples in from a noted plantsman and propagator, and developing the Acer Glade in Foggy Bottom, I have become more attached each year to the amazing *Acer palmatum* 'Shin-deshōjō' (try and say that name quickly twenty times!). In time it makes a small, elegant tree with finely divided leaves, which transform from red to pink over many weeks in spring, gradually turning green. Who says nature isn't magic? Planted in the Acer Glade, it is protected from spring frost, but also has room to grow. Needless to say, 'Shin-deshōjō' lights up this newly planted area each year.

For some years, my favourite and most obvious Japanese maple in the garden was this *Acer palmatum* which I obtained labelled as 'Effigy'. Later, I found the correct name which is 'Fireglow'. It was visible from our sitting room window and in summer the purple leaves are lit by the morning sun. Because I had planted taller conifers to the east of the garden, on cold spring nights the frost on the leaves had usually gone by the time the sun reached it. Then I had the trees removed to make way for our tree house, not considering that the sun the following spring would strike the new growth of 'Fireglow' much earlier in the morning…

…and the emerging young leaves did catch a severe frost the following May, resulting in several branches dying back. A word of advice… don't give up too soon, as even if it looks dead, quite often young shoots still may appear later in the spring or summer. If you look closely, you will notice that two of the thicker stems have been pruned. Now moved, *Acer palmatum* 'Fireglow' is recovering and continues to glow in the sunlight.

↑

Not all Japanese maples belong to the species *palmatum*, the Latin translation in the Oxford Dictionary meaning 'shaped like an open hand' and in Hillier's Manual: 'lobed or divided in hand-like fashion, usually five or seven lobed'. *Acer japonicum* has between seven and eleven lobes and the closely related *Acer shirasawanum* with broader, more rounded leaves has eleven. All very interesting, but a selection of the latter has always been rather special to me since I saw one of some considerable size and age in Holland. This is *A. s.* 'Aureum'. From 1968 as I began the garden, I have enjoyed seeing the elegant structure gradually develop, as well as the broad, golden yellow leaves. It featured in an early planting in a small bed near my house, later in another area called the Acer Glade where it has struggled on heavier, poorly drained soil in winter, and too dry in summer. The third and more successful planting, the small tree you see in this photograph is on well-drained, moist soil in half shade, protected from spring frosts. And the name of the bed? The somewhat utilitarian 'Opposite the Old Kitchen Garden Bed'. Since the old kitchen garden will soon become a Japanese-style garden, perhaps I might find a nicer name.

Growing plants in containers is almost another book, and although I have planted and experimented with various woody and non-woody subjects in pots for use on patios and terraces, this book concentrates more on plants in the garden. With that preamble, it might seem unnecessary to show a Japanese maple in a container. Suffice to state that these maples adapt extremely well to being grown in pots, and it is quite a good way to start growing on smaller plants before planting in the garden – and somewhat less expensive too! This twenty-year-old *Acer palmatum* 'Dissectum Viridis' is shown in spring with fresh, green, finely dissected, red-tipped leaves. It started as a small plant and has been potted on over the years into larger and larger containers (I don't intend to repot it into anything bigger!). Because of its low, wide spreading habit, the container has been carefully lifted so that the lower branches can naturally turn downwards, creating an eye-catching specimen. The autumn colour is striking if you can catch it before the weather takes off the leaves. Here you can more clearly see the wooden pedestal that we have used to lift and position the pot.

02
10

Bulbs that Suit the Garden

As it comes… a slightly scruffy but entirely natural combination. The moment many of us wait for… the harbingers of spring; aconites, *Eranthis hyemalis*, and snowdrops, *Galanthus* 'S. Arnott', are in flower at the base of a silver birch with *Bergenia* 'Bressingham Ruby'. The reason there are so many of this large-flowered snowdrop in the gardens at Bressingham is that I was lucky enough to be given a large clump of *G.* 'S. Arnott' around 1975. I divided the clump into about twenty-five single bulbs and planted them that autumn. Every few years I made many more from these clumps, so now we have a wonderful show in spring. We keep the propagation going so that the show just gets better… and we can hopefully encourage others to do the same.

In the beginning, I had enough going on establishing a garden with woody plants and perennials to bother with planting bulbs. That said, I did scatter a large number of *Narcissus* 'King Alfred' on the area of lawn near our house, as well as many *Crocus*. The daffodils are still there, now with a few other varieties, but the *Crocus* were long ago dug up and eaten by our extremely active and voracious grey squirrels – an unwanted invasive species imported a century or two ago from America. As the garden has developed, I have incorporated bulbs into positions where they combine with other plants, woody or perennial, and already you will have seen the extensive use of *Scilla bithynica* and *Galanthus* 'S. Arnott'. Generally speaking, small 'bulbs in the borders' can be a problem when you come to dig perennials up to divide or move.

We tend to categorise certain plants and that is certainly the case with bulbs. Whilst the delineation seems quite clear between bulbs and other plants – bulbs have a distinct root system denoted by their name and usually include the similar corms – other herbaceous plants are not so easily defined. In gardening, we mostly apply the term 'bulb' to dry bulbs which are sold in autumn and spring. We refer to bulb growers and bulb catalogues, and probably Holland in the same context… Daffodils (*Narcissus*), tulips (*Tulipa*), snowdrops (*Galanthus*), *Alliums* etc. In spring it may be lilies (*Lilium*), gladioli (*Gladiolus*) and *Crocosmia*. In the 'gardening season' – now the more promising season of spring since nurseries began to grow plants in pots to sell to garden centres and retail nurseries – you can purchase bulbs (many of which are perennials with a bulbous root system) alongside other plants and plant together as you wish. Or you can have more time after deliberating and consulting with your bulb catalogue and order for delivery in autumn. After that little treatise, I refer you a few bulbs and how we have used them in Foggy Bottom.

Spring has arrived for many when the daffodils finally burst into bloom, here in Foggy Bottom in mid-March. For others, the daffodils will be earlier or later according to which area and country you live in. At Foggy Bottom we have quite heavy soil and although the daffodils have not spread very widely, they have not declined from increasing competition from tree roots or grass. This is one of the best ways of naturalising daffodils, but to allow the tops to die down naturally after flowering you must let the grass grow around them until perhaps late June. Although that eventually runs the risk of the grass around them to suffer or let other plants seed in, this to me is a risk worth taking for the joy that such a bright display of colour can bring. By August the grass (with a contribution of rain or irrigation) is back to the same standard as that which surrounds it.

← This Fuji cherry, *Prunus incisa* 'Shidare' (which in Japanese means 'weeping'), was a small plant when I received it from Japan many years ago. Now, although it has grown into a rather ungainly looking plant for much of the year, it more than makes up for that with a wonderful show each spring of pink-centred, small white flowers. We have it placed where it can be seen from a distance and have gradually tried to enhance the spring display by planting bulbs around it. The snowdrops have finished flowering, now it's the turn of the daffodils and the Siberian squill, *Scilla siberica,* beneath. We have tried to keep the area directly beneath the cherry clear of weeds or grass which might smother them.

The genus *Chionodoxa* seems as though it should have a worthy common name… and it has! 'Glory of the snow' refers to its main mountainous habitat where flowers appear on snowy slopes. Imagine the show! We seldom have snow in Foggy Bottom and generally snowdrops have finished flowering when the most popular species photographed here, *Chionodoxa luciliae*, comes into flower. This is a bulb best planted in sun with good drainage, but it is quite versatile and contrasts with many spring flowers such as the clusters of rich pink bell-like flowers of *Bergenia* 'Bressingham Ruby'. The *Chionodoxa* seeds and gradually spreads, and if you move a clump of *Bergenia* elsewhere in the garden it is no bad thing for some *Chionodoxa* to travel with it.

This is a clump of a rather little known but first-class *Scilla* known as the Bithynian squill. Why Bithynian? Because it comes from Turkey and the Balkan Peninsula. The Balkan Peninsula? This is turning into a geography lesson but underpins my belief that it is helpful and interesting to know the origins of species that you choose to plant in your garden, which also provides some guidance as to the conditions the plant prefers. And for your information if you aren't aware, the Balkan Peninsula has a coastline in the north-eastern Mediterranean and contains several countries: Greece, Macedonia, Serbia, Bosnia, Croatia and Romania – and those you do know. *Scilla bithynica* has established itself in our garden, flowering a good month before the common bluebell (British and European species), *Hyacinthoides non-scripta*.

Does this action seem familiar to you? Looking through a glossy autumn bulb catalogue, I came across a wonderful picture of *Fritillaria persica* and on impulse added three bulbs alongside others that I was ordering. It wasn't until the bulbs arrived that I had to fully consider where in my low-lying garden, which is badly drained in winter, this exotic plant might thrive. After all, *Fritillaria persica* in its native habitat in Syria, Iraq and Iran is used to hot, dry conditions. So, I planted them in a position of full sun at the base of a tree, a *Robinia*, which usually ensures good winter drainage. I was pleased that the *Fritillaria* succeeded and for many years has made a striking show each spring, so much so that I am now able to remove some bulbs in the early autumn to try elsewhere.

The *Camassias* mostly originate from North America and are rather opposite in their cultural preferences to *Fritillaria persica*. They are a late spring – almost early summer – flowering bulb and related to the *Scillas*. They do well in grass where not too dense, preferring moisture and happy in part shade. They have become more popular in recent years, perhaps because they blend so well with perennials and provide early colour. This clump flowering at Foggy Bottom is *Camassia leichtlinii* 'Caerulea'.

The most ornamental onions, known for large, rounded heads often on tall stems have one main drawback as most who have grown them will know. Their leaves often die back well before the plant has finished flowering, spoiling the drama and possibly embarrassing the garden owner in front of visitors… So, plant your tall *Alliums* in amongst other perennials and grasses where they can peek above their surroundings. Ideally contrast them with other foliage such as a deep green, sharply pointed *Crocosmia*, an early flowering *Geranium* like the white 'Galactic', and a frothy plumed *Stipa tenuissima*. This is *Allium* 'Globemaster'. Its lilac purple flowers have faded, but the definition of the heads and distinctive form is still every bit as impressive. Lastly, when planting, give your *Alliums* enough space to grow and place where they are unlikely to be invaded by vigorous perennials and grasses.

02
11

Raising the Canopy

Over time, most gardeners will be faced with the need to carry out some pruning of trees, conifers or shrubs in the garden. The gardener's attitude might fall into two or more categories. One being, "Just let things grow" or two, "Let's hack this tree/shrub down or get rid of it". There is a third way, which is generally more creative for the gardener and slightly more comfortable for the subject. 'Raising the canopy' sounds less aggressive, more artful and may describe it best.

In a large garden it's possible to use plants to frame a scene which remains for a period, offering a view that is later obliterated by foliage as perennials and grasses grow and trees come into leaf. Here is a case in point. It is early spring as we look between a small *Acer griseum* on the left and a shrub that has turned into a small tree on the right, *Prunus incisa* 'Kojo-no-mai'. The view above a drift of *Erica* × *darleyensis* 'Arthur Johnson' narrows between two upright conifers to the columnar *Taxus baccata* 'Fastigiata Robusta' onto a Japanese cherry in the far distance, *Prunus incisa* 'Shidare', dazzling white in the afternoon sun.

↑
The bushy, round shaped pines are good garden value from when you first put them in your garden, most having been propagated from witches' brooms found on larger conifer species. Some, like this *Pinus mugo* 'Ophir', being one of the naturally dwarf European mountain pines, is not only compact, but has bright lemon-yellow needles in winter. This specimen is around forty years old and taking up too much space in the All Seasons Bed, so now in early spring I have been on my hands and knees to start pruning away the lower branches. Thinning smaller side branches will make this look older and give it more character – and avoid it looking like a mop head (no self-respecting conifer wants to look ridiculous). And of course, rather than taking up the whole space, I can now fill in beneath – which I did, planting the lesser used *Ophiopogon planiscapus* which makes a dense carpet of green leaves.

Here's one I did earlier… *Pinus sylvestris* 'Lodge Hill' began life as a witches' broom in the upper branches of a Scots pine, *Pinus sylvestris*, in Surrey, England. It was found and propagated by nurseryman Don Hatch. I bought a small plant from Don in 1973 and planted it in Foggy Bottom. In time of course, if you can draw a line in your mind's eye from the outer branches to the ground, the conifer without pruning would be at least 3–4 m (10–15 ft) in diameter. I had a couple of choices, a) take it out, or perhaps better, b) prune away the bottom branches to increase its stature but reduce its ground space, creating an opportunity to plant something else beneath. Now on a misty spring morning 'Lodge Hill' is creating its own drama. →

We are looking toward the Acer Glade which is gradually being adapted to a woodland garden leading to our new Japanese-style garden. In the foreground is a seldom seen form of the Canadian hemlock, *Tsuga canadensis* 'Fantana'. It is some years old since first planted as a semi-prostrate bushy plant. It has expanded upwards and outwards and is now a conifer of some substance and grace, having 'limbed up' gradually and made space for shade loving plants; *Hosta* 'Big Mama', *Rodgersia podophylla*, *Geranium* × *cantabrigiense* 'Cambridge' and behind, a large drift of the shuttlecock fern, *Matteuccia struthiopteris*.

I wasn't sure that this would work, but these three specimens of dwarf blue spruce, *Picea pungens* 'Globosa', had grown into each other and the lower branches were looking decidedly untidy and dying back. As ever, I considered the options, a) get rid of them, or b) create a feature… you can always dispose of them later if lifting the canopy doesn't work. The blue spiky foliage is so distinctive and once I had removed the lower branches, I could see that planting contrasting lower plants around them could make for an arresting and colourful combination. Two years later in summer, two of my favourite perennials *Rudbeckia fulgida* var. *sullivantii* 'Goldsturm' and the orange *Crocosmia* 'Spitfire' contrast vividly with the silver-grey foliage of the forty-year-old *Piceas*.

One of the 'small' trees that really does grow on you is Young's weeping birch, *Betula pendula* subsp. *pendula* 'Youngii'. I originally bought this as a small weeping tree to plant amongst heathers in the Mini-Pinetum. It was grafted at about 60 cm (2 ft) high, where you notice the trunk is thicker. Without pruning severely each year it was bound to want to grow into a tree. Pruning away lower branches enables planting beneath – the heathers are still flowering each winter – allowing interesting vistas to other parts of the garden. Here, it handily blocks the rising sun on a late summer's day, mist is in the air and a pale blue *Agapanthus inapertus* is in flower.

If you bought a small plant in a pot labelled as 'Nana', → you would have every right to think that it was a small plant suitable for a small garden or a rockery. And this *Chamaecyparis pisifera* 'Filifera Nana' was small once… but forty years later it's beginning to take up a lot of space. In my view and given the passage of time, this, like many other bushy conifers, is far more interesting when at this age; they are pruned to resemble a tree or perhaps a cluster of trees. They then don't completely block your view and look more mature than 'blobby'. Just pruned, within a year or so this specimen will blend into the surrounding planting.

02
12

Rivers – Going with the Flow

The new, dark purple leaves of *Heuchera* 'Prince' help to hide at least some of the scruffy foliage of *Allium hollandicum* 'Purple Sensation' which was planted a year or two after the snowdrops. But they too make a dramatic contribution to the river and help carry the eye into the two beds and all the way to the pendulous blue Atlas cedar, *Cedrus atlantica* 'Glauca Pendula', in the far distant Sad Bed. The bulbs will completely die back on their own, but we generally clean them up after flowering so that the *Heuchera* can enjoy the limelight once more.

Okay the title sounds a bit flippant and the idea a bit of a gimmick, but the more I have used and experimented with plants as a sort of river, the more sense it has made in gardening terms. There is much made of a 'naturalistic style' of gardening, of 'getting back to nature' and of course, the seemingly valid attempt to create wildflower gardens. Though most protagonists have had to admit to the fact that unless you are happy to just let your garden go wild, 'natural' takes a lot of work and planning, usually followed by the need for continual maintenance. There is no doubt that fashion affects gardening, plants and styles will come and go (whoever thought of conifers and heathers as fashionable?) and the word 'fashion' itself, now in the digital age, has arguably been replaced by 'on trend'.

In design terms, back to Gertrude Jekyll, drifts of plants were common parlance and still describe a group of plants whose spread and length is much longer than width. 'River' is also sometimes used to describe a much longer planting but is seldom defined further. So, my definition is that a river of plants should be low growing and have a long period of interest, particularly compared with plants either side of it. Those are basic considerations and in some of the examples, mostly in Foggy Bottom, I will show and explain further what I mean.

"I feel calm and excited all at once and the urge to recreate this effect is real!"

↑
Seldom is an idea entirely new, so on the one hand you could be seen to copy, or more positively to follow a good idea and adapt it to your garden or situation. American nurseryman Kurt Bluemel was a good grower of ornamental grasses and referred to a planting of Japanese grass, *Imperata cylindrica* 'Rubra', in his garden in Maryland as 'A River of Blood'. It was impressive as a spectacle – the name, although descriptive, less appreciated!

In a revised planting in what had previously been called the Conifer Bed, the All Seasons Bed, I planted a long river of Japanese blood grass. Planted in the spring of 2009, now early autumn, the *Imperata* is obvious as it snakes between conifers. The ice blue perennial on the right is *Mertensia asiatica*, and in the distant centre are the white plumes of *Pennisetum villosum*.

If impact is something you strive towards achieving with your → planting, then this early autumn view of *Imperata cylindrica* 'Rubra' in the All Seasons Bed might be hard to beat. Two years after planting and looking from north to south, the light shines through the crimson bladed grass whose coloured leaves intensify from late summer into autumn. The deep green pine in the foreground is *Pinus heldreichii* 'Smidtii', far left is *Pinus mugo* 'Ophir'.

Fifteen years later, you are seeing the still functional river now reduced to a stream and largely in the shade. To 'function', the *Imperata* is to not only maintain its attractively coloured leaves, but to lead the eye to the distant planting at Crossways Corner. Again, this is late summer as *Pennisetum* is coming into flower and white heads of the *Hydrangea paniculata* 'Dart's Little Dot' are fading to pink. You may be able to spot another grass river in the Crossways Corner bed… →

In summer, the large brilliant white heads of *Hydrangea arborescens* 'Annabelle' draw the eye, as does the drift of *Agapanthus inapertus* 'Summer Blue Bells' intermingled above it. More subdued but playing a role is the low grass, *Hakonechloa macra* 'Albovariegata', forming a river to the other side of the bed, contrasting with the dark green 'stones' of *Pinus heldreichii* 'Smidtii'. In the foreground, the bronze-leaved form of *Carex comans*.
↓

A Prince Among Rivers

This could well be not only the longest river of *Heuchera* 'Prince' in the world, but the only one. Rather hidden in Foggy Bottom, I first planted this river of the purple-leaved *Heuchera* over fifteen years ago. Here, making a line for the eye to follow from the Snake Bed across into the All Seasons Bed beyond – a total distance perhaps of 30 m. The insignificant flowers were removed so that the foliage would make a greater contrast in autumn against golden yellow *Rudbeckia fulgida* 'Viette's Little Suzy' and the autumn leaves of the Siberian Birch, *Betula davurica*, in the distance.

↓

↑

Same river, but could we suggest now covered in ice? You can hardly see the purple *Heuchera* leaves due to the masses of snowdrops in flower, all *Galanthus* 'S. Arnott'. They seem to relish the lighter, moister soil in this lower part of the garden. Now in winter, grasses and woody plants edge the river.

More Plants for Rivers

I am almost cheating with this river as it flows not through or into a border, but along the edge. On the other hand, it demonstrates how useful a plant *Stachys byzantina* 'Silver Carpet' is for both situations. It needs full sun and good drainage to maintain density without dieback, but this group (or grass edged river) has been planted in those conditions for several years. It looks good for most of the year and here in the Book Bed it makes a striking contrast in height, foliage and colour to *Sedum* 'Matrona', *Ageratina altissima* 'Chocolate', *Hakonechloa macra* 'Alboaurea' and the just visible *Geranium* 'Rozanne'.

This was the first river of *Geranium* 'Rozanne' I planted → around the time we introduced this indispensable perennial at the RHS Chelsea Flower Show in 2000. Not having the right position to plant one in Foggy Bottom, we planted *G.* 'Rozanne' in a long, broad river in what was the new Summer Garden at Bressingham. Twenty years later, the perennials and grasses around it may have changed, but *G.* 'Rozanne' is still there and almost perfect in the role. Why 'almost'? It is low growing (bluer than most rivers) and in flower from June until autumn frosts. But being brutally honest it doesn't have much, if any, interest from December to April when new growth begins. Until recently, this part of the garden has not been open to the public through winter, but I should plant it up with bulbs …a river of *Galanthus* and *Chionodoxa* perhaps.

Initially, I had planted this garden with quite a few *Miscanthus* which arose to create higher 'banks' to the river (it helps to get into the spirit of the river when you fully imagine the geography). Many of them became too dominant so other perennials and grasses were planted as an alternative. The russet red mounds belong to *Helenium* 'Rubinzwerg' and a contrasting focal point at the end (or is it the beginning?) of the river is the purple-leaved *Cercis canadensis* 'Forest Pansy'.

I read somewhere that *Anaphalis triplinervis* was one of the few grey-leaved perennials to succeed in shade, so I decided to give it a try. I used the popular *A. t.* 'Sommerschnee' (Summer Snow) to create a river which main period of display would be late summer and autumn. Grey-leaved from spring with white everlasting flowers in summer, it meanders amongst *Aster amellus* 'Veilchenkönigin' (Violet Queen) in the foreground and *Rudbeckia fulgida* 'Viette's Little Suzy' as banks, leading to a purple-leaved *Cotinus* in the background. The combination worked quite well, but I'm not sure the *Anaphalis* was as happy as it might have been in sun.

One of the first frosts of the autumn might spell the end of most perennials and many grasses, but in this partnership both plants take on a new seasonal role. Frost is easing from the black-leaved *Ophiopogon* as the morning sun begins to highlight the dying foliage of the formally green *Hakonechloa macra*. Through winter you have brown foliage paling to beige (neither of those words can be made to sound exciting), giving a more striking contrast to the carpet of black *Ophiopogon* until the *Hakonechloa* begins a new year with fresh green shoots the following spring. Minimalist it may be, but the changing, dramatic effects of winter weather – wind, rain and frost – add to the garden, all aided by changing light… and perhaps a few snowdrops planted alongside.

↑

Ophiopogon planiscapus 'Nigrescens' is carpet forming, evergreen (or ever-black), adaptable to shade, part sun in countries with hot summers, full sun in cooler climates – the perfect plant for a black river. A plant I have used extensively at Bressingham. Here beneath a Japanese maple and a *Hamamelis*, a relatively short stretch of *Ophiopogon* joins a woodland path (where we are standing) to a lawn. Ferns, *Pulmonaria* and *Hostas* either side give a long period of interest.

A cool early morning in April. Close to a ground frost but a cooler night air has given a misty start to the day. The rising sun to the east is trying (and will win the battle) to disperse the mist. On a morning like this, you take note of the still leafless, deciduous trees and the spectral forms of the evergreen conifers. Soon the brightness of the sunlight will allow colour into the garden, but perhaps some of the mystery and magic will be lost until the evening.

02
13

Trees are the Future

To say I've grown up with trees is true in two ways. Firstly, as a child in Cambridgeshire, Bressingham, Vancouver Island, Ontario and back to Bressingham, they were everywhere around me, or I them, climbing their branches or playing beneath, trees were always taken for granted. Bressingham Hall dates to 1820 and we suspect some of the magnificent old oak trees were planted at the same time. Whilst 200 years might be considered seriously old, what about trees that date back more than 2,000 years? Although I knew of them and had even planted some in 1964, it wasn't until 2000 that I visited the giant redwoods, *Sequoiadendron giganteum,* in the High Sierras of California. Respect! Truly awesome in the real sense of the word.

But what did I know about trees?

So, here comes the second part. Although I thought of myself as having developed and planted a garden, trees were just one of the types of plant I used alongside conifers, shrubs (including rather a lot of heathers), perennials and grasses. I collected trees and shrubs to shelter, bring shade or to show off other plants. Developing from an empty meadow bare of anything but grass, the results of planting anything was going to take time. That story is largely shown and told in the third section of this book, but let's concentrate on trees. As they get bigger and more mature, and I get older (and possibly wiser), my appreciation of trees increases. I share some of my impressions in the following captions.

Birds are singing lustily. The air is warmed by the sun and it's almost too late for a spring frost. April showers are still about in early May. A darkening sky. A wind on the trees before the squall. All the ingredients are there, capturing the fresh foliage of the deciduous trees. I resisted the urge to say 'fresh green' since whilst all here in Foggy Bottom are fresh, not all are green. From left to right (ignoring the scruffy blue spruce at the base which has now gone), the slender form of *Populus tremula* 'Erecta' whose early purplish leaves have faded to a green bronze. Sweep past the birch and behind you will see the bright golden yellow *Acer platanoides* 'Princeton Gold', a distinct selection of the Norway maple. In stark contrast to the maple and silver birch, to the right is *Chamaecyparis lawsoniana* 'Dik's Weeping'. I hate to tell you, but this has been removed too.

Looking for a different angle to view the garden, I came → across this interesting aspect of mainly trees and shrubs in late spring. Look past the deciduous *Azalea* to the left and fresh leaves on the Japanese maple to the right, and in the centre you will see a tree that takes little sideways space. This is the pendulous form of the giant redwood, unsurprisingly named *Sequoiadendron giganteum* 'Pendulum'. Most of the weeping redwoods develop their own character with age and you can see how with a little imagination they are sometimes likened to dinosaurs. Other mature forty-year-old conifers can be seen in the background.

It's late September and signs of a golden autumn are touching a river birch, *Betula nigra*, near the hidden pond. Behind, the leaves of the Amur maple, *Acer tataricum* subsp. *ginnala*, have already turned a deep crimson. The darker greens of taller trees, oaks, ash, alder and poplar in the background belong to a woodland just beyond the garden. The more 'exotic' plants used in the midground are from left to right; *Chamaecyparis lawsoniana* 'Globus', *Taxodium distichum*, narrowly pyramidal *Alnus glutinosa* 'Aurea', and *Betula nigra*. In the lower foreground with golden leaves dulled by the shade is *Physocarpus opulifolius* 'Angel Gold', and to the right, two plants of *Cornus sericea* subsp. *occidentalis* 'Sunshine'.

There's a certain balance to this photograph of Foggy Bottom → in autumn. Shapes and colours of shrubs and conifers fill the middle part of the All Seasons Bed, finally catching the view which at another level encompasses the taller trees behind. As leaves fall away, conifers come into their own aided by the extra light from branches empty of foliage, until they burst into growth in spring. *Stipa tenuissima* is the wavy grass in the foreground.

↑ Does the fact that this photograph was taken on the twelfth day of the twelfth month in 2012 hold any significance? No, but it is a rather eerie scene, almost entirely created by fog and frost on trees and plants in the garden. Colours are subdued with all the plants looking like they have been lightly sprinkled with baking flour, covering the grasses in the foreground to the giant redwoods behind. Centre is *Platycladus orientalis* 'Flame' whose summer golden yellow has turned deep bronze in winter frost.

← Feeling the cold? With no hint of sun this scene is yet to sparkle, but light snowfall with little wind has coated the trees and shrubs with a lining of snow, contrasting with the lower sides of the branches. An almost immediate transformation to a 'white out'. This is near the pond, the bridge itself laden with snow, delicate yet congested branches of the swamp cypress, *Taxodium distichum*, on the island. A river birch, *Betula nigra*, to the right.

The (Almost) Unbelievable Redwood, Guardian of the Garden

'Here's one I planted earlier' is a cliché that often comes to mind when I think about the way these giant redwoods came to be. I never imagined that when I sent a packet of seeds home to Bressingham, whilst working at the 1960 Winter Olympics at Squaw Valley, California, that over sixty years later I would be able to look up to the magnificent giant trees 40 m from our house! I planted the five young seedling plants in 1964, then about 90 cm (3 ft) tall, in an area later to be called Adrian's Wood. Now two of the five original trees are over 33 m (100 ft) high and tower over Adrian's Wood and Foggy Bottom, poking above the canopy of several much older trees around.

To comprehend their stature, start by looking at the white plumes of pampas grass (about 2 m high). Then follow the silver birch up past the tree house and you eventually come to the three redwoods as they grow skywards, the branch tips touched by frost left by the early morning fog. The central tree, equally tall but further away, is the coastal redwood, *Sequoia sempervirens*.

This tree was once a seed in a packet… strange, remarkable, but true. Standing at the base I am amazed again at the size and solidity of this great tree, *Sequoiadendron giganteum*, looking past it to a pathway leading to the entrance to Foggy Bottom. Here showing up in autumn is the crimson foliage of *Acer rubrum* 'Brandywine', a much more recent addition.

Trees That Stop You In Your Tracks

← Two special trees seem to have found a happy spot in Foggy Bottom. Growing close to other trees they are shown from their best side, but somewhat bare branched behind. Growing on the north side of Rosemary's Wood, perhaps the only thing they have in common is their pendulous habit and age. Both are about forty years old and were moved from other parts of the garden. On the left is a good form of Brewer's weeping spruce, *Picea breweriana*, a native to western North America. Here in light shade, it gets sufficient moisture in the summer. From the dark green of the spruce, passing the pink *Rhododendron* in the background, is an unusual weeping golden beech, *Fagus sylvatica* 'Aurea Pendula'. In early years it struggles to make an upright leading shoot and if an upright form (it can be trained to a rounded shape), help from a cane is appreciated. This plant arose as a chance sport or shoot on a green-leaved *Fagus sylvatica* 'Pendula' around 1900. It is prone to leaf scorch in summer sun, which explains why I moved it to the shade ...but also near enough to the pond so it could reflect on us.

↑
And just as it was looking spectacular ...but that's at the end of the story. The often-called wedding cake tree has green leaves and is an attractive plant given room to grow. The variegated form *Cornus controversa* 'Variegata' is trickier but is one we would all like to grow successfully. In my experience, this small tree is not easy to please. It can sulk if too dry, weep if it gets hit by a spring frost, bend in an unnatural way in a windy position or, as this one did, expire after a flood in April. Just as well I managed to get some photographs, wishing a plant we had nurtured for some years a long life. Some things are not meant to be.

A few pointers would be more helpful... This is a grafted plant which needs staking when young and to be allowed to develop a framework of branches with a main upward leading shoot. It requires free draining soil and shelter from spring frost and wind. When happy, it grows well.

↑
An early evening in midsummer draws shadows across the mown grass, highlighting a mix of shapes, forms, leaves and flowers. Left is a flowering Chinese dogwood, *Cornus kousa* var. *chinensis*, amassed with creamy bracts smothering the leaves. This can vary from seed and may not flower for a few years, so you can be very pleased if you end up with a tree as showy and full of flower as this forty-year-old specimen. There have been a great number of cultivars bred and selected in the past few years, some with very large, and even pink, flowers. I have collected and planted many selections in Foggy Bottom, but few can make the impression that this tree makes in early summer.

Immediately behind are three dark green Italian cypress, *Cupressus sempervirens*, stiffly erect and living up to the cultivar name of 'Totem Pole'. In the background, a maple, pine and blue spruce still allow the sun to highlight the weeping *Sequoiadendron giganteum* 'Pendulum', seemingly in two minds as to which way to go.

← Plant a *Crocosmia* like the scarlet 'Lucifer' around this showy Indian bean tree, *Catalpa bignonioides* 'Aurea', and the resulting vibrancy against the golden leaves might be breathtaking. Although I do plan for a wow factor, it might be an overkill of colour, so I planted it with cooler perennials and grasses. The *Catalpa* is enough of a show-off anyway with large, pointed leaves and a broad canopy creating a summer long display. You could grow this in a smaller garden as it takes well to pruning back to the main branches in late spring. The *Miscanthus* is *M. sinensis* 'Super Stripe'.

Late autumn in Foggy Bottom, standing near the pond and looking north sees the last leaves defiantly clinging on. The morning sun is just catching the golden leaves of a tree that will get more spectacular each year. We are looking at a ten-year-old plant of *Nyssa sylvatica* 'Autumn Cascades' on the right, a selection that arose in Australia which has added variety to the relatively small range in this genus. The species is a North American native commonly known as the tupelo or sour gum and is renowned for its wonderful golden autumn leaves. As I carefully prune away the lower branches it will make an impressive weeping specimen several times its present size near the pond. As you look further into the garden, the conifers begin to become more dominant and provide vital structure for the long winter period, as well as shelter for birds. The tallest trees in the distance with their tips in the sky are from left to right; *Abies procera* 'Glauca' from western North America, a widely branched *Cedrus deodara* from the edge of the Himalayas, and *Chamaecyparis lawsoniana* 'Howarth's Gold' found in Port Orford, Oregon, US. Popular in the UK, they are known as Lawson's cypress, whereas in the US, they are known as the Port Orford cedar. Botanically, it is a 'false cypress' and not a true cypress or a cedar.

Timing is everything. It could be that Matt hadn't yet completed the tree house, that Rosemary and I were away, that the snow wasn't the 'right sort', that the sun didn't shine and that I didn't have a good camera. It's not until you capture a glorious moment like this that you think how fortunate everything was to be in place. Bressingham in Norfolk, England, doesn't often get snow and sunshine, or even snow and no sunshine. Any of the above could happen, but let's marvel at the splendour and the warmth of the scene, despite the snow. Shrubs in the foreground bend under the weight of snow, a silver-white birch frames the newly completed tree house, and above, emerging like a powerful rocket, the indomitable giant redwoods who are well used to such conditions every winter.

Still foggy at Foggy Bottom, December 1990.

PART THREE

LOOKING BACK

Tennis Court Garden, 1966.

03 01

Creating The Foggy Bottom Garden 1966–85

It seems almost unbelievable to view Foggy Bottom today, its plants and relative maturity, and to imagine how it started fifty-seven years ago. For me, it has been a growing experience in both senses of the word. The garden has been a very big part of my life, more so in later years, but it has not been my whole life. My wife Rosemary and sons Jason, Matt, and Richard all lived with the garden being developed around them. It was a space for play, and later a place for our sons to earn some pocket money. Foggy Bottom was named after my travels and grew out of my experience, later as a trial garden for our nursery business and a showpiece as part of The Bressingham Gardens. Rosemary sadly died of cancer in 2014. Although she had worked hard in the garden and knew many of the problems of running it at times, the fact that she often expressed her opinion in later years that Foggy Bottom was "a little piece of heaven", meant much to me. To some extent, her abiding statement underpins my ambition to continue the garden as a place that would have resonated with her, which means something special to others as it always will be for me.

In The Beginning…

After four years abroad and working on a nursery in Denmark, I returned at my father's request to join the family business, Blooms Nurseries Ltd in Bressingham. That was in August 1962, the same month my brother Robert came home from his five years of working on various farms in England. I don't think getting married and finding a home was on our radar at that time and it was very normal to live in your parents' home. It was convenient too as Bressingham Hall had plenty of rooms and there was no commuting to work beyond a hundred-yard walk. I had no thoughts of a garden, and why would I? My father had just finished creating his five-acre Dell Garden in front of the Hall, devoted to hardy perennials grown in a novel way …in 'island beds'. From 1953 to 1962 he had travelled Britain and Europe, collecting and exchanging plants with nurseries, botanic gardens and garden owners to amass around 4,500 varieties. He planted them back at Bressingham in the former meadows between the A1066 road and Bressingham Hall where we lived. It was a labour of love and passion which my father had waited long to create, first establishing a wholesale nursery in 1926 in Oakington, Cambridgeshire, then moving to the village of Bressingham, Norfolk, in 1946.

Although I had considerable admiration for what my father had achieved by the age of fifty-six, I also wanted to find my own niche within the business, then specialising in hardy perennials and alpines – or rockery plants as they are also known. Although I was happy to learn more about perennials, I started propagating conifers and heathers, seizing an opportunity to grow a range of plants that were a) rather undeveloped in the garden market, b) offered more year-round interest than perennials, and importantly for me c) were a group of plants which my father was unfamiliar with! Of course, he had set me a difficult path to follow, and my knowledge was still very limited at that time, but considering I was only twenty-two that is hardly surprising. I have no doubt that at times I was a slight nuisance to him. I asked if I could plant a few conifers among the alpine beds in his garden, to which he reluctantly agreed. By the following year we agreed that I could start another garden, adjacent to the Dell Garden, where I could experiment with planting 'dwarf' conifers and heathers together. This was on light loam just south of a grass tennis court I had developed, planning to play on summer evenings after work. Unfortunately, work largely won out and even more so as I got more involved with our business. But this relatively small garden was my chance to experiment and was the basis of Foggy Bottom and what was to come. Much like my father had done with perennials, I started to visit other nurseries, learning more about propagation and collecting plants (mostly conifers) that we didn't have.

Thirsting for new challenges, I discussed with my father the possibility of planting another area at the lower end of the meadow from my garden next to the tennis court. I suggested that we could expand the gardens to include this area in the future. In the meantime, we dug a pond, and in 1964 I started planting trees… mostly conifers. I planted about thirty of the fast growing × *Cupressocyparis leylandii* – which were then becoming popular as an evergreen hedging plant – as a shelter belt for some rather choicer conifers like the giant redwoods and Douglas fir. After planting in 1964 and 1965, it would be another thirty-five years before it was brought into the main garden. This is another story, but this area eventually became known as Adrian's Wood. In 2000, the 60 ft high Leyland cypress were cut down and removed, thus dramatically exposing the giant redwoods that looked over Adrian's Wood to the east and Foggy Bottom to the west. But even in 1964, I had not met Rosemary and had little idea that the meadow to the west was to become our home and garden for the rest of our lives.

I met Rosemary, my wife to be, at an International Club dance in Cambridge in late 1964. Rosemary lived with her parents in Cambridge and liked the countryside even though she was a 'town girl'. Suffice to say, since being in a partnership was unheard of in those days, we were very happy to get married and planned a wedding for October 1966 in her local church in Trumpington. But first we had to consider where we might put our house and garden.

1966

A memorable year, and more memorable as time goes on. Why? Well, to a great many English people it was the one and only year that England won the football World Cup. That happened in July, and at that time we certainly thought England would win again. Not many people know this but 1966 was also the year that we built our house, moving in when only two rooms were finished, and the year I planted the first tree in our garden. This was the beginning of our Foggy Bottom Garden.

The beginnings in spring 1966.

← Bricks and mortar disturb the green Waveney Valley meadows in 1966. We found a plot of land in a meadow south of Bressingham church and 300 yards from the closest neighbour. This was a Victorian vicarage which had a five-acre meadow stretching to an established tree line and ditch which marked the northern edge of our (at that time) one-acre garden. Look at the flat lowland meadows edged by willows and to the left of the photograph (not in sight) was a mixed woodland. All this was prone to flooding in winter. The single storey house, designed by Rosemary and I with the help of an architect, was being built by local tradesmen only at weekends. We became the labourers at times as I mixed cement and Rosemary pointed bricks. On the afternoon that England won the World Cup, I was helping carry tiles to the builders putting on the roof.

↑
Looks like a house! Although we designed our home to look slightly 'ranch style', in reality it's a bungalow (the builder in local Norfolk said, "it's low and you 'bung' a low roof on it"). More to the point, the sitting room and bedroom windows look to the south over a flat, treeless six-acre meadow – the view still to be developed. Our neighbour's property is on the other side of the trees.

Snowy Winters

These photographs were taken in February between 1968 and 1971 and are reminders that it was more usual than not to have frost and snow over several periods of winter. They're also a reminder of how lonely our home looks, isolated in the north-eastern corner of the meadow. Lastly, a memento that if the cattle were inside for the winter, our working pony, Tinker, was happy to trudge toward us on a foggy, frosty early morning, not having an inkling that a pond was to be dug near the wood behind. The snow-covered meadow is now the Foggy Bottom Garden. A lot of planting and growing is to be done, though at this point I had no plans to expand the garden beyond the house.

In 1971 I was lucky enough to get a ride in a helicopter (I knew I wouldn't be believed if I said this photograph was taken from a tall stepladder!). The aerial view shows our house and garden five years from building it, tucked in the corner of the meadow as described. The curved beds surrounding the house is our garden and the colourful lines are stock beds containing conifers from which we could take cuttings for the nursery. The area above the house in this picture would eventually become Adrian's Wood and the empty meadow to the right will become the Foggy Bottom Garden.

Taming the Meadow

On a rather dull day in 1973, looking west from the main entrance of what was to become Foggy Bottom, you can see my initial markings denoting the beds. These were sprayed with a knapsack and lance using the chemical paraquat which kills the grass. Foggy Bottom was going to need a great many plants and a lot of time to achieve a three-dimensional structure. What an opportunity I had ahead of me!

Collecting Conifers

The garden grows, but what was to go in it? Ever since I had returned to our nursery from Denmark in 1962, I was eager to learn as much as I could about conifers and how to propagate them. So, from 1963 to 1970 and afterwards, I followed my father's footsteps in one aspect at least… he had become obsessed with collecting perennials whilst developing his Dell Garden and I became obsessed with collecting conifers …particularly the dwarf and slow growing type that might fit most gardens. Like Alan, I started in England and spread outwards. Unfortunately, I didn't keep all the records, but I still have the accession notebook I made with handwritten entries from 1962 until 1972. Some of the early plants went into larger pots, some into what would become the Fragrant Garden south of the tennis court, and some into the area that would become Adrian's Wood. Once moved into our house, I had plants to put into the garden which I had already collected, but this was just the tip of the iceberg…

Collecting more conifers…

The main sources for finding conifers were the few nurseries that offered anything different to the normal limited range. Most popular at the time in Britain was the Lawson's cypress, *Chamaecyparis lawsoniana*, a species native to a relatively small area in Oregon on the West Coast of the United States. Not widely popular there, it's interesting that this false cypress should become the most used group of conifers in British gardens. Well (and not many people know this) here's how it happened… Discovered in 1854, growing inland in the Siskiyou Mountains close to Port Orford, the species grows in its native habitat to 150–200 ft. The botanical name given was *Chamaecyparis lawsoniana*, named after Scottish nurseryman Charles Lawson, commonly called 'Lawson's'. Further plants and seed were distributed throughout Britain, varying in size and habit, from which many new cultivars were named. I planted and trialled many in Foggy Bottom and several remain.

…and more

I visited gardens and nurseries, getting cuttings from some and buying plants from others where available. Hillier Nurseries in Hampshire was one of the most famous for trees, shrubs and conifers, and Harold Hillier (later Sir Harold Hillier) had an interest and authored a small booklet on dwarf conifers. Visiting the gardens and nursery in 1964 I met the enthusiastic plantsman Roy Lancaster for the first time, then employed as Harold's assistant. Roy gave me a brief tour of Jermyn's House and Harold Hillier's Garden, then introduced me to expert propagator Graham Adcock. I was happy to come away with a few rare plants (rare to me anyway) and a bit more knowledge.

Another source of advice and knowledge was a specialist conifer nursery recently established by a retired civil engineer who had a passion for conifers. This was Humphrey Welch, and his small nursery was set on a sandy slope in Devizes, Wiltshire. The garden surrounding his house was called the Pygmy Pinetum. It was good of him to accept a fact-finding visit from a potential rival, and although he was known to have a grumpy demeanour, over time we got on quite well. His 1966 book *Dwarf Conifers: A Complete Guide* was erudite and the most comprehensive publication on the subject for over twenty-five years. I'd like to think the growing popularity of dwarf conifers benefitted him too.

← 1973. Once the beds were marked out, we trialled a new implement which my brother Rob had imported from Germany called a Willibald, resembling a giant rotovator but with curved 'spades'. This almost mimicked hand digging and was ideal to turn over the heavy soil which afterwards the weather would break down. The area around the house was now full, and later in the spring I could start putting the first plants into the newer garden.

↑
1973. The garden behind (or in front of) the barbed wire fence was finished and full, the ideas for combining slower growing conifers with heathers seemed to be working, providing year-round colour and ground cover. Now to the meadow on the other side of the fence…

1974. Although I was a long way from getting the first beds planted, the next year I was able to take in another acre or two of the meadow, here being marked out with canes before spraying. When I look back, it looks very ambitious! →

↑

Soil and preparation, 1976. First the Willibald digger, then the frost and then we brought in piles of soft sand from a nearby lower meadow. It was only then that nursery helper, Bill Saunders, could start digging. The soil here was a heavy loam. Without sand or compost it would solidify to a dense clay and be sticky and difficult to work. Some planting had already been done by spring and we weren't to know that this was going to be the longest, hottest year on record and for many years after.

↑
Rivers of grass, 1977. From the first plantings around the house, looking south from the house roof, you can see the gradual progress of planting as well as the design and style of the garden. With the vegetable garden now moved (almost out of sight in the distance), Rosemary, not entirely joking, said she now had to get on her bike to reach it... The pathways were wide and sweeping, the garden planting informal, I attempted a 'natural' look knowing of course it was anything but. Vistas would become more evident once the structural plants had grown a lot more. Top left is the fence and the remaining southern part of the meadow … and soon that area too would be brought into Foggy Bottom.

An enthusiasm for plants and gardens seemed apparent following a visit from Peter Seabrook and BBC *Gardeners' World* who had recently filmed at Foggy Bottom. Or was it just the television? This was the first of many September 'Open Weekends' that we held from 1977 until 1984 after we had started the Bressingham Plant Centre. We were initially rather unprepared for the volume of cars, many of which had travelled more than a hundred miles. Traffic hold ups meant that at peak, a queue of more than two miles was formed along the A1066 road into Diss before we could get the cars into our meadow to park! This period was in the middle of the expanding growth of suburban Britain, with empty gardens waiting to be filled. This also led to the rapid development of garden centres. New plants and ideas were in their ascendancy for an ever-wider group of gardeners. From visitor's faces, it seemed they were much more focused on the garden than the photographer on the roof... →

The last frontier, 1977. Standing in the remaining meadow, I have marked out the proposed edge of a pond, yet of course to be dug. Over time this area will be transformed beyond recognition. The bridge and shaded garden are to be on the left.

Digging in, 1977. A few thousand years ago this whole valley was beneath a lake of water. It is alluvial soil lying on a sandy base, much lighter loam than the upper part of Foggy Bottom, but neutral rather than acid. The digger is moving the spoil from the pond to create a bank behind near the wood, leaving an island in the middle. This was not an island bed, but if you camped, you could have a bed on an island... This is the lowest part of the garden, but I wasn't sure the pond would hold water in the summer without putting in a liner. We'd have to wait at least a year to see.

↑ Shape, form and colour. In March 1979 you can see more established, 'joined up' planting in the distance, the newer plantings in the foreground already blending with the older. The ideas were simple – create height and contrast between one or more conifers and large groups of heathers. These would generally include acid loving, summer flowering heathers (*Calluna* and *Erica*) and winter flowering heaths (*Erica*). It's quite acceptable to just call them heathers! At that time there was an increasing choice of new introductions in both groups, some with yellow or golden foliage – always popular in Britain. Attractive year-round, many take on a more vibrant colour in winter. Note the distance between the heather plantings is at least 45 cm (18 in), although this may vary according to the size and vigour of each cultivar.

← 1979. Here on the north side of the central beds (later to be called the Mini-Pinetum) and a few places elsewhere, I had used peat blocks to create different levels where I intended to plant some *Rhododendrons* and acid loving shrubs like *Gaultheria* and *Vaccinium*. Though it might take time, much of this area would become shadier. The bags contained peat (which was widely used then) and later the equally acidic composted pine bark.

1979. Without explanation this photograph won't tell you much, but it reminds me of several things:

a) The pond level in February is quite low, so without an impervious liner it is unlikely to hold water in summer. That's going to cost a lot of money…

b) A circle of trees has now been planted which would eventually blend with the existing woodland and hide the gate and the Gap Meadow beyond.

c) The high-powered electric cables? Unless these were moved it would severely restrict the planting I had done. Years before, we had given the Electricity Board a wayleave to cross our land to feed electricity to another area. The high-power wires had to be kept well clear of tree branches and foliage, and anything encroaching would need to be removed. Fortunately, using a clause in the contract, the Electricity Board were willing to move the cable further down and through the woodland below at their cost. I thank them to this day!

d) What a transformation compared with this area today over forty years later (see p. 135).

← Conifers and heathers in a large garden, March 1980. Daffodils, mostly the variety *Narcissus* 'King Alfred', in the distant right in front of a mix of conifers, including the fast growing and very popular Leyland cypress, × *Cupressocyparis leylandii*. This area will become Adrian's Wood and somewhere amongst them are the giant redwoods. Almost all the conifers and heathers in the foreground are now replaced by nature of time and change.

↑ Filling the gaps, October 1980. The roof of our house had a very low incline, enabling me to safely stand on it and photograph the whole garden. At this early stage I could see all the way to the pond and the woodland behind. The heavy-duty electric cables are still there, and you can get a sense of why I wanted them moved.

Nursery beds, 1970.

The Conifer and Heather Garden Period

It seems worth exploring this period in which Foggy Bottom was (and was seen as) a garden primarily planted with a wide range of conifers and heathers. The advantages that were evident to me at the time were that, once established, they were relatively trouble free and provided year-round colour. As my collection of conifers grew, I could learn more about them …and in six acres of garden I had that opportunity, and importantly, would be able to pass on that experience. It soon became evident that knowledge of ten-year growth rates would mean some revision of what constituted a dwarf, slow growing or large conifer. Many were not what they said on the label or in books, and at thirty to perhaps fifty years (without pruning to restrict growth) how tall might a so-called 'dwarf' conifer get? The most popular Lawson's cypress in Britain, *Chamaecyparis lawsoniana* 'Ellwoodii', was described in Humphrey Welch's book in 1966 as growing to 3 m (10 ft). In my first book on conifers published in 1972, *Conifers for Your Garden*, I estimated 'Ellwoodii' as eventually growing to 4.5–6 m (15–20 ft). My last book on conifers published in 2017, *Gardening with Conifers*, was based on even greater experience, so I had to raise it to 7–10 m (23–33 ft). Most people would not live and garden in the same place for fifty or more years, therefore may not have to deal with the inevitable consequence of planting too close. But what is too close? Depending on the plant's growth, eventual size and its distance between others, 'overplanting' might occur after five or more years as trees, conifers and shrubs grow beyond their original allotted space. In further sections of this book, we'll see what some of the answers might be.

Mother Plants

The company Blooms Nurseries Ltd, founded by my father Alan Bloom, was primarily a wholesale grower built on a reputation of growing hardy perennials. Now we also started supplying garden centres across Britain with an increasingly wide range of conifers that had previously been largely supplied from Holland. So, we needed to build up the quantities of conifers that we propagated and grew for sale, all of which would go into pots and containers. As I obtained plants, either buying them in or more often propagating our own, I planted the 'mother plants' in Foggy Bottom to the west of the house. Straight rows looked great in nursery beds, but not in the garden. However, this does allow you to see the wide difference there is in colour and habit amongst conifers. This area was eventually turned into garden.

1978. Stop right there! This shows an ideal stage of growth, a patchwork of colour and balance of the plants shown. The heathers are planted in groups and still retain their individual habit and the conifers are still in scale and offer a contrast. But of course, everything keeps growing! Note the blue needled fir on the left, *Abies procera* 'Glauca Prostrata', contrasting with the bronzed foliage of winter flowering *Erica carnea* 'Vivellii' and *Cedrus deodara* 'Nana Aurea' above, which I had found in France. The yellow in the foreground is *Calluna vulgaris* 'Beoley Gold' surrounding three plants of green *Thuja occidentalis* 'Danica'. To the right, contrasting with orange foliaged *Calluna vulgaris* 'Sir John Charrington', are three plants of the same blue spruce, *Picea pungens* 'Montgomery'.

1981. This was a period when I was trying to show the variety you could have with conifers and heathers as my collecting continued and more were planted in the Foggy Bottom Garden. This photograph was taken in late summer when the bell heather, *Erica cinerea*, was in flower but before the *Callunas*. Green grass, the lawn just cut and edges trimmed, sets off the other colours. Outstanding on the right are plants of *Picea pungens* 'Globosa'. →

↑

1984. The dark green patches are groups of winter flowering heathers; the buds are already developing here in late summer. In the foreground is the truly dwarf *Chamaecyparis lawsoniana* 'Pygmaea Argentea', its creamy foliage contrasting vividly with *Erica cinerea* 'C.D. Eason', one of the bell heathers. The two taller conifers, *Cedrus deodara* 'Nana Aurea' (not dwarf as the name implies!) left, and *Abies procera* 'Glauca Prostrata' (not prostrate as the name implies – see *What's In a Name?* p.332) right, will become quite a feature for many years. Eventually both will have to be trimmed to stop them growing into each other. Between them is a summer flowering heather *Calluna vulgaris* 'Robert Chapman' which, like many, is grown more for year-round foliage colour than for flowers.

Vigorous healthy-looking conifers in the prime of youth! Here in March 1985 amongst the surrounding heathers are three distinct forms. A more vigorous form of the Japanese Hinoki cypress than usually seen, *Chamaecyparis obtusa* 'Graciosa', maintains a good green colour in winter. The golden Scots pine, *Pinus sylvestris* 'Aurea', shows its best winter colour, gradually turning back to green in summer. A distinctive form of the Bosnian pine rather unimaginatively called *Pinus heldreichii* 'Groen' (Green).

← Spot the flower! Foggy Bottom in early summer against a bright, but cloudy sky in 1985. For this short period of time there are no heathers or any other plants in flower, yet the garden is lit by the colourful foliage of both conifers and heathers. The house is nearly hidden, and the backdrop of Leyland cypress could be ominous! The brightest conifers are forms of the Colorado blue spruce, *Picea pungens*. In the foreground, *P. p.* 'Globosa'.

← Here on a sunny day in January 1986, the *Cedrus deodara* 'Nana Aurea' and *Abies procera* 'Glauca' have grown a bit more and the heathers have completely carpeted the ground. Enhanced by frost in the foreground is the burnt orange winter foliage of *Calluna vulgaris* 'Robert Chapman'.

The Changing Garden

By 1980, just under fifteen years since the house was built and the garden started, we had dug the pond and reached the woodland below. The north half of the garden was now mostly planted with conifers and heathers, but as more shade was created it was time to start filling in gaps and find room for shrubs and perennials. With the nursery now growing an increasing range of dwarf shrubs, I needed to trial these too. Although the Dell Garden had an enormous collection of perennials, I wanted to blend some of them in with woody plants in Foggy Bottom. I was beginning to travel more regularly to other countries in Europe and to the US and Canada; nurseries there became a source for new plants for both nursery and trialling at Foggy Bottom.

A much wider range of conifers was now available (see *Hard Grafting* p.331) and I was anxious to improve my own knowledge by growing a wide range of some of the standard but less showy shrubs such as *Weigela*, *Philadelphus* and *Deutzia*. I had already made some inroads in my collections of shrubby *Potentilla*, *Berberis*, *Euonymus* and *Spiraea*, as well as more acid loving evergreens: *Rhododendron*, *Azalea*, *Camellia* and *Pieris*. I used the garden to learn as much as I could about plants as garden plants. So often as a nurseryman you would learn much about propagation and growing, but little about a plant beyond its selling age of two or three years. I was also aware that with six acres of 'trial grounds' to fill, I was able to collect and use plants which were helpfully considered a legitimate business expense.

Security guard looking over Potentilla fruticosa 'Red Ace' exhibit at RHS Chelsea Flower Show, 1976.

Chelsea

Bressingham Gardens became our retail mail order business in 1966 and initially listed perennials from the gardens. We started to exhibit at the RHS Chelsea Flower Show in May each year and the mail order developed rapidly. Gradually, more conifers were added to our range and appeared in the catalogue, but it was not until 1976 that we also had an exhibit devoted to conifers. Each variety was not only labelled with the correct name, but with the age of the plant so that the growth rate of each could be seen. This was also the year we had a small solo exhibit with several plants of a new shrub, *Potentilla fruticosa* 'Red Ace', the first colour break in plants that, until then, had normally been white or shades of yellow. Since someone had attempted to steal cuttings of the plant at a previous show, resulting in national publicity, it seemed a good idea to employ a uniformed security guard to protect 'Red Ace', which the RHS agreed to. The additional publicity did us no harm!

New Plants

Alan Bloom with his helper, Percy Piper, had raised some outstanding perennials, but their introduction tended to be low key, particularly since in the mid 1960s perennials had yet to become widely popular. Although forcing plants was done by many growers for the Chelsea Flower Show, in the early days we tended to lift mature plants from the garden or nursery. This meant that some of the most exciting Bressingham perennials such as *Helenium*, *Kniphofia*, *Crocosmia* and *Phlox paniculata* flowered too late to make an appearance at the show. I felt we were now embarking on an introduction of new plants... or at least one new plant at the Chelsea Flower Show each year. It could be a perennial, a shrub or a conifer, but would require planning since we needed to have sufficient plants to offer our mail order customers, as well as wholesale to garden centres. Each one has a story of course, and although all these new plants were trialled in the gardens, there isn't room to fit the individual stories into this book.

Hard Grafting

The British were considered a nation of gardeners, not like the Dutch who could be called a nation of nurseries. Apart from a few specialists, British nurseries were not practised in the art of grafting plants, particularly conifers. The Forestry Commission, responsible for a great many national conifer forests, were concerned that diseases might be imported if some of the main groups of conifers that they grew – pines, spruce and firs – could be imported without strict plant health regulations. So, when

I first started collecting cultivars, we could only import six of each of these plants and otherwise find what we could in Britain. Having visited several nurseries in Holland, Germany and France, I was beginning to compile a list of wants, hoping that since we were (after 1973) a member of the European Union the plant health regulations would be similar for all countries soon. This restriction was finally removed in 1978, giving us and other UK nurseries a potential boost. To take advantage of this freedom of movement, we imported conifer specimens from the specialist conifer nursery zu Jeddeloh in Germany and our Dutch supplier Kromhout in Boskoop. This resulted in one of the biggest exhibits of conifers ever seen at the RHS Autumn Show in London. We tried to create interest and excitement about a range of plants seldom considered, exhibiting specimens of many different pines (*Pinus*), spruce (*Picea*), firs (*Abies*) and cedars (*Cedrus*). This was followed with a large 'conifer only' exhibit at the Chelsea Flower Show in May 1979.

What's In a Name?

What would you do if you found a conifer seedling that looked like a flat or prostrate fir as it grew? One that also had golden yellow foliage, brighter in winter than summer? You felt it should be propagated for others to enjoy, so you needed to give your new plant a name. Few would argue that 'Golden Spreader' described it perfectly, so *Abies nordmanniana* 'Golden Spreader' was introduced in the 1960s and soon was in demand. However, it was slow to propagate as it had to be propagated by grafting. But back to the name… As their plants got older, many gardeners discovered that they put on a leading shoot, soon making a pyramidal shaped tree. 'Golden Pyramid' now seems a more appropriate name, though 'Golden Spreader' it must remain.

This fir is a great example of how names can be misapplied. Another, *Pinus mugo* 'Gnom' (Gnome) was evidently intended to be dwarf, but on good soil in Foggy Bottom I had to get rid of my specimen when it reached about 3 m (10 ft) high and equally wide at twenty-five years old. I obtained three plants of *Cedrus deodara* 'Nana Aurea' from France, which seemed to be a better colour than the one I had got in England under the same name, but it was not a dwarf nor particularly slow growing. I let one grow, but it had to be cut down and removed when it reached about 10 m (33 ft), for another I trimmed it every year to keep it an attractive plant.

Lastly, when you graft a conifer (usually one which doesn't root from cuttings) you take a cutting (scion) from your named specimen which will then be grafted onto a prepared seedling called an understock.

The latter is usually a seedling of a naturally fast growing conifer, whilst the scion may be from a dwarf conifer (I hope you are still with me?). For example, *Abies procera* 'Glauca Prostrata' would be grafted onto *Abies procera* or another seedling fir. It may be flat growing for a few years, but eventually the vigour of the understock encourages the scion to assert itself and start growing up (as a casual observer it seems like a 50/50 partnership). Now it is your decision. To keep your plant flat growing, prune away any upright leading shoots. To make it more pyramidal, let it grow and prune side shoots to improve density.

Centre stage is the rather large Pinus mugo 'Gnom' and the golden conifer to the right is Cedrus deodara 'Nana Aurea' – another misnomer, 1994.

03
02

Growing Up – Foggy Bottom Changes Character 1986–99

The Garden Grows

I enjoyed planting the Spring Garden, which has never been open to visitors – though that was the original intention. It was planted in an area behind what became the Long Bed and was ideal for spring flowering *Rhododendrons*, *Pieris* and other shrubs whose early flowers could have been damaged by spring frosts. Behind the Norfolk reed fence to the right, formerly a nursery stock bed of conifers in rows, was our private family lawn where on Open Days we could concentrate on playing football or other games with our three sons. Here you can see I am in the middle of a project, building levels with peat blocks, planting and mulching with composted bark …I did clear the plastic bags up. Over thirty years later this is now a rather overgrown woodland garden. Perhaps that's why it isn't open…

The beginning of the TV Bed. Planted either side of a *Lavatera* are young, rather skinny *Cedrus atlantica* 'Glauca Pendula' plants being trained over some canes. The eventual shape of this will almost resemble (with some imagination) a TV screen. Perennials will be planted in front.
↓

Did someone say this was overplanted? Yes, I did, many times and increasingly year after year as all the trees, shrubs and conifers grew upwards and outwards. One by one, plants would have to be moved or replaced as I redesigned parts of the garden. It is now late summer and to name a few from left to right; the blue needles of *Pinus parviflora* 'Negishi' contrast with *Cedrus deodara* 'Golden Horizon', purple *Berberis* × *ottawensis* 'Auricoma' behind, and bright pink *Calluna vulgaris* 'H.E. Beale' on its right. The deep yellow-leaved tree is *Gleditsia triacanthos* f. *inermis* 'Sunburst' in front of the blue *Picea engelmannii* f. *glauca* which contrasts against the tight column of *Cupressus glabra* 'Sulphurea'. Lower to the far right is the striking deep pink of *Calluna vulgaris* 'Peter Sparkes'. Sadly, all have now gone. Partly to commemorate them we decided to call this the Sad Bed, though it was later named as such because all the plants in it were weeping… (see p.93).

The Constant Need For Re-Designing

← I had planted up one small corner where I thought the New Zealand flax, *Phormium tenax*, and cultivars would be protected in case of freezing winter weather, sheltered by conifers. Having seen them first in 1976 at the Chelsea Flower Show, I had the opportunity to visit growers in New Zealand in February 1978. They were certainly colourful and the foliage evergreen in the wider sense of the word. I was also led to believe that they were hardy, but as I have learnt over time, hardiness is a relative term and must be considered from different aspects. To my chagrin and the company's cost, nearly all our plants were wiped out in the garden and on the nursery during a severe cold period in the winter of 1979–80.

← 1986. Same corner, same conifers, but eight years older. The *Phormiums* have gone, but here I thought I would try a collection of ornamental grasses with *Kniphofia* to add summer colour. Behind, you can see the blue leaves of a *Eucalyptus* which I thought made a good backdrop, particularly if pruned regularly and kept fairly bushy. I have never really liked using labels in Foggy Bottom, mainly because they could be distracting (and annoying when photographing plants). However, I had to overcome this antipathy as not only were the labels helpful to visitors, but with over 3,000 different plants in the garden, helpful to me and the gardeners too.

← A year later, the grasses have filled in and the bright vermilion of *Crocosmia* 'Lucifer' lights up the corner. Having seen some examples elsewhere where grasses were planted as a standalone collection and with my trial in Foggy Bottom, I wasn't convinced that growing several grasses together was the best way of using them.

← There will be more on catastrophes in the garden later (see p.387), but in August 1987 we had a continuous downpour where 90 mm (3.5 in) of rain fell in one day, flooding the lower third of Foggy Bottom. There's little that can be done after the event except record it – hence an opportunity to photograph this nice reflection. But the most interesting discovery, since the water stayed for nearly two weeks, was that the bright golden yellow *Rudbeckia fulgida* var. *sullivantii* 'Goldsturm' flowered throughout. Long considered in Britain to be a sun-loving perennial, which did well in fairly dry situations, I was curious to check the detailed origins of the species, *Rudbeckia fulgida*, which I only knew was a North American native. I was able to refer to Albert Rickett's extensive work to find this description "July to October: in woodland and meadows and even in swamps from Florida to Mississippi northward to New Jersey, Michigan and Missouri". So, surviving and thriving in the Foggy Bottom 'swamp' was hardly beyond this plant's ability and this experience considerably added to my knowledge and appreciation of a perennial already in my top ten.

A roof with a view. Taken from our house roof in August 1987 (an advantage in big views is that there is hardly a weed to be seen!), your eye is taken down the sweeping grass pathways, many of the beds planted with heathers interspersed with conifers of different sizes, shapes and colours. Though an attractive tree, the dark green pine (left) had been given the name *Pinus heldreichii* 'Compact Gem'. Perhaps a gem but not compact for long. Centre towards the right is the graceful pendulous-tipped golden needled cedar, *Cedrus deodara* 'Nana Aurea', heading for the sky. In order to keep the garden and planting balanced, both would have to go eventually. →

He who rises fastest… In Britain, most gardeners will know what you are talking about when you mention a Leyland cypress. It is one of the fastest growing conifers for temperate climates and 90 cm (3 ft) a year is not uncommon. However, when it first appeared in garden centres in the late 1960s it seemed the ideal conifer for most who wanted to plant an evergreen hedge as a division between their own property and their neighbours. × *Cupressocyparis leylandii* admirably fulfilled their first desire "to grow in two or three years to 180 cm (6 ft)", but not the second "to slow down when it reaches that height". The Leyland cypress was not programmed for that since without annual pruning it will keep growing vigorously and could soon block out light in a small garden. Not the cypress's fault, but it inadvertently became an issue and the matter taken to court by some neighbours for being the cause of a legal dispute…

When you see how large the trees are in this planting in Foggy Bottom, you can imagine that it wouldn't have been long before it could be a danger to our house in a high wind. I had planted some conifers behind so that when these trees came down, we still had some shelter and interest without being in danger or overcrowded. In the far distance you can see some even taller specimens; they too would eventually have to be culled.

The Creation of a New Area for Planting

Marking out methods. In the earliest planning of Foggy Bottom when a 'blank canvas', I had used a knapsack sprayer to walk along the planned borders. In 1985, I didn't want to scar the grass since I might have wanted to adjust the edge of the new bed. So, I used canes (which could be adjusted and moved) to design an informal plan and edging which would blend with others nearby. Here, I planned to plant a winter feature which, though distant, could be seen from our house. More garden to plant and weed, but less grass to cut!

Another view, this time towards the neighbouring Gap Meadow and the main entrance gate. To the right of the gate is the bed previously marked out with canes, now planted primarily for winter interest in 1987. You can see the electric cables have now been moved to cross the woodland below the garden.

The recently planted Winter Bed (now the Entrance Bed) in early winter, the display in 1989 primarily from dogwoods; crimson stems of *Cornus alba* 'Sibirica' and orange stems of *C. sanguinea* 'Winter Beauty', and silver birch. Already there's a lot of colour to enjoy and later winter flowering heathers will add a vibrancy to the display. At this time, the view to our home is clear of taller conifers and the colourful planting could be enjoyed from our sitting room.

About fifteen years after planting, conifers and heathers in a → winter scene at Foggy Bottom made a striking combination with an amazing array of forms and colours at this normally dull time of year. Pines and spruce dominate the centre, *Pinus sylvestris* 'Aurea' (centre right) leads the eye to the tall × *Cupressocyparis leylandii*, about eighty yards away in the background. In the foreground is *Juniperus horizontalis* 'Banff', one of many prostrate junipers I had planted in the garden. With almost any size of garden, enjoy it as it grows, but be aware nothing stays the same. Here, I could see congestion was coming and would soon need constant change.

↑

A view that puts our house in context with the garden and vice versa. Winter heathers are flowering amongst a patchwork of foliage and contrasting heights and shapes of conifers. You can almost hear the bees buzzing as they gather nectar, they must be very happy! Look again and you can see the Leyland cypress in the background surrounding Adrian's Wood, ominously reaching for the sky.

The Juniper Explosion

Not a literal explosion of course, but I had seen the prostrate and semi-prostrate conifers planted widely in the United States for ground cover, as well as upright selections of American species like *Juniperus virginiana* and *J. scopulorum*. Junipers are known to be hardy and relatively easy to propagate, so I started to collect them from contacts all over the world. I was interested in all forms that might be good garden plants. Many such as *J. s.* 'Skyrocket' and 'Gray Gleam' were narrow and upright in habit. I had to trial them in our conditions since many junipers liked good drainage year-round, which couldn't be guaranteed in Britain. The only British native was the common juniper, *J. communis*, but as with most British natives it seldom means that they are solely native to Britain! *J. communis* for instance spreads throughout Europe and is also native to northern North America. By 1980 we listed about seventy different *Juniperus* species and cultivars in our Bressingham Gardens mail order catalogue. Although many of these were first-class plants, like many conifers they gradually became unfashionable as perennials began to increase in popularity.

You can imagine that in such a large garden as Foggy Bottom and over many years, certain areas, certain views and certain plants get photographed many times. But every so often you suddenly see a view from a different position you hadn't seen or considered before. And now, looking back at photographs after many years with many of those plants changed or gone, you get another perspective. Caught here on a December morning in 1989 is perhaps the epitome of Foggy Bottom in its 'Conifer Garden' era, conifers from foreground, centre and background. Taken close to our house, the foreground is filled with droplets of water on *Juniperus* × *media* 'Pfitzeriana Aurea' (planted to disguise a manhole cover, which it did extremely well) and various colours, textures and shapes of conifers as you look into the distance. From this vantage point you see a condensed view of conifers, but not the spaces between.

The Mediterranean Bed

Moving conifers became a constant but seasonal undertaking as plants outgrew their original allotted space, or I saw a better place for them to fit. This was an area we were going to plant with mostly sun-loving perennials, but it needed structure and year-round interest too. Here, gardener Michel Boutet is helped by a student and me in moving and planting a very awkwardly shaped and prickly *Juniperus communis*. It was found on local heathland by Gunther Horstmann, a nurseryman in northern Germany, and simply named *J. c.* 'Horstmann'. Spring or early autumn are good times to move conifers, and the bigger the plant the more important it is to have a good root ball.

← I had just raided some perennials from our nursery, placed them in the back of our Audi and, being dry in the garden, used this very convenient transport to save time and effort to get the plants on site. It wasn't a practise I made into a habit since we had a tractor and trailer, and barrows, but when time is short…

← I called this the Mediterranean Bed (now the Book Bed), not for a planting of purely Mediterranean species, but for the fact that it was mostly in sun on well-drained soil. *Achillea*, *Miscanthus*, *Gaura*, *Crocosmia*, the *Juniperus communis* 'Horstmann' (right), and *Buddleja* 'Pink Delight' beyond are all combining to make a colourful late summer show.

↑

From the northern vantage point of this recent 1990 planting, you can look south to the woodland, the new pond hidden on the right. A new colour breakthrough from Holland was the distinctly pink *Buddleja* 'Pink Delight', on its right the slender branched tree *Gleditsia triacanthos* f. *inermis* 'Sunburst'. In the foreground is a combination of perennials; the wispy plumed grass *Stipa tenuissima*, *Crocosmia* 'Vulcan', *Artemisia ludoviciana* 'Silver Queen', *Coreopsis verticillata* 'Golden Gain' and the brilliant white, double flowered *Leucanthemum* × *superbum* 'John Murray' (also then known as 'Summer Snowball'). This was the first bed large enough to really add a new element to the garden and I was keen to introduce both perennials and grasses …but with the garden nearly full where would I find the space?

← You win a few, you lose a few, but we hope we always learn. There were a few gaps in our Mediterranean Bed in 1997 and I had obtained some colourful new 'hardy' *Chrysanthemums* from Italy in the spring. This bed seemed the obvious place to plant them. It's a long wait until October, but these ground covering, free flowering plants were worth waiting for as they came into bloom. They had beautiful autumnal shades which we hoped would last for weeks. But living in a 'frost pocket', sharp frosts came early that year and the show was ended abruptly. Many of the plants died in the winter due to poor drainage and freezing temperatures. Ah well, worth a try…

The Volcano Bed

When I was seven years old, my father emigrated to Canada → with our family to Vancouver Island and then to Toronto, where I saw some magnificent scenery which has remained in my memory. This was probably one reason from childhood why I had loved the subjects of geography and geology. I was subsequently lucky enough to see dramatic scenery around many continents where my fascination with the natural world continued. Perhaps this makes a tenuous connection with one of my first attempts at creating an imaginary topographical feature in Foggy Bottom in 1990… the Volcano Bed (now the Front of House Bed). Plants of *Stipa tenuissima* form the vegetation on the slopes of the volcano, whilst orange red spikes of *Kniphofia* 'Bressingham Comet' represent molten lava as it flows river-like down (and great imagination is needed here…) a mountain slope in South Norfolk!

↑

We can learn about plants from books, but given an opportunity much more can be learnt from personal experience. This is the Volcano Bed after the lava (*Kniphofia* 'Bressingham Comet') has finished flowering, but the relatively short-lived grass, *Stipa tenuissima*, adds waves of movement amongst the largely static conifers and heathers in this early winter scene. The cones of *Abies procera* 'Glauca' balance on the blue needled side branches. Not everyone knows this, but the firs (*Abies*) hold cones above the branches, whilst the spruce (*Picea*) has cones that hang beneath.

↑

Who could resist getting the camera in action when such dramatic scenes are created by the winter weather? Taken in 1991, it's good to look at thirty years later as we will probably never quite get this combination again; hoar frost and grasses make an unforgettable partnership. In the foreground are three silver-coated clumps of *Carex flagellifera* and beyond, the now frozen river of *Stipa tenuissima*, seemingly caught as foaming torrents down the precipitous slope!

The Year-Round Garden

You can always count on the white stuff to create drama in the garden. In 1991 the planting of the Winter Bed down near the entrance to Foggy Bottom shows how colourful and dramatic the stems of *Cornus* can be highlighted against the carpet of snow. *C. alba* 'Sibirica' is in the foreground with orange stemmed *C. sanguinea* 'Winter Beauty' beyond; outstanding and introduced to British gardeners by our nursery.

I was becoming increasingly intrigued with the shrubby dogwoods as they seemed to offer so much to the gardener over a very long period in winter when not much else is on show. This view looks through the black stems of *Cornus alba* 'Kesselringii', introduced in Germany in 1907 from seed sent from Saint Petersburg Botanical Garden in Russia. If given the name 'Black Beauty', perhaps this distinctive dogwood would be more widely known and used.

↑

I planted *Eucalyptus niphophila* in the Long Bed in April 1991 in a newly prepared area. The misnamed *Pinus mugo* 'Gnom' on my left with dark green needles is getting in the way and would soon go. The view through the Spring Garden is filled in with plants, but the *Eucalyptus* is still garden worthy and has now matured into a tree with attractive bark.

This was a fairly well-drained area of the garden where I could use sun-loving plants, perennials and grasses too with a backdrop of trees, conifers and shrubs. Initially at least, the bright gravel from local pits showed them off and looked quite distinct from other parts of the garden.

↓

↑

I should have known better! Whilst I had used gravel to surface another smaller alpine garden near the house, this Mediterranean area was covered in gravel both as a mulch, but also to make it look the part. This photograph almost needs the caption "This is how you do it Dad" my youngest son Richard said as we spread on the shingle with our buckets. It looks good for a year or two, but the gravel gets disturbed and the weeds seed freely into it – settling beneath the gravel where the retained surface moisture gets them off to a good start.

The devil is in the detail and so it was with these very different plants. In the foreground I planted the small mosquito grass, *Bouteloua gracilis* (having at long last found out how to say it, I preferred the original species name *B. oligostachya*), named not because mosquitos are deterred or attracted to them, but because the inflorescences dancing on stems resemble the insect. It is a sun-loving North American grass which grew well in my father's well-drained garden but succumbed in mine after a couple of wet winters. Some years later, I was amazed and delighted to see it thriving on top of the Grand Canyon in Arizona, where drainage is seldom an issue!

The *Hemerocallis* 'Stella de Oro' arose through the highly developed breeding of daylilies in the US, where literally hundreds of varieties were introduced each year before a wider range of perennials became available. A dwarf repeat-flowering selection 'Stella de Oro' was raised by Walter Jablonski in 1975 who, stuck for a name, famously named it from a Cuban cigar box on his desk. A great plant for any garden in sun, though flowering will reduce unless it is divided and replanted every two or three years.

Two Kinds of Winter Colour

This area has been transformed as time and growth demands, but as we planted more perennials and grasses in Foggy Bottom, we were able to experiment with a greater diversity in planting combinations. As ever, I was keen to consider the winter element with shrubs, perennials and grasses. These two photographs were taken on quite different winter days and show two parts of the same east-facing bed.

Are there hoar frosts in the Mediterranean? Probably not, but of course this bed name was just for our benefit to help us remember roughly what was where. Primarily, this is a wonderful frosty morning when moist air is frozen dramatically on perennials and grasses, transforming something ordinary into the extraordinary. To help you locate the next photograph, look at the rather indistinct shrub in the left background of this view. →

← You don't have to wait for a hoar frost to enjoy the colours of the plants in this combination. Left is the bright gold of *Thuja occidentalis* 'Holmstrup Yellow', a *Pinus mugo* with a few cones, a pink and white heather, *Erica* × *darleyensis*, and the interesting twisting stems of coppery red are those of *Salix* × *sepulcralis* 'Erythroflexuosa' (the name once learnt, never forgotten), a willow best pruned each spring.

A New Attached Bed

↑

It is always easier and sometimes more appropriate to start with a blank canvas – or a vacant area of soil. Let me explain... As a garden and its plants mature, a small plant may struggle for survival let alone be noticed. It is also likely to be out of scale with the plants around it. So, in 1991 in this cleared and extended bed, I was planning to create an almost standalone group of dwarf and slow growing plants which were waiting in the wings for an appearance.

There was a pathway made of 'sawn' concrete logs which over time looked reasonably real. Unlike the real thing, they didn't rot. The planting looks too close now ...and it was.

↓

↑

From the size of the mature planting behind, you can see what I mean about scale. I started to put out some of the plants knowing this was likely to be a temporary position for some who would go on to be greater plants.

Almost a year later and mulched with a coarse grit (finer than the gravel used in the Mediterranean Bed), the planting had a reasonable balance and I had managed to fit in a few alpine plants and small grasses.

↓

Perennials and grasses were creeping into the garden by design, not accident! I mostly used them at the front of beds with taller trees, shrubs and conifers at the rear. A planting on the corner of the bed which became Rhus Corner shows *Hylotelephium* 'Herbstfreude' (Autumn Joy) displaying flattish heads of pink flowers, contrasting with the sharp spiked leaves of *Yucca filamentosa* 'Variegata'. A *Miscanthus sinensis* is in flower on the right, the foliage tinged red as autumn nears. In the distance is a large expanse of grass and then the edge of the pond. Ideas were forming for another planting in the broad stretch of lawn in between… →

↑

Now spring, the *Cornus* in the Winter Bed are beginning to shoot, so it's time to cut them back hard so they perform their best in the autumn and winter. The group of three *Pinus mugo* 'Winter Gold' are shooting too but are still a vibrant feature before gradually turning green. Three different *Erica carnea* varieties make colourful carpets as they follow the edge of the bed. Left is *E. c.* f. *alba* 'Springwood White', introduced as long ago as 1926, the aptly named *E. c.* 'Myretoun Ruby', and *E. c.* 'Pink Spangles' almost out of sight. The deep blue is one of the best lungworts, *Pulmonaria* 'Lewis Palmer'.

↑

A garden that grows on you would certainly apply to what you are viewing here in early autumn. I had much admiration for the dark green pine on the right, *Pinus heldreichii* 'Compact Gem', but its presence was too dominant and overpowering. A more recent addition, *Calocedrus decurrens* 'Berrima Gold', which is just behind the crimson foliaged shrub, *Euonymus alatus* 'Compactus', is stunning with its vibrant autumn colour. Time to grit the teeth and remove the pine. Foreground left is a selection of the Cornish heath, *Erica vagans* 'Mrs D.F. Maxwell' at the base of *Picea pungens* 'Globosa'.

←

As an early winter scene, this east-facing bed in Foggy Bottom had a diversity of plants, from perennials and grasses in the foreground to the structure of trees and shrubs behind. In a flat meadow it offered some form of topography. However, it dawned on me that without some drastic action this could become an overgrown and dark woodland. I hadn't planned it yet, but in fifteen years' time all the conifers in this view would be gone.

A Sad Story…

"Who's got the best job then?". That was my comment → when we moved an established specimen of *Cedrus atlantica* 'Glauca Pendula' across the garden to its new position. Jason, my eldest son is on the left, Michel our main gardener in the red t-shirt, and nursery staff were needed to drag the large root ball about a hundred yards. It wasn't only suspicion that had me believe they were amused at my predicament holding the top of the tree as the six 'young' men pulled the sheet, but it was a joint effort using undoubted and willing 'manpower' that achieved our objective.

Initially, the cedar was planted and watered in, but → its importance as a living sculpture would need more time and some designs around it. In the meantime, the groups of bright pink *Calluna vulgaris*, 'H.E. Beale' and 'Peter Sparkes', made an excellent contrast to the weeping blue cedar.

← Finally planting what was to become the Sad Bed, in which I was to plant some other trees of pendulous habit. It seemed obvious that we should give it that name since nearly all the plants in it were weeping… and I must take full responsibility for it.

← Late autumn in Foggy Bottom and the late afternoon light was amazing, the lowering sun seeming to saturate a redness onto the autumn leaves of *Cornus sanguinea* 'Winter Beauty' and other plants. Although this colour looks artificial, it was nature caught by a camera in which timing was everything. I should know because I was there…

↑ …and I was here too a few weeks later, soon after a light snowfall had blown in, alighting on the upright coppery stems of the *Cornus*. Magic in the eye of the beholder!

The weather can completely transform a garden in winter, and it's obvious that snow can do that on its own. This was a heavy fall which stayed on many branches, small clumps on upright branched conifers and a carpet of white on the semi-prostrate juniper in the foreground. It's late afternoon and you feel certain that there's going to be a frost tonight as the fog gradually filters among the conifers down towards the wood and the pond. A magic moment in time.

↓

The Snake Bed Comes to Life

Whilst Rosemary and I had made a three-week visit (part holiday, part business) to South Africa, Michel had been digging this completely new bed in the large expanse of grass north of the pond. This was going to be primarily planted with perennials and grasses, and I had recently bought several new varieties of *Miscanthus sinensis* from Germany which I wanted to trial. This bed, being reasonably moist in summer, should be ideal for them. We were to call this the Snake Bed. No snakes, but if you look at the canes I had placed, they form a snaking line against and through where I would weave perennials and other grasses. The *Miscanthus* are mostly planted but are only showing the old stems above the soil.

Even in the first autumn the *Miscanthus* I had planted had nearly all flowered and showed promise to come. In autumn and winter, it is a distinct advantage to be able to look toward the distant sunlight, which can brilliantly light up certain plants like the inflorescences of the varied *Miscanthus*. Of course, low in the sky the light can at certain times of the day be just too bright to look at or photograph. →

Looking from the south at another section of the Snake Bed → you can see how much colour some perennials still offer in October. The *Miscanthus* plumes are in the background and in front, two *Asters* (most now called *Symphyotrichum*, a name which runs off the tongue much more easily… not!). Lastly, the wonderful *Persicaria amplexicaulis* 'Taurus' which, like others of this species, would flower until Christmas if there was no frost. This photograph firmly asserts the rights for perennials and grasses to contribute to Foggy Bottom, long held and largely known as a conifer and heather garden.

Perennials and grasses usually come to maturity in a much ↓ shorter time than conifers, heathers or other shrubs, hence this view of the Snake Bed in late summer only three years after planting. Repetition of *Rudbeckia fulgida* var. *sullivantii* 'Goldsturm' and *Eupatorium maculatum* 'Gateway' seems to add continuity in this long bed. *Helenium* 'Bruno' in the centre was named by my father after his pipe tobacco.

Adrian Bloom in February 2000 photographed by his son Richard Bloom.

03
03

Making Decisions – The Need for Change 2000–20

Facing The Facts

Looking at both photographs, the inescapable fact is that twenty years after planting, we had to start making decisions on which plants to thin out …and get on with it quickly. Richard, my youngest son and now a top-class horticultural photographer, was taking a picture of his dad standing in front of what was then called the Conifer Bed, shortly before many of the conifers were removed.

Why, you might ask, did I not originally plant at a wider spacing? The answer is that as a collector of conifers from all over the world, I wanted to learn how well they grew in our climate and how distinct they were as garden plants. I also didn't want to overcrowd other parts of the garden where I was creating longer term designs. So, rather than having many conifers sitting in pots, I found room to plant them in the Conifer Bed (now the All Seasons Bed), a relatively small island bed in the middle of the garden. By this time, there were about 500 species and varieties of conifers in Foggy Bottom, including over a hundred in this bed alone. As you can see, whilst they offered a multitude of shapes and colours here in winter, they were definitely overcrowded.

Three is a crowd if you only want two of anything. And if you garden with any group of plants – particularly woody plants – without acres of space, you almost always plant too closely. This is a subject on its own, but one I have tried to deal with for the last thirty years in Foggy Bottom and is ongoing. It is a challenge and decisions are not made lightly. From the perspective of those who love plants and gardening, you can spoil yourself. Enjoy collecting and planting ...but if you want to keep a balance, prepare to be brutal to some plants by thinning out and convincing yourself that you are being kind to those that remain. For garden designers, the selection of plants needs to be more considered, looking further ahead. The designed garden must bear in mind future growth when selecting plants, a consideration which is likely to restrict choice. Of course, in all gardens, maintenance needs to be considered; weed control, pruning, perhaps grass cutting, and at some stage, replanting. The latter also applies for 'natural' plantings of perennials and grasses, as not all, however much you plan, have been created equal. Whilst selections of plants for combinations and larger plantings can happily exist for a period, adjustments will inevitably need to be made, curbing some and replanting others. This is not to undermine the joy of plants and gardens, but to add reality to the vision and potential excitement.

Transforming the Conifer Bed to the All Seasons Bed

So where is the vision in overplanting? Vision is applied to those looking far enough ahead to see what the final picture will be. But if it is all part of an experiment, judging the success of a vision can only be perceived in hindsight. At what stage can we judge? In Foggy Bottom, even after fifty years, the jury is still out. But individual projects can be judged after a shorter time span. As it grew, this view had gradually become a scene to enjoy and record. Though it had a lot of impact, I knew the background would have to change radically with the removal of many colourful conifers in the Conifer Bed. Now, all those conifers have gone as well as many of the *Miscanthus* in the Snake Bed in front. My answer to people who ask, "Don't you feel sad when you have to part with attractive plants?", is "Sometimes", but I usually think "Great, we can create something else and try some different plants!", hoping that my knowledge and experience can produce something new and dramatic. From a need to change to the completion of an idea, the journey is not achieved overnight, but the following images will give you an idea of the process.

← "There are some nice conifers there!", I can hear you say. And yes, you are right. In fact, some I have never been able to replace, such as *Juniperus chinensis* 'Variegated Kaizuka' and a fine specimen of *Picea pungens* 'Hoopsii'. These two (and others) were too big to move and since I wanted to retain the rounded pine to the left, *Pinus koraiensis* 'Winton', the blue spruce would have to go. Had I planned a year or two ahead, I would have taken cuttings of the variegated juniper to grow some young replacement plants, but sometimes decisions can't wait. Do make a note of *P. k.* 'Winton', as it becomes an important part of the soon to be All Seasons Bed, the new name for the Conifer Bed.

This gives a better idea of the removal of conifers and the canes I had put out to enlarge the bed. We needed a small digger to dig out stumps and roots so that we would be able to prepare the soil before planting. This area of the garden had some of the best and most easily worked soil in the six acres of Foggy Bottom. Many a time had we wished all was the same, but that's the challenge of gardening.

Mike Murton was our farmer and driver of the only tractor on our 300-acre farm but had to turn his hand to many other jobs. He took some pride in cutting trees down and through experience was very good at it. We occasionally had to call in a tree surgeon when a larger tree within the garden needed dismantling rather than felling, dropping each branch from the top down so as not to damage other plants nearby. In this exciting action shot Michel is helping to stabilise the ladder, but these days would sensibly and legally be required to wear a safety helmet!

A load of composted bark is being unloaded by Jaime and Michel, whilst I am leaning on my spade and keeping a keen eye on proceedings. Richard Bloom is the photographer, and he had used the steps in the background to capture the previous elevated shot. The conifer in the distance behind the ladder is an *Abies koreana* which blew down in a storm a few years later. At the end of February, new crimson purple shoots of *Acer tataricum* subsp. *ginnala* (left) glow against a woodland backdrop. Not many people would have noticed that…

Evergreen conifers need light and air around the complete plant to remain fully furnished with foliage. If grown too closely to other conifers, they will 'go blind' and lose their leaves or needles. Most will never regrow from that area of the plant. What to do? As you might imagine, I had several conifers in this bed that had become one-sided, and I wanted to keep some if possible… In the case of *Abies nordmanniana* 'Golden Spreader', this was the answer. Opposite the blind side of the *Abies* we planted a bare-sided Canadian hemlock, *Tsuga canadensis* 'Verkade Recurved', a unique selection with densely held dark green leaves and somewhat brittle branchlets. They grew toward each other and made an attractive combination. →

← In 2005 planting begins. You can get your bearings of the All Seasons Bed today (covered more in depth on p.69) by noticing the fresh spring leaves of *Betula davurica* to the left. Behind *Pinus longaeva* 'Sherwood Compact' is the tall, bushy *Erica australis*, its purple-pink flowers making a late spring show. Not many people know this but *australis* means 'south', not a plant originating from Australia! Centre right and making new growth is *Pinus mugo* 'Ophir', and behind is our key conifer, *Pinus koraiensis* 'Winton', which I have already pruned from the base. You will see *P. k.* 'Winton' many times as a focal point as this planting develops.

It looks like someone has been at work… arranging and planting is the most enjoyable process for most gardeners. In the case of the All Seasons Bed, I had to decide what to remove, what to leave and what to bring in, considering how new plants might fit with others for now and for a number of years ahead. From the Sad Bed in the background, you can see the pyramidal *Picea glauca* 'Alberta Blue'. There are too many other conifers to name, but two newly planted selections in the centre are *Cedrus deodara* 'Feelin' Blue' and *Abies concolor* 'Wintergold'. The small grass-like shoots of *Imperata cylindrica* 'Rubra' are planted as a river which will flow through the whole bed, and here in late spring you have little idea what impact they might have. To 'mop up' names, *Pinus koraiensis* 'Winton' is on the right, and the plants in pots with creamy white shoots are *Erica* × *darleyensis* 'Jenny Porter'. →

Now in early summer, the tips of *Imperata cylindrica* 'Rubra' are making a vibrant appearance amongst the plants it flows past. I couldn't resist planting the creeping, silvery-blue *Mertensia maritima* in the foreground, although I knew it might be short-lived. It needs full sun and good drainage. This position offered the first requirement, but in our often-wet winters perhaps not the second. →

A year later in late summer, you can see the planting in relation to distant beds. In the distance is the Snake Bed where the maroon heads of *Eupatorium maculatum* 'Gateway' almost match the colour of the *Imperata*. It now looks clever, but that wasn't even planned… →

In looking at the summer and autumn views, we need to remember this bed was not called the All Seasons Bed for nothing – this is where the winter flowering heathers and conifers come in. Photographed in late winter after the *Imperata* has been cut back, *Erica carnea* 'Myretoun Ruby' replaces the grass with the glow of its flowers. Maybe the *Cedrus deodara* 'Feelin' Blue' is feeling a little less blue now… →

Plants From Across the World

Elements of Change as the Garden Grows

Having travelled and collected conifers and other plants from across the world (developing markets abroad for the Blooms of Bressingham brand at the same time), I found new plants in New Zealand, Australia, Japan, the United States, Canada, as well as Europe. I then had to find space to grow them. Foggy Bottom was a large trial garden, but though 'large' by most people's standards, it didn't compare with the greater garden areas of RHS Garden Wisley, The Savill Garden at Windsor, or the Royal Botanic Gardens, Kew.

I was collecting and gardening with a view to demonstrate what I hoped would be good garden plants. My father Alan, with his Dell Garden and amazing collection of perennials, always had our business and the gardener customer in mind. That was very much my objective too. That said, I knew that many of the larger trees, conifers and shrubs used in Foggy bottom wouldn't be suitable for most gardens in the UK, nor would they be ones that we'd want to grow on our nursery. I had to admit that I was also taking this opportunity to widen my knowledge about plants... particularly those I was not familiar with. These thoughts were at the back of my mind, but the driving force was to create a garden that over time might speak to everyone, to both inspire and serve as a source of ideas which could be replicated...

Of course, not all trials were successful. You win a few, you lose a few! Well, quite a few as I have realised looking at images of Foggy Bottom taken some years ago. Here, I am standing on our low incline house roof taking photographs. The date is July 1993 and for my interest as much as yours I will list what is still there and what has gone, from left to right... An asterisk (*) denotes if the plant is still with us.

Picea pungens 'Thomsen'*, a blue spruce raised in Denmark at the point of perfection with a few ripe cones at the top of the tree. *Thuja plicata* 'Stoneham Gold', gold tipped and one of my early favourites from Rogers Nursery, Eastleigh, Hampshire. *Chamaecyparis pisifera* 'Filifera Aurea'*, a golden thread cypress, behind which is a bluish-leaved *Lonicera korolkowii*, nice but too vigorous. Dark green *Pinus heldreichii* 'Compact Gem', obviously misnamed and would get too big and cut out light. The smaller conifer near the purple shrub is *Abies koreana* 'Silberlocke' from Horstmann Nursery in Germany, it had attractive curved needles as a young plant but reverted to type with age. *Cedrus deodara* 'Nana Aurea' from France, a name that attracted me and though a good plant it certainly was not 'Nana' (dwarf). Sad perhaps, but not necessary to create the continuing garden.

The Best of Times

Certain plants had not improved with age and in this case, it is primarily down to cultural reasons and maybe climate change. I was aware that Brewer's weeping spruce, *Picea breweriana*, is used to a high rainfall, originating from the West Coast of America. Here on the driest side of England it would need adequate moisture to do well. I had come across a particularly good form in Germany and planted a small specimen in the lower part of the garden. Here it is about twelve years after planting with a collection of perennials and grasses around it. There's no denying which is the main plant! The golden foliaged conifer behind was removed, but roots from the Austrian pine behind and other trees began to take more than their fair share of moisture (they probably didn't see it that way). Although we had irrigation available during very dry periods, it had not been enough to prevent the conifer from being under stress and shedding some of its lower branches. Luckily, I have another *P. breweriana* in a more favourable position in Foggy Bottom, so if this has to go, I still have another making a display elsewhere.

The Worst of Times

Another North American native conifer commonly known as the Engelmann spruce, *Picea engelmannii* f. *glauca*, had to be removed as it was not only taking up too much space, but was also overcrowded by other plants. Like most conifers when growing in a forest or not having sufficient light around it, it had shed its lower branches. As a standalone specimen it is an attractive species with grey-green needles giving a bluish cast, softer to the touch than the Colorado blue spruce, *Picea pungens*. We called in long-time tree surgeon Sean Hickey and his son Shane (who is up the tree) to remove each branch, then remove the trunk in short lengths so all could be carted away. Then in most cases we dug round and cut the largest roots using a winch to pull out the stump, then cut it up and removed. It was considered necessary to remove most stumps to prevent potential attack from the dreaded honey fungus, *Armillaria mellea*. This area was to become the Acer Glade, being the most sheltered area in Foggy Bottom from early morning spring frosts.

The Big Picture

Until my son Matt built the tree house, the best elevation to get a view of the garden was from the roof of our home, now mostly hidden from visitors (by intent!). From here, an overview from the Front of House Bed down to the woodland below is visible. This photograph shows the development and growth of the plants in the east side of Foggy Bottom, with the Gap Meadow on the left. It had always been my intention to have wide pathways leading the eye to distant plants as focal points, the grass acting as a broad river of green. Note in the foreground the use of *Hosta* 'Shade Fanfare' in a ribbon from the dwarf blue spruce, *Picea pungens* 'Globosa', to around the base of the purple Japanese maple, *Acer palmatum* 'Fireglow'.

There were several objectives in collecting plants for Foggy Bottom, some of which have been stated already. Year-round colour was, and is, a prime objective so every season is important. I still marvel when visiting New England in 'fall', fiery tones of autumn leaves breaking out across the landscape. Of course, even in the different states of New England, some seasons are better than others. An early sharp frost or gale force wind happens in both locations but finding trees and shrubs to rely on for autumn colour in Britain is difficult. There are regional differences as well as diverse conditions and climate on our small island.

Here from the roof of our house at Foggy Bottom, you see early autumn with every promise that it will be a colourful one. Fine, mostly sunny days that are not too dry and cool nights (even a light early frost or two) all help. A mix of deciduous plants such as *Euonymus*, *Berberis*, *Spiraea*, *Cornus* and *Hamamelis* will assist, and many selections have been made of cultivars that colour better than others. Seedlings of the American native sweetgum, *Liquidambar styraciflua*, vary in habit and degrees of autumn colour. Raised, grown and selected in Surrey, England, for having reliable red-purple leaves, *L. s.* 'Worplesdon' can be recommended in Britain.

Some other trees for autumn colour in the UK climate are selected forms of the Japanese maple, *Acer palmatum*, ornamental cherries, *Prunus*, and silver birch, *Betula*. Of course, there are many more! If you mix other coloured foliage plants such as *Cotinus* and *Physocarpus*, alongside some ornamental grasses – including the often-maligned pampas grass *Cortaderia selloana* – and very late flowering perennials, you can have many ingredients to make a colourful autumn display. Returning after that dissertation to the view, it is evident that the trees on the left-hand side of Foggy Bottom have now blocked off the view to the Gap Meadow, so the garden is fully enclosed.

Changing The View

A Short-Term Balancing Act

In a span of more than fifty years, 'short-term' probably means five to ten years. This area is the Front of House Bed, photographed in 2008 ten years before the image on p.42. This is in July and the plants in flower stand out boldly; *Rosa* 'Knock Out' in the foreground, *Hydrangea quercifolia* 'Snow Queen' on the right, and behind with a few vibrant flowers is *Crocosmia* 'Lucifer'. The balance to me in this grouping comes from every inch of the soil being covered. Though plants mingle and work off each other, they still stand out as individuals. From the left, the pink flowered *Spiraea japonica* 'Magic Carpet' nestles alongside the rounded bush and silvery upturned needles of *Picea sitchensis* 'Tenas'. Obviously home to many spiders, the semi-upright *Picea omorika* 'Pendula Bruns' is looking as though it hasn't yet decided which way to go. The golden fragrant *Jasminum officinale* 'Fiona Sunrise' competes with an ivy for dominance over the stump of a onetime *Juniperus chinensis* 'Robusta Green'.

← A few months later, taking a step or two to the left, I was able to pick up a 'borrowed' view from the private area of the garden. From the back, this brings in the vivid blue spruce, *Picea pungens* 'Hoto', in front of which is the deep purple-leaved *Cotinus coggygria* 'Royal Purple'. Mid-distant behind the golden-leaved jasmine are a couple of witch hazels; *Hamamelis* × *intermedia* 'Jelena' and 'Feuerzauber'. This has been one of my favourite autumn combinations in the garden, but at the time of writing this book, things now need changing again.

From Enclosure to Letting in The Light

Starting with an open and at times very windswept meadow, my first action and design was to gradually create an enclosed environment. Trees and conifers would shelter tender plants from the wind, and (eventually) as a visitor entered the garden, it would be like venturing into another world, a self-contained environment, quiet, peaceful, and perhaps therapeutic. The first garden area around our house was relatively easy to disguise as our private area, whilst keeping the atmosphere in the rest of the garden as part of the whole. But the journey to the point of full enclosure of the garden, as shown on these pages, took more than thirty years. The various sized island beds would have structural plants generally toward the centre, the islands becoming three-dimensional as the plants grew. Views and vistas would primarily be along the green pathways and showy plants would be planted to draw the eye. The idea was that since you couldn't see through the beds, you would walk to a point at the end before you got another or perhaps several views. Oh the excitement! It added interest to a garden which started life as a featureless meadow.

Having achieved enclosure, the second phase was to open up the quickly growing garden on the verge of becoming crowded. It was obvious well before this stage that unless severely restricted and controlled, Foggy Bottom was never going to be 'finished'. If you love plants and gardening, why would you want that?

← As well as removing trees (mostly conifers), redesigning and replanting, we needed to create glimpses through the beds to others beyond, borrowing plants in the distance to enhance a view. Now that trees and conifers were growing skywards, it was easier to draw them in. We also made more pathways that could lead you through to another planting. To some extent this has worked, but creating more pathways meant that more maintenance and planting would be required. It's an ongoing process and that's when we could do with more gardeners to help!

Early morning view from the pond in early winter across sun-spotted trees to the redwoods in Adrian's Wood.

PART FOUR
...AND NOT TO FORGET

04
01

The Gardeners Over Time

Family First

In the early years as the garden around the house developed, I was able to do most of the digging and planting myself. Although we called it Foggy Bottom from the beginning, the garden stood above the low meadow and where mist gathered on certain days. So, although the name is very appropriate, it was an import from a place in the United States! Rosemary and I moved into our unfinished house after a brief honeymoon in October. A green meadow surrounding us. In the first few years, I mostly worked to build and plant the garden at weekends. In February 1969, Jason was born and followed not too long after by Matt in January 1971, and Richard in July 1973. "Was born" seems not to express the vital and painful role Rosemary played in giving birth and having the prime responsibility of raising our sons, particularly in their early years. From 1970 as new joint Managing Directors, my brother Rob and I got more and more involved with the rapid growth and development of our family business Blooms Nurseries Ltd.

This was also still very much family time as the children grew, attending the local Bressingham Primary School where I had gone twenty years earlier, but only for a year in 1950–51. The garden may have been growing as I planted more conifers and heathers in an experimental fashion, but it was still a place for all our family to enjoy. By 1974 the garden near our house was full of plants and growing quickly together. I needed more space!

Here, stylish as ever, Rosemary stands beside the large and quite distant (from our house that is) vegetable garden, a newly planted *Thuja* hedge behind her. In the distance, the white shine of the polyhouse which was the Foggy Bottom Garden shed for many years.

There was still room in the garden barrow for the all-important watering can as well as our three sons, Matt, Richard and Jason. This was almost as much fun (well not really) as splashing each other in a pop-up swimming pool. That certainly takes us all a long way back to other magical moments. For the gardeners looking beyond our mini swimming pool, please note the parched garden, planted beds, bags of composted bark and hosepipes.

Help from the first Foggy Bottom gardener

It is difficult to chronicle in detail the help provided in the garden, but in the early days I relied on a few people from the nursery to come and keep the weeds down in the spring. I did most of the setting out and planting myself at this stage and knew that it would take some time to fill the bare meadow and start to plan ahead. Broad pathways of grass would eventually lead the eye in long vistas, and slowly, the bare soil would become covered. Rosemary cut the grass with a small ancient tractor and helped me with the weeding. We both developed a vegetable garden, first on heavy soil at the back of our house and later at the far side of the garden where the soil was easier to work. Throughout the development of the garden, Rosemary helped where she could and was always a part of it. It will always be memorable to me that as it matured, she came to look upon the garden in our more relaxed moments as being "a little piece of heaven".

Rosemary's parents, Stan and Iris, used to visit regularly on Sundays from the family home in Cambridge usually for a roast lunch, expertly cooked for the family by Rosemary. She also had her own ideas and projects and for a while kept chickens in the meadow below before it became garden. Judging by the healthy-looking vegetables just picked from the vegetable garden, it was very productive, whilst Rosemary has collected some free-range eggs. Matt is just happy to be there! The hens were locked up at night as to avoid becoming a meal for the foxes. The cattle in the Gap Meadow are as ever inquisitive, sometimes if you walked through the meadow they panicked, dangerously so.

The presenter Peter Seabrook and film crew with Adrian in Foggy Bottom, the garden now more established, April 1985.

Gardeners and Helpers

I was lucky to be able to continue developing Foggy Bottom, but until we had a full-time gardener, a policy of beg, steal or borrow was undertaken in order to keep on top of things. I much preferred the latter… Of course, it is not to be forgotten that plants mostly came free via the nursery. I could, and did, continually make the argument that Foggy Bottom was a trial garden, as was my father's Dell Garden, which would eventually benefit our business.

Our first full-time assistant, Bill Saunders, wasn't really a gardener, but he wasn't afraid of hard work and there was plenty of that for him from the start. He was a straight-talking Brummie and did a lot of soil preparation work but knew little about plants. He was joined on occasion by Frenchman Michel Boutet, who was working on the main nursery. Michel had gained a wide experience of propagation and other nursery work, having worked on French and Swiss nurseries as well as the well-known Hillier Nurseries. Michel and Bill had to share a small polyhouse as their garden shed and in close quarters. They were very much opposites in their nationalities, background, work experience and interest in gardening. Unsurprisingly, there were times when they didn't see eye to eye, but I think they came to respect each other and did a good job as gardeners. As the garden grew, so did their association with it. Michel became full-time at Foggy Bottom in 1981 and Bill left in 1985.

Michel Boutet preparing the new Snake Bed in Foggy Bottom, February 1996.

Michel became Head Gardener, always enthusiastic about his work and knowledgeable, particularly on woody plants. He had to put up with basic conditions for some years, but seldom complained. He also accepted and enjoyed the challenge of digging and preparing conifers and moving them (on his own if the specimen wasn't too large). I considered myself very lucky to have been able to start a garden when I was twenty-seven and develop it over time, but it had to come second to the business. So, once Michel was here, at least I knew that maintenance was being carried out and plants were being watered. Additional help came from students, and if we had a bigger job to undertake 'The Conifer Gang' came down, led by Brian Tate and his younger helpers.

In 2000, we got sufficient finances together to have our Garden Store built in the north-west corner of the garden. Although practical, it seemed a great luxury for the gardeners and I managed to add another office where, if I needed to, I could get away from phones etc. to write articles or books. Writing these had to be fitted in at the extreme hours of the day, early mornings or late evenings.

From 2000, the gardens were open to the public daily, along with the Steam Museum which was now a charitable trust. We had opened up a pathway through Adrian's Wood and I started to develop the Summer Garden and the Winter Garden from 2004. Eventually, this extended The Bressingham Gardens to seventeen acres in total.

Strictly speaking, I was always really the Head Gardener for Foggy Bottom, but I had limited time to fulfil the day-to-day practical work required. When Michel left in April 2003, I appointed a young man who had some horticultural training, but not much experience. It turned out to be a mistake for both of us as unfortunately he had an illness which resulted in absence for weeks at a time, eventually he left to get

You are never too young to learn, take my word for it! Anja takes a moment to comfort Julia in the pram before continuing to edge and weed one of the beds in Foggy Bottom with Martin.

long-term treatment. We needed a replacement quickly and were glad that Martin Raven was able to join us as Assistant Head Gardener, helped initially by Alison. Soon after Alison left, a young Polish woman called Anja joined us and together they made a good team. Neither had any training as gardeners or had been working in horticulture, but they did a good job whilst gradually learning about plants and how things were done. They formed a good working partnership and when Anja started a family, we adjusted the hours and were as flexible as possible. Occasionally, if Anja couldn't get a babysitter, she would bring her daughter Julia with her. In 2019, Anja went back to Poland and had her second child, continuing her life there.

Is it from Mars? Is it a giant snail? No… it's a hot air balloon inflating in the Gap Meadow on an early July morning in 2014. It's getting ready to take TV presenter Christine Walkden on a ride over The Bressingham Gardens and into the Waveney Valley.

The fastest growing evergreen × *Cupressocyparis leylandii* was grown and sold by the million, planted as hedges and windbreaks across Britain. I had planted these in 1967, and twenty years later felt it necessary to take them down as they were on their way to be over 100 ft (and less than thirty feet from our house). Michel appears to be holding the ladder steady whist Mike Murton is cutting down chunks of the main stem, having cleared all the branches first. It was the first of about thirty tall Leyland cypress we felled in the next few years.

As the plants, trees and conifers grew in the garden, some could be moved, some pruned (mostly down to me), and some removed entirely. Estate and Farm Foreman, Mike Murton, who used a chainsaw well, helped dismantle trees when the time had come to thin them out or cut them down. In more recent years, this role was carried on by his successor, Kenny Roberts. All have played their part and I am pleased to thank them as being part of what has been the long Foggy Bottom journey. Beyond that, we have called in expert tree surgeons at different times to remove trees that had grown too close to others, that were too big or likely to get too big, and some that blocked a view. Taking plants out for such a purpose undoubtedly gives a greater appreciation of what you chose to keep.

Kenny, often working with Martin, would help with felling trees that didn't require a qualified tree surgeon. Sometimes, as with this *Chamaecyparis lawsoniana*, the tree was left with a high trunk so it could be winched over, the root exposed, then cut up and removed. We didn't want to take the risk of the stump being attacked by the notorious honey fungus which might then spread more widely.

You'd need to be confident as a tree surgeon to gradually scale this blue Atlas cedar, *Cedrus atlantica* 'Glauca', (which I planted around 1970) cutting the branches as you ascend until you get to the top of the now narrow trunk. You'd also need a head for heights when getting to the top, chainsaw hanging. In a close situation where there is not space to fell a tree, the tree surgeon must gradually dismantle the tree as he descends, leaving a stump, in this case 3 ft high. This is all that remains of the fast growing cedar, which due to brittle branches had regrettably become a danger to garden visitors.

In the last five years there has been more trees coming down in Foggy Bottom than being planted, a necessary procedure if the garden is not to be overcrowded. *Chamaecyparis lawsoniana* 'Dijk's Weeping' was a distinctive conifer, selected in Holland for its blue-green foliage and weeping habit. It was not improving as it got to middle age and had to make way for more worthy and younger plants. Matt wanted the whole trunk to use as timber later. Here he is riding the heavy 'bronco' before being carted away by tractor and trailer.

In 2019, I got to sit down and have a pleasant conversation with plantswoman and TV presenter Carol Klein in Foggy Bottom. We were featured in a series called *Great British Gardens* for Channel 5. The great thing about this series is that all four seasons are covered and therefore relevant to all who are interested in creating a garden for year-round interest.

I certainly should leave some room to mention our volunteers, now becoming such a valuable resource for many gardens who simply couldn't manage without them. As people vary, each volunteer has their own reason for helping, and there are a range of benefits that they can gain too. We value their help and appreciate that they are giving their time, but for all, matching skills and physical abilities needs careful management. It is early days still, but we are setting up a small team to develop this programme for the future. Since COVID-19, there seems to be much more awareness of nature and gardening, and the benefits of working amongst living things.

You are never too old! … Except when you are. We are always pleased to welcome volunteers and they often stay and become part of Foggy Bottom's story. And it was just so with Len Speller, who despite heart problems was with us for five years, and more recently, Gerry Branigan who arrives fully equipped with his own barrow and tools and gets stuck into whatever is asked of him. Here is a picture for posterity! Our valued monthly expert gardener, Will Twentyman, is on his knees having just dug around the *Betula nigra*. Before he could say help, Gerry and Michel Boutet were there helping to push and pull the stump over. Michel, now in his mid-seventies, still comes as a volunteer, and in a note he wrote to me in 1999 said, "Every time I come here, I really enjoy the peace and the colourful tableau". Michel of course was part of that.

And whether this is the right place to say, I am glad to share most of the garden with its visitors. We have a notebook that visitors can write in after their visit and the comments mean a lot to the gardeners and to me. As one might expect, some comments are underwhelming such as "Very nice", others show their excitement "Wow, wow, wow!". Then quite often there is someone to whom, like us, think that Foggy Bottom and all the other gardens here at Bressingham are something special, "Stunning, memorable, a true paradise. A place which is now on our 'favourites' list to be visited regularly now that we are retired. Inspiring ideas too to take home and emulate". (Thank you R.C. and T.C. and please visit many times again!). Surely for those of us that open gardens to the public, this is what it is all about?

We can review the past which can't be changed and preview the future which can. I can and will hope to take a leading part in the Foggy Bottom Garden as long as I am able. But it is every bit as important to consider the future and how the garden will fit in with the next generation. Foggy Bottom is my garden, but one of five including the Dell Garden created by my father Alan. Together, they are seventeen acres and come under the title of The Bressingham Gardens. An ongoing challenge!

Before COVID-19, 'furlough' was a word unknown and hardly used. Now, it doesn't require explanation. The pandemic was a time where many, 'locked at home' had more time to enjoy and work in their garden, and if they had a chance, perhaps learn more from experience. It was also an opportunity for me to tackle a project at Foggy Bottom that we would be unable to achieve with our full-time gardeners. We had an excellent response and with the help of some enthusiastic volunteers we were able to complete the first stage of our project. The project followed a long-held idea to create a winter walk that would link elements of seasonal interest, particularly *Cornus*, silver birch, *Galanthus* and plantings of mostly winter flowering heathers. Josh Tye, a young and knowledgeable new employee, volunteered to lead the project each Saturday morning for several spring weeks. Many visitors will hopefully benefit in future from their generosity and hard work.

04
02

Fifty Years of Weather

Visitors from outside of the United Kingdom ask about the soil and the weather in Foggy Bottom. Both have been covered to some extent so far, but with regard to the weather, I would say we seldom experience, nor have experienced, extremes compared with many parts of the world.

Drought

Within the UK, the climate varies more than people might think in terms of rainfall, wind and temperature. I agree wholeheartedly with the science of global warming, although there can be facts that seem to conflict. Though evidence shows a gradual but definite change in climate, and we seem to break high temperature records regularly, I distinctly remember what was recorded as the hottest, longest summer on record in Britain in 1976. I had just started the expansion of Foggy Bottom into the meadow in front of the house and had to irrigate constantly, as well as restrict planting that year until after September 19th when the weather finally broke in our part of the country.

July 1976 was the beginning of the hottest summer on record in Bressingham and much of England. The grass is suffering from heat and drought, a sprinkler is vainly trying to keep up. This was the year that I began to take in a five-acre meadow as part of the future Foggy Bottom Garden. New areas had been prepared and a few conifers placed in the new beds. In the distance is the house and developed garden, a colourful window box drawing the eye. But burnt grass and a small sprinkler better reflects the beginnings of drought.

Blue sky, scorched grass and the mop head of an umbrella pine on the right might have you thinking this photograph was taken in Italy rather than on the edge of the Foggy Bottom Garden. The *Pinus pinea* is one of a few plants that I brought back as seed in a cone from Italy, and in sun (occasionally provided in England) with good drainage they have made excellent trees.

Eucalyptus felled by Storm Doris, February 2017.

Wind

Looking at the topography of Britain, the Atlantic Gulf Stream brings in wind to the west side of the country, dropping most of the moisture in the hills (we call them mountains, though all except two are below 4,000 ft), the middle and eastern sides getting far less annual rainfall. For instance, Liverpool on the western side of England gets around thirty-two inches a year, whilst Bressingham gets only twenty-two inches, a third less.

Likewise, strong gales are much more prevalent near western coasts, from Cornwall in the south, north to Wales, and to the coast and islands of Northern Scotland. In October 1987 whilst I was on a lecture tour enjoying the fine 'fall' weather in Pennsylvania, the UK experienced the worst, most severe gales – missed by the (later, highly embarrassed BBC) weather forecasts – which swept up across Northern France to Southern England and through East Anglia. Swathes of trees came down like ninepins in forests, woods and gardens. Wakehurst in Sussex, managed by the Royal Botanic Gardens, Kew, and RHS Wisley in Surrey were just two notable gardens affected. At Bressingham, many trees came down, but we were let off lightly compared to some. At other times and in more recent years, strong tornado-like winds have taken the tops out of trees in Foggy Bottom, and a large *Eucalyptus* came crashing down, narrowly missing our Garden Store building.

Floods

One of our worst extreme weather occurrences is extensive flooding. Foggy Bottom is situated in the lower meadows of the Waveney Valley, which sounds and often can be idyllic. Though not the source for our garden name, it is in a low-lying position which leads to it being quite foggy at times, as you may have noticed. August 1968 and August 1987 were two of the worst years for floods. In 1968, the hardly started garden was on higher ground near our house. The flood of 1987 occurred after nearly four inches of rain fell in twenty-four hours and the shallow river valley and river itself was blocked on its journey to the North Sea. Less than 60 ft above sea level here at Foggy Bottom, that was only a drop of 2 ft a mile. During an October visit to New England, Rosemary and I were stranded in Portland Maine after thirteen inches of rain fell in twenty-four hours! Even more fell inland, yet it didn't produce long-lasting or serious flooding. Had that occurred in Foggy Bottom, we would probably still be standing on the roof of our house waiting for rescue!

August 1987. It's nice to get the canoe out on a summer's day, but not when your garden is flooded. Rosemary Bloom is practising her paddling skills before going down the usually unnavigable River Waveney to Diss three miles away. Summer flooding, if the water stays many days, does more damage than in winter when plants are dormant.

In 2020 our worst flooding came, luckily in winter and just before Christmas, remaining for several weeks into 2021. Though relatively few losses are still happening. Can we expect more regular flooding in future? Who knows! It might be wise to consider the choice of what is planted… and where they should go.

December 2020. The Waveney Valley is hardly a valley, nor as it 'flows' through Bressingham is the Waveney much of a river. In parts, it is more like a ditch congested with reeds and unmanaged vegetation. So, when heavy rain falls for a long period, the water cannot get away and the valley floods. The water table is high and the adjacent woodland and meadows as well as the lower end of Foggy Bottom, being only 150 metres from the river, is flooded. Nothing much can be done until the water gradually subsides, except perhaps take photographs to record this unplanned landscape. Snowdrops lie beneath, amazingly soon to emerge (we hope post-flood), but the six white *Betula papyrifera* 'Saint George', the enlarged pond and summer house are highlighted in this watery view.

December 2020. An aura of mystery seems to be reflected in this unusual and dramatic scene in Foggy Bottom. Where there is grass, now there is water. The winter sun highlights the trees above ground, which are mirrored in the new lake below. The main tree in the centre is the Hungarian oak, *Quercus frainetto*, which I planted in 1978. The summer house is stranded, waiting for better times.

Winter

What I have yet to cover is temperature, highs and lows. Low winter temperatures used to be regularly below freezing, -10°C, and for several days. So much so that I could get out my speed skates and skate on our ponds (the one in Foggy Bottom was too small, though I did give it a try and our children learnt to skate on it). Certain plants like *Agapanthus* were not considered hardy and had to be covered with leaves or foliage each winter. What were then seen as less-hardy perennials are now not covered at all. Losses of plants on our heavy soil are more from winter wet and poor drainage than frost. But I knew right from the beginning that Foggy Bottom is in a 'frost pocket'. It is a fact of nature that cold air 'drains' to the lowest point, so it has not been surprising that spring frosts here can be very damaging to new growth. From as early as late February until late May, early morning frosts are possible. The period of new growth for plants, trees, shrubs and perennials extends throughout that period. At the same time, the sun rises earlier each day as spring advances. Ground or air frost on plants situated in shade may do little to no damage. Add the warming laser-like rays of the early sun to frosted shoots or flowers exposed to them and severe scorching might result. Older, more substantial plants will likely survive and reshoot some weeks later, younger plants might be killed. *Camellias*, *Rhododendrons*, *Magnolias,* and other early spring flowering plants are best planted where the early morning sun cannot reach them. This would also include the beautiful, but notoriously difficult plants to keep happy, Japanese maples. Please excuse the pun, but whether we like it or not, weather will always have an important role in gardening!

Phormium tenax and cultivars lost to a cold frosty spell in winter 1979. We also lost many on the nursery since we couldn't place the container plants under cover. Not the first time that optimism was overcome by realism!

Adrian Bloom skating on the pond in Foggy Bottom, 1994.

Trees, shrubs and grasses (and the roof of our home) are dramatically transformed as it snows. Watching snow fall is both mesmerising and therapeutic, muffling sound and blanketing all with small white flakes of unbelievably complex texture and design. Rarely are we able to fully observe this natural transformation to our own environment, let alone record it. This is another reason to be glad of the seasonal changes that affect our plants and gardens.

'The best of both worlds' might apply to being in the warmth of the house whilst observing the snow transforming your view of the garden outside. This scene was captured on a wintery day in Foggy Bottom from our front window, capturing the drooping heads of *Miscanthus sinensis* 'Morning Light' in the foreground and the larger landscape beyond, framed by the structure of trees and conifers. This *Miscanthus*, in my experience, is one of the best for keeping its shape through most of the winter.

04
03

Introducing Native Wildflowers to Foggy Bottom

Wildflowers and weeds have a lot in common; they are often related and usually self-distributed by seed in habitats that suit them. It has often been mentioned, and most horticulturists agree, that creating a wildflower garden or meadow in any sustainable fashion needs a lot of planning to make it work. It is important to remember that nearly all the plants in our gardens originated somewhere as wild plants, even though subsequent breeding has considerably widened our choice. In normal circumstances (unless overcome by compulsion), we will choose suitable cultivated plants for our garden and try to match their soil and situational preferences. Most of us want our plants to be 'happy' and will attempt to find a place where they will thrive best. The same should apply to our selection of wildflowers for any given situation. We shouldn't dig up or take seed from plants in the wild landscape, so those on offer should come from recognised and approved sources. That's the general rule, however, seed obtained from other gardeners and organisations is allowed.

What is a British native wildflower? Let's take a small divergence to explain the origins of British wildflowers, and my answer is possibly a contender for the now well-known statement "not many people know that". The fact is there are very few British native species that are exclusive to these islands. Most exist in other parts of Europe too. Even the English oak (*Quercus robur*) is not purely English, the Scots pine (*Pinus sylvestris*) does not only originate from Scotland, nor the Welsh poppy (*Meconopsis cambrica*) from Wales. The term 'wildflower' seems to suggest that since the plant is wild it will grow anywhere. Much work has been done in recent years to select plants which share a similar habitat and catalogues generally offer collections for particular areas, sites and soils. Native British wildflowers are wonderful in the right setting where they grow naturally of course, even if our range of species is limited. I am often reminded that the number of truly native plants in Britain is a measly 2,200. France has double that, Japan and Italy have around 6,000 each, the United States 15,000, and China 30,000. Not many people know that either!

There are many distinct habitats in the UK, coastal areas (in your mind just do a quick circle of the UK coastline to comprehend the diversity of situations) and inland. Wet, dry, well-drained, open meadow, woodland, shade, acid, alkaline or neutral soils are all factors to bear in mind when introducing ornamental wildflowers into the garden. A small amount of trial and error of new native plant introductions is useful too. Plants may sulk if not in an appropriate place, or they may rapidly spread if you have got it right. If successful, the latter may eventually be as problematic as the former and on this I have gained some valuable experience over the years. I felt some years ago that with a large garden to fill, it would be good to introduce a few wildflowers to create a 'natural' feel, particularly in areas I hadn't yet planted up. Most are still with us, some on the verge of being weeds!

I will only mention a few, but the subject of perennials, wildflowers and weeds is one worth returning to in the future. Not all is as it may seem…

Common name: *Campion, also known as red campion*

Botanical name: *Silene dioica*

Origin: *Woodlands across much of Europe*

Flowers: *Pink; Spring and early summer*

Conditions: *Partial shade, moist but well-drained soil*

Height: *Variable, approximately 80 cm (2–3 ft)*

We started by sowing seed of *Silene dioica* in our lower woodland in areas we had yet to plant. It wasn't long before they were well established and ready to spread elsewhere in the garden. A small leafy clump occurs in the first year. The next spring, floppy stems reach up looking for something to lean on. Without support they are generally untidy. Here the campion is seen at the base of a forty-year-old *Rhododendron yakushimanum* 'Koichiro Wada' coming into flower, with *Hosta* 'Shade Fanfare' in front.

Common name: *Common foxglove, sometimes called finger flower*

Botanical name: *Digitalis purpurea*

Origin: *Western Europe including the UK*

Flowers: *Generally pink to purple, occasionally white; Summer*

Conditions: *Sun or shade where not too dry*

Height: *Variable, 90–180 cm (3–6 ft)*

↑
A few of these foxgloves were planted, the rest have naturally seeded. In June, few other tall, spiked plants are at this stage of growth, so, although they will be dug up later, the line of white spires lightens this planting and draws the eye into the distance.

White goes with almost any other colour of flower or foliage. Not only is there something pure about white, but in the right setting it is more striking than anything else. It also has a presence when late spring or early summer foliage is fresh and abundant. Hence my use of the white foxglove, *Digitalis purpurea* 'Alba'. Here you can see a group located in a shady open spot in Foggy Bottom, self-sown, but previously thinned out. Spikes of white flowers rise above *Hostas* and *Brunnera* with a backdrop of shrubs. Bumble bees in particular love to gather pollen from foxgloves and when doing so, stand out clearly against the white petals. To keep the majority of the *Digitalis* in Foggy Bottom white, we remove all pink or purple plants as soon as they're visible. All *Digitalis* provide copious amounts of seed when flowering has finished, which usually falls adjacent to the parent plant. Spreading your foxgloves to another part of the garden couldn't be easier. Cut the stems carrying the seed pods before fully ripe and dry them off on paper, either shake the seed from the pods where you want them to be or scatter the minute seed from a jam jar …and wait.

Remember that no plant is perfect… Foxgloves are biennial – which means that they flower in their second year – so thinning is a good idea. You can also lift and replant your seedlings in early autumn if you prefer to place them. They can also become a bit thuggish if too close to other plants, smothering smaller or less vigorous growers. Common or not, overall, this version of our common foxglove makes an important addition to the garden.

← **Common name:** *Bluebell or English bluebell*
Botanical name: *Hyacinthoides non-scripta*
Origin: *Western Europe*
Flowers: *Violet blue, sometimes pink or white; Spring*
Conditions: *Partial shade, moist but well-drained soil*
Height: *30–45 cm (12–18 in)*

Considered an ancient woodland plant, bluebells are a favourite each May when fragrant violet blue flowers carpet woodland floors. It is a coloniser and though a wonderful plant to enjoy, it can be invasive in conditions it likes – this is normally on heavy, reasonably moist soil. But in this photograph, it has spread from beneath the *Cornus alba* 'Aurea' where I planted it to a more open, sunny position. Great in a woodland, great in a garden that has plenty of woodland and open spaces … perhaps use with care in the smaller garden.

It is important to note that *Hyacinthoides non-scripta* in its truest form has bell-like flowers on one side of its flower spike. The Spanish bluebell (*Hyacinthoides hispanica*) has flowers around the stem and are more often sold as a flowering plant in garden centres. The two can naturally cross or hybridise, usually to the detriment of both. Partisanship is not unusual, and attempts are constant to fight off more vigorous ornamental Spanish bluebells and preserve the English bluebell in its natural state. A bit like the Armada, but in today's world possibly more serious…

← **Common name:** *White comfrey*
Botanical name: *Symphytum orientale*
Origin: *Turkey, now naturalised in Britain and much of Europe*
Flowers: *White bell-like; Summer*
Conditions: *Most soils in sun or even dry shade*
Height: *60–90 cm (2–3 ft)*

Seeing *Symphytum orientale* adorn the grounds of Knightshayes Court in Devon some years ago, I obtained a few plants. Unsurprisingly being a free-seeding plant, it is still a feature in spring in various parts Foggy Bottom. It is quite attractive, perhaps more as single plants or groups rather than in a mass. Although it looks at home against a background of *Rhododendron*, seedlings in the wrong place need to be removed before they become too well established. What seems like an attractive plant in isolation somehow looks weedy in a larger planting.

Common name: *Honesty, penny flower*

Botanical name: *Lunaria annua*

Origin: *Central Western Europe, now widely distributed*

Flowers: *Purple, mauve, reddish pink or white; Late spring and early summer*

Conditions: *Sun or shade, moist but well-drained soil*

Height: *90–120 cm (3–4 ft)*

I had grown the perennial *Lunaria rediviva* but it didn't do well. Although a variegated form *L. r.* 'Honour Bright' was impressive – discovered and named by plantsman Bernard Tickner – it reverted to green rather too easily. Seeing a large and striking group of the annual, *Lunaria annua*, its reddish-purple flowers outstanding in a small suburban garden (my son Richard's garden at the time), I put in a request for some seed later in the year. Now, patches of these vibrant flowers light up the garden in early spring when not much else of the same colour is about. You must keep an eye on it as young seedlings emerge, thin out if necessary and pull up if too close to a more precious plant. The broad leaves serve to show the purple-red flowers, which later become amazing transparent seed heads beloved by flower arrangers.

I also value the brightly variegated → *Lunaria annua* 'Variegata'. As the name suggests, it is an annual which should be more widely known and grown. Plant in shady undisturbed corners and it will be a surprising spring delight.

The Chinese muntjac is seen here in the middle of winter close to our home looking for food (I assume). Of small stature, it is usually seen on its own, sometimes in pairs. Very widespread in and around Foggy Bottom and elsewhere in Britain. In time they create a daily track in the garden, where largely unseen (it hopes) it can snack on various plants on its route. If culled, two or three more soon turn up.

04
04

Wildlife in Foggy Bottom

Gardens are generally a haven for all sorts of wildlife, but a bit like weeds, some are more welcome than others. Some are more easily kept out or controlled than others. If your garden is in the countryside, the wildlife may well consider your garden as part of their territory and are hardly likely to differentiate our precious plants from any others. Since there is no common language or form of communication to enable us to reason with them, cunning and sometimes brutal ways need to be considered.

Wildlife and animal welfare has become a big issue and, as always, a balance needs to be achieved where possible. I won't mention all forms of wildlife that visit Foggy Bottom, but from mammals to birds, amphibians to insects, we have our fair share.

In the horticultural world, Latin names are the common language which I have gradually come to know and use. It is important to recognise that all life is denoted in Latin, but wildlife is generally referred to by common names (except in professional circles). You might, however, see me break out in the former occasionally where the Latin name is useful.

Our mammal list starts with the very large (and thank goodness only very occasional) red deer, the agile and graceful roe deer and the much smaller muntjac from Asia. Having no natural

predator since wolves were wiped out centuries ago, all have multiplied enormously. Foxes, stoats and weasels are all seen in the gardens and are predators to smaller rabbits, possibly hares, and sometimes a lazy unobservant pigeon. That's wildlife and seldom is there an even balance.

Rabbits are rampant, scratching roots and new plantings, and chewing back emerging and defenceless plants. Over a long spring and early summer, fast breeding wood pigeons are a menace to certain plants, particularly the early shoots of *Asters*, *Phlox paniculata* cultivars and a few others. Crows, magpies and jays also make their presence felt in the distance but are rarely seen, and the repetitive call of the cuckoo can be heard. A couple of magpies can sometimes be spotted looking uncomfortable on foot as they waddle around the house, ever observant and looking for food.

↑
In the early days of developing Foggy Bottom, we rarely saw rabbits although they were in nearby fields. How is it we care for hares but revile rabbits? Hares live above ground and breed more slowly. They also have more appeal for their spring antics and comic character. As with this rather hidden burrow just a few metres from the house, rabbits make holes in the garden where they can multiply and are invasive in their habits, chewing and scratching plants. I have yet to catch a hare in action chewing back plants, although I have my suspicions that they probably do.

A rather showy evergreen (or ever-yellow) grass, *Carex oshimensis* 'Everillo', has been chewed almost to the point of non-existence by deer, rabbit or hare. I wasn't there to see who it actually was, but it was evident that I should have covered this with wire.

Smaller birds are almost always welcome, blackbirds, thrushes, robins, wrens and bluetits are among the most common. And in the tops of the tall ash trees in the woodland behind the house, noisy crows command their territory, chasing off a pair of buzzards circling majestically above. Kestrels and sparrow hawks are always welcome too and in a beautiful moment, a tawny owl flies silently by looking for prey hiding in the grass.

We see frogs, toads and hedgehogs, beneficial to any garden and in many places under threat as our climate changes and their habitats are lost. In our area of Britain, we have long lost the native red squirrel to the more aggressive grey squirrel. Since the British have no doubt been responsible for introducing rabbits to Australia, we can hardly blame the Americans for introducing their grey squirrel to England (it was actually the English who first brought them over in 1876 or earlier). They are quick to multiply without a predator and find new things to chew on every year, nuts to bury in autumn and dig up in spring. They can also be vicious if cornered!

Also introduced and tiresome (that is understated!) is *Muntiacus reevesi*, the Chinese muntjac. We hear their dog-like rasping bark at night and sometimes in the day. With their heads mostly close to the ground, they tend to snack on plants as they do their daily foraging exercise. The roe deer has both grace and beauty but has a reach of at least 120 cm (4 ft), twice that of the muntjac. This needs bearing in mind when protecting plants with guards, barriers or fencing. Another less obvious protection which I had heard of being used elsewhere is a piece or shavings from a bar of soap, preferably of considerable fragrance. As deer are not connoisseurs (we believe), it can be as cheap as you can find! We put the soap in small bags and attach to canes above or amongst the foliage of the plants we want to protect. If I now asked you, "What is the most asked question from visitors?", you might guess the answer. I have been tempted (and occasionally do) reply with, "Soap helps to keep the garden clean". A few years ago, when a large flock of crows settled in the tall ash trees, we discovered the bags of soap had been attacked, with most of the soap eaten or carried away …by the crows? A flock of crows had until recently been called 'a murder'. We had no intention of considering such a terminal solution, but from eating that much soap you would like to think that it might at least give them indigestion!

"Yew've got to be joking!" was the first reaction to seeing the skilful pruning job done by a bunch of marauding roe deer. Knowing that the deer like eating the leaves of yews (*Taxus*) – which is a poisonous plant to humans – we had intended to put up tree guards, but the deer got there first. The plants are the columnar *Taxus baccata* 'Fastigiata Robusta' and you can see how far the deer could reach – over 120 cm (4 ft). I don't much like 'lollipops' in the garden, but this might be a new challenge! There is little doubt that we don't want to experience constant damage to specimen trees, nor do we want to have protective fences around every conifer, shrub or tree which are enjoyed by deer. Selection and compromise will be necessary, almost certainly coming from one side…

↑
The weeping Weymouth pine, also known as the Eastern white pine from North America, *Pinus strobus* 'Pendula', has every reason to weep after lower branches and needles were chewed by the roe deer. Not often seen in Foggy Bottom, these deer were driven to the relatively higher ground when their woodland habitat was flooded. More than once, I disturbed a small group of beautiful but nervous roe in the garden. Of course, in hindsight they were only hungry and seemed to know what plants they liked, some certainly less usual than what they were used to; *Cornus*, *Viburnum*, *Rhododendron*, even holly and *Prunus*, plus a few other conifers.

Could I have planted this *Bergenia* in a better place? Subject to flooding, spring frosts and winter food for the deer. This is down near the pond and if left to its own devices it would be totally garden worthy. The tell-tale sticks and bags denote fragrant soap chunks, placed there as a deterrent for deer. It mostly seems to work. →

← The evergreen *Rhododendron* 'Princess Anne' has small leaves and early soft primrose-coloured flowers. This was a forty-year-old specimen given a short back and sides by roe deer in early April. Accentuating the positive, the plant will recover and at least the deer couldn't reach most of the top.

↑

Red deer exist happily in forests and woodland edges all around our area. Looking at the damage early one winter morning caused by one jousting with this old and rather rare pine, *Pinus pumila* 'Jeddeloh', we were happy when the small group moved on. The wide spreading formidable antlers of the powerful male made short work of my forty-year-old specimen. Of course, it was unexpected, and the damage caused was the end of this plant, but my greatest regret was not being there to see the deer. To get a good photo would have been even better.

The Canada geese on their annual visit stand proudly on the bank, the female on the right looking more relaxed than the watchful male. When his head dips and stretches it means "Don't get too close!", but they dutifully remained for a photo opportunity.

Does the Canada goose come from Canada? Originally yes, but they have settled in Europe and elsewhere. Although some consider them as aliens, we welcome the very refined and garden appreciative pair (we believe) who arrive annually to Foggy Bottom. They command the waters of the pond and create an open nest on our island, much to the disgruntled mallard ducks who previously had that privilege. For a few weeks they are in residence, the male patrolling whilst the female incubates her eggs. Less than a week after their progeny hatch, the geese are gone for another year, not even stopping to tidy up after themselves.

A bridge over troubled water? We built it for paying visitors but had our suspicions that others were using it too. Here's confirmation on the snow-covered bridge that this convenience is helpful to all, although we haven't fully identified our winter visitors. →

↑ A pheasant caught in the act, digging and eating an established *Arum*, so intent on the tasty bulbous perennial that it didn't notice me at the window. These *Arums* can seed around and become a nuisance plant inevitably in the wrong place.

↑ This pheasant thought an easier way of getting some food was to sit on the bird table and wait!

Our last 'invasive' wildlife species that has an annual presence in Foggy Bottom is the pheasant. Originally from eastern Asia, it has been in Britain since Roman times – the pheasant should therefore be considered a native. Not thought of as the most intelligent birds, usually one or two that are sensible or lucky, walk or fly clear of the guns of shooting parties that occur on a farm in neighbouring Suffolk. The southern boundary of our Norfolk land is the River Waveney. Norfolk and Suffolk (North folk and South folk), says it all. The cock pheasant is gloriously colourful in autumn and winter, and you would think an easy target. They often scratch vigorously around and have a particular fondness for certain bulbs, *Crocus* and *Fritillarias* among them. They also dig out the deep-rooted *Arum italicum* which is sometimes helpful if they did a proper job and didn't leave such a mess.

Shy moles prefer to stay underground and rarely break the surface, but on our alluvial soil the black hills are easily seen. With meadows either side of the garden, incursions rather than invasions are almost bound to happen. Also, our irrigation of Foggy Bottom during dry periods keeps worms turning, which moles are likely to seek out.

← The underground network of tunnels is seldom seen, but sometimes the moles are adventurous and in the right conditions prove they can move more quickly just beneath the surface of the lawn. You can hardly notice except for the spurts of black soil. If not dealt with, the disturbed grass soon turns brown.

There just wasn't any appetite to show a picture of a slug. But looking at this *Hosta*, slugs have their Christmas earlier since by the end of June they had tucked into the soft early growth of *H.* 'Christmas Candy'. I left the label near the plant, so the irony was not lost. The question really must be, where does the plant and name come from? *Hostas* are of course completely dormant by Christmas, and you would imagine here in Foggy Bottom little of 'Christmas Candy' would be recognisable long before then…

Caterpillars munching on the leaves of a birch tree (*Betula apoiensis* 'Mount Apoi') in late summer.

And then there are occasionally snakes, mice and voles and myriads of insects which come with the seasons. The seemingly evil vine weevil attacking roots and as adults, leaves. Snails and particularly slugs are considered bad (can anyone convince me that slugs have a useful purpose?), whereas caterpillars, butterflies and moths are considered beneficial. Bees, though concerns exist about their future, love the plants in Foggy Bottom and are active for most months of the year. In summer, they particularly enjoy the diversity of over 4,000 species and cultivars in the nearby Dell Garden.

↑
Even though we don't get many butterfly species in Foggy Bottom, I seem unable to retain the names of the more common butterflies except the cabbage white (which doesn't make a great picture). Here is a red admiral opening its wings on a *Buddleja*.

↑
A peacock butterfly alighting on an *Allium*, the artfully painted false 'eyes' on the wings hoping to confuse predators.

← You can imagine that we get many bees in Foggy Bottom, small and large. They are a study on their own and play a very important role in nature and its interconnectedness. Jaime Blake, curator of the Dell Garden, and his wife, my half-sister Anthea, keep bees and produce a Head Gardener's honey, the nectar taken from the thousands of flowering plants in all the gardens. The noisy but humble bumble bee enjoys the flowers and bracts of the *Eryngiums*. Seen from above, this is *Eryngium* × *zabelii* 'Big Blue' in Foggy Bottom growing above *Stachys byzantina* 'Big Ears'. Sometimes caught out late in the cooler evenings, they sleep in the bracts of the flowers until woken by the warmth of the following morning sun.

We sometimes get unusual visitors, and the animals are not always wild. One warm July day a group of cattle came to the gate at Foggy Bottom. Matt held them up at the entrance and can be seen here on the phone to the ticket office, "They *herd* that Foggy Bottom was worth visiting and want to know if they can get group entry?".

Aphids and ants, the latter some say will gradually take over the world. What did I leave out? Well perhaps those we see as considerably less beneficial such as mosquitos, horse flies and ticks, the latter deposited by deer. Wasps, seemingly fewer in number in recent years, have a role to play, though without research I'm not quite sure what that is. Frogs and toads breed at the pond edge every year but are seldom seen in the garden. With climate change, our warmer winter temperatures allow the survival of many more insects crossing the channel, Brexit or no Brexit.

Overall, Foggy Bottom is a haven for many forms of wildlife, for which taking a broader view we must be grateful. Nature has its own rules which we are not always to know and seldom able to control. We can be glad that in most of England we don't have to consider animals like porcupines, wild boar, buffalo or bear… the latter was last seen (so a local story goes) in the upper Waveney Fens a few hundred years ago.

04
05

The Houses that Matt Built

My son Matt has a skill that he only occasionally gets to use creatively. I have been fortunate that over the years he has been able to use some of those skills in Foggy Bottom, and some of the results will be there for people to enjoy for many years to come. Matt embarked on a career as a timber framer both in the UK and North America, and like many people in gardening or horticulture, a career (even career doesn't quite seem the right word) which is seldom entered for monetary reward. It is a trade, relying on skills crafted over time – like gardening. If you are talented and have a passion, it can be immensely rewarding to be close to the natural world and to create using mostly natural products.

In the Dell Garden, my father had been able to find the time to build walls, a bridge and a summer house made from flint stone, known locally as Norfolk flint. Apart from a limited amount of sandstone, flint is the only natural stone in the county. It's not an easy stone to build with because of its variability in size and shape, but his work has produced natural-looking structural features which considerably enhance his garden creation.

The Bridge and Decking

In Foggy Bottom, positioned at a lower level in the Waveney Valley, we needed a more imposing bridge over our new natural-looking, but artificial pond. As much as I had dreamed of having a sparkling stream running through Foggy Bottom, flowing and gurgling its way to a clear pond on the edge of woodland, the reality was somewhat different. Our ditch nearby brought floods in the winter and dried up in the summer, so no natural stream was possible. Dug in 1978, water drained away

The bridge and decking in midwinter.

from the pond and was only contained in following summers after a butyl rubber-like pond liner was laid in 1980. Matt was on hand at the time to help some local contractors to build our wooden bridge and decking. A few years later, Matt had to re-do some of the work and build another stretch of decking, allowing visitors to walk into the centre of what was to become a largely spring flowering garden, Rosemary's Wood.

A new entry into Rosemary's Wood.

The Summer House

The summer house near the pond and on the edge of Rosemary's Wood.

The summer house was the first main structure Matt built in the garden, made with wood from our woodland and farm, as was the case with most of his Bressingham creations. We had discussed what we wanted and asked Matt for his ideas. Situated a little higher than some of the land around which could be prone to flooding and needing some footings, he drew up a plan of the building. Matt managed to build the summer house in between his travels to India, Australia and the United States, and although some of the work was heavy and he required some assistance with the lead capping, he did it all himself. Matt used green English oak and was meticulous about the detail and fitting the joints. The summer house now looks as though it has been in the garden forever. It serves as a refuge against the weather, a destination for visitors, and perhaps above all as a focal point in the garden from almost any aspect observed. Standing in the entrance, looking out also frames a great view of Foggy Bottom.

This view from the summer house at the lower end of Foggy Bottom gives a broad spectrum of the informal layout of the garden and its mix of plants. The lawn, regularly mown, acts as a pathway or 'green river' dividing and linking the several varied sizes of island beds. In recent years, unfortunately the area near the pond has been prone to flooding in winter. In time, it may be that climate change will create more challenges for future gardeners.

The long view down to the summer house, its roof covered in snow.

↑

Matt putting Western red cedar *(Thuja plicata)* shingles on the roof of the tree house.

The Tree House

The tree house is in our private part of Foggy Bottom and so not open to the public. It is hardly surprising that eager, adventurous children are disappointed when they and their parents find it is not accessible for visitors. Nor is it strictly a tree house, which tends to denote that the house is situated in a tree. Needless to say, it was carefully planned and built by Matt over three years whilst he was working in Cumbria and studying for his MSc. It is an amazing structure and aesthetically pleasing from whatever angle it is viewed from. Of course, the purpose was also to create an opportunity for a very different and striking view of the garden since we have no hills, nor second floors to our house to get an elevated vista. I have no hesitation in suggesting that on a quiet summer's evening it is a great place to see the garden and enjoy a gin and tonic, cocktail (shaken, not stirred), beer or glass of wine!

The early morning winter sun throws its beams against all it touches, making the tree house look like a UFO that has landed from another planet!

↓

A perfect fit. Since it is not open for visitors, the tree house is part of a 'borrowed' landscape which all visitors can see from the main garden.

Rosemary's Spire

Rosemary, my wife and partner for fifty years who died in May 2014, will of course always be remembered by myself and our sons and many others beside. What could be a fitting tribute to her? Rosemary's Wood and the oak spire within it were something tangible and that area of the garden, despite its early neglect, seemed a perfect place. The spire, conceived and built by Matt, is something we all agreed would represent her long and loving contribution to the garden and family. Once again, Matt selected branches from oak trees that had fallen on our land, using the curved branches to joint together as one. His concrete footing would ensure a strong and permanent base and prevent strong winds, occasional tornados and gales from blowing it down. The spire would soon come to belong in the garden, the slender outline reaching for the sky.

Cutting and fitting oak together to achieve a seamless curve.

Matt and Richard bring the spire to Foggy Bottom.

A scaffold was needed to complete the spire.

The Japanese-Style Building

What to call the building? Despite checking with various sources (including Japanese), we haven't come up with a perfect description, hence 'Japanese-style building'. The surrounding area will similarly not be an exact replica of a Japanese garden. I had made three previous trips to Japan from 1978, but these were mostly for our nursery business, both importing and exporting new plants. I always found visiting this very different country an unbelievable experience, from its fascinating history, social and cultural differences as well as its topography and climate. But it wasn't until Matt and I made a trip together in October 2016 that I had a chance to visit many gardens, and for Matt to study some of the structures that adorned them. It was a fascinating journey for both of us and I treasured the opportunity to travel together.

I admire the constraint used in most Japanese Gardens and their minimalist use of plants to create an atmosphere for meditation. For several years, I had the idea of creating a separate Japanese-style garden in Foggy Bottom. The site would be on the west side of the garden where the (now old) vegetable garden was shaded by trees. Matt was soon interested in the possibility of a building that would reflect our experience and fit the new garden which would be open to the public. It was equally important to me, as to Matt, that the building would be a structure like no other. The thought that he would construct a work of art was never in doubt… although for valid reasons at the time of writing it has yet to be completed (as has the garden!). There are plenty of other things to get on with of course, and I remind myself of the adage… the best is always worth waiting for!

Matt in the workshop preparing the joints for the top roof.

The site for the Japanese-style garden and the building under construction. All together an exciting development!

One of the seeds that went on to greater things, the straight trunk heading up to the sky, over 100 ft at present. Not bad progress for a sixty-year-old conifer. It has probably grown faster in the milder climate of Britain having been given a longer growing period here than in its native habitat.

1960, just before the Winter Olympics at Squaw Valley, California, elevation over 5,000 ft. A nineteen-year-old Adrian Bloom (who was a speed skater, but not competing in the Olympics) with recently made friends and US team members, Dick Hunt and Bill Disney, both Californians. Bill was a silver medallist in the 500 metres, considered a sprint. At this point, the seeds of the giant redwood, *Sequoiadendron giganteum*, were destined for Bressingham, not knowing their destination, nor what might become of them!

The Redwoods

More Than A Seed

Aged nineteen, whilst was working in Squaw Valley, California, and training with some of the US speed skating team, I had no idea what my future might be. It's a long story to be kept brief here. I travelled in the US for two years from 1959 and planned to see the Olympic Games in the High Sierras of California, not far from Lake Tahoe. I had heard about the giant redwoods, but not seen them (and wouldn't for another forty years). But the Squaw Valley gift shop was selling packets of seed, so I purchased one as a souvenir, sent it home and asked my father if his helper Percy Piper would sow them. Perhaps if the seed had germinated when I came back, I could plant them.

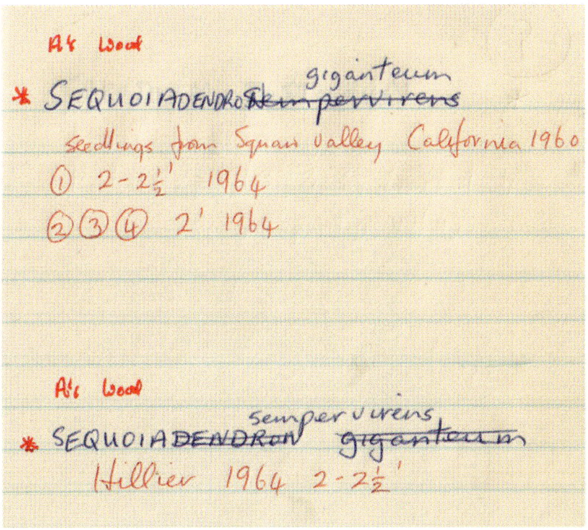

Adrian wrote this in his record book after planting the four redwoods raised by Percy Piper. The similar-sized coastal redwood, *Sequoia sempervirens*, over 100 ft, is also nearby in Adrian's Wood.

To most visitors and I, the dark cones of *Sequoiadendron giganteum* seem part of the Foggy Bottom Garden. The trees appear at home in the background, taking a paternal interest in what they see below from their lofty heights.

After working in Switzerland and Denmark, and a winter skating in Norway, I returned in August 1962 to begin my career as a nurseryman at Bressingham. In 1964 we dug out a pond and I started planting up trees on the southern and western sides. Amongst those that I planted were five plants of the giant redwood, *Sequoiadendron giganteum*. This was still called Wellingtonia by many British gardeners, the name given soon after the plant's discovery in 1852 to commemorate one of Britain's great heroes. However, it wasn't within the right of the British to do so and a more appropriate name was eventually given to honour a Native American chief called Sequoyah.

The trees were planted and the area was sheltered, as I had planned, by about thirty × *Cupressocyparis leylandii*. Then in 1967 I started my own garden, Foggy Bottom. As we had other things to do, the woodland garden was left for thirty-three years and was largely hidden, fighting for dominance (or perhaps survival) with the Leyland cypress. It must have been grateful when the Leyland cypress were cut down in 2000, as I designed a linking pathway to the Dell Garden through what was to be called Adrian's Wood. Since most plants in the wood originated from North America and I had long realised how many good plants that included, I thought we should dedicate all future planting to fit under that theme.

It wasn't my intention to line up these two redwoods, but as both grew, they seemed to welcome each other's presence. Of course, (and here I might be thinking too much…) planted earlier and going straight up, *Sequoiadendron giganteum* was always going to look down on its weeping cousin *S. g.* 'Pendulum' in the foreground. The species was only discovered in 1852 and the first pendulous selection arose not long after as a seedling in France dated 1863.

The Watching Redwoods

So now to the best part. At the time of planting my redwoods, I had no idea that we were going to build our home within sight of them, and for several years I hardly noticed them amongst the fast growing Leyland cypress. That all changed as we cleared the wood for the pathway and planted more North American plants. On slightly higher ground than Foggy Bottom, three trees have attained over 100 ft and tower over it, very much seeming to be part of the garden. Truly awesome and majestic, I can hardly believe that the seeds I sent home in a small packet have brought so much awe and amazement to me and many others. The last part of the story is that I have now cleared a few trees and conifers blocking the view to the small grove of redwoods. When washing the dishes or sitting in my study, I can look out and see these magnificent trees, as if in the High Sierras, their trunks bare and branchless 30–40 ft and only fifty yards away! Serendipity indeed!

Fog and frost combine to create a dusting of white which unlike snow, doesn't completely hide the foliage. In winter, the weather provides some of the most dramatic scenes which need capturing for others to appreciate.

And another remarkable thing... Over the tops of shrubs and trees, and at least a hundred yards away, our giant redwoods are still reflected in our pond. To me, that is amazing and at times like these I'm glad I bought that packet of seed. There ought to be a parable somewhere there!

Early morning against the rising sun, Rosemary's spire naturally fits into the garden.

Afterword

A few thoughts from the Head Gardener

Of course, the Foggy Bottom Garden is not magic, but the result of a lifelong endeavour from me and the help of many others. I am lucky to still be here and be able to look at the future, continuing to make changes and necessary developments. It is challenging and ultimately rewarding.

Occasionally, I can stand back and see Foggy Bottom, despite its flaws, as a wonderland. It is a temporary and fragile garden, because without continual maintenance it would soon become an overgrown wilderness. The so-called 'balance of nature' seldom favours all within it. When I think about it, this wonderland has been created using plants from all over the world. And like humans, each has a background, a DNA and a story. Plants in Foggy Bottom originate from the East; China, the Himalayas, Japan and Korea, from the West; Canada, the United States and Mexico, and southern temperate zones; Chile, Argentina, South Africa, Australia and New Zealand.

Earlier introductions, giving us an ever-widening range of garden plants, often followed movements and explorations in wider Europe, the Mediterranean, the Middle East, Russia and Scandinavia, even Iceland and Greenland. Later introductions then added a human element, continuing ever more rapidly in recent years by chance discovery, selection and breeding to produce new cultivars. Putting this potpourri of plants in some form of order, largely to look reasonably natural and happy in their environment, has and continues to be the most enjoyable and interesting aspect in developing Foggy Bottom. At the same time, recognising that with growing plants there is seldom a sight of the finished 'article'. A couple of examples…

The so-called dwarf Serbian spruce, *Picea omorika* 'Nana', was (like many other conifers given such indicative names) supposed to not grow taller than 3 m (12 ft). I planted one in 1976 which was about 60 cm (2 ft) high, now it has reached nearly 10 m (33 ft). Unlike some, it is still an attractive plant and will stay.

Another is our native birch, *Betula pendula*, which I was told had a lifespan of around fifty years. A five-year-old plant was planted in 1966 when our house was built. It is now a large, healthy tree at over sixty-years-old and looks like it will be good for several more years. One lifetime is not enough… and as ever, the devil is in the detail, observing and recording.

The Future of Today's Gardens

I often reflect on gardens and gardeners past. This is not the place to give that thought the time and space it deserves but take for example, the classic early French and Italian gardens. Formal, clipped hedges, parterres, bedding replaced each year, roses pruned and clipped. Then the Japanese, representing a more natural, but tightly measured landscape. Without doubt, the point is that these gardens have lasted because they have been controlled. Many of the great gardens of Britain either follow one of the above or are in large Capability Brown landscapes where the 'garden' is more like an estate parkland.

Will the 20th century be seen as The Garden Century? When gardening became a truly national pastime for millions of people worldwide; driven by the growth of suburbia and the rise of garden centres. Gardens of all shapes, sizes and specialities arose. Some in the UK planned with considerable investment, like the Eden Project and RHS Wisley, others through the interest and passion of one or more individuals. Inevitably, although there will be many more that could be mentioned, I would consider plantspeople like Margery Fish, Alan Bloom and Beth Chatto as outstanding examples. The latter mostly pioneering the use of hardy perennials, which can be cut back each year to begin anew, but division and maintenance is necessary to keep them looking attractive. Gardens like Foggy Bottom, that rely on a wide range of woody plants, offer a different challenge over many years and into maturity.

Above all, it seems to me that it should be up to all of us who have had the opportunity to grow and garden through the latter part of the 20th century, to pass on knowledge, enthusiasm and inspiration to a younger generation of gardeners and horticulturists. I'm not sure we are succeeding, but I hope this book might at least illustrate what a garden can represent.

Adrian Bloom

Index

ANNUALS & BIENNIALS

BULBS

CONIFERS

FERNS

GRASSES

PERENNIALS

SHRUBS & TREES

Acknowledgements

My special thanks to Rosie May, who as my assistant and computer wizard has helped turn the probable into the possible.

Many thanks to John Chandler for our easy working relationship and for designing such a beautiful book. Thank you to Richard Bloom for some of the images in the book and to other photographers who used my camera to take photographs of myself and the family over the years.

I would also like to thank all those who have signed the visitor book in Foggy Bottom, some of the comments of which we have reproduced throughout the text. In many cases these refer to Foggy Bottom but also include the rest of the seventeen acres of The Bressingham Gardens.

Published in Great Britain 2023 by
Foggy Bottom Books

A CIP catalogue record for this book is available
from the British Library.

ISBN: 978-1-9196042-1-3

Images used in this book were taken by
©Adrian Bloom unless otherwise stated.

Designed by chandlerbookdesign.com

Printed in Great Britain by
TJ Books Ltd, Padstow, Cornwall.